Rapid increases in international economic exchanges during the past four decades have made national economies very open to the world economy by historical standards. Much recent economic analysis has been devoted to exploring the effects of such internationalization on macroeconomic policy options, national competitiveness, and rewards to various factors of production. Since economies and politics are so closely linked, there is reason to expect profound political effects as well: in particular, domestic politics in countries around the world should show signs of the impact of the world economy. The central proposition of this volume is that we can no longer understand politics within countries – what we still conventionally call "domestic" politics – without comprehending the nature of the linkages between national economies and the world economy, and changes in such linkages.

This volume focuses on the effects of the internationalization of national markets on domestic politics. Internationalization refers to an exogenous reduction in the costs of international transactions that can be empirically measured by the growth in the proportion of international economic flows relative to domestic ones. We examine the effects of internationalization on the policy preferences of socioeconomic and political agents within countries toward national policies and national policy-making institutions. We also analyze the effects of internationalization on the national policies and policy institutions themselves.

D0449156

Internationalization and Domestic Politics

CAMBRIDGE STUDIES IN COMPARATIVE POLITICS

General editor
PETER LANGE Duke University

Associate editors
ELLEN COMISSO University of California, San Diego
PETER HALL Harvard University
JOEL MIGDAL University of Washington
HELEN MILNER Columbia University
RONALD ROGOWSKI University of California, Los Angeles
SIDNEY TARROW Cornell University

OTHER BOOKS IN THE SERIES

Catherine Boone, *Merchant Capital and the Roots of State Power in Senegal, 1930–1985*
Donatella della Porta, *Social Movements, Political Violence, and the State*
Roberto Franzosi, *The Puzzle of Strikes: Class and State Strategies in Postwar Italy*
Ellen Immergut *Health Politics: Interests and Institutions in Western Europe*
Thomas Janoski and Alexander M. Hicks, eds., *The Comparative Political Economy of the Welfare State*
David Knoke, Franz Urban Pappi, Jeffrey Broadbent, and Yutaka Tsujinaka, eds., *Comparing Policy Networks*
Allan Kornberg and Harold D. Clarke *Citizens and Community: Political Support in a Representative Democracy*
David D. Laitin *Language Repertories and State Construction in Africa*
Doug McAdam, John McCarthy, and Mayer Zald, *Comparative Perspectives on Social Movements*
Joel S. Migdal, Atul Kohli, and Vivienne Shue *State Power and Social Forces: Domination and Transformation in the Third World*
Paul Pierson, *Dismantling the Welfare State: Reagan, Thatcher and the Politics of Retrenchment*
Yossi Shain and Juan Linz, *Inerim Governments and Democratic Transitions*
Theda Skocpol, *Social Revolutions in the Modern World*
Sven Steinmo, Kathleen Thelan, and Frank Longstreth, eds., *Structuring Politics: Historical Institutionalism in Comparative Analysis*
Sidney Tarrow, *Power in Movement: Social Protest, Reform, and Revolution*
Ashutosh Varshney, *Democracy, Development, and the Countryside*

Internationalization and Domestic Politics

Edited by

ROBERT O. KEOHANE
Harvard University

HELEN V. MILNER
Columbia University

CAMBRIDGE
UNIVERSITY PRESS

Published by the Press Syndicate of the University of Cambridge
The Pitt Building, Trumpington Street, Cambridge CB2 1RP
40 West 20th Street, New York, NY 10011-4211, USA
10 Stamford Road, Oakleigh, Melbourne 3166, Australia

© Cambridge University Press 1996

First published 1996

Printed in the United States of America

Library of Congress Cataloging-in-Publication Data
Internationalization and domestic politics / edited by Robert O.
    Keohane, Helen V. Milner.
        p.   cm. – (Cambridge studies in comparative politics)
        ISBN 0-521-56264-3 (hc). – ISBN 0-521-56587-1 (pb)
        1. International economic relations.   2. World politics – 1989–
    3. Comparative government.   I. Keohane, Robert O. (Robert
Owen).
    1941–   . II. Milner, Helen V., 1958–   .   III. Series.
    HF1359.I5877   1996
    337 – dc20   95-41396
                                                                CIP

A catalog record for this book is available from the British Library

ISBN 0-521-56264-3 hardback
      0-521-56587-1 paperback

Contents

Preface   *page* vii
Contributors   ix

PART I Theoretical Framework

1 Internationalization and Domestic Politics: An Introduction   3
   HELEN V. MILNER AND ROBERT O. KEOHANE
2 The Impact of the International Economy on National
   Policies: An Analytical Overview   25
   JEFFRY A. FRIEDEN AND RONALD ROGOWSKI
3 Internationalization, Institutions, and Political Change   48
   GEOFFREY GARRETT AND PETER LANGE

PART II The Industrialized Democracies

4 Capital Mobility, Trade, and the Domestic Politics of
   Economic Policy   79
   GEOFFREY GARRETT
5 Economic Integration and the Politics of Monetary Policy in
   the United States   108
   JEFFRY A. FRIEDEN
6 Internationalization and Electoral Politics in Japan   137
   FRANCES McCALL ROSENBLUTH

PART III Internationalization and Socialism

7 Stalin's Revenge: Institutional Barriers to
   Internationalization in the Soviet Union   159
   MATTHEW EVANGELISTA

8   Internationalization and China's Economic Reforms   186
    SUSAN SHIRK

PART IV International Economic Crisis and Developing
         Countries

9   The Political Economy of Financial Internationalization in
    the Developing World   209
    STEPHAN HAGGARD AND SYLVIA MAXFIELD

PART V Conclusion

10 Internationalization and Domestic Politics: A Conclusion 243
    HELEN V. MILNER AND ROBERT O. KEOHANE

Notes   259
References   279
Index   303

Preface

This project has had a long gestation. We first discussed editing a book on "what happened to interdependence theory" at the American Political Science Association meetings in Atlanta, 1989. The conversation led to the more ambitious plan of putting together a working group on internationalization and domestic politics, in which students of international relations and comparative politics would engage in a serious dialogue about these issues.

With the support of the Social Science Research Council, we convened a group for planning meetings at Columbia University in March 1990, and at the Center for International Affairs, Harvard University, in September 1991. At those meetings we benefited from memos and comments from several scholars who did not become further involved in the project, in particular David A. Baldwin, Peter J. Katzenstein, Ian Lustick, and Walter W. Powell. Encouraged by the ideas expressed in those meetings and by widespread enthusiasm for the project, we commissioned papers for a larger meeting at Oxnard, California, in November 1992, cosponsored by the Institute on Global Conflict and Cooperation of the University of California. At that meeting, we benefited from the insights especially of Ellen Comisso, Kiren Chaudhry, and Timothy McKeown, who made presentations, as well as of commentators Alessandra Casella, Benjamin Cohen, Albert Fishlow, Haruhiro Fukui, Peter Gourevitch, Yasheng Huang, Miles Kahler, David Lake, John Odell, Manuel Pastor, Philip Roeder, Richard Rosecrance, Arthur Stein, and Michael Wallerstein. Lisa Martin provided valuable comments after the meeting.

The authors met again at the University of California, Los Angeles in June 1993 for final discussions of the individual papers and how they fit together in a volume. Jeffry Frieden and Ronald Rogowski bore significant organizational and logistical burdens, with the able support of their assistant Roland Stephen, both for this meeting and the one at Oxnard.

After making a presentation to the Board of Editors of *International Organization* in September 1993, we submitted the manuscript to *International Organization*. In the extended review process that followed, we received valuable comments from the editor, John Odell, and two anonymous referees, who read the whole manuscript twice, as well as from referees for specific manuscripts. Although *International Organization* disappointed us, in the end, by deciding not to accept this volume as a special issue, we wish to recognize the substantial improvements in this work that were prompted by the exhaustive reviews provided by the journal. Readers of both *International Organization* and this volume may now make their own judgments as to whether the journal made the correct decision!

In the last stages of revision, we benefited from timely reviews by referees for Cambridge University Press and another fine university press, and from the valuable assistance of Alex Holzman, our editor at Cambridge University Press. However, our greatest debt is to our colleagues in this project, who provided criticism of our own contributions, constructive suggestions about the volume as a whole, and even moral support. We are particularly indebted to Matthew Evangelista, Jeffry Frieden, Stephan Haggard, and Peter Lange for valuable comments on an earlier version of our introduction. All of the contributors exhibited enormous patience and great cooperative spirit during a long drawn-out process. We are especially grateful to Geoffrey Garrett, Stephan Haggard, and Sylvia Maxfield, whose papers were accepted by *International Organization* at an early stage but agreed to delay publication while we tried, in a second round, to have the whole volume accepted as a special issue. This project has truly been a collective one. One of its major benefits for us has been the opportunity it provided to make new friends and enrich old acquaintances among some of the most serious scholars, and most engaging people, we know.

Contributors

MATTHEW EVANGELISTA
Department of Government
Cornell University
Ithaca, NY 14053

JEFFREY A. FRIEDEN
Department of Government and Center for International Affairs
Harvard University
1737 Cambridge Street
Cambridge, MA 02138

GEOFFREY GARRETT
The Wharton School
University of Pennsylvania
Philadelphia, PA 19104

STEPHAN HAGGARD
School of International Relations
University of California, San Diego
9500 Gilman Drive
La Jolla, CA 92093

ROBERT O. KEOHANE
Department of Government and Center for International Affairs
Harvard University
1737 Cambridge Street
Cambridge, MA 02138

PETER LANGE
Department of Political Science
Duke University
Box 90204
Durham, NC 27708

SYLVIA MAXFIELD
Department of Political Science
Yale University
PO Box 3532
New Haven, CT 06520-3532

HELEN V. MILNER
Institute of War and Peace Studies
Columbia University
420 West 118th Street, #1309
New York, NY 10027

RONALD ROGOWSKI
Department of Political Science
University of California, Los Angeles
Los Angeles, CA 90024-1472

FRANCES McCALL ROSENBLUTH
Department of Political Science
Yale University
3532 Yale Station
New Haven, CT 06520-3532

SUSAN SHIRK
Institute on Global Conflict and Cooperation
University of California, San Diego
La Jolla, CA 92092

PART I
Theoretical Framework

1

Internationalization and Domestic Politics: An Introduction

HELEN V. MILNER AND ROBERT O. KEOHANE

Rapid increases in international economic exchanges during the past four decades have made national economies very open, by historical standards, to the world economy. Much recent economic analysis has been devoted to exploring the effects of such internationalization on macroeconomic policy options, national competitiveness, and rewards to various factors of production. Since economics and politics are so closely linked, there is reason to expect profound political effects as well. in particular, domestic politics in countries around the world should show signs of the impact of the world economy. The central proposition of this volume is that we can no longer understand politics within countries – what we still conventionally call "domestic" politics – without comprehending the nature of the linkages between national economies and the world economy, and changes in such linkages.

"Internationalization" is a broad concept used by a variety of writers in a variety of ways. In Chapter 2, Jeffry Frieden and Ronald Rogowski attempt to introduce some precision into its analysis by distinguishing between observable flows of goods, services, and capital, on the one hand, and the "exogenous easing of international exchange that such flows reflect," on the other. Measurable flows, such as the vast increases in international capital movements over the past few decades, reflect more basic shifts in the costs of international relative to domestic transactions. Indeed, shifting opportunity costs are more fundamental than the flows themselves: the *potential* for international movements of capital, in response to shifts in interest rates or changing expectations about exchange rates, can exert profound effects on national economic conditions and policies even if no capital movement actually takes place. Hence, as Frieden and Rogowski recognize, an adequate analysis of internationalization cannot begin with international flows, but must probe the sources of these transactions.

However, "the exogenous easing of international exchange" is less directly observable, whereas flows of goods, services and capital can be measured, however imperfectly. In this volume, therefore, internationalization is measured by such indicators as changes in trade as a proportion of gross domestic product (GDP) or the ratio of a country's net foreign investment to its total domestic assets. *Internationalization, as used in this volume, refers to the processes generated by underlying shifts in transaction costs that produce observable flows of goods, services, and capital.* As documented below, international trade, investment, and currency trading have grown dramatically during the last two decades, especially relative to the size of national economies; hence, internationalization, as we define it, has grown.[1]

Frieden and Rogowski devote some attention in their chapter to the sources of internationalization. This volume as a whole, however, focuses not on the causes of internationalization but on its effects. Internationalization affects the opportunities and constraints facing social and economic actors, and therefore their policy preferences – not necessarily the basic values that actors seek (power, money, or virtue as they define it) but their choices about which policies will best achieve their fundamental goals. Internationalization also affects the aggregate welfare of countries, their sensitivity and vulnerability to external changes, and therefore the constraints and opportunities faced by governments. As incentives change through internationalization, we expect to observe changes in economic policies and in political institutions. Possible changes include the liberalization of foreign trade and investment policies, the deregulation of domestic markets, shifts in fiscal and monetary policy, and changes in the institutions designed to affect these policies.

Political institutions reflect domestic actors' policy preferences, since they are intentionally created to guarantee the pursuit of particular policies. But they also have independent effects: they create rules for decision making, help to structure agendas, and offer advantages to certain groups while disadvantaging others. Over time, strong institutions may even shape actors' policy preferences. Since institutions have effects, people have preferences about institutions as well as about policies; and these preferences will be linked. If an independent agency seems less likely to provide tariff protection than the legislature, free traders should favor appointment of the agency while protectionists should oppose it.

The central explanatory variable throughout this volume is internationalization, which involves an exogenous reduction in the costs of international transactions that can be empirically measured by the growth in the proportion of international economic flows relative to domestic ones. We recognize throughout, however, that the effects of internationalization are mediated through domestic political institutions. The dependent variables are twofold:

1 The policy preferences of relevant socioeconomic and political agents within countries toward national policies and national policy-making institutions, as reflected in their political behavior; and
2 National policies and national policy institutions themselves.

This volume is built around two core sets of propositions, which are elaborated in Chapter 2 by Frieden and Rogowski and Chapter 3 by Geoffrey Garrett and Peter Lange. Frieden and Rogowski focus on the policy preferences of socioeconomic actors, Garrett and Lange on the institutional side of the story. The empirical chapters examine both sets of arguments in light of evidence from countries around the world.

Frieden and Rogowski argue that internationalization affects the policy preferences of actors within countries in broadly predictable ways, based on the economic interests of the actors. Most obviously, it expands the tradables sector within an economy, thus reducing the amount of economic activity sheltered from world market forces. *Ceteris paribus*, internationalization should therefore increase the sensitivity of national economies to world market trends and shocks.[2] More significantly, internationalization affects the relative prices of domestically produced goods or domestically owned factors, compared to each other and to foreign goods and factors. Since changes in relative prices have implications both for growth and for income distribution, socioeconomic actors advantaged by these price changes will press for increased openness, while disadvantaged groups will seek restrictions, subsidies, or protection. Each of the empirical chapters evaluates this first proposition: that changes in policy preferences will reflect changes in relative prices.

Yet internationalization affects policies and institutions differently from country to country: the existing institutional context conditions the incentives facing interest groups and politicians. Thus the second fundamental proposition of this volume is that political institutions can block and refract the effects of internationalization. Political outcomes cannot be predicted simply on the basis of economic interests. Coalition formation depends on strategic judgments and maneuvering, and often cannot be predicted from policy preferences alone.[3] Moreover, decisions on whether to work through existing institutions or to press for radical institutional change depend not merely on economic policy preferences and strategic judgments, but also on exogenous factors.[4]

In Chapter 3, Garrett and Lange discuss how preferences, policies, and institutions relate to one another. Given a set of domestic political institutions, an increase in the size and productivity of the exposed sector of the economy (the tradables sector) will not, in general, be accompanied by a comparable increase in its political influence. Garrett and Lange suggest, through a set of stylized models, that nondemocratic regimes should react more sporadically than democratic ones to changes in internationalization; and that variations in the responsiveness of democratic regimes will be related to the strength of labor unions, the electoral rules, the number of veto players, and the extent of political independence of key bureaucracies such as central banks. They conclude with a discussion of the conditions under which democratic governments, seeking reelection, will pursue strategies of institutional change. Although no single, well-specified deductive theory exists to guide us through the institutional thickets, a number of interesting hypotheses can be formulated about the connections among preferences, policies, and institutions.

The empirical chapters assess how different forms of internationalization have affected the policy preferences of actors and have produced changes in domestic coalitions, policies, and institutions. These chapters also discuss many instances in which that impact was mediated and in some respects fundamentally altered by national political institutions. Chapters 4–6, by Geoffrey Garrett, Jeffry Frieden, and Frances Rosenbluth, discuss Europe, the United States and Japan, followed by Chapters 7–8, by Matthew Evangelista and Susan Shirk, on the Soviet Union and China. Chapter 9, written jointly by Stephan Haggard and Sylvia Maxfield, analyzes the effects of financial internationalization in selected developing countries. Our own arguments are presented in Sections III and IV of this introduction and elaborated in the concluding essay of this volume.

This volume is firmly within the "second image reversed" tradition (Gourevitch 1978). Its distinctiveness derives from the juxtaposition of theories of policy preferences based on microeconomics, on the one hand, and arguments that emphasize how existing institutions shape the effects of internationalization, on the other. In a broad sense this volume presents a dialogue between international political economy, heavily influenced now by economic models, and comparative politics, driven these days by the "new institutionalism." Our work therefore reflects attempts in political economy to integrate these two distinct types of theories.

In this volume, both the political economists and the institutionalists assume that political actors are, broadly speaking, rational. Politicians respond to incentives, which are provided both by institutions and by the opportunities and constraints of the world economy. Thus, the debate in this volume is *not* between rationalistic and nonrationalistic approaches. It *is* about the relative importance of the constraints and incentives imposed by the world economy, on the one hand, and the constraints and incentives inherent in preexisting national institutions, on the other. It is also about how these international and domestic constraints interact.

The next section of this introductory chapter reviews earlier work on international and domestic political economy, explaining how this volume relates to it. Section II provides some evidence on the various dimensions of internationalization during the past twenty years. In Section III we put forward some hypotheses about the impact of internationalization on domestic politics, which are then juxtaposed, in Section IV, to hypotheses about institutional sources of resistance to the linear effects of internationalization. We conclude by emphasizing the essential point of this volume: that internationalization is having profound effects on domestic politics, although the forms that these effects take vary cross-nationally due to different institutional as well as political-economic conditions.

I. EARLIER STUDIES OF THE EFFECT OF THE INTERNATIONAL ECONOMY

Two substantial literatures have addressed the broad issues we raise in this volume. During the late 1960s and early 1970s, studies of international "interdependence" focused on the ways in which greater economic linkage among countries could affect them (Cooper 1968, 1972; Deutsch and Eckstein 1961; Keohane and Nye 1972; Rosecrance and Stein 1975; and Waltz 1970). As this literature developed, it became more precise about the meaning of interdependence and its relationship to the concept of power, adapting concepts that Albert Hirschman (1945/1980) had developed a generation earlier (Baldwin 1980; Keohane and Nye 1977). Interdependence, this literature argued, altered the nature of world politics by changing the context and alternatives facing countries. In that respect, the essential point of this work was similar to the argument made here. Missing from this literature, however, was a systematic analysis of how interdependence affected domestic politics.[5] Keohane and Nye, for instance, limited their analysis in *Power and Interdependence* to the international level and thus "had to view interests [of states] as formed largely exogenously, in a way unexplained by our theory . . . [yet] changes in definitions of self-interest . . . kept appearing in our case studies" (Keohane and Nye 1987: 739). Our study of "internationalization" in this volume attempts to build on the interdependence literature by exploring the impact of interdependence on politics within countries.

Responding to this neglect of domestic politics in the work on interdependence, a new literature, beginning in the late 1970s, argued that international forces had decisively affected the internal politics, and hence the foreign policies, of major countries. By affecting interests and power, international developments could affect the coalitions that form in domestic politics (Gourevitch 1978; Katzenstein 1978). However, since the early, innovative literature on these issues was not firmly grounded in economic theory, the causal linkages between international-level changes and domestic politics were rarely made explicit.

More recent work has attempted to address these problems and to extend this "second image reversed" tradition. Four arguments about the diverse effects of international economic forces on domestic politics are prominent in recent work. In *Commerce and Coalitions,* Ronald Rogowski has used the Stolper–Samuelson theorem to argue that changes in international trade flows affect national political coalitions and cleavages by changing the returns to factors of production (Rogowski 1989).[6] Grounding his analysis in the Heckscher–Ohlin approach to international trade, he has argued that the factors that gain and lose from the external changes form distinct political coalitions that mark the major political cleavages within states. Hence showing what shifts in the level of trade occur and which factors gain and lose from these trade flows generates hypotheses about the national political cleavages within countries.

Factors of production, however, may be tied to the economic sectors in which they are used: that is, factors may be "specific" to sectors, or industries. Insofar as such specific factor models are applicable, coalitions will be based on sectors rather than on factors of production. Politics will not pit labor versus capital along class lines, or city versus countryside, but will be oriented toward cleavages such as those between producers of tradables and nontradables, exporting and import-competing sectors, or multinational and purely national firms. Following the argument of Alexander Gerschenkron, Peter Gourevitch showed that during the last quarter of the nineteenth century, countries' "production profiles," defined by "the preferences of societal actors as shaped by the actors' situation in the international and domestic economy," help to explain their trade policies (Gourevitch 1986, especially chapter 3).[7] Changes in trade flows and the competitiveness of sectors will therefore reshape national preferences and thus alter domestic politics. International openness, as Jeffry Frieden (1991b) has argued, may shift political disputes from interest rates toward exchange rates, and pit international traders and investors, who favor stable exchange rates, against import-competing manufacturers of tradeable goods for the domestic market, who favor depreciated currency values.

In a complex modern economy, however, the gains from trade may be even more specific, accruing to particular firms rather than to either broad sectors or factors of production. Coalitions will then rest on the convergence of firms' interests. For instance, in *Resisting Protectionism,* Helen Milner (1988) has argued that different degrees of export dependence or multinationalization of production by firms affect their preferences toward the regulation of international transactions and hence national policies.

Finally, different levels of integration into world markets may influence the character of national political institutions. David Cameron (1978) showed that exposure to the international economy during the 1960s and 1970s was associated with large public sectors; and Peter Katzenstein interpreted the corporatist structures of small European states as designed to provide "an institutional mechanism for mobilizing the consensus necessary to live with the costs of rapid economic change" (Katzenstein 1985: 200), although the exact form taken by these institutions varies with those states' historical experiences.

Other observers have also noted variations in national responses. First, a number of authors have claimed that countries' responses will depend heavily on the partisan composition of the government in office: left-wing governments will react differently to economic pressures than will their right-wing counterparts. The partisanship of governments matters since each party has a different program that appeals to a different electorate. To win or keep office requires keeping one's core constituents happy. This argument is based in part on the literature on macroeconomic policy-making, which shows that a rational partisan model of the economy is a powerful predictor of policymakers' behavior. In this model, governments controlled by left-wing parties expand the economy when they come to office, while right-wing governments contract the economy after winning office. However, in a highly internationalized economy, these simple relationships do not hold. Alesina and Roubini find that small, highly trade-dependent countries do not show evidence of rational partisan macro-economic cycles, suggesting that very high levels of internationalization constrain the use of macroeconomic policy (Alesina and Roubini 1992; Alt 1985).

Second, the organization of labor and financial markets seems to matter. Garrett and Lange argue that successful policies of left-wing or right-wing governments depend on compatible social constellations. Left-wing governments succeed best where labor is strong and centrally organized, while right-wing policies work best where labor is weaker and more fragmented (Alvarez, Garrett, and Lange 1991; Garrett and Lange 1986). Paulette Kurzer (1993) focuses on financial linkages between economies of small European states and world markets, seeking to show, in a study of Belgium, The Netherlands, Austria, and Sweden, that these financial linkages are important determinants of the success of social democratic corporatism.

Third, political institutions make a difference. For the developed countries, a score of studies focused on economic policy make this point (Hall 1986; Katzenstein 1978; Shonfield 1965; Zysman 1983). Katzenstein, for instance, argues that how nations respond to external economic pressures depends on whether their political institutions are "strong" and able to insulate policymakers from immediate political pressures or "weak" and more permeable to societal influences. Countries with long traditions of professional bureaucracies, like France and Japan, will react differently than will countries lacking such well-developed, distinct state institutions, such as the U.S. and United Kingdom. Of particular importance for this volume is the argument that some countries, because of their political institutions, can insulate themselves from societal pressures. This implies that even though internationalization may be growing and the policy preferences of domestic actors changing, central policymakers will not respond to such changes, or will respond in their own fashion.

Virtually all of the work on this topic, whether stressing partisanship, labor or financial markets, or state institutions, casts doubt on the argument that countries will respond to internationalization simply as a function of its effect on their relative prices. No matter how seriously one takes the propositions in Chapter 2 about the impact of internationalization on actors' preferences, it is clear that this impact is mediated by domestic political factors, which reflect diverse historical experiences.

II. INTERNATIONALIZATION: THE EVIDENCE

Economic transactions across national boundaries have expanded dramatically over the last two decades. Hence internationalization, as we empirically identify it, has increased. Such internationalization can be expected to increase integration between domestic and international markets, where integration is defined in terms of the convergence of prices of goods, services, and capital in those markets. Although internationalization and integration do not perfectly covary, and measures of price convergence are hard to construct, the correlations between short-term interest rates have become quite high recently, returning to levels only seen in the Gold Standard period. (Frankel 1991; Zevin 1992: 46–55). Since our concern is with the political effects of flows across borders, rather than with their effects on integration, we sidestep the issue of the relationship between internationalization and economic integration.

International trade flows

Data on world trade document a major dimension of internationalization.[8] During the first fifteen or twenty years after World War II, measures of trade openness (such as ratios of import volumes to real income) recovered to levels above those of the 1930s and 1940s, but did not reach levels as high as those of the period before 1914 (McKeown 1991). Since the early 1970s, however, world trade has increased dramatically relative to previous levels, and relative to domestic product. Import volumes as a percentage of real GNP in industrial capitalist countries, which remained between 10 and 16 percent throughout the ninety years between 1880 and 1972, increased to almost 22 percent during the 1973–87 period (McKeown 1991: 158). Between 1972 and 1991 the average rate of import growth into the Organization for Economic Development and Co-operation (OECD) area was slightly over five percent, compared to an average increase in real total domestic demand (both expressed in 1987 dollars on the basis of 1987 GDP weights) of only three percent (OECD 1992: tables R10 and R8, pp. 210, 208). That is, imports grew over these two decades at a rate about 65 percent higher than growth in domestic demand. Much of this trade occurred through multinational enterprises: roughly 40 percent of United States imports, 25 to 30 percent of Japanese imports, and thirty percent of British imports occurred as intrafirm transactions during the early 1980s (McKeown 1991: 168).

The long-term patterns are documented in Tables 1 and 2, which show changes in the ratio of merchandise exports to GDP for sixteen developed countries between 1913 and 1987, at current and 1985 prices, respectively. With few exceptions this ratio fell between 1913 and 1950, and rose both between 1950 and 1973 and between 1973 and 1987. However, there is also a great deal of country-by-country variation. In 1973, half of the countries listed in the table still had ratios below those of 1913, on the basis of current prices; even in 1987, five countries had lower ratios than in 1913. However, the period after 1950 is marked by sustained increases in the export/GDP ratio for all countries, with the exception of Australia, when measured in current prices.

The more recent export records of the Newly Industrializing Countries (NICs) are equally relevant for documenting the internationalization of national economies. Six countries are often regarded as the first NICs: Brazil, Mexico, Hong Kong, South Korea, Singapore, and Taiwan. Although trade preferences extended by rich countries did not favor these economies over other developing countries, their gross domestic products and exports grew dramatically in the 1970s, unlike those of many of their counterparts. These six countries accounted for 3.5 percent of world gross domestic product and 1.9 percent of world exports of manufactures in 1964–5, but accounted for 6.2 percent of world GDP and 8.7 percent of world exports of manufactures by 1983 (OECD 1988: tables 1.1 and 1.4, pp. 11 and 14). Their exports to OECD countries, which had been less than half their imports from those countries in 1964, exceeded their imports by 1983 (OECD 1988: figure 1, p. 17). Between 1964 and 1985, imports to the OECD countries from the NICs grew at an average annual rate of 23.6 percent, compared to 13.6 percent for all imports (OECD 1988: 18) As a result both of this export boom and falling oil prices, the proportion of South to North merchandise exports comprising manufactured goods rose from 15.2 percent in 1980 to 53.3 percent in 1989; in that same period, the percentage of Southern nonfuel exports consisting of manufactured goods rose from 45.1 to 70.9 (Wood 1994: table 1.1, p. 2). The record of the NICs demonstrates that during the 1970s and 1980s, the world economy was sufficiently open that even in the absence of any special treatment some poor countries could achieve rapid rates of export and income growth.

The expansion of international capital markets

In the past twenty years, capital markets have grown increasingly internationalized. Global capital flows of all types have expanded dramatically, far

Table 1. *Ratio of merchandise exports to GDP at current market prices*

	1913	1950	1973	1987
Australia	18.3	22.0	13.7	13.5
Austria	8.2	12.6	19.0	23.2
Belgium	50.9	20.3	49.9	59.8
Canada	15.1	17.5	20.9	23.9
Denmark	26.9	21.3	21.9	25.4
Finland	25.2	16.6	20.5	22.5
France	13.9	10.6	14.4	16.8
Germany	17.5	8.5	19.7	26.4
Italy	12.0	7.0	13.4	15.4
Japan	12.3	4.7	8.9	9.7
Netherlands	38.2	26.9	37.3	43.6
Norway	22.7	18.2	24.4	25.7
Sweden	20.8	17.8	23.5	27.6
Switzerland	31.4	20.0	23.2	26.6
UK	20.9	14.4	16.4	19.3
USA	6.1	3.6	8.0	5.7
Arithmetic average	21.2	15.1	20.9	24.1

Source: Maddison 1991: 326.

faster than domestically. As one economic text claims, "If a financier named Rip Van Winkle had gone to sleep in the early 1960s and awakened two decades later, he would have been shocked by changes in both the nature and the scale of international financial activity. In the early 1960s, for example, most banking was purely domestic . . . Two decades later, however, many banks derived a large share of their profits from international activities" (Krugman and Obstfeld 1988: 622).

Three factors created this revolution in the world's capital markets: deregulation of capital markets and finance by governments; the rapid growth of world trade and investment, which has generated huge financial flows; and technological innovation, making the movement of capital faster and cheaper (Turner 1991: 11–12). These changes are mutually re-inforcing: the growth of international investment has prompted governments to deregulate capital movements, which in turn has facilitated investment and technological change (Goodman and Pauly 1993).

All aspects of finance have been internationalized in the past twenty years. By the end of the 1980s, gross international capital flows rose to $600 billion annually (Turner 1991: 9). International capital inflows to the industrialized countries (mostly from other industrialized countries) rose from an annual average of $99 billion in 1975–7 to $463 billion in 1985–9, nearly a five-fold increase. For developing countries, international flows doubled from $52 billion in 1975–7 to $110 billion in 1985–9 (Turner 1991: 23).[9] Net

Table 2. *Ratio of merchandise exports to GDP at 1985 prices*

	1913	1950	1973	1987
Australia	10.9	7.7	9.5	12.4
Austria	5.2	4.0	12.6	20.0
Belgium	17.5	13.4	40.3	52.5c
Canada	12.9	13.0	19.9	23.8
Denmark	10.1	9.3	18.2	25.8
Finland	17.0	12.7	20.5	23.0
France	6.0	5.6	11.2	14.3
Germany	12.2	4.4	17.2	23.7
Italy	3.3	2.4	8.7	11.2
Japan	2.1	2.0	6.8	10.6
Netherlands	14.5	10.2	34.1	40.9
Norway	14.6	13.5	27.4	34.0
Sweden	12.0	12.2	23.1	27.0
Switzerland	22.3	9.8	21.3	28.9
UK	14.7	9.5	11.5	15.3
USA	4.1	3.3	5.8	6.3
Arithmetic average	11.2	8.3	18.0	23.1

Source: Maddison 1991: 327.

capital inflows to the developing countries reached $151.3 billion in 1993 (BIS 1995: 146). Net short-term international bank flows also quintupled in the last two decades, growing from $11.5 billion annually in 1975–9 to almost $62 billion by 1989 (Turner 1991: 75). Total net lending in world markets exploded; it averaged $100 billion per year in the late 1970s and $342 billion yearly by 1990. By 1992 the stock of international bank lending had reached $3.6 trillion, seven times the level of 1978.[10] Foreign exchange trading more than doubled between 1986 and 1989, when it amounted to $650 billion daily, which was about 40 times the average daily volume of world trade. By 1992 the volume of such transactions had increased to almost $1 trillion per day (Turner 1991: 34, 9–10; Eichengreen 1993). Thus while increases in international trade of goods and services have far outstripped the growth of domestic production, the movement of capital around the globe has grown even faster than that of trade.[11] "The growth of international capital movements has dwarfed the growth in trade. The stock of international bank loans, for example, has grown from 5 percent of GDP of countries in the OECD in 1973 to about 20 percent of OECD GDP in 1991" (*Economic Report of the President*, 1993, p. 281.)

International portfolio and direct investment have also grown. In 1979, annual international transactions in equities averaged about $73 billion; by 1990, this had grown twentyfold to $1500 billion (Turner 1991: 53). By 1989, furthermore, the total worldwide stock of foreign direct investment (FDI) was $1.5 trillion in a $20 trillion world economy (United Nations *World Investment Report 1991:* 3). Global inflows of FDI surged to $185 billion that same year, compared with annual averages of $53 billion in 1980–4 and $28 billion in 1975–9 (Turner 1991: 39). Aggregate foreign direct investment outflows in 1994 reached a new record of $230 billion as well (BIS 1995: 66). In the 1980s, direct investment outflows grew at an "unprecedented rate" of 30% annually, three times faster than the growth of trade and four times faster than the growth of world output (United Nations *World Investment Report 1991:* table 1, pp. 3–4). In the aggregate, FDI accounted for one percent of all the OECD GNP by the end of the 1980s; it was only 1/2 percent in 1980 (Turner 1991: 30–2). FDI grew more rapidly than domestic output and more than domestic investment. The ratio of FDI to gross domestic capital formation rose from 2.9 percent in 1980–2 and 3.4 percent in 1985–7 for the developed countries. As with the other aspects of finance, foreign direct investment has become a more important component of almost all economies.

Of course, the fact of huge capital flows is neither a necessary nor a sufficient condition for the true integration of capital markets, in which real covered interest rates should equalize. Where no barriers to transactions exist, interest rates could converge as a result of information flows and expectations, without much actual capital movement; conversely, one can at least imagine a situation in which barriers to capital mobility, preventing true economic integration, persisted alongside substantial flows.[12] Nevertheless, one would normally expect an association between capital mobility and actual flows of financial assets. Other studies, such as those by Frankel and Zevin cited earlier, do show that at least for short-term instruments, covered interest rates have become very highly correlated. The level of internationalization existing now is close to the very high levels experienced during the Gold Standard years of the late nineteenth century.

In any event, these data show that internationalization, as we have empirically defined it, is well under way: international transactions are of increasing importance in the world economy. No country can escape the effects of this dramatic change. But the degree of openness of a given economy depends also on national policy. It is still possible, at least temporarily, to insulate a country from the world economy, although the opportunity costs of doing so may be high. Cuba and North Korea illustrate this point. Moreover, the impact of the world economy on countries that are open to its influence does not appear to be uniform. Differences in factor endowments, group organization, national institutions, and the political strategies of leaders have all helped produce diverse national responses to common international trends. Understanding the effects of internationalization thus requires analysis of its impact both on policy preferences and incentives more generally, and also on political reactions of socioeconomic groups to its effects and the way that political struggles over openness are mediated by domestic institutions.

III. HYPOTHESES ABOUT THE POLITICAL EFFECTS OF INTERNATIONALIZATION

Our analysis of the effects of internationalization begins by distinguishing between its impact on policy preferences, as discussed by Frieden and Rogowski in Chapter 2, and its impact on the constraints and opportunities faced by governments. We begin with policy preferences.

Internationalization and policy preferences

In general, internationalization is expected to generate new coalitions revolving around the differential effects of greater openness. Producers closest to their countries' comparative advantage are expected to favor policies that promote increased openness, while disadvantaged producers should oppose them. Hence the winners and losers from internationalization should have conflicting interests. However, other cleavages exist – for instance, between tradables producers favoring devaluations and nontradables sectors opposing them, or between owners of specific factors, whose capital is immobile, and holders of liquid assets. Furthermore, changes in policy preferences alone will not tell us how policies and institutions will shift as a result of internationalization: we also need to know what the effects of internationalization will be on the relative political influence of various actors.

It seems clear that the economic as well as political effects of internationalization are neither simple nor uniform. Although internationalization may exert some broadly similar effects across countries, its differential effects are likely to dominate. Two sets of these are apparent. First, capital and trade flows will have different effects on national economies. Economic theory points out that these two factors will have significantly different economic effects.

Reductions in barriers to capital mobility provide for enhanced investment opportunities and allow countries to diversify country-specific productivity shocks. Increased capital mobility can thus be expected to enhance the volatility of investment. At the same time, the ability to use the current account for international borrowing and lending facilitates consumption smoothing. Hence *enhanced capital mobility should be associated, ceteris paribus, with smoother consumption and more volatile investment* . . . Turning to goods markets, international economic integration of goods markets intuitively allows national economies to specialize in (final) goods in which they have some comparative advantage. A reduction in trade barriers (for example, import tariffs or NTBs) . . . will lead to geographical concentration of industries and to export specialization . . . Succinctly, *increased goods mobility should be associated, ceteris paribus, with increased output volatility* (Razin and Rose 1994: 50–1).

Given the different economic effects of goods versus capital mobility, we expect the two different forms of internationalization to have distinct effects. As noted above, greater capital flows in contrast to goods flows will create different types of shocks to an economy. This suggests, for example, that the political crises experienced by countries should differ depending on their type of international exposure.

The other way in which internationalization can have differential effects is a function of the different endowments of countries or the specificity of their sectors. In general, as Frieden and Rogowski argue, internationalization will lead to relative price changes among factors or sectors – depending on the model one uses – and this may lead to changes in their policy preferences and eventually in political coalitions. But how this process unfolds depends on the particular economy. For example, in a capital-rich economy, internationalization may induce owners of capital to push for even greater levels of openness; in a capital-poor economy the outcome should be the reverse. While we expect that the general process of internationalization will alter relative prices, thus changing groups' policy preferences and leading to new coalitions, we do not expect all countries to come to look alike as a result of this process. The similarity we do expect is that, in a variety of ways, the interests on which domestic political coalitions rest will be increasingly shaped by international economic forces. Domestic debates and coalitions will become more focused on international policy issues as internationalization progresses: policies involving international trade, exchange rates, and foreign investment should not only spark increasing political debate but occupy an ever greater amount of domestic political interest.

Internationalization and government policy

We can be more specific about two political effects of internationalization that affect government policies. Increased international trade and capital movement between economies raises the proportion of each economy exposed to world market pressures (the tradables sector) and is therefore likely to increase the sensitivity of the domestic economy to international price trends and shocks. Internationalization thus means that economic shocks from abroad will be more fully and quickly translated into the domestic economy, as the Mexican devaluation crisis in late 1994 and early 1995 suggests. Economic shocks from abroad will generate political crises, often of such magnitude that they reshape national policies and institutions fundamentally. Our first hypothesis is that mounting internationalization will increase the likelihood that polities experience large economic shocks that lead to political crises. These are the very same crises that, as institutionalists have noted, create the "political space" necessary for political entrepreneurs to fundamentally reorganize domestic politics (Goldstein 1989; Haggard 1988; Hall 1989).

Second, internationalization affects the autonomy of governments' policy choices by undermining the efficacy of some policies. "Countries which reduce international barriers to either goods or capital sacrifice domestic autonomy in the hope of a higher standard of living" (Razin and Rose 1994: 48). Both fiscal and monetary policy may be affected; as Bryant argues, "after an increase in interdependence, a given-sized policy action in one nation will typically have greater spillover effects on variables in the rest of the world, whereas less [sic] of the impacts will remain in the nation initiating the action" (Bryant 1980: 181).[13] As the Mundell–Fleming theorem shows, under fixed exchange rates increases in capital mobility render monetary policy less and less useful domestically; it becomes simply a tool for maintaining the exchange rate. This may be one reason why West European states are willing to consider monetary union now; their desire for fixed exchange rates in the face of massive capital mobility has left them little room for independent national monetary policies.

The "standard open economy macroeconomic model," which makes a series of assumptions about the nature of the economy, points out that with floating exchange rates and complete capital mobility, fiscal policy may lose some of its efficacy, especially when compared to a world of less mobile capital (Mussa 1979). Market reactions to fiscal policy in the short run affect domestic interest rates and the exchange rate in ways that tend to offset the effects that it would have had in a closed economy. In contrast, changes in monetary policy tend to have a bigger impact under these conditions than with fixed rates. In open economies, the very size of the impact may deter expansionary monetary policy for fear of capital flight. That is, even if monetary policy could make a difference, monetary autonomy may be constrained (Andrews 1994; Goodman and Pauly 1993). As even the United States with its relatively insulated markets is coming to realize, internationalization changes the costs of policy options. The Federal Reserve Chairman recently said in explaining his decision not to lower U.S. interest rates, "A consistently disciplined monetary policy is what our global financial system increasingly demands and rewards . . . While there are many policy considerations that arise as a consequence of the rapidly expanding global financial system, the most important is the necessity of maintaining stability in the prices of goods and services and confidence in domestic financial markets. Failure to do so is apt to exact far greater consequences as a result of cross-border capital movements than those which might have prevailed a generation ago" (*New York Times,* 21 June 1995, A-1 and D-9).

This loss of policy autonomy may place special pressure on left-wing, social democratic governments. If left-wing governments favor expansionary monetary and fiscal policies to create full employment, then their policy preferences may be more constrained than those of right-wing governments who give stable prices priority over full employment (Alesina and

Roubini 1992; Hibbs 1987). With floating exchange rates, high capital mobility may render expansionary fiscal and monetary policy ineffective (or even counterproductive); and under fixed rates, capital mobility makes monetary policy less usable and may constrain expansionary fiscal policy as well.[14] On the other hand, contractionary policies or ones that aim for price stability may be rewarded by markets. Hence, the constraints of openness on macroeconomic policy appear to benefit right-wing governments at the expense of their social democratic competitors, since the options of expansionary monetary and fiscal policy become much more costly. However, as Garrett points out in Chapter 4, fiscal policies that upgrade a country's trade competitiveness, such as government investment in human capital and infrastructure, may be an alternative route for social democratic governments. Leftist corporatist governments may be best-positioned to follow such trade-enhancing investment policies.

If the hypotheses discussed above and summarized below are true, internationalization would have far-reaching effects on domestic politics. As it progressed, the policy preferences of groups would change; new coalitions would form; and the potential for changes in domestic policies and institutions would grow.

PROPOSITION 1:   *As internationalization progresses, the tradables sector will expand and the economy will become more sensitive to world market price trends and shocks. The likelihood of major domestic policy and institutional reforms will grow as internationalization makes the economy more vulnerable to externally generated economic shocks.*

PROPOSITION 2:   *Internationalization will undermine the autonomy and efficacy of government macroeconomic policy. It will more seriously constrain the behavior of left-wing governments than of right-wing governments. Capital mobility will have more far-reaching consequences than trade openness.*

Corollaries

Frieden and Rogowski's argument implies that internationalization will affect even autarchic economies, since it is not flows per se but changing opportunity costs that exert the major effects. Barriers between the domestic and the world market create a differential between home and foreign prices, which exacts aggregate opportunity costs from the economy as its efficiency is lowered, and which differentially penalizes sectors that would be competitive on world markets. Closure benefits those factors of production that are relatively scarce (or uncompetitive sectors) and hurts abundant factors (and competitive sectors). Groups that could gain from openness (for example, owners of the abundant factors) should increase their pressure on the government to change its policies; on the other hand, potential losers will lobby hard to preserve the status quo. If actors have secure property rights and can rationally anticipate these potential gains and losses – two major caveats, as we will see – political pressures from actors in closed economies should parallel those emanating from similarly situated actors in open ones. Hence as internationalization proceeds, the opportunity costs for countries with autarchic economies will mount, new coalitions should arise and pressures for policy change will grow. Hence we have:

Corollary 1: *Internationalization should affect even countries whose economies are not open.*

A second corollary hypothesis begins with the recognition that internationalization implies greater mobility for capital. If capital is less costly to move from country to country, then those owners of capital who can "exit" can use the threat of exit to magnify their political influence, or "voice" (Hirschman 1970). Credible threats from capital to move put additional pressure on political leaders to preserve what Charles E. Lindblom (1977) once called, in a domestic context, the "privileged position of business." As a recent study of social democracy in four small European countries declares, "the most persistent dilemma for labor is that increased mobility of capital has also increased the power resources of capital. The effect of this mobility is that managers and owners of financial assets and transnational corporations are favored, and labor is hurt" (Kurzer 1993: 12). In Chapter 4 of this volume, Garrett concurs that "the easier it is for asset holders to move their capital offshore, the stronger the incentives for governments to pursue policies that will increase rates of return on domestic investments" (Garrett, p. 88). In their analysis in this volume of capital market liberalization in four developing countries, Stephan Haggard and Sylvia Maxfield observe that "episodes of capital account opening appeared to be motivated by the efforts of political leaders to reassure creditors and investors." (p. 234). Internationalization of capital markets thus should increase the political leverage of internationally mobile capital.
    Hence we have:

Corollary 2: *Internationally mobile capital will gain political power, relative to labor and political officials, as internationalization proceeds.*

Some discussions of internationalization raise the question of whether countries' policies will tend toward convergence. Convergence, however, is not a central theme of this volume. In theory the opening of markets for goods, services and capital should lead to the convergence of prices. Markets may punish countries that adopt price-distorting policies: interest rate premia or adverse effects on efficiency may eventually force their governments back to more conventional policies. The current vogue for "neoliberal" economic policies – the combination of financial anti-inflation measures, trade and capital market liberalization as well as the reduction in government intervention domestically – is sometimes cited as evidence of this process of convergence.

However, as we have emphasized, the political impacts of internationalization vary depending on the context, such as which factors and sectors are advantaged, the adaptability of political institutions, and the vulnerability of the economy to internationally induced crises. Furthermore, as Lange and Garrett emphasize and we also stress in the next section, existing institutions profoundly affect the kinds of effects which given patterns of internationalization exert. Painted with a broad brush, movements toward neoliberal policies may look similar, but when each country's portrait is painted in more detail the changes appear quite different. In Chapter 4, for example, Garrett argues that left-labor governments have maintained a significant capacity to maintain differential policies from their more conservative counterparts, despite internationalization. Such governments may well pursue expansionary fiscal policies even in the face of interest rate premia imposed by market actors. "Convergence" is not a precise concept, and the evidence about it that we have been able to muster is ambiguous. Nevertheless, it is an important topic that requires more research.

IV. RESISTANCE TO THE EFFECTS OF INTERNATIONALIZATION

If all of these hypotheses were true, the impact of internationalization, especially on social democratic governments, would be severe indeed. Yet observations of past political change should make us wary about expecting that internationalization would have such direct, one-sided effects. Indeed, it is highly unlikely that unions, political parties, and other organized interests disadvantaged by internationalization will passively accept their fate, or that governmental decisions about how to react to contacts with the world economy will be dictated by neoclassical economic theory.

Political leaders have a degree of latitude in how they respond to internationalization. In large part, this range of choice is a function of the domestic institutional framework in which they must operate. In general, preexisting domestic institutions may allow actors to resist the pressures generated by internationalization. Institutions may enable actors who would lose from internationalization to halt any such change. Institutions may facilitate the organization of groups opposed to change, or give them privileged political access. They may deny political representation to groups benefiting from the changes advanced by internationalization. Existing institutions may make new policies literally unthinkable. Domestic institutions may simply be able to block any changes from occurring even in the face of internationalization.

We can identify three different effects of domestic institutions on the process linking internationalization to domestic politics: (1) They may block relative price signals from the international economy from entering the domestic one, thus obscuring actors' interests; (2) they may freeze coalitions and policies into place by making the costs of changing these coalitions and policies very high; and (3) they may channel leaders' strategies in response to international economic change.

First, and at the earliest stage, domestic institutions can block price signals emanating from the international environment. Particularly in countries with central planning or heavy state intervention, government policies and institutions may serve as a "wall" between the domestic economy and the international one. Relative price changes may occur, but they may not be felt domestically because of the state's intervention. While we expect these countries to experience the effects of internationalization through the growing opportunity costs of autarchy, they may be able to afford these costs for a long time. As Garrett and Lange point out, the more authoritarian and stable a political system is, the longer its leaders can resist responding to the pressures created by internationalization. Others have also noted that the imposition of capital controls is more likely in "strong" governments characterized by long-lived, majoritarian governments, which can better insulate themselves from the costs of imposing such measures (Alesina, Grilli, and Milesi-Ferretti 1994).

Second, preexisting political institutions may negate or modify the influence of the world economy by "freezing" coalitions and policies into place. International price signals may enter the domestic economy, but politics may remain frozen in timeworn patterns. Groups with access to the centers of political power may retain their advantages despite internationalization; groups denied such access may be unable even in the face of internationalization to gain it. Furthermore, those people who would gain from change may not interpret the price signals correctly or may be uncertain about the extent of their prospective gains, while entrenched groups may be more intent on defending their interests.

Much as Lipset and Rokkan described the "freezing" of party systems in European countries, other institutions may lock coalitions that support existing policies into place (Lipset and Rokkan 1967). Policies adopted earlier may also remain because the institutions built around them make changing them too costly for any rational actor. Here the claim is that new coalitions and interests cannot easily form; the higher the costs of entry into the political system, the greater the resistance to change. Certain forms of electoral laws may also effectively freeze old coalitions in place, as Garrett and Lange argue.

The third mechanism by which domestic institutions may affect the impact of internationalization is to channel state strategies designed to respond to international-level changes. This process is less dramatic than the two prior ones, but perhaps the most important in the long run. The choices of strategies, coalitions, policies and the timing of reforms have differed substantially from country to country. The domestic political institutions of a country heavily influence these choices. For instance, countries lacking an independent central bank may have to use different policies and strategies to reach their objectives than do ones with an independent central bank; and governments whose societies have coherent unions and employers' associations that are used to collaborating with one another have options not available to governments presiding over fragmented labor markets. Prior policy choices and institutions condition which particular strategies and policies leaders select to respond to the pressures of internationalization.

All three effects of institutions are evident in at least one of the country cases that follows. These cases were chosen to provide maximum variation on the context in which internationalization was occurring. If internationalization is indeed a systemwide, global process, then all countries should in some measure be affected by it. Varying the type of political system, geographic region, level of development, cultural and historical background should enable us to see whether it is having such global effects, and how much they depend on the context. Are all countries undergoing a systemic transformation in their political coalitions, policies, and institutions? Or do prior political institutions block or channel this change, while political leaders remain relatively free to choose their particular strategies for dealing with internationalization? The tension between domestic institutions and international pressures has been a constant one. But is there now some linear trend whereby internationalization inevitably leads to the effects outlined in Section III? Or can domestic actors and institutions intervene and retard or reshape such international pressures?

CONCLUSION

The internationalization of the world economy seems to be having profound effects on domestic politics worldwide. As the world economy changes, so do incentives for governments, firms, and organized socioeconomic groups within countries. Pressures to alter policies, and associated institutions, mount. This volume systematically examines these changes and documents the resulting patterns of behavior in advanced industrialized democracies, the state-socialist systems before radical institutional changes took place in them, and selected countries of the Third World. That the politics of advanced capitalist democracies and developing countries are affected deeply by changes in the world economy is hardly surprising, although the variety of such effects is impressive. It is perhaps more novel to show, as Evangelista and Shirk do, the profundity of the political and economic effects on state socialism from changes in the capitalist world political economy.

While the primary focus of this volume is on the interplay between internationalization and domestic institutions, other factors clearly affect how governments respond to international pressures. Governments can influence the constraints imposed by the international economy both through unilateral and multilateral action. In the presence of trade openness, government policy often focuses on improving the competitive advantage of a country's industries, thus promoting the rapid adaptation of the economy to internationalization. As the industrial growth of Japan and South Korea illustrates, under propitious conditions such policies may be successful (Haggard 1990; Krueger 1992; Wade 1990). Such national industrial policies can also run into dead-ends, as in Sweden during the 1980s. Even if underlying factor endowments can only change significantly over several decades, there are good reasons to believe that governments (for good or ill) have had significant impacts on patterns of competitive advantage within shorter time periods. Government policy may not be limited to targeting "winners," but may encompass a wider range of measures to increase total factor productivity by improving factor conditions, increasing demand, and affecting firm strategies (Porter 1990: ch. 6, 617–82). The central question today, however, is whether such strategies can persist in the wake of extensive capital mobility. The key difference for governments today is that, unlike their predecessors in the period from 1945 to 1980, they confront unprecedented levels (and speeds) of capital mobility, which make the reaction of international financial markets a major consideration in policy formulation.

Our argument also has to be complicated by considering the cumulative results of collective international state action. Indeed, since the end of World War II the world economy has been altered quite fundamentally by institutional innovations, fostered by powerful states, that have reduced transaction costs, thus fostering internationalization. Some of these innovations have been public and multilateral, such as the evolution of the General Agreement on Tariff and Trade (GATT); others have been private or unilateral. All have been affected directly or indirectly by the policies of powerful states and hence by international politics. Particularly important have been the tariff reduction rounds under the GATT, which have changed the relationship between home prices and world prices by lowering barriers to exchange. Economic actors within GATT countries confronted new opportunities for gain and threats of loss as the tariff cuts opened markets. Countries outside the GATT also faced new opportunity costs; as the size of the global market increased, so did the costs of being outside the world trading system. The creation of the European Economic Community and its expansion into the European Union as well as the collapse of the Bretton Woods fixed exchange rate system in the early 1970s also altered the world economy. Each of these events has promoted the growth of economic transactions across borders. They have also affected world market prices of goods and services, and hence led to shifts in the relative prices of domestic and world goods and services. These changes have had cumulative effects, increasing the opportunity costs to competitive sectors in countries not fully integrated into the GATT system or into the European Union.

Political choices and strategies thus play a role in our arguments both as reactions to internationalization and in shaping changes in the world economy. We do not view internationalization as an apolitical process characterized simply by adaptation to technologically driven change. On the contrary, powerful states and the international institutions that they control help to shape changes in internationalization, subject to the constraints of economics and technology. During the 1980s, for instance, intense political pressure was exerted by advanced industrialized countries on developing countries to open their economies. International financial institutions, such as the International Monetary Fund and the World Bank, intensified their emphasis on conditionality; the GATT codes of the Tokyo Round moved away from unconditional most-favored-nation treatment toward demands for reciprocity from developing countries; and the United States, using Section 301 of the Trade Act, pressed hard for liberalization of foreign investment regulations, and for protection of intellectual property. Along a variety of dimensions, the national economic regulations of developing countries were called into question by powerful states. As always in the world economy, power mattered.

In sum, the fact that since the 1970s countries all over the globe – including ones as diverse as Vietnam, India, China, South Africa, Chile, and Mexico – decided to reduce trade barriers, to open their capital markets, to reduce government intervention in the economy, to privatize state-owned enterprises, and to scale back social welfare policies suggests the powerful pressures exerted by the forces of internationalization. But a reading of the empirical papers also demonstrates that internationalization is not the only story. Internationalization may induce differing outcomes in each country as each polity reacts somewhat differently to the opportunities and constraints created. In the conclusion we will examine the generalizations developed here in light of the evidence presented in the following chapters.

2

The Impact of the International Economy on National Policies: An Analytical Overview

JEFFRY A. FRIEDEN AND RONALD ROGOWSKI

By virtually any measure, cross-border trade and investment have grown at extraordinary rates over the past thirty years. Representative trade statistics for the industrial economies and the newly industrializing countries (NICs) are presented by Milner and Keohane in the Introduction to this volume. Among the poorest states, as well (the forty-three countries that the World Bank classifies as "low-income," with per capita GNP of $610 or less in 1990), merchandise exports grew on average by 5.2 percent annually between 1965 and 1990 (computed from World Bank 1992: table 14). Cross-national flows of capital, as Milner and Keohane also indicate, increased even more sharply, roughly quintupling among the industrialized countries and doubling among the developing states in the single decade between the mid-1970s and the mid-1980s.

Increases of these magnitudes in international transactions – or more precisely, as we argue below, the exogenous easing of international exchange that such flows reflect – have affected domestic politics in virtually every country. Some of the ways in which they have done so are obvious, for example, controversies over trade agreements, common markets, non-tariff barriers, migration, and investment. Other impacts are less obvious but perhaps even more profound, including widespread repudiation of tax, regulatory, and macroeconomic policies that inhibit international competitiveness. This chapter attempts to elucidate how economic integration affects domestic politics, policies, and institutions by using international trade theories to generate testable propositions about the preferences of important groups within societies.

In Sections I and II, we define our independent and dependent variables: respectively, what we mean by exogenous easing of international exchange and what political outcomes we are trying to explain. Section III argues

The authors acknowledge useful comments and suggestions from Barry Eichengreen, Geoffrey Garrett, Robert Keohane, and Helen Milner.

that exogenous easing affects politics chiefly by way of its impact on relative prices and on the directness with which world prices are transmitted into the domestic market (or, more precisely, into the domestic opportunity structure). Section IV outlines the ways in which exogenous easing – and, more generally, international relative price trends – affects aggregate national welfare and related policies. In Section V, we explore the impact of such trends on domestic actors' preferences for governmental policies. Section VI discusses briefly the role of institutions. Section VII summarizes our argument and is followed by a conclusion.

I. THE INDEPENDENT VARIABLE

Increasing levels of international trade and investment reflect a deeper change: an exogenous decrease in the costs, or an increase in the rewards, of international economic transactions. Growing global trade and financial flows are an observable result of the changed costs and rewards of doing cross-border business. Of the many underlying causes of such change, we regard five as particularly salient.

Transport costs obviously affect the rewards of international economic exchange: much of the great increase in international exchange in the nineteenth century is commonly attributed to the vastly cheaper transport that canals, railroads, and steamships afforded (cf. Rogowski 1989: 21–2). Similarly in the last quarter-century, improved aircraft, containerization, and trucking have eased international trade. A second element of cost may be broadly called *infrastructure:* systems of international communication, settlements, credit, insurance, and forward markets that reduce the overall expense associated with international trade and payments. Some of these are technological in origin; others, such as integrated financial markets, result from combined economic, technical, and policy developments. A third major category of costs is *government policies* toward trade and investment. Most obvious are such barriers as tariffs, quotas, capital controls, and "voluntary" export restraints; but some policies, such as a stable international monetary system, reduce costs. Chief among the factors that may exogenously increase the returns to international trade are the growing significance of production processes characterized by *economies of scale* and growing cross-national disparities in *total factor productivity.*[1] This is not an exhaustive list of factors exogenously affecting the costs and rewards of international economic activity, but it includes important elements of any such list.

We mean by "exogenous easing" of international exchange an overall *decrease in the costs, or increase in the rewards, of such exchange:* either an exogenous reduction in the technical, economic, and political barriers to trade, investment, migration, or payments; or an exogenous change in production processes or endowments that increases the returns to international, as opposed to domestic, economic activity. The past thirty years, for example, have almost certainly been marked by a decrease of almost all relevant costs and, at least in many sectors, an increase in international returns; hence this period is one of exogenous easing of international exchange. Two introductory points are in order:

1 Movements of services and capital are analogous to those in goods and can be subjected to similar tools of analysis. For purposes of simplicity, we focus on trade in goods, with a few illustrative asides concerning financial and investment flows. In terms of exogenous easing, we emphasize changes in the cost and rewards of carrying out international trade in goods. The general argument does not vary appreciably if extended to the movement of capital or labor, although this is substantially more complex. There are differences worthy of note, but we largely ignore them to avoid overwhelming the argument with nuance and detail.

2 We focus on, and regard as central, changes that are not only exogenous to any one nation's policy but that resist manipulation by any one government. Governments often choose to try to isolate their economics from world markets, with effects that we analyze below. However, so long as they lack global dominion, they can do little about technical innovations that diminish costs of international communication and transport, institutional innovations that make international transactions less risky, production processes that guarantee increasing returns to scale, or other states' decisions to raise or lower barriers to exchange and investment. Of course, the policies of all governments are in the final analysis endogenous to the global political economy; but for our purposes and as a first approximation it is adequate to maintain the presumption that countries, and groups within countries, take as given the policy choices of the world's leading governments.

II. DEPENDENT VARIABLES

We are ultimately interested in understanding the economic policies enacted by individual states. Even small countries' governments can set policy within their borders, and this is a unique and important power. Moreover, although no one government can fully dictate the international environment, some national policies, especially of large countries, affect the international economy in important ways.

We are interested not only in the policies adopted by governments, but in the political institutions within which these policies are debated and by which they are implemented. According to one view, institutions themselves are but "congealed tastes" (Riker 1980: 445), intentionally created to guarantee the pursuit of particular policies. Others hold that institutions simply aggregate interests in ways that make it unnecessary to recalculate continually the balance of political forces; and still others assign a much greater independent weight to institutions – the view taken by Garrett and Lange in this volume. In all three views, institutions matter; and those interested in economic policies must also be interested in the institutions that make those policies.

Inasmuch as policies and institutions respond to the political pressures brought to bear by individuals and groups, it is also important to understand the policy and institutional preferences of these social actors.[2] This includes comprehending why actors aggregate politically in a particular way (say, by region) rather than another (say, by industry). Ideally, for example, we seek to predict what trade policy a particular firm, sector, or group will favor.

Given that socioeconomic and political agents have preferences about policies, and political institutions affect the adoption and implementation of policies, it follows that private agents must have preferences about institutions themselves. If an independent agency is more likely to provide tariff protection than one dependent on the executive, those who prefer high tariffs should want an independent agency while free traders should not. So our second-order set of dependent variables is the policy and institutional preferences of important socioeconomic and political groups.

A third-order set of things to be explained falls out of those set forth so far. If we want to understand policy and institutional outcomes in the first instance, and the policy and institutional preferences of socioeconomic and political actors in the second instance, it follows that we desire implicitly to understand the actual relationship between political institutions and policy outcomes. It only makes sense to ask about preferences and outcomes over *both* policy and institutions if the relationship between them is not immediately obvious; therefore we need to examine how institutions affect policy outcomes.

The dependent variables of interest in this project are thus threefold. The independent variable throughout is exogenous changes in the costs or rewards of international economic exchange. In rough logical order, the dependent variables are:

1 the policy preferences of relevant socioeconomic and political agents within countries toward national policies and national policy-making institutions;
2 given these preferences, the adoption or evolution of national policies and of national policy institutions;
3 given preferences, policies, and institutions, the relationship between a given set of institutions and a given set of policies.

Our proposed explanatory apparatus focuses on the first set of dependent variables, the policy preferences of socioeconomic actors. We by no means regard the others as unimportant, but we feel on firmest ground in making projections on the basis of an existing literature in economics and political economy. Geoffrey Garrett and Peter Lange, in their contribution to this volume, explore the institutional side of the story at much greater length.

In the next section we explain in greater detail why we find it useful to summarize the independent variable – changes in the costs and rewards of

international economic transactions – as reflected in their chief consequence, changes in relative prices. In the sections after, we explain the
relationship between relative price changes and the policy preferences of
economic actors.

III. THE EXPLANATORY LINK: INTERNATIONAL ECONOMIC TRENDS AS MOVEMENTS IN RELATIVE PRICES

Changes in the international economy can usefully be regarded analytically
as changes in relative prices; and changes in relative prices have predictable
effects on the policy preferences of socioeconomic actors. First, we defend
the view that for analytical purposes we can treat international economic
trends – including exogenous easing of international trade – as changes in
relative prices.

Virtually all developments of interest to economic agents have to do with
relative price changes. *Prices* matter because they are the basic signal by
which economic information is transmitted, and therefore the proximate (if
not the underlying) determinant of wages, rents, and profits. *Relative*
prices matter because prices have meaning only in relationship to each
other, for example, how many bushels of wheat trade for one yard of cloth,
or how many hours of labor for one automobile. If all nominal prices
suddenly and magically were multiplied or divided by 100, nobody would
be better or worse off (leaving aside computational and relabeling problems).[3] Finally, a large and widely accepted literature tells us *how* relative
price movements affect the fortunes of economic agents.

Two kinds of changes in relative prices are of particular importance. First
are broad trends in world prices, most notably for our purposes the *price*
convergence that is brought about by an exogenous decline in trade barriers. Second are *price shocks,* changes in world prices that ensue from, *inter*
alia, transient shortages and surpluses, technological innovation, and political disruptions. Price convergence is straightforward: in isolation, wheat is
cheaper (trades for less of other goods) in land-abundant Argentina than in
land-scarce England. As trade between two such regions becomes easier,
wheat becomes dearer in Argentina, cheaper in England; absent such artificial barriers as tariffs and quotas, prices in both countries converge toward
a "world" price.[4] Price shocks are theoretically more complex[5] but, particularly since 1973, empirically quite familiar: a world glut of wheat, the
discovery of some cheaper source of nutrition, or a multitude of other
causes may depress the world price of wheat, and consequently its price in
every region where it is traded, relative to other products.

Virtually every change in the international economy that has drawn the
attention of historians, theorists of international relations, economists, and
journalists, can be recast in terms of one or both of these kinds of price

changes. Technological innovation, international cartels, fiscal or monetary policies of major states, wars hot and cold, booms and busts – all matter in the international economy to the extent that they shift world prices and/or alter the relation between domestic and world prices.

Even where governmental policy contravenes such price changes – by tariffs, subsidies, rationing, price controls – the changes affect "shadow" prices, which define actors' economic opportunities. Two examples help clarify this point. (1) If, as was typical in the Communist economies, official prices of many consumer goods are set below market-clearing levels, "shadow" prices (those at which markets would actually clear) define incentives for black market activity, queuing, and payments for queuing by others. (2) Many African governments set farmers' prices below world levels; but world prices, as transmitted through neighboring countries or along seacoasts, determine incentives to smuggle, sell on the black market, or migrate to a less restrictive state (Bates 1981). As we discuss more fully below, an exogenous easing of international trade paradoxically can affect most strongly the relatively *closed* economies that try hardest to shelter themselves from international markets.

It is often useful to disentangle the component parts of an exogenous easing of international trade, for particular aspects of it may have more nuanced effects than the overall trend. The cheapening of ocean-going transportation was especially important to the world steel industry, as it allowed low-cost production of steel at relatively great distances from sources of iron ore; this mattered greatly for Japan, whose steel industry relied on imported raw materials. Developments in shipping, however, had far less (if any) impact on the microchip industry. Telecommunications advances probably had a more direct impact on capital movements than on trade, and contributed to the explosion of world financial markets that has played so central a role in affecting monetary and financial policies (on the LDCs, see Haggard and Maxfield). The cheapening of oil transport by means of pipelines and supertankers in the 1950s and 1960s, and the consequent dependence of many economies on petroleum as an energy source, meant that the OPEC oil price hikes had a devastating effect on some oil-importing countries, especially in the developing world, even while they enriched the oil exporters. Economies of scale have mattered more in chemicals and automobiles than in textiles or food processing (Krugman and Obstfeld 1991: 139). It is important to keep such specific trends in mind, so as not to conflate artificially a series of economic developments into one broad tendency that obscures more than it reveals.

Nonetheless, in the past three decades both general and specific propensities have come together to reduce the costs and increase the benefits of international trade and payments. A combination of technological change, national policies, and other developments have dramatically increased the degree to which markets are linked across national borders. The next section discusses the impact of this trend on economic activities and interests at the aggregate national level.

IV. RELATIVE PRICES AND NATIONAL ECONOMIES: EFFECTS ON AGGREGATE WELFARE

To provide a baseline for analysis, we first analyze the impact of an exogenous easing of international trade generally, and of specific international price shocks, on the aggregate welfare of entire societies. In the next section, we discuss effects on the individuals and groups that constitute nations. In both instances, we rely on the insights of modern theories of international trade. However, these theories are primarily concerned with explaining economic outcomes for societies as a whole, while we are interested in their implications for the policy preferences and political behavior of groups and nations.

First, an easing of international trade increases the impact of global economic trends on domestic political economies – even, we reiterate, where government policy keeps the national economy relatively closed. This is because a decrease in the costs of trade, or an increase in its relative rewards, *raises the share of tradable goods* in each country's economy. By definition, a good is nontradable if the difference between local and international price is less than the cost of moving it. In the eighteenth century, for example, long-distance transport was so expensive that only such low weight-to-value ratio goods as spices and jewels were "tradable" across oceans; in the nineteenth century, cheaper carriage transformed commoner and bulkier goods, such as grain and lumber, into tradables.

As described above, this effect operates even where economies remain relatively closed, by way of the impact of shadow prices on the opportunity costs of particular economic activities. One prominent example is how easier international exchange magnifies the potential domestic effects of price shocks, understood as fluctuations in *terms of trade,* the ratio of export to import prices. As more of a country's products become tradable, favorable or unfavorable shocks to the world price of a good produced locally or imported extensively – Saudi oil, Canadian wheat, Japanese automobiles – affect national welfare more profoundly.[6]

Easing of international exchange heightens the transmission of world economic trends to domestic political economies. In so doing, it intensifies actors' preferences concerning governments' foreign economic policies. We hypothesize that exogenous easing leads to the "import" of global economic trends into domestic politics. This might manifest itself in myriad ways, many of which we discuss below, but we expect most generally that easier trade at the global level will lead to an analogous "internationalization" of domestic political economies, in the sense of strengthening the national political ramifications of world economic developments. Specifically, we hypothesize that issues related to the world economy will grow more salient in all countries. As a corollary, insofar as internationally correlated economic developments become more important to all countries, the political dynamics of these concerns will grow more coordinated cross-nationally as international exchange becomes exogenously easier.

In addition to increasing the domestic political salience of internationally related issues, exogenous easing has relatively clear social welfare effects. First, as noted earlier, easier trade inevitably leads to economic pressures for *price convergence* among countries.[7] This affects aggregate welfare directly, for as domestic and world prices converge, the distortionary effects of protective barriers rise. This can perhaps best be understood by considering a country that is relatively closed to world trade. The country bears costs by producing goods at home that could be purchased more cheaply abroad. One set of costs is purely *distributional:* consumers of goods whose domestic price is higher than the world market price lose, while producers of such goods gain. A second set of costs, however, is to *aggregate* social welfare. The price distortions created by protection lead resources to be allocated to activities that do not represent their most efficient possible use. Physical and human capital are invested in industries that are profitable only because they are protected; without protection, these factors would flow toward industries closer to the country's comparative advantage. These deadweight (social welfare) costs represent income lost to society as a whole.

The welfare cost of closure to the economy as a whole varies with the difference between (a) the "landed" price of protected goods (world price less transport and other costs of trade) and (b) the domestic price created by national protective policy. Generally speaking, the bigger this "wedge" between domestic (protected) prices and effective world market prices, the greater the efficiency costs of protection (and the greater its redistributive impact). This is because the greater the price gap, the more "inappropriate" the allocation of the country's resources (relative to its comparative advantage).

The costs and rewards of international transactions affect the size of this price "wedge," and thus the welfare costs of closure. As international trade becomes easier, "landed" prices of the country's real or potential imports fall and the effective world market price of its exports (that is, the price other countries pay at the source) rises.[8] If the domestic price of protected goods remains the same, the gap between world market and domestic prices increases, and so does the efficiency cost of protectionist policies.

An illustration from capital markets may prove useful. Capital controls that keep national interest rates below world interest rates will (all else equal) reduce savings and raise borrowing to socially undesirable levels. The efficiency costs are a function of the gap between onshore and world market interest rates; the bigger the gap, the bigger the distortions. If an exogenous shock – financial crisis, macroeconomic trends – raises world interest rates, the gap between world and national interest rates grows, the difference between the politically controlled allocation of resources and that expected in a financially open economy increases, and the efficiency costs of capital controls rise accordingly.

As either the cost of international economic transactions or the world price of a good or service declines, the opportunity cost of economic closure rises. The easier or more potentially profitable it is to trade, invest, borrow internationally, the more a society forgoes by adopting policies that reduce cross-border economic activity. These costs are the *static efficiency costs of closure,* and are increasing in the ease of international economic exchange.

In recent years, analysts have begun paying more attention to the potential *dynamic* costs of closure. A large and growing literature has tended to look beyond short-term efficiency costs to focus on the longer-term impact of insulating a national economy from global trends. There are many different strains of this literature, but most agree that participation in world trade and payments has a complex and cumulative positive effect on national economic growth.[9]

Perhaps most importantly, international economic exposure stimulates domestic economic agents to adopt and adapt new technologies. In relatively closed national markets, incentives to innovate are limited by weak competition. Any firm selling into world markets, however, is forced to match its global competitors in technology, quality, and marketing. Inasmuch as much modern economic activity involves learning by doing and other – potentially intangible but clearly significant – processes that tend to exhibit increasing returns to scale, the widening of markets available to national producers allows (indeed, forces) them to develop new expertise that would be unlikely in a closed national market.[10]

Much of what analysts have in mind here is captured in the view that economic growth can only be understood by incorporating "total factor productivity" (TFP), a residual left *after* the consideration of increased labor and capital productivity.[11] TFP includes knowledge, technological adoption and adaptation, organization, and much else; and a country's welfare may depend as much on how it develops and uses these skills as on its endowments of land, labor, and capital.[12] Many believe that TFP growth has become increasingly important to complex industrial production, especially that associated with microelectronics;[13] and that the difficulties of very closed developing and Communist economies had to do not primarily with their inefficient uses of land, labor, and capital, but rather with their near-total inability to generate the growth in TFP that results from innovation, technological creativity, and better managerial organization (Krugman 1994b: 64–9). It may well be that, to the extent that *any* high-tech sector (telecommunications, computers) is sheltered from world competition, it rapidly becomes technically outmoded in ways for which there simply is no short-term "fix."

In any case, and whatever the precise mechanism, easier international exchange increases the gap between nationally protected (or taxed) and world market prices for goods and services. Where imports are protected, exogenous easing increases the difference between world market and protected prices, transferring more income from consumers to producers and encouraging more (and more inefficient) investment in industries whose products could be imported at ever lower cost. Where exports are taxed, easier international exchange similarly increases the distance between (artificially depressed) returns accruing to national export producers and those potentially available on world markets, analogously leading to *under*investment in goods that the country could potentially sell profitably abroad.

It is important to reemphasize that these expectations hold even, and indeed especially, in *very closed economies*. We focus not on how open a national economy is to foreign trade and payments, but rather on exogenous developments in the global economy. If we examined only the former aspect, the argument would be trivial: more open economies are more sensitive to world economic developments. The point here is different. The easier are international economic transactions in general, the greater the social cost of sustaining economic closure for any one country, and the greater the social impact of global economic trends on any one country – no matter how economically closed the country in question. This cost, and this impact, may be mediated through dense networks of government policies and programs, as in many of the former Communist countries and LDCs, but they operate nonetheless; and, given that distortions are greatest where protective barriers are highest, the aggregate benefits of liberalization will be greatest precisely in the most closed economies. Conversely, the losses to such economies from continued closure, exacerbated by forgone dynamic gains and gains in TFP, are greatest; and, over time, are likely to multiply into overwhelming demand for change.

Finally under this rubric, we note that impediments to trade can be (in the infamous phrase of some recent U.S.–Japanese negotiations) "structural," rather than flowing consciously from trade policy. Entrenched patterns of regulation, government purchasing, even taxation and jurisprudence, can effectively discourage cross-border exchange or investment and thus can create quite as effective a "wedge" between world and domestic prices as any tariff. An exogenous easing of international trade may make structural barriers costlier in terms of aggregate welfare and thus increase social pressure for liberalization in the broader sense of deregulation and harmonization of standards.[14]

These considerations lead us to quite specific, empirically testable conjectures, namely that an exogenous easing of international trade will (holding all else equal):

1 increase pressure within each country to liberalize international trade and payments, including dismantling structural impediments to trade;
2 create such broad political pressure as an increasing function of the degree to which the national economy was previously closed; and
3 generate such aggregate pressure for change as an increasing function of the degree to which the economy has readily exploitable gains from trade available (such as high levels of total factor productivity).[15]

Governments may well resist pressures to liberalize, however, for policymakers rarely have incentives to behave as benevolent social planners. Aggregate benefits are offset by concentrated costs; long-term social dividends, by short-term pain. Policymakers may well hesitate to reform, bearing instead the cost of slower (or even negative) long-term growth. Postponing our consideration of institutional issues to a later section, we nonetheless note here that whatever attunes policymakers to broad social interests or gives them longer time horizons will make them likelier to internalize the benefits of increased international trade. Speaking concretely, we expect that larger constituencies, more broadly based (for example, "catchall") parties, a more participatory franchise, longer average terms in office, and more stable partisan loyalties will weight decisions more in favor of aggregate welfare considerations.[16]

International price shocks, no less than price convergence, affect aggregate national welfare – again, even in closed economies.[17] A fall in the relative world price of a country's exports, or a rise in the price of its imports, is by definition a deterioration in its terms of trade, and reduces national income.[18] Such terms-of-trade shocks affect the welfare costs of closure in ways closely analogous to price convergence. Take a country whose policies reduce exports of a particular good, perhaps by protection on imported inputs or by an export tax. If the world relative price of this good suddenly rises, the national welfare cost of the export-inhibiting policy also rises.[19] Put more generally, an improvement in terms of trade raises the static national welfare costs of closure; a deterioration in terms of trade lowers those costs.[20] From these considerations we advance the following counterintuitive hypothesis:

All else equal, pressure for increased participation in the world economy will rise when a country's terms of trade *improve*; when terms of trade *decline,* pressure for less exposure to global economic trends will increase. This link will become more manifest as international trade becomes exogenously easier (and hence as international price shocks are transmitted more directly and deadweight costs of closure rise).

Up to now we have looked at how exogenous easing affects a country's aggregate economic performance. Important as this may be, it is a commonplace of political economy that what is good for national welfare may bear little relation to the policies actually adopted. There are of course settings, mentioned above, in which politicians worry about the consequences of economic trends for the country as a whole, but it is more common for political pressures to emanate from social groups rather than from the entire society. National economic effects are often secondary to the impact of easier international exchange on domestic economic and political agents. It is to this topic that we now turn.

V. INTERNATIONAL PRICES AND NATIONAL ECONOMIES: EFFECTS ON ECONOMIC ACTORS AND GROUPS

An easing of international exchange – a reduction in the cost of international transactions – is beneficial for those who consume goods or services associated with international exchange, such as exporters, importers, and consumers of imports. Conversely, such a reduction in international transaction costs hurts those competing with imports.

Internationalization lowers prices paid by consumers of imported goods and raises prices received by producers of exported goods; and it lowers prices received by producers of import-competing goods. (The argument again holds, *mutatis mutandis,* for international payments and investment, but we again restrict discussion here to trade in goods.) The first two categories benefit and the last is harmed. As easier trade widens the price wedge between domestic prices (protected or taxed) and world market prices, it increases the incentives of import competers to lobby for trade protection and the incentives of potential exporters and import consumers to resist or remove policies that hamper the free movement of goods they wish to purchase or sell.

To move beyond this point, we must be able to predict who will export, who will consume imports, and who will face competition from imports. This is especially important in very closed economies, where – as already noted – the impact of easier trade may be felt most strongly but massive distortions obscure the identity of potential gainers and losers from liberalization. While it is probably not difficult to anticipate that regions with valuable natural resources will gain by economic opening – oil- and uranium-producing areas of the former Soviet Union, for example – it may be far from obvious whether those in more differentiated lines of production – Brazilian steel producers, Uzbek cotton farmers, Czech textile manufacturers – will win or lose.

We can think of a country as having a comparative advantage in the production of particular goods. Those whose products are most in line with the country's comparative advantage stand to gain most from easier world trade; those "farthest" from comparative advantage (at greatest comparative disadvantage) stand to lose most. Exogenous easing of trade raises the benefits available to those close to the national comparative advantage, but also raises the costs that threaten those far from it. Three main trade theoretic perspectives, which are better regarded as complementary than as mutually exclusive, endeavor in essence to identify who is closer to, and farther from, the national comparative advantage; and thus who will gain, and who will lose, from easier international exchange.

A powerful and influential approach to the problem is that stated, within the context of the Heckscher–Ohlin trade model, by the Stolper–Samuelson Theorem (Stolper and Samuelson 1941). The Heckscher–Ohlin approach concludes that a country will tend to export goods intensive in the factors it has in abundance, and to import goods intensive in factors in which it is scarce. The Stolper Samuelson extension finds that in each country returns rise absolutely, and disproportionately, to owners of factors that are required intensively in the production of goods whose prices have risen; and they fall absolutely, and disproportionately, to factors required intensively in the production of goods whose prices have fallen.

Wheat, relative say to steel, is land-intensive; steel is labor-intensive.[21] The Stolper–Samuelson Theorem tells us, in essence, that if wheat rises in price relative to steel, landowners in general (and not just those currently engaged in wheat production) will be absolutely better off (able to buy more of all goods); and that workers in general (not merely those currently employed in the steel industry) will be absolutely worse off. Rents are bid up, and wages are bid down, across the board. Moreover, a change in the product price occasions a magnified change in the relevant factor price(s): a ten per cent increase in the price of wheat relative to steel occasions an increase of more than ten percent in land rents relative to wages.

The Heckscher–Ohlin approach leads to one subset of propositions about the distributional effects of easier international trade. It implies that exogenous easing raises the domestic prices of goods whose production is intensive in the given country's abundant factors and lowers domestic prices of goods intensive in the country's scarce factors; hence easier trade benefits a country's abundant factors but harms its scarce factors. In this view, exogenous easing of trade – which makes the benefits or costs of trade that much larger – raises the incentives for owners of abundant factors to attempt to liberalize trade, and for owners of scarce factors to work to restrict it. We expect to see, in this context, easier trade associated with intensified conflict between laborers, landowners, and capitalists over foreign economic policy and liberalization generally – with the specific battle lines depending on national factor endowments.

A common alternative, or supplement, to the Stolper–Samuelson view looks not at distributional effects on broad productive factors, but at more narrowly defined factors specific to particular uses. This so-called specific factors (or Ricardo–Viner) approach emphasizes the sector-specific impact of changes in relative prices. Factors specific to particular uses bear the full weight of price changes in their distinctive products. If land in a particular region is suited only for the cultivation of wine, then its price varies with the (projected future) price of wine, not with the price of agricultural products generally. Physical or human capital that is similarly specific (for example, useful only in the production of aircraft) is similarly product-linked.[22]

The Ricardo–Viner perspective suggests that many factors of production are quite specialized, so that we often observe sectoral, rather than broad factoral, effects of changes in relative prices and in analogous political behavior. The U.S., for example, is by most measures capital-abundant and labor-scarce. Price convergence, or a terms-of-trade shift in favor of capital-intensive products, should benefit U.S. capital and harm U.S. labor; but if both labor and capital in an import-competing sector are specific, both are harmed: the American automobile industry is perhaps the most obvious example. Steven Magee (1978) has argued that the sectoral pattern has more often characterized postwar American trade lobbying.

Most concretely, this approach implies: (a) that pressure for or against liberalization will vary with the *specificity* of the relevant actors' assets (most notably their human and physical capital); (b) that sectors will divide between those relatively competitive on world markets and those relatively uncompetitive; and (c) that political cleavages will be sectoral rather than factoral. By definition, nonspecific assets are readily redeployed in response to changing prices and accrue neither windfall profits nor surprise losses. Only owners of sector-specific assets, in the Ricardo–Viner perspective, have incentives to lobby for sectoral protection (if faced with import competition) or for liberalization (if faced with export opportunities).

This subset of propositions clearly diverges from those of the Heckscher–Ohlin approach and leads to different empirical expectations.[23] Not the country's factor endowments, but the specificity of the particular industry's human and physical capital, and its position in world trade and payments, would predict the likely pressure for or against liberalization. Rather than sharpening battles between laborers and capitalists, easier trade would lead to greater conflict between internationally competitive and uncompetitive *industries,* uniting workers and managers alike behind sectoral demands.

A third perspective is associated with aspects of firms and industries related to the scale economy and total factor productivity considerations mentioned above. There may be a *dynamic* distributional impact analogous to the scale economy and TFP welfare effects of easier trade. Such things as a larger scale of output, learning by doing, and technological adaptation can make the firms and industries involved particularly capable of taking advantage of economic opportunities. In this sense, effects of international relative price changes build on themselves.

In sectors characterized by internal economies of scale (EOS), by definition the sheer scale of the firm's production is crucial to its costs and competitiveness.[24] In such sectors, the opening of world markets increases the advantage of larger over smaller firms, and this advantage grows as access to markets expands. For example, it is conjectured that in an integrated European market only four or five automobile firms, all located within a radius of perhaps 200 kilometers, might survive (Krugman 1991). Inasmuch as the already largest firms are most likely to be able to implement the redeployment of assets and physical relocation necessary to reap fully the larger scale economies, political support for integration is expected from these firms; conversely, smaller firms will be less enthusiastic.[25] To the extent that autoworkers' skills are firm-specific, or that they will incur costs (for example, a new language) to move to a larger, surviving firm, their preferences will parallel their employers'.

A similar case is learning by doing, especially as applied to international trade. The ability of a firm to tap into world markets may depend on networks of suppliers and customers, information about market conditions, and a wide variety of other complex and firm-specific factors. A firm without access to world markets has no incentive to develop this informational and other capital. But if the net benefit of engaging in world trade increases substantially, the firm may be drawn into gradually developing this expertise. And if the knowledge and networks so built are cumulative, each easing of international exchange will be magnified by its accretion to an existing stock of characteristics crucial to international competitiveness. In this way, firms and industries already involved in global economic activities – trade, lending, investment, licensing – may have a substantial cost advantage due to their past actions, and this will amplify their preference for further economic openness.

The converse can also obtain: the substantial adjustments needed to enter into international economic activity may increase opposition to openness from those who most need to make such adjustments. Where, for example, the ability to participate in global trade and payments requires a full-fledged reworking of a firm's managerial and marketing organization, the firm is more likely to resist being thrown into the international marketplace more than if such a reworking were unnecessary. Where, as in the former Soviet economies, virtually all firms face drastic and uncertain restructuring, the resistance is likely to be massive.

In other words, there may be adjustment and informational costs associated with increased (or decreased) participation in world trade and payments. Such "dynamic" costs – retooling complex management structures, retraining employees, rebuilding supplier and customer networks – may be very hard to project or measure, but they may also be extremely important in determining preferences toward international economic policy. Those for whom a liberalization of cross-border economic activity would imply more costly adjustment are less likely to support it; those faced with lower prospective adjustment costs, all else equal, are more likely to look favorably on liberalization. Concretely, we expect that, in sectors characterized by economies of scale (e.g., chemicals and office machines, but not shoes or foodstuffs), support for liberalization will vary with: (a) firm size and (b) existing international contacts and experience (cf. Milner 1988).

These several perspectives agree that exogenous easing of international trade must affect, and usually intensify, domestic political conflict; they disagree, at least for the short run, about precisely *how* domestic politics is affected. Yet each perspective generates eminently testable propositions; and, pitted against each other, the several approaches adumbrate an interesting and fruitful program of research.

At present, for example, developed countries are characterized by an abundance of physical and human capital but a paucity of unskilled labor; LDCs are abundant in unskilled labor, poor in physical and human capital; and most NICs offer an abundance of both human capital and unskilled labor and are deficient only in physical capital. In the Heckscher–Ohlin perspective, exogenous easing of international trade increases potential benefits to capitalists and skilled workers in the advanced countries, to skilled and unskilled workers in the NICs, and to unskilled workers in the LDCs – all of whom are predicted to mobilize on behalf of liberalization. At the same time, easier trade threatens unskilled workers in advanced economies, local capitalists in NICs, and owners of both physical and human capital in LDCs – all of whom will heighten their demands for protection or compensation. Wood (1994) has argued that we observe exactly this in the economic history of the last twenty years.

In the Ricardo–Viner perspective, specific kinds of exogenous easing, and specific price shocks, matter more. As cheaper transport encouraged trade in petroleum in the 1950s, for example, coal owners and workers in many countries mobilized to demand protection and subsidies; auto workers and owners, whose markets would expand with cheaper oil, agitated in most cases to keep markets open; and political leaders, eager to minimize deadweight costs, sometimes suppressed the coal miners quite brutally and at high short-term cost (cf. DeGaulle 1971: 347–51).

The EOS perspective emphasizes the peculiarities of sectors characterized by increasing returns to scale.[26] To the extent that a given industry is so characterized *and* that capital within it is even moderately specific, an exogenous easing of trade is expected to precipitate conflict between large and small, and between internationally experienced and inexperienced, firms (and, where human capital is also specific, their employees); the former in each case pursuing liberalization, the latter likelier to be protectionist. It would, for example, be quite useful to see whether firm size better predicts attitudes toward European unification in, say, the British chemical industry (EOS) than in the British food-processing sector (non-EOS).

In addition to the broad impact of exogenous easing of trade in and of itself, particular relative price shocks affect the preferences of domestic socio-economic groups. We should note, moreover, that changes in one relative price can have an indirect influence on a wide range of economic actors. A "ripple" impact affects producers of goods that are complementary or substitutive to the directly affected products. The oil price rises of the 1970s expanded demand for coal and natural gas (substitutes) but depressed demand for heavy, fuel-inefficient automobiles (a complement) and hence for steel. It is often crucial to trace through such widening "ripples."

Perhaps the best known example of a specific relative price shock is the one often described as "Dutch disease," after the impact of postwar natural gas discoveries on the Netherlands. The general phenomenon is an unanticipated resource inflow, typically associated with increased export volumes or values.

The process is conventionally depicted as beginning with the discovery of a natural resource, but for our purposes it could just as easily be a major increase in the world price of an already known natural resource. This leads funds to flow into the country, and toward the natural resource sector involved. This is good for the booming sector, for obvious reasons. The resource inflow also has an important collateral (or ripple) effect on aggregate demand: those in the booming sector now have more income at their disposal, and this raises domestic demand. Inasmuch as the demand is for nontradables, such as housing, it stimulates the nontradables sector, such as by causing the price of housing to rise. However, as the prices of the booming resource and of nontradables rise, domestic tradables producers face increased input costs and therefore heightened import competition. The result is analogous to that of a real appreciation of the exchange rate, and is typically observed as "deindustrialization" – whether in the modern Netherlands or sixteenth-century Spain.[27]

In this context, a substantial increase in the world price of a commodity leads producers of the exported good, and those in the nontradables sector, to want policies that allow them to realize the full force of this positive terms-of-trade effect. However, those in the nonbooming tradables sector (typically manufacturing and agriculture) want the government to counter the negative direct and indirect impact on them of the resource inflow – whether by means of protection, subsidies, or something else. There may also be debates over the potential appropriation of the rents accruing to the now more valuable resource.

To take a prominent example of this process, a major rise in the price of oil is expected to lead owners of oil-producing properties to push to capture the full value of their windfall. Nontradables producers will welcome the inflow of resources as it increases demand for their output. Tradables producers outside the oil sector – industry and agriculture, typically – will press the government to protect them from the real appreciation and import surge that would ensue without mediating policy.

An exogenous easing of trade, then, has highly differentiated effects on economic agents within countries. It leads to intensified demands for freer trade and investment on the part of those firms and individuals closest to their country's comparative advantage. In one view this impact is primarily factoral: it helps labor-intensive manufacturing sectors in a labor-rich country, for example. In other views, the effects are principally to sectors and firms with unique advantages over those elsewhere, whether these advantages are associated with scale of output or with firm-specific knowledge or managerial capabilities. On the other hand, easier trade sharpens the desire for protection on the part of those farthest from their country's comparative advantage, on whatever basis this may be calculated. Similar effects are expected in the event of a onetime increase or decrease in a world relative price; and easier trade increases actors' sensitivities to such price shocks.

Again we emphasize that we expect these effects even in relatively closed economies. Exogenous easing should, in this view, increase the pressure for trade liberalization from individuals, firms, and industries that could compete globally – even in highly insulated developing and Communist countries. So too should specific price shocks create pressures from particular potential beneficiaries and losers, even where governments have typically tried to shield domestic economies from such global price trends. Whether these expected pressures lead to actual changes in policy is a function of complicated coalitional and institutional conditions, discussed briefly by us below and at greater length by Geoffrey Garrett and Peter Lange in their contribution to this volume.

VI. THE ROLE OF INSTITUTIONS

We begin with the fundamental insight of Becker (1983), that deadweight costs offer opportunities to political entrepreneurs: by building the coalitions that can overcome even entrenched or institutionalized resistance, they can capture for themselves part of the resultant gain in aggregate social welfare. Hence the greater the deadweight loss from a prevailing arrangement, the likelier it becomes that some political entrepreneur will succeed in changing it. Applied to these issues, the Beckerian insight implies: the greater the exogenous easing of trade, the likelier it becomes in every country – including particularly, we reiterate, those previously most closed to the world economy – that liberalization, and where necessary liberalization-favoring institutional reform, will occur.

How smoothly reform progresses (or, indeed, whether it is possible at all under the incumbent regime) is determined in our view chiefly by three factors: (a) the breadth of existing constituencies and coalitions; (b) the credibility (based on experience) of the regime's commitments; and (c) the time-horizons of major decision makers. These broadly institutional aspects, we note, are both exogenous (reformers face a set of established institutions) and endogenous (reformers are motivated to change those institutions in ways that favor, or entrench, liberalization).

(a) As we noted briefly above, politicians are likelier to internalize aggregate welfare and thus to minimize deadweight costs the more they are accountable to, and depend for their continuance in office on, the whole society.[28] A franchise that is limited to landowners, or to the *nomenklatura,* will privilege those groups' interests even at great cost to the larger society. An electoral system in which each representative answers only to a small geographic constituency guarantees that s/he will weigh the constituency's interest over that of the country as a whole. A political party that represents a narrow economic interest will be less attuned to aggregate welfare than a more "encompassing" (Olson 1982) rival. In the specific case of an exogenous easing of international exchange, we hypothesize:

1 On average, democratic regimes will liberalize more readily than nondemocratic ones.[29]
2 Among equally democratic regimes, and among different elective bodies within the same country, the tendency to liberalize will increase as the number of distinct constituencies decreases.
3 All else equal, the likelihood of liberalization will decline with increasing partisan fragmentation (as measured, for example, by Rae 1967).[30]

In the U.S., hypothesis (2) suggests that the President (elected in effect from a single national constituency) will normally support openness more than the Senate (elected from fifty constituencies); the Senate, in turn (and abstracting from its bias toward sparsely settled states), will be more free-trading than the House. Certainly the authors of the Reciprocal Trade Adjustment Act of 1934 and of the "fast-track" procedure for ratifying trade agreements hoped, by delegating significantly greater powers to the Presidency, to favor the odds of freer trade.

Among the total set of democracies, (2) implies that countries that elect from a very few parliamentary constituencies will liberalize more readily than ones that employ many single-member districts; and the evidence to date appears to support this proposition (cf. Garrett and Lange, this volume; Lohmann and O'Halloran 1994; Mansfield and Busch 1995; Rogowski 1987).

(b) While aggregate welfare gains from trade insure that, with appropriate side payments, liberalization can make everyone better off, many actors are unprepared to believe that promised side payments will be made. To the extent that political leaders can credibly commit to compensation, support for liberalization can be organized more easily and more cheaply. Here history matters: a government that has consistently kept its promises will have greater credibility, and hence will be better able to liberalize successfully to meet an exogenous easing of international trade. Among plausible operational proxies for a government's credibility are: the risk premium on its financial obligations; the independence and neutrality of its judiciary; whether its constitutional provisions are enforceable through some neutral body, such as a constitutional court; and survey responses of its citizenry to questions about political trust. All else equal, we would expect easier liberalization in countries where the rule of law is entrenched and respected, and where both the currency and government-backed bonds are trusted.

(c) It is often argued (as in Grilli, et al. 1991) that longer time-horizons (as gauged by average time in office) make politicians less likely to run deficits. Plausibly, secure leaders will discount the future less and be more willing to incur short-term costs for longer-term social gain. In the U.S., as in many other countries, independent agencies have arisen with some influence over national policy toward cross-border transactions; and insofar as they are less subject to day to day political pressures, they may be more likely to take the lead in pursuing the long-term aggregate interest. With respect to trade policy, we hypothesize that, under an exogenous easing of trade:

1 The longer the average life of a cabinet in a given country, the likelier the country is to liberalize.
2 Within a country, a cabinet is likelier to liberalize the stabler its majority or the more fixed its term of office.
3 The more influential are agencies relatively independent from direct political pressures in the making of international economic policy, the likelier is liberalization.

VII. THE EXPECTED IMPACT OF EXOGENOUSLY EASIER TRADE

It is worthwhile to recapitulate salient effects of easier international transactions. Again, we focus on the implications for the policy preferences of socioeconomic actors.

National effects

At the aggregate level, an exogenous easing of exchange increases the proportion of tradables in the national economy, magnifies pressure for the convergence of domestic to world prices, and augments susceptibility to world price shocks. Even where the government does not remove barriers to cross-border trade and payments, easier access to international economic activity increases the susceptibility of domestic economic actors to international conditions. In this way, an exogenous easing of trade increases the impact of the international economy on national politics. We expect such a change to be associated with an increase in the domestic political salience of international economic issues – whether or not the country actually opens to world trade and payments as the net benefits of cross-border transactions increase.

Easier trade also raises the static and dynamic costs of isolation from world markets. That, in turn, generally raises the pressure to reduce barriers to international trade and payments. Such pressures will, all else equal, tend to be greater where economies have previously been most closed, and where opportunities for the realization of untapped gains from trade thus are greatest.

The degree to which policymakers respond to the higher efficiency costs of closure will depend on a wide variety of factors, most of them institutional. We anticipate that exogenously easier trade will produce a generally higher level of social pressures for the reduction of barriers to cross-border economic activities. Governments will be more likely to respond to such pressures to the extent that they more accurately represent the broad social interests in the aggregate; can make credible commitments to compensate potential losers; and have relatively longer time-horizons.

Distributional effects

At the more disaggregated level, less costly or more rewarding international exchange has a differential impact on domestic groups. Easier international exchange encourages specialization and may well be welfare-improving overall, but societies are divided between those likely to benefit and to lose from such greater specialization.

Economic actors best able to take advantage of newly available opportunities for international trade and payments are expected to support policies that allow them to realize the fullest possible benefits associated with broadened economic horizons. These may include the liberalization of trade and the capital account, macroeconomic policies that encourage global trade and payments, attempts to regulate or harmonize standards in such a way as to facilitate cross-border commerce and investment, and a whole host of other initiatives.

On the other hand, those who anticipate that the greater specialization attendant upon higher levels of international economic activity will make them redundant can be expected to press for policies to protect them from global economic trends. Again, this extends from such broad policies as trade protection to such narrower ones as regulation. The more past policy has sheltered these sorts of groups, the more severe is the threat of international competition and the fiercer is the likely opposition to removing previous protection.

This leads to the expectation that exogenous easing of trade will be associated with increased demands for liberalization from the relatively competitive, and with increased demands for protection from the relatively uncompetitive, groups. The operationalization of this hypothesis is potentially variegated, for different trade models predict different things about the economic actors likely to win and lose from increased international trade and payments.

In the Heckscher–Ohlin view, the principal actors are such broad factors as land, labor, and capital. Owners of locally abundant factors are the winners from internationalization and will demand liberalization, while owners of locally scarce factors seek protection. In the Ricardo–Viner perspective, relevant divisions are on sectoral lines: the steel industry, wheat farmers, the banking industry. Those industries best (least) able to compete internationally for whatever reason are expected to cohere *as industries* in demanding (opposing) liberalization. Inasmuch as scale economies and other such (often intangible) characteristics of firms and sectors are important, large and internationally experienced firms are expected to be the principal supporters of liberalization. These three viewpoints may all be valid in different sectors and over different intervals of time, but they do give rise to disparate empirical expectations.

Specific price shocks

Particular relative price shocks also affect the preferences of domestic socio-economic groups. Those for whom a global shock implies a potential windfall are expected to push for policies that allow them to capture that benefit. Those on whom the shock has a negative effect, on the other hand, will want policies to protect them from it. Simple as this may seem, the full political economy effects of such price shocks can be great, as their impact ramifies throughout the economy. The example of "Dutch disease" shows how many economic interests and policy preferences can be affected by the change in just one price, especially when it is an important component of the country's export profile.

Exogenous easing of international exchange, then, affects policy preferences both toward such broad issues as trade liberalization and toward such narrow concerns as particular regulatory policies. Its effects on the preferences of private actors can be understood in a reasonably coherent way, on the basis of the expected impact of easier trade on the relative prices facing particular producers and consumers of goods and services. These preferences, of course, go on to be mediated by existing political coalitions and institutions, in ways that we have sketched above and that are treated in greater detail by Geoffrey Garrett and Peter Lange.

CONCLUSION

We emphasize that the framework presented here is neither exhaustive nor all-encompassing. We have ignored many factors that affect the policy preferences of individuals and groups. We have attended only summarily to the impact of institutional arrangements on policy outcomes and have ignored the origins of the institutional arrangements themselves.

The analytical approach developed here does not tell us, in itself, what policy outcomes to expect from a given set of international economic changes. It does not, for example, imply that increased interdependence reduces the probability of war or insures the triumph of particular foreign policies or modes of domestic governance. Indeed, it is largely a plea to eschew impressionistic generalizations, instead attending consciously to the interests and incentives facing all relevant individuals and working up from that point to expectations about their behavior. The presentation of these foundations, we hope, will help scholars interested in the domestic effects of international economic trends to carry out systematic research.

3

Internationalization, Institutions and Political Change

GEOFFREY GARRETT AND PETER LANGE

The internationalization of markets has commonly been associated with wide-ranging changes in domestic politics in the past two decades, but the precise nature of these linkages has remained opaque. Recently, however, numerous scholars have developed rigorous "open polity" analyses of the impact of international change on politics and policies within nations. At the highest level of aggregation, Ronald Rogowski's *Commerce and Coalitions* focuses on coalitional politics in countries with different endowments of land, labor and capital (Rogowski 1989). Jeffry Frieden's *Debt, Development and Democracy* investigates the reaction of different economic sectors to changes in international market conditions (Frieden 1991a). In *Resisting Protectionism*, Helen Milner discusses the political consequences of the changing competitive positions of individual firms (Milner 1988). Frieden and Rogowski's contribution to this volume synthesizes the underlying logic of such arguments by linking the interaction between changes in relative prices in the international economy and the specificity of domestic actors' assets, on the one hand, with changes in these actors' domestic policy preferences and the political coalitions they form to advance those preferences, on the other hand.

This line of research provides a parsimonious approach to analyzing the impact of integration into the international economy on the preferences

We would like to thank the members of the working group on internationalization and domestic politics, and especially Jeffry Frieden, Stephan Haggard, Robert Keohane, and Helen Milner for comments on earlier drafts of this paper. Thanks also to Robert Bates, Judith Goldstein, David Soskice, and Barry Weingast for helpful discussions. Garrett gratefully acknowledges the financial support of the Hoover Institution, Stanford and the Research School of Social Sciences, Australian National University, Canberra. Lange would like to thank the Center for Advanced Study in the Behavioral Sciences for the support it provided while he was working on this project and the members of the Center's Summer Institute on "The Impact of Global Trends on Domestic Political Economy" for their discussion of an earlier draft. Special thanks to Ilene Grabel, Lori Leachman, Doug McAdam, and Beth Simmons for their comments as work on the paper proceeded through various iterations.

and coalitional behavior of domestic actors. It should be noted, however, that scholarship in this vein pays relatively little attention to the relationship between preference change and policy outcomes, much less to the mechanisms by which they might be related. The implicit political model is that of "economic pluralism" – in which policy outcomes are a function of political conflict shaped by the preferences of different actors, weighted by their market power and their propensity for collective action. As a result, it is assumed that the effects of internationally generated changes in the constellation of domestic economic preferences will be quickly and faithfully reflected in changes in policies and institutional arrangements within countries. If one understands which economic interests have gained economic strength, one knows which have gained political power, and in turn how policy is likely to change.

There is something missing from this account of politics – institutions. Today, few would dispute that – at a given point in time – institutional conditions have a significant bearing on political processes. The causal status of institutions in the dynamics of political change is less clear. Much of the rational choice branch of the "new institutionalism" does not explicitly address this issue because its primary objective is to analyze the consequences of a given set of institutions. Where the question of dynamic change is broached, a functionalist orientation dominates game theoretic work. Institutions arise to mitigate market failures, be they generated by informational needs, commitment problems, prisoners' dilemmas, or cycling majorities (Krehbiel 1991; Milgrom, North, and Weingast 1990). How such institutions were created is less important than the functions they perform (Bawn 1993; Lohmann 1995).[1] In contrast, the historical-structural branch of new institutionalism is directly concerned with intertemporal issues, and it is avowedly antifunctionalist (Thelen and Steinmo 1992). From this perspective, institutions invariably outlive the constellations of interests that created them and hence they provide barriers to market-driven policy change (Goldstein 1993). The analytic power of historical institutionalism, however, is lessened by its failure precisely to delineate the causal mechanisms underpinning institutional inertia and its influence on outcomes.

We seek in this article systematically to examine how and why extant institutions mediate in the relationship between internationally induced changes in the policy preferences of domestic actors, on the one hand, and political outcomes (both policy and institutional change), on the other. Our analytic framework is essentially game theoretic, but we endeavor to avoid the functionalist reasoning common to this paradigm without resorting to the fuzzy logic of historical institutionalism. The following section outlines our basic theoretical argument. We then introduce a stylized example of an internationally generated change in the structure of a national economy of the type envisaged in most open polity models such as that of Frieden and Rogowski in this volume – an exogenous increase in the portion of the economy that is exposed to international competition. The subsequent sections analyze how this change can be expected to affect domestic politics under a variety of institutional arrangements. We concentrate on two types of institutions: "socioeconomic institutions" that organize interests in the private sector and "formal institutions" that aggregate these interests in the public arena and determine the responsiveness of governments to them. The final substantive section of the paper considers the possibilities for endogenous institutional change in different types of polities. We conclude by discussing the epistemological status of institutional theories in the social sciences.

I. INTERNATIONALIZATION, INSTITUTIONS, AND POLITICAL CHANGE

Our basic understanding of the relationship between changes in the international economy, domestic institutions, and political outcomes is delineated in Figure 1. Stage I represents the type of stimulus commonly associated with economic internationalization – a change in the constellation of actors' preferences in the domestic economy. We will not discuss this process further since it is the primary concern of Frieden and Rogowski's paper. We concentrate, instead, on the ways preference changes can be expected to be filtered through political systems with different institutional attributes to affect the policy choices of national governments. We ask not "how will a change in the structure of the international economy affect the preferences of domestic actors?" but rather "how will governments respond to these changes in preferences?"

Let us begin with a simple understanding of government behavior. Political leaders clearly have objectives they would like to further (from ideological goals to maximizing the perquisites of holding power). Nonetheless, the proximate objective of all governments is to retain office – irrespective of whether the mechanisms for deposing governments are elections, palace coups or popular revolutions. In the economic sphere, this entails seeking both to redistribute wealth in favor of the government's core political constituencies and to preside over an expanding societal pie (Hibbs 1987; Kramer 1971; Londregan and Poole 1990).[2]

Playing the distributional game will tend to dominate the government's agenda over concerns about aggregate economic performance. Politicians cannot afford to ask what is good for society as a whole in the long run, lest they lose power in the interim. The simplest way to avoid this fate is to distribute benefits to the groups whose support brought them to office – even if this has significant costs for macroeconomic performance

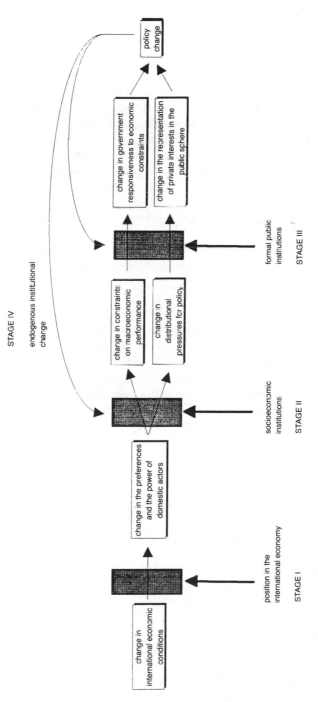

STAGE IV

endogenous institutional
change

STAGE I

position in the
international economy

socioeconomic
institutions

STAGE II

formal public
institutions

STAGE III

change in
international economic
conditions

change in the preferences
and the power of
domestic actors

change in constraints
on macroeconomic
performance

change in
distributional
pressures for policy

change in government
responsiveness to economic
constraints

change in the representation
of private interests in the
public sphere

policy
change

Figure 1. The international economy, domestic institutions, and political change

(Cox et al. 1984). In the economists' long run, "maladapted" government strategies will invariably change. But for extensive periods it is likely that political imperatives may diverge considerably from the path of economic efficiency.

Consider the example of agriculture. Governments in democratic and non-democratic countries alike often pursue agricultural policies that are manifestly inefficient. Governments in subSaharan Africa curtail exports and dump food on the domestic market to appease urban constituencies in order to reduce the prospect of coups and urban unrest (Bates 1981). Conversely, agriculture is heavily protected in many western countries despite the inefficiency of domestic producers because of institutional arrangements (such as representation based on geography rather than population) that privilege rural interests. The reason that these policies endure is obvious – from the perspective of incumbents with short-term time-horizons, these policies are politically expedient.

This general model of government behavior tells us very little about variations in the strength of distributional pressures for policy change and in the macroeconomic constraints under which governments operate. Clearly, the constellation of societal preferences and coalitions will affect distributional pressures and macroeconomic constraints – as economists pluralists have documented. We concentrate, in contrast, on the mediating role of institutions between raw preferences and government behavior.

In Stage II of our model, "socioeconomic institutions" both condition the distributional policy demands resulting from changes in economic actors' preferences and influence the macroeconomic outcomes associated with different combinations of government policies and international economic conditions. These institutions clearly affect the political clout of actors in the private sector. As Frieden and Rogowski make clear, the ability of actors sharing common interests to overcome collective action problems is critical to their effective political capacity, and institutions can play important roles in facilitating collective action.

Socioeconomic institutions also have significant consequences for economic performance, however (Olson 1982). The most systematic work concerns labor market institutions. Calmfors and Driffill argue in an influential study, for example, that the relationship between labor market institutions and economic performance is U-shaped (Calmfors and Driffill 1988). Where unions are very weak, market pressures will lead to strong economic growth and low inflation and unemployment – consistent with neoclassical expectations. Outcomes are hypothesized to be considerably worse where individual unions are strong but collectively uncoordinated because they will push up wages regardless of the deleterious consequences for the economy as a whole or for the employment prospects of nonunionized workers. Finally, Calmfors and Driffill argue that wage militancy will be mitigated – and hence macroeconomic performance will be improved – by the presence of powerful central labor confederations and national-level bargaining arrangements.

We extend this argument by considering the likely consequences for both distributional policy pressures and economic performance of different combinations of international economic conditions and labor market institutions. Our basic hypothesis is that the better existing socioeconomic institutions perform under changing conditions in global markets, the greater is the latitude for governments to maintain policies that further their distributional interests – even in the face of a change in the balance of societal preferences away from these policies. In these circumstances, the policies governments wish to pursue from a distributional standpoint are also compatible with good macroeconomic performance – creating an effective cushion against pressures from newly empowered actors for policy change. This dynamic helps explain the strong continuities in economic policy in countries with strong and coordinated labor movements in the past decade – such as Austria and to a lesser extent Germany and Norway – notwithstanding the dramatic and unfavorable changes in the international economy that took place in the 1980s.

Our second set of institutional arguments concern the impact on government behavior of variations in formal political institutions in the public arena (Stage III). Again, these institutions affect both the macroeconomic constraints under which governments operate and their responsiveness to distributional pressures for policy change. We make four specific points.

First, the responsiveness of governments to changes in domestic preferences will vary significantly with regime type. The easier it is for opponents to challenge the policies of the incumbent government, the more responsive will the system be to changes in societal preferences (Barro 1973). One should thus expect – in the wake of a similar change in domestic preferences – political change to be faster and smoother in stable democracies than in more authoritarian regimes (where the entry barriers to politics are higher).

Second, the more institutions privilege groups that form the core bases of support for incumbent governments, the stronger are the incentives for governments to maintain policies and institutions that benefit these constituencies (even if these are of declining market power). Consider the example of rural interests in contemporary industrial democracy. Where the political system overrepresents rural interests (relative to their economic importance and even to their population), agriculture has been able to win significant trade protections – as in Japan under the single nontransferable vote (Rosenbluth), or in the United States with geographic representation in the Senate.

Third, the responsiveness of policy and institutional change to a given change in societal preferences will be inversely correlated to the numbers of veto points in a political system (Tsebelis 1995). For example, "gridlock" in the American political system is a natural outgrowth of the checks and balances inherent in the separation of powers between the presidency and the two houses of congress. Similarly, Italy's historical governance problems were at least partially attributable to its low threshold proportional representation electoral system, to the fragmented party system this encouraged, and to the interaction between this party system and the relatively weak executive provided for under the Italian constitution. At the other extreme, the ability of governments in Westminster systems to act quickly and decisively – but not always prudently – is infamous.

Finally, the more authority over policy rests in the hands of independent bureaucratic agencies, the less policy change should be associated with a given change in the constellation of preferences in the private sphere (Moe 1990). Here, the archetypal case is that of an independent central bank committed to price stability, such as the German Bundesbank. Under such conditions, the ability of the government effectively to stimulate the economy is limited because the central bank will counteract the expansionary effects of deficit spending with higher interest rates – as the German social democrats found out in the later 1970s and early 1980s (Scharpf 1991).

The central conclusion we draw from our analysis of Stages II and III is that in many instances the course of policy change will differ markedly from that anticipated by economic pluralism. Existing institutions can generate powerful pressures for governments to persist with policies that are favored by the constellation of interests that initially supported their ascent to power, even if the power of these interests has declined, and even if this has deleterious consequences for macroeconomic performance.

In these circumstances, governments may have incentives to change the institutional structure of their polities so as to mitigate the tension between distributional politics and economic performance (Stage IV)[3] (Keohane 1984; Krasner 1983). However, such endogenous institutional change is costly in the short run – because it will harm the interests of the government's existing constituencies. We argue that governments will only be likely to pursue a strategy of institutional change when they are risk accepting, when conjunctural conditions (such as the health of the international economy) are favorable, and when there is a long time until the government will be held accountable for their actions by the citizenry.

II. A HYPOTHETICAL TWO-SECTOR ECONOMY UNDER INTERNATIONALIZATION

In order to develop our arguments about the role of institutions in processes of political change, we introduce a hypothetical case of the type of change in the structure of a national economy envisaged by Frieden and Rogowski and captured in Stage I of our model. Having generated expectations about policy change from the perspective of economic pluralism (the null hypothesis for our analysis), we then explore whether and how institutions can be expected to alter these expectations.

Consider an economy that can be divided into two sectors – goods and services that are tradable and those that are not. In the tradables sector, national producers of goods and services compete in international markets. They are price takers, that is, there is a world market price that they cannot influence.[4] Employment and output in this sector are thus a function of international demand and the domestic sector's productivity relative to foreign competitors.[5] The nontradables sector comprises economic activity that is largely unconstrained by conditions in the international economy. Examples include the public sector, the construction and retail industries, and other goods and services for which it is hard to create international market.[6] Employment and output in the nontraded sector are primarily influenced by domestic demand and by the economic policies of governments. There is, by definition, no "world market price" for products that are not traded.

At time t_0, the tradables sector of this hypothetical economy constitutes 30 percent of economic output and employs 30 percent of the population – or more accurately, supports 30 percent of the labor force and their dependents (Table 1). The remaining 70 percent of output and population are in nontradables. Productivity is therefore the same in the two sectors at t_0. In the wake of exogenous changes in the international economy (for example, a reduction in transportation and communication costs), the economic structure of our hypothetical country at t_1 is different in two ways. First, the portion of output in the traded goods sector increases from 30 percent to 70 percent. Second, productivity in this sector increases dramatically (because of gains from scale economies and comparative advantage). As a result, the population split at t_1 marginally favors nontradables, 51–49 percent.

Given that output and population weights were the same in each sector at t_0, it is reasonable to assume that government policy would have been tilted at this time in favor of the nontraded sector – regardless of one's theoretical orientation. We speculate that four types of policy would likely have characterized the economy at t_0. These constitute the "Keynesian welfare state" (KWS) prevalent in western Europe in the 1960s (Shonfield 1965), but they also resemble the strategies used in many developing countries at the same time (albeit with less emphasis on welfare provision):

• heavy reliance on Keynesian demand management (to smooth domestic business cycles)

Table 1. *International change and domestic economic interests*

Sector	Economic structure	t_0	t_1
tradables	output	30%	70%
	employment	30%	49%
nontradables	output	70%	30%
	employment	70%	51%

- the imposition of capital controls (to increase the effectiveness of domestic demand management)
- industrial policies (to bolster output and employment in designated sectors)
- substantial public provision of welfare and other social services (to redistribute wealth to poorer segments of society)

Expectations about policy at t_1, however, will vary significantly according to the political economic model one deploys. Economic pluralism would strongly suggest that the dramatic increase in the portion of economic output generated by tradables should be associated with a substantial move away from the KWS. From the perspective of the traded goods sector, deficit spending and expansionary monetary policies are not helpful because they do not stimulate demand in international markets and may only stimulate imports. Indeed, domestic expansions might be counterproductive because they can be expected to result in higher real interest rates, an appreciation in the real exchange rate, lower international competitiveness, and ultimately lower profits and employment in tradables. Restrictions on cross-border capital movements represent significant losses from the inefficient allocation of investment. Industrial policies and the welfare state must be paid for by taxes to which the traded goods sector would contribute disproportionately (given its productivity) – further reducing the sector's international competitiveness.

The fundamental claim of this paper, however, is that the relationship between changes in economic structure and public policies is contingent upon extant institutional conditions. In the following two sections, we develop this argument with respect to the organization of socioeconomic interests and to formal institutions in the public sphere. Our conclusion is that the range of institutional arrangements under which policy change will accord with the expectations of economic pluralism is very narrow.

III. THE ORGANIZATION OF SOCIOECONOMIC INTERESTS

The institutional organization of socioeconomic interests mediates between changes in the constellation of market-driven preferences in the private sector and public policy in two ways. First, socioeconomic institutions affect the types of distributional demands societal actors place on governments. Second, socioeconomic institutions influence the macroeconomic constraints under which governments operate. In this section, we focus on the impact of variations in the ways workers are organized in the industrial democracies, but the argument could be extended to developing countries or to the organization of business (Haggard 1990; O'Donnell 1974; Soskice 1990).

We divide labor market institutions into three types. The first most closely approximates a "free" labor market: unions organize a small portion of the total labor force and collective bargaining is primarily at the plant or firm level (as in Canada, France, and the U.S.). In the second category, unions organize a significant portion of the labor force at the industry level, and individual unions are strong. However, there is little interunion coordination of wage bargaining, either because central labor confederations are weak or because no union is able to act as a "wage leader" for the rest of the economy (as in Belgium or Italy). The final "corporatist" category is characterized by high levels of unionization and either a single powerful and centralized labor confederation (as in Austria) or a single union that acts as the wage leader (such as IG Metall in Germany)[7] (Golden and Wallerstein 1994).

Table 2 illustrates our expectations for economic policy and macroeconomic performance under these three types of labor market institutions in our hypothetical economy at t_0 and t_1. We expect that there should be a secular decline in the propensity of governments to pursue Keynesian welfare state policies at t_1 as a result of the strengthening of the traded goods sector. However, the government's commitment to the KWS increases with the power of trade unions at both t_0 and t_1.

Consistent with recent work, we hypothesize that performance will be significantly better at t_0 in countries either with very weak labor market institutions or with strong and centralized ones than where individual unions are strong but collective bargaining is decentralized (Calmfors and Driffill 1988). At t_1, the former two sets of institutions can be expected to allow countries to reap the advantages of increased trade (in terms of scale economies and comparative advantage), but this will be substantially reduced in the "strong and decentralized" category as the result of distributional tensions between tradables and nontradables.

To explain these hypotheses, recall that governments that want to retain office will try both to deliver distributional benefits to the constituencies that most strongly support them and to preside over improving macroeconomic outcomes to attract new constituencies. At t_0, the KWS is likely to be both politically effective (with respect to retaining the support of the nontradables sector) and economically efficient (since most of the economy is insulated

Table 2. *Economic interests and labor market institutions*

		Labor market institutions		
Outcomes	Dominant sector (by economic activity)	Weak and decentralized	Strong and decentralized	Strong and centralized
policies[a]	t_0 - nontradables	5	3	1
	t_1 - tradables	6	4	2
performance[b]	t_0 - nontradables	3 =	5	3 =
	t_1 - tradables	1 =	6	1 =

Note: Numbers represent rank orders, ties are indicated by " = ."
[a]Commitment to the Keynesian welfare state and capital controls.
[b]Economic aggregates such as growth, inflation and unemployment.

from international competition). This equilibrium is destabilized at t_1, however, because economic performance will now be heavily dependent on the competitiveness of tradables in global markets, and there is potentially a tension between the politically effective and the economically efficient.

The logic of wage setting in the traded and nontraded sectors is very different (Garrett and Way 1995). The welfare of workers in tradables is directly affected by their competitiveness in global markets. To retain their jobs, those employed in the traded goods sector must thus constrain their wage demands to the imperatives of competing in global markets. In contrast, the proximate determinant of employment is government preference rather than global competitiveness, and there are powerful incentives for governments to prop up employment in nontradables during hard times.[8] As a result, workers in the nontraded sector know they can push up their wages with much less fear of losing their jobs than can workers in the traded goods sector. Moreover, those in tradables will be particularly hard hit by wage increases in nontradables and supportive government policy. This is because higher deficits and inflation will put upward pressures on interest rates and the real exchange rate, decreasing the competitiveness of national products in international markets.

This dynamic is potentially very damaging to the macroeconomy. Labor market institutions, however, will have a powerful influence on whether and how it is played out. Consider each of the three types of institutional arrangements in turn.

As we have already suggested, where trade unions are weak, the growing weight in the economy of the traded goods sector would be expected to be faithfully translated into pressures for policy change. Thus, in our hypothetical economy, societal pressures for policy change at t_1 would reflect more closely the preferences of the traded goods sector than was the case at

t_0. More importantly, where unions are very weak, a reduction in the KWS will reduce the ability of workers in nontradables to push up wages by imposing domestic competitiveness pressures on them. If governments don't smooth business cycles and choose to cut industrial and welfare policies, the fear of unemployment will loom larger for the nontraded sector. Full-blown examples of this pattern policy-performance nexus are scarce in the industrial democracies because organized labor continues to play a significant role in most countries. However, the closest approximations to this type of strategy in the 1980s were Britain and New Zealand.

Increasing the strength of individual trade unions in our two stylized sectors (without a powerful confederation to coodinate them) does not alter their policy preferences. However, this institutional modification significantly increases the capacity of workers in the nontraded sector to resist the policy changes preferred by the tradables sector through action both in the labor market and in the political arena. Under these conditions, even though the structure of the economy has changed significantly between t_0 and t_1, one would expect much less – and less coherent – change in economic policies, and poorer economic performance.

These expectations follow directly from the weak labor type. The primary difference between the free labor market and that characterized by strong but uncoordinated unions is that in the latter case workers in nontradables have not only the incentive but also the ability to push up their wages. These employees benefit from wage militancy – even though this has negative externalities for the rest of the economy. Moreover, nontradables workers have the power to thwart government attempts to impose market disciplines on them (by cutting the KWS). Public sector unions, for example, can not only offer resistance in the market through strikes but can also exert considerable pressures on policy. While individual unions have no incentive to coordinate their actions to promote public goods such as international competitiveness, they are likely to form an implicit (and sometimes even explicit) negative coalition against policy reforms that would damage their interests.

We would thus anticipate that economic policies would be sticky at t_1 where unions are strong but decentralized, and that economic performance would deteriorate. Instead of realizing the gains from increasing exposure to international market forces, this institutional configuration would turn these potential gains into real costs – in virtue of the ability of strong unions in the nontraded sector to resist policies that would allow the economy as a whole to benefit from internationalization. This scenario was played out in Britain and Italy in the late 1970s (Gourevitch 1984; Lange, Ross, and Vanicelli 1982) and in Denmark and Sweden in the late 1980s and early 1990s (Iversen forthcoming).

Finally, let us consider the case of labor market institutions in which workers are organized under a single umbrella confederation that has effective authority to negotiate a wage agreement for the whole labor force. This institutional arrangement mitigates the deleterious consequences of differences in wage setting dynamics across sectors. The leaders of centralized labor movements have an interest in maximizing total employment in the economy, and they are acutely aware of the negative externalities of wage militancy in specific sectors. Wage growth that increases unemployment is unacceptable. From their perspective, the best wage setting regime is thus one in which increases in nontradable wages are constrained by those in tradables (determined by their international competitiveness). This is the Aukrust model that has long been deployed in Austria, to a lesser extent in Norway and Germany, and in Sweden until the mid-1980s (Flanagan, Soskice and Ulman 1983).[9]

The policy and performance consequences of an increase in size of the tradables sector under this type of labor organization are more complex than for the other categories. On the one hand, union leaders understand the critical role played by the traded goods sector in employment growth. One might thus expect them to advocate the neoliberal policy reforms favored by the tradables sector. On the other hand, the central confederation is also concerned with the welfare of nontraded sector workers who require compensation for the dislocations associated with liberalization. The leadership of a monopoly union confederation can therefore be expected to lobby for a mix of policies that can maintain external competitiveness while promoting solidarity among all workers.

The types of policies favored by a monopoly union at t_1 would thus be twofold. First, they would compensate workers in nontradables for the wage restraint imposed through centralized collective bargaining with expansionary and welfarist policies. Second, they would try to facilitate structural adjustment in the economy – that is, the movement of jobs to and within the tradables sector. This could be accomplished by eliminating policies that distort efficient investment, while simultaneously promoting active labor market and other interventionist supply-side policies (such as public investment in infrastructure and research and development) (Garrett and Lange 1991; Katzenstein 1985).[10] In turn, these policies would likely generate economic performance similar to that in the case of very weak unions.

IV. FORMAL POLITICAL INSTITUTIONS

The preceding section explored how socioeconomic institutions condition the impact of an internationally driven change in the structure of a national economy by influencing both the distributional policy demands emanating from the private sector and the macroeconomic constraints under which governments operate. This section considers the impact of formal institutions in the public sphere on the responses of governments to these distributional demands and macroeconomic constraints. Our analysis is divided into four subsections. The first two discuss the formal avenues of access to the policy making process available to societal interests. We begin by exploring differences between broad regime types, and then focus more narrowly on variations among democratic polities. The final two subsections investigate the responsiveness of political systems to demands for policy change. We begin with the consequences of variations in the number of institutional actors whose support is required to generate a policy change. We then discuss the effects of the insulation of bureaucratic agencies from societal pressures.

Regime type and government change

The most basic institutional determinant of government responsiveness to a change in the constellation of societal preferences is the ease with which incumbents can be replaced. The lower the costs of opposing the government, the more likely governments will be unseated if they pursue unpopular policies, and hence the more responsive to changes in societal preferences should we expect incumbents to be. This suggests that the dynamics of political change are likely to vary significantly between democratic polities characterized by high levels of political competition and authoritarian and totalitarian regimes.

Figure 2 presents a conception of political change in democracies, authoritarian regimes, and totalitarian systems in our hypothetical economy – compared with the baseline of economic pluralism in which changes in the balance of economic power between sectors would be reflected faithfully in policy changes. Recall that at t_0 nontradables constituted 70 percent of output and population and economic policies were characterized by frequent recourse to Keynesian demand management, capital controls, industrial policy, and extensive public provision of welfare and other social services. At t_1, the balance of economic power tilted strongly in favor of tradables as a result of changes in the structure of the international economy, and economic pluralism would predict that this would lead to a dramatic decline in the KWS.

Holding constant socioeconomic institutions, one should expect policies more closely to approximate the expectations of economic pluralism in democratic polities than in other systems. The reason for this is at the core of modern democratic theory. If an incumbent government pursues policies that are unpopular, it will be replaced at the next election. Anticipating this, government leaders will try to change policy in advance to avoid losing office. If they do not succeed, their replacements surely will change policy.

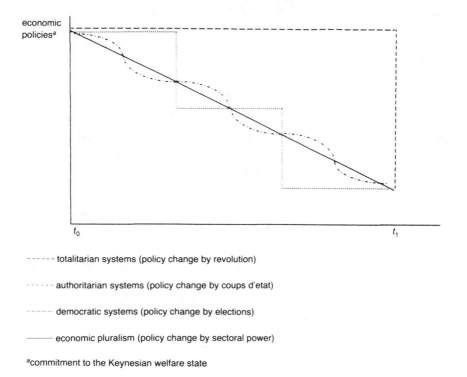

------ totalitarian systems (policy change by revolution)

- - - - - - authoritarian systems (policy change by coups d'etat)

········· democratic systems (policy change by elections)

————— economic pluralism (policy change by sectoral power)

[a]commitment to the Keynesian welfare state

Figure 2. Policy change across regime types

The trajectory of policy is unlikely to track changes in public opinion perfectly – due to ideology, incomplete information about electoral preferences, or other factors. Nonetheless, the process of policy change should broadly accord with changes in societal preferences. It should be noted, however, that in democracy preferences are weighted according to the number of voters sharing them, rather than their economic importance.[11] As a result, the move away from the KWS in our hypothetical economy at t_1 should not be as smooth as would be expected under economic pluralism.

Policy change is likely to be more sporadic in nondemocratic regimes where legal and constitutional procedures for replacing governments are less developed and where there may be significant sanctions imposed on opposition to the incumbent government. The threshold for policy change will be significantly higher in such systems. One should expect relatively long periods of policy stability (even as popular opposition to the incumbent's policies strengthen), followed by bursts of rapid policy change associated either with a change in government or a fundamental realignment in the incumbent's support bases. This should be most pronounced in totalitarian systems where opposition is illegal and coercively sanctioned and where the state is organized into a monolithic party (as in the communist bloc during the cold war). In such cases, popular revolution is virtually the only mechanism for policy change in directions supported by the bulk of citizens. It will therefore be much delayed, but when it occurs, the pace of change will be very rapid indeed.

The existence of competing elite factions in nondemocracies – such as independent militaries or leaders with distinct ethnic or regional support bases – can be expected to increase the responsiveness of governments to changes in societal preferences. Coups d'état, or the fear of them, will make policy more responsive to changes in popular preferences than in totalitarian regimes. But the absence of transparent and predictable mechanisms for government change means that the process will inevitably be less smooth than in competitive democracies. This pattern has been the historical norm in the twentieth century for many countries in Africa, Asia, and Latin America.

Preference aggregation in democracies

Two central properties of democracy are that governments must submit to the will of the people in periodic elections and that all citizens' votes count equally. There are many ways, however, to translate votes into representation. This can have significant implications for how "the will of the people" is manifested in public policy (Rae 1971). [12] In this subsection, we compare the likely outcomes associated with the change in the structure of our hypothetical economy from t_0 to t_1 under different electoral formulae. Table 3 considers five different scenarios. In the baseline case of economic pluralism, government policy is determined by the relative economic contribution of the two sectors (rather than by any formal political mechanism for aggregating preferences).

In the remaining cases, preferences are aggregated through formal electoral mechanisms, all of which base representation on the numerical strength of groups sharing common interests, rather than on their economic power. Let us assume for the moment that the formal political system is characterized by a unicameral legislature, that a single party exists to represent the interests of the two sectors, and that everyone in each sector will vote for his or her party. Four different scenarios are entertained. First, under list proportional representation (as used in most of western Europe), the fraction of the electorate in each sector will be translated almost perfectly into seat shares in the legislature. [13] Second, similar outcomes may ensue under plurality voting in single member districts (as in Britain and New Zealand), but only where support for the two parties is highly geographically concentrated (for example, all of the tradables sector voters at t_0 are located in only 30 percent of the districts) (Gudgin and Taylor 1976). [14]

Table 3. *The aggregation of economic preferences in democracies*

		Method of preference aggregation				
Time	Sector	Economic Pluralism	Proportional representation	Single member districts (concentrated)	Geographic units (federalism)	Single member districts (uniform)
t_0	tradables	30%	30%	30%	30%	0%
	nontradables	70%	70%	70%	70%	100%
t_1	tradables	70%	49%	49%	30%	0%
	nontradables	30%	51%	51%	70%	100%

Third, proportionate representation could also be generated under a system (as in the U.S. Senate and other upper chambers in federal systems) where seats in the legislature are apportioned not on the basis of population, but rather according to political divisions (such as states). However, this will only be the case under a highly restrictive set of circumstances: each "state" contains either only nontradables or only tradables sector voters; and, the number of states of each type is commensurate with the overall distribution between the two sectors in the whole country (as is assumed to be the case at t_0 in Table 3). The final scenario is single member districts with an even distribution of nontradables and tradables sector voters in each district. In this case, one party will win all the seats. For example, at t_0, the nontradables party would win every seat (by a margin of 70 percent–30 percent).

Thus, where the productivity of sectors is equal, there will generally be little difference between outcomes under economic pluralism and a variety of democratic methods for aggregating citizens' preferences. The situation changes dramatically, however, where sectors differ in productivity. Recall that our baseline is economic pluralism which suggests that at t_1 the interests of the traded goods sector would be dominant in virtue of its predominant contribution to economic output (70 percent), and economic policy would move considerably away from the KWS.

As the second panel of Table 3 makes clear, all democratic processes will be biased in favor of the nontraded sector – in virtue of its lower productivity and hence the downward stickiness in the portion of the citizenry in this sector. The extent of this bias will be smallest under national list proportional representation and single member districts (when voters in each sector are highly geographically concentrated). But even here, assuming that decision making in the legislature is by simple majority rule, the nontradables party will always be able to pass the legislation it prefers – in this case to maintain existing KWS policies.

The party of the nontraded goods sector will have a larger legislative majority (70 percent) where seats are granted to geographic units – assuming the system is designed to represent political entities rather than people. Hence, there will be no redistricting between t_0 and t_1 even though the portion of the population in the nontradables "states" will have declined from 70 percent to 51 percent.[15] Finally, in the classic case of exaggerated majorities under single member districts with voters for each party split evenly over all constituencies, the nontradables party would win all the seats at t_1 – with 51 percent of the vote in every district.

This simple example shows that democratic elections will always bias policy outcomes in favor of less productive sectors, in virtue of the one person–one vote principle. The size of this bias will vary with electoral rules, but democratic elections will always give more power to nontradables than would be the case under economic pluralism. This forces incumbent politicians to confront an unpleasant reality. The policies that their constituents prefer are likely to be harmful to economic performance and to disenchant the more productive sectors of the economy. Nonetheless, pursuing policies that are efficient over the longer run will jeopardize a government's hold on power in the short term. We discuss how governments might mitigate this tension in Section V on endogenous institutional change.

The responsiveness of government – veto players

Students of American politics have long recognized that the sharing of power between the presidency and congress creates a strong status quo bias. Recently, others have made similar observations about bicameralism and presidentialism in other countries (Shugart and Carey 1992; Weaver and Rockman 1993). Tsebelis has generalized these arguments by suggesting that the responsiveness of policy to a change in societal preferences is inversely related to the number of formal "veto players" in the political system – that is, the number of institutional actors whose assent is required for a policy change (Tsebelis 1995). This argument rests on the reasonable assumption that the interests of veto players will differ so long as the ways they aggregate preferences are not the same. For example in the U.S., only the president has a truly national constituency. "All politics is local" in the House of Representatives. Representation in the Senate is based on political geography rather than on population.

The implications of this argument for the dynamics of political change in our hypothetical economy are clear. The magnitude of policy change associated with the increasing influence of tradables on the course of policy would be negatively correlated with the number of veto players. Within democracies, responsiveness would increase the greater concentration of legislative and executive authority. Hence, policy could be expected to be more responsive to changes in preferences in Britain – with a single veto player, the House of Commons – than in Germany – where legislative authority is split between the two chambers, the Bundestag and the Bundesrat – than in the U.S. – where the president can veto congressional decisions. Similarly, one could argue that in nondemocracies, the military, the secret police, and other parts of the state apparatus may sometimes be sufficiently independent to act as veto players. Where this is the case, one should expect the pace of policy change to be slower than in more centralized systems.

The responsiveness of government – bureaucratic autonomy

For at least a decade, scholarly efforts to "bring the state back in" have asserted that bureaucratic agencies exert an independent influence on politics that is not captured by models based purely on societal demands (Evans, et al. 1985). The twin notions underpinning this research are that considerable authority is delegated to bureaucracies, and that the preferences of bureaucrats are different from those of elected politicians. Bureaucrats will not change the way they make and implement policy in lockstep with the preferences of governments or societal actors. While this argument is plausible, the literature has been plagued by a lack of clarity about causal mechanisms and a paucity of rigorous empirical tests.

The same cannot be said for recent work in economics on central bank independence (Cukierman 1992).[16] The basic argument in this literature can be summarized briefly. Governments always have an incentive to inflate the economy to stimulate demand and employment. Economic actors know this, however, and build inflationary expectations into their current behavior. As a result, expansionary policies will have no impact on real aggregates, but will only increase inflation. Delegating monetary authority to an independent central bank constitutes a credible commitment that will remedy this "time inconsistency" problem. The consequence will be lower rates of inflation rates at the "natural" level of unemployment. Consider two scenarios.

In the first case, the government effectively controls monetary policy because the central bank has little independence (as in Britain). Here, private economic actors anticipate that the government will always inflate the economy (at 5 percent per annum, for example) in an effort to boost demand and employment. As a result, actors will base their behavior on the assumption of inflation. If employers and workers construct forward wage contracts on the expectations that the real wage should remain constant, this will mean that next year's contracts will be for a 5 percent increase in nominal wages. Corporate profits will thus remain constant in real terms and no new jobs will be created. But prices throughout the economy will have gone up by 5 percent.

Now consider the case where the government delegates all authority over monetary policy to the central bank and mandates through legislation that central bankers will pursue the objective of price stability (annual inflation of 0 percent, in the extreme case) by raising interest rates even if this generates higher unemployment in the short run (as in Germany or contemporary New Zealand). Since all economic actors know that this is how the central bank will act, they will adjust their behavior accordingly. Forward wage contracts that protect the real income of workers will now have 0 percent nominal wage increases. As in the dependent central bank example, real corporate profits will be unaffected by nominal wage developments, and no new jobs will be created. However, prices will remain stable. Thus, the delegation of monetary authority to an independent central bank can cut inflation without harming the real economy.

What are the implications of central bank independence for our hypothetical economy? In order to answer this question, it is crucial to note that the impact of central bank threats to fight inflation by increasing real interest rates will differ between the traded and nontraded sectors (Franzese 1995). Recall that employment and output in tradables is directly a function of competitiveness in global markets, but this is not the case for those in the nontraded sector. Thus, if the central bank raises real interest rates, this will lead to an appreciation of the real exchange rate – and hence to a decline in the competitiveness of the traded goods sector. The same policy will have much less impact on nontradables, however, and it will also decrease the costs of imports consumed in this sector.

Thus, the macroeconomic consequences attributed to independent central banks in much of the literature only apply directly to tradables. Threats to raise interest rates will not lead workers in nontradables to reduce their wage militancy. If anything, they benefit from higher real interest rates that increase the exchange rate and hence their ability to buy imports.

Table 4 presents our expectations about economic policy and macroeconomic performance in our hypothetical political economy under high and low levels of central bank independence. At t_0, nontradables are dominant. Where the central bank has little independence from government, this should result in very strong KWS policies. Increasing central bank independence, however, would somewhat constrain the government from pursuing these policies – for example, by imposing an interest rate premium on the running of budget deficits. In this case, the macroeconomic consequences of central bank independence would be dire. The combination of loose fiscal policies and tight monetary policies would greatly benefit nontradables but undermine the competitiveness of tradables. Thus at t_0, performance would be better where the central bank was controlled by the government, which would be able to coordinate fiscal and monetary policy effectively to manipulate domestic demand.

The situation would be quite different at t_1. Increasing the economic power of the traded goods sector would decrease the government's commitment to the KWS. Moreover, economic performance would improve the more independent the central bank. At t_1, central bank threats to increase real interest rates would be very effective on the large traded goods sector, and government fiscal policies would also tend to be relatively tight. Under these conditions, inflation would always be low and output and employment would be driven by the competitiveness of tradables in global markets.

Summary

The purpose of this section has been to delineate how formal political institutions mediate in the relationship between societal preferences and

Table 4. *Economic interest and central bank independence*

Outcomes	Dominant sector (by economic activity)	Independence of central bank	
		high	low
policies[a]	t_0 - nontradables	2	1
	t_1 - tradables	4	3
performance[b]	t_0 - nontradables	4	3
	t_1 - tradables	1	2

Note: Numbers are rank orders.
[a]Commitment to the Keynesian welfare state and capital controls.
[b]Economic aggregates such as growth, inflation and unemployment.

political outcomes. We have shown these mediating effects are likely to be highly consequential – in terms either of which societal preferences get heard in the public arena and of how responsive the political system will be to those interests that are effectively represented.

V. ENDOGENOUS INSTITUTIONAL CHANGE

The preceding two sections have shown that in our hypothetical case of the domestic consequences of economic internationalization the course of policy change will only accord with the expectations of economic pluralism under a restrictive set of institutional conditions. Specifically, we have argued that an increase in the economic importance of the traded goods sector will only be associated with concomitant decreases in the use of Keynesian demand management, capital controls, and industrial policies and welfare provision where the following institutional requirements are met:

- the political system is democratic (government officials are responsive to new policy demands)
- labor unions are weak and decentralized (nontraded sector unions cannot veto policy changes that are detrimental to them)
- the electoral bias against economically powerful sectors is minimized (list proportional representation is likely to be best)
- political authority is concentrated in a single institution (there is little threat of gridlock)
- the central bank is independent from the government (promoting competitive behavior in the tradables sector)

Such a political economy does not exist. Our analysis suggests that democracy is a precondition for economic pluralism (because it decreases the entry barriers for newly empowered interests). But within the major democracies, the United States satisfies only the weak unions and central bank independence criteria; political authority is dispersed and geographic representation in the Senate is biased against economically powerful interests. Germany has an independent central bank and an electoral system that generates proportional representation, but its unions are strong and the political system is bicameral and federal. Japan has weak unions and concentrated political authority, but its central bank is not insulated from political control and its electoral system is biased in favor of rural interests. Perhaps Switzerland most closely approximates the institutional desiderata for the policy predictions of economic pluralism to hold, but policy change in Switzlerland is thwarted by the Proporz norm in cabinet government formation, the wide use of referendums, and the power of cantons.

At this point it should be noted, however, that our analysis has assumed that the institutional environment in which governments operate is fixed. What happens if this assumption is relaxed to allow for the possibility that governments can change institutions in addition to policy? In this section, we examine this politics of endogenous institutional change.

Let us begin by adding some institutional details to our hypothetical economy. Assume that the institutional setup at t_0 is one that is likely to generate strong KWS policies: labor market institutions are strong but decentralized; nontradables' interests are overrepresented in the decision-making realm; there are multiple veto players in the system; and the central bank has little independence from government. If these institutions are not changed by t_1, policies will still be favorable to the nontraded sector, and aggregate economic performance will decline.

It is under these conditions that governments have an incentive to engage in institutional change to strengthen the position of the tradables sector. This is because there is a tension between the existing distributional pressures to pursue the KWS and the macroeconomic consequences of these policies.[17] While the government might be able to maintain power in the short run – by continuing to pursue policies that benefit nontradables – over time the deterioration in macroeconomic performance that will result from these policies will come to jeopardize the government's ability to maintain power. The benefits of institutional reform, however, are unlikely to be reaped immediately. In our hypothetical example, long run economic performance could be increased by weakening the power of organized labor. But in the short run, this is likely to hurt the nontradables sector by raising unemployment, with significant costs to the government in terms of lost support from this large sector.

How should we expect governments to solve this dilemma between retaining power in the short run but prejudicing their hold on power over time (by maintaining the existing institutions) and improving their long-run

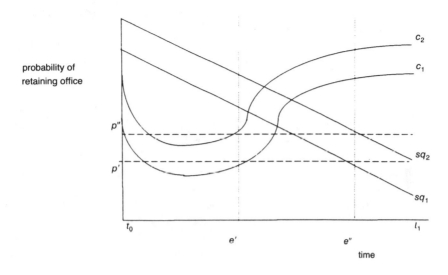

p - the probability of retaining office desired by government
sq_1, sq_2 - the utility of not undertaking institutional reform
c_1, c_2 - the utility of undertaking institutional reform
e', e'' - the period of time before the government will be accountable to the electorate
The subscripts 1 and 2 refer to unfavorable and favorable conjunctural conditions, respectively.

Figure 3. The politics of institutional change

prospects at the risk of losing office in the short run (by undertaking institutional change)?

Consider the following example (depicted graphically in Figure 3). The primary concern of governments is to ensure that their probability of maintaining power does not fall below a given threshold level. There are two types of governments – those that are highly risk averse (p'') and those that are more risk accepting (p'). The more risk accepting governments will be more prepared, at the margin, to sacrifice some of their confidence about their prospects for retaining office in the name of other objectives. All governments discount the future; thus doing whatever will maintain power today is weighed more heavily than acting to retain power tomorrow.

Governments can pursue two strategies. They can either maintain the institutional status quo and pursue policies that favor nontradables (sq), or they can change institutions and pursue policies that favor the traded goods sector (c). The utility to the government of pursuing sq declines in linear fashion with time. In contrast, the utility of pursuing c is curvilinear. For a period after an institutional change is made, the government's probability of retaining office will decline. At some point, however, pursuing c increases the government's prospects of staying in power (eventually the benefits of institutional change dissipate).

Governments are only accountable for their policy choices at certain times. For convenience, we simply distinguish between a shorter and a longer window of freedom for government action – e' and e'', respectively. In democracies, this period is determined by electoral laws; in nondemocracies, government would have expectations about their window of opportunity until their policies are evaluated by the citizens based on the power and mobilization of opposition forces. In all political systems, governments will base their strategic choices on the expected utility of maintaining or changing the institutional status quo only at the time when they are accountable to the citizenry.

Finally, conjunctural conditions – such as the health of the international economy – can be expected to have an independent impact on the government's probability of retaining office. In Figure 3, we distinguish two simple cases, in which conjunctural conditions are either unfavorable (denoted by the subscript (1) or favorable (2).

We consider this to a reasonable model of the parameters that are likely to affect a government's decision about whether to pursue a strategy of institutional change that is likely to be costly in the short run but beneficial over the longer run. The model yields some interesting comparative statistics.

The simplest observation is that it is more likely that governments will choose to pursue strategies of institutional change: the less risk averse are governments; the longer is the period of time until the government will be held accountable for its actions by the citizenry; and, the more favorable are conjunctural conditions. However, this logic isn't linear. In our model, governments only compare the expected utility of different strategies at specific times in the future – when they expect to be held accountable for their record in office. Four different scenarios should be considered.

1 The expected utility from c is less than the government's desired threshold p at time e, whereas the expected utility from sq is greater than p: in this case, there is no incentive for the government to change institutions. In Figure 3, this is the case for e' and p' under unfavorable conjunctures.

2 The expected utility from c is greater than the government's desired threshold p at time e, whereas the expected utility from sq is less than p: there is no incentive for the government not to change institutions. This is the case for e'' and p' with unfavorable conjunctures.

3 The expected utilities from c and sq are both above the government's desired threshold p at time e, but c is greater than sq: the government could clearly pursue sq in this case, but so long as it cares at all about the future, there is no reason to think it wouldn't engage in institutional change (e'', p'' with favorable conjunctures).

4 The expected utilities from c and sq are both above the government's desired threshold p at time e, but sq is greater than c: this is the most difficult choice a

government could face. Nonetheless, we would still expect the government to pursue institutional change under these conditions (e.g., p'', e' and favorable conjunctures).

We believe that these decisions capture important elements of the decision making environments that governments have faced in the real world. For example, Thatcher's Britain provides a good example of how both favorable conjunctural conditions and accepting attitudes to risk can lead a government to pursue a strategy of institutional change even though this is costly in the short term.

The British conservative government realized that weakening organized labor was very important to the efficacy of its neo-liberal policy goals (Garrett 1993). Allowing unemployment to rise was the most direct way of weakening organized labor, but this was likely to have significant electoral costs in the short run. Nonetheless, the government was prepared to accept the risk that this would lead to electoral disaster (as the opinion polls through 1982 predicted). Moreover, the government was able successfully to implement its strategy for attacking the unions in the early 1980s – and to reap the rewards into the 1990s – because conjunctural conditions mitigated the costs of unemployment. Most notably, the implosion of the Labour party in 1980 – and the Social Democratic party that spawned – meant that the Conservative government could retain its majority in the House of Commons on only slightly over 40 percent of the popular vote as the opposition parties split anti-Conservative vote.

The other important implication of Figure 3 is that increasing the period until a government must be accountable to its citizens will increase the government's propensity to engage in economically efficient institutional changes. This clearly suggests that democracy will be more resistant to such endogenous institutional change and hence less prosperous – than nondemocracies. But this will only hold if the nondemocratic government is a "benevolent dictator" – if given the opportunity to change institutions, it will do so in ways that are good for society as a whole in the long run (in terms of improving aggregate economic performance). Some have suggested that this has been the case with respect to the economic successes of the East Asian NICs (Wade 1990).

However, for each example of economic success without democracy in East Asia there is another instance of economic failure based on maladapted policies and institutions (most notably in the former Soviet bloc). The reason for this is simple – governments in most nondemocracies aren't benevolent dictatorships dedicated to improving aggregate economic performance. Rather, they have their own constituencies they wish to favor with policy. As was suggested earlier in the section on formal institutions, the absence of democratic elections is likely to increase resistance to policy change dictated by changes in cconomic structure. One should expect this resistance to be at least as great in the case of institutional change.

In sum, this section suggests that there are significant barriers to the types of institutional reforms that would need to be undertaken if the policy expectations of economic pluralism are to be borne out in practice. It seems most imprudent to assume that institutions are epiphenomenal and hence irrelevant to processes of political change. Thus, bringing the prospect of endogenous institutional change into our model of politics doesn't alter the fundamental conclusion of this paper: preexisting institutional conditions will have a marked bearing on how a change in the preferences of societal actors will affect government behavior.

CONCLUSION

The basic objective of this article has been to show how "institutions matter" in dynamic processes of political change. In so doing, we hope to have integrated two bodies of work that have hitherto tended to talk past each other. On the one hand, students of international relations have recently begun to explore the linkages between economic internationalization and the preferences and likely political behavior of domestic actors, but they have tended to pay little attention to the institutional context of politics within nations. Frieden and Rogowski's article in this volume is an excellent synthesis of this approach. On the other hand, modern comparativists have studied the effects of political institutions on public policy, but in so doing they have often downplayed the importance of the rapidly changing international environment in which domestic politics is embedded. The international-comparative divide is increasingly anachronistic. Today the clear challenge for scholars is to combine the insights of both perspectives without losing sight of their unique contributions.

We have sought to accomplish this task by working with an "open polity" model to analyze the mediating effects of domestic institutions between internationally driven changes in the preferences of actors in the private sphere and public policy outcomes. We have placed national governments at the center of the analysis and asked how variations in institutional conditions – in both the private and public realms – can be expected to affect the responses of governments to an exogenous increase in the size of the traded goods sector. Our central conclusion is that the range of scenarios in which processes of political change can be effectively explained without an explicit institutional dimension is very narrow. The null hypothesis of economic pluralism – that changes in the constellation of preferences in the private sphere will be quickly reflected in commensurate changes in public policies and institutions – can be rejected under almost all of the institutional conditions examined in this paper.

Thus, adding an explicit institutional dimension increases our analytic leverage over the political consequences of economic internationalization. However, this research strategy has significant consequences for theory building. Studying the impact of international economic change on the preferences of domestic economic actors lends itself to parsimonious theorizing – as the work of Frieden, Rogowski, and others attests. This is not the case for institutional approaches.

There is no simple "grand theory" of political institutions. Rather, specific institutions have different effects. For example, the policy consequences of labor market institutions and central bank independence are complex and require close attention on their own. Moreover, the effects of these institutions are unlikely to be independent of each other – the impact of central bank independence on wage setting, economic policy, and macroeconomic performance, for instance, is likely to be influenced by the labor market institutions that accompany it (Franzese 1995). But in order to understand such interactive processes – and hence to build more encompassing institutional theories – it is necessary first to isolate their independent effects.

Thus, the process of theory building with respect to the effects of political institutions is likely to be a laborious one, necessitating careful analysis of a whole series of relatively small but nonetheless significant relationships before any clear "big picture" may emerge. But if important variations in domestic political outcomes can only be explained by supplementing an analysis of preferences and preference change with attention to the institutional context of politics, this is an endeavor well worth the effort.

PART II

The Industrialized Democracies

4

Capital Mobility, Trade, and the Domestic Politics of Economic Policy

GEOFFREY GARRETT

The increased international integration of goods, services, and capital markets among the advanced industrial countries in the past two decades is widely viewed to have exerted powerful pressures for convergence in economic policies toward those that promote the freer play of market forces (Andrews 1994; Goodman 1993; Kurzer 1991; Lee and McKenzie 1989; Notermans 1993; Scharpf 1991). The relative closure of the international economy from the end of World War II until the mid-1970s afforded governments the luxury of pursuing expansionary and interventionist economic policies – the "Keynesian welfare state" (KWS) – without undermining aggregate economic performance, and there were obvious reasons why such policies were particularly appealing to the left and organized labor. But the space to pursue such policies evaporated, so goes the conventional wisdom, in the ever more integrated and competitive international economy of the latter 1970s and 1980s.

In contrast, others claim that the association between left-labor power and the KWS increased with integration into the international economy – measured in terms of exposure to trade – at least through the late 1970s (Cameron 1978; Katzenstein 1985). Moreover, this contention has been buttressed by recent research in economics on the endogenous sources of

This paper has taken a long time to reach publication. I have been thinking about the issues it broaches for many years, both in my own work and in collaborations with Thomas Cusack, Peter Lange, Deborah Mitchell, and Christopher Way. My intellectual debts to them are manifold. Special thanks are also due to Thomas Cusack and Andrew Rose for providing much of the data, to Jeffrey Frankel for tolerating my repeated questions about capital mobility, and to Jeffry Frieden for pushing me (and helping me) to think harder about the interaction between macroeconomics and domestic politics. I would also like to thank Jonathan Bendor, Bruce Chapman, Steve Dowrick, Peter Hall, Robert Keohane, Keith Krehbiel, Helen Milner, Adrian Pagan, Douglas Rivers, and David Soskice for helpful comments on various aspects of this paper. Finally, the financial support of the Hoover Institution, Stanford, the Research School of the Social Sciences, Australian National University, Canberra, and the Wissenschaftszentrum, Berlin, is gratefully acknowledged.

economic growth and on the macroeconomic consequences of labor organization. "New growth" theory contends that active government involvement in the economy (for example, public spending on education, physical infrastructure and research and development) may actually increase productivity and hence competitiveness by providing collective goods that are undersupplied by the market (Aschauer 1990; Barro 1989; Lucas 1988; Romer 1990). It has also been argued that the beneficial effects of government involvement in the economy are accentuated where powerful and centralized organized labor movements can reduce the wage militancy that might otherwise be associated with such policies (Alvarez 1991). From this perspective, governments in countries with powerful left parties and trade unions ("social democratic corporatism") might respond to internationalization with more interventionist and expansionary policies – because these may both redistribute wealth and social risk to workers and the poor and enhance competitiveness in international markets.

There are thus two very different ways of thinking about the impact of economic internationalization on domestic politics, and these generate diametrically opposed hypotheses about the course of economic policy in the global economy. On the one hand, those who focus on changes in the structure of the international economy assert that increasing trade and capital mobility lead both to a secular decline in the KWS and to a cross-national convergence in policies. On the other hand, concentration on domestic factors suggests that the KWS may not have been undermined by market integration and that cross-national variations in policy may endure, if not increase, with economic internationalization.

This paper assesses the merits of these two approaches by analyzing the interactive effects of economic internationalization and left-labor power on economic policies for fifteen advanced industrial countries – Australia, Austria, Belgium, Canada, Denmark, Finland, France, Germany, Italy, Japan, The Netherlands, Norway, Sweden, the United Kingdom, and the United States – over the period 1967–90.[1] Unlike previous work on the relationship between internationalization and domestic politics, the impact of capital mobility, as well as trade growth is considered. The data on trade unions are drawn from new research that permits meaningful intertemporal comparisons of the strength of organized labor (Golden and Wallerstein 1994). Finally, a range of macroeconomic policy indicators is examined: government spending, budget deficits, capital taxation[2] and interest rates.

The analysis shows that the relationship between market integration, domestic politics, and economic policy is more complex than the existing literature maintains. On the one hand, there is some evidence that internationalization, *ceteris paribus*, has decreased government activism. For example, both increasing trade and increasing capital mobility led to reductions in budget deficits across the industrialized countries. Furthermore, there is also some support for the proposition that increased internationalization has mitigated the relationship between left-labor power and interventionist policies. Specifically, while the independent effect of increasing left-labor power was to increase capital taxation, at higher levels of trade this relationship was reversed.[3]

This does not mean, however, that the conventional wisdom about the demise of leftist alternatives to free market capitalism in the face of economic internationalization forces is unambiguously correct. Far from it. First, the structural foundations of social democratic corporatism have been remarkably stable. In the period under analysis, there was no secular decline in the political power of the left, nor the strength of organized labor, nor any noticeable diminution in cross-national differences in left-labor power. If domestic conditions were conducive to the KWS in the 1960s, there is little reason to believe that they should have been less so in the 1980s.

Second and more importantly, the evidence on fiscal policy conflicts sharply with the convergence thesis. The coincidence of strong left parties, strong trade unions, capital mobility, and high levels of trade led to greater government spending and the running of larger deficits. The association between social democratic corporatism and the KWS was significantly stronger at the beginning of the 1990s than it was in the late 1960s. The left and organized labor had to pay a price for fiscal expansions – in terms of higher interest rates – and these interest rate premia increased with greater capital mobility. Up until 1990, however, these interest rate premia were not large enough to prompt governments in countries with powerful left parties and trade unions to abandon fiscal activism.

These interest rate premia may in time come to erode the social democratic corporatism – KWS nexus. While countries with strong left parties and trade unions have long been highly exposed to trade, they have also had relatively closed financial markets. Capital mobility increased significantly in all countries between the late 1960s and 1990. But today there are still more controls on cross border capital flows in countries dominated by the left and organized labor than in those with weak left parties and unions. If and when the remaining capital controls are removed in these countries, and if the financial markets continue to demand higher interest rates for lending in these countries, at some point governments will be forced to cut spending and deficits. But this limit to fiscal expansions was not reached in the 1980s.

The remainder of the paper elaborates these points. The next section describes changes in trade, capital mobility, the power of left parties, and the organization of labor movements since the mid-1960s. The third section develops hypotheses about the interactive effects of market integration and domestic politics on economic policy. These are then tested empirically in the fourth section. The final section re-assesses the debate about economic internationalization and domestic politics in the light of the paper's findings.

I. INTERNATIONALIZATION AND DOMESTIC POLITICAL CONDITIONS

There can be little doubt that the international integration of national economies increased substantially from the mid-1960s to 1990. With respect to trade, average exports plus imports in goods and services (for the fifteen countries studied here) grew as a portion of gross domestic product (GDP) from around 45 percent to over 60 percent (see Figure 1, right hand scale). Moreover, much of this growth was accounted for by increases in trade with countries outside the Organization for Economic Cooperation and Development (OECD) (left hand scale). Imports from the Organization of Petroleum Exporting Countries (OPEC) accounted for around 15 percent of total OECD imports between the first and second oil shocks, but this portion subsequently declined with falling oil prices. In contrast, imports from the Newly Industrializing Countries (NICs) of East Asia and Latin America grew steadily throughout the period, to constitute almost 10 percent of all OECD imports by the end of the 1980s.

It is harder to measure the integration of capital markets. The most obvious indicator of financial integration – the dramatic rise in international capital flows since the mid-1970s – is not favored by economists. Greater cross-border capital movements could be the product of any number of changes in the investment environment in addition to reductions in the barriers to cross-border capital movements. A variety of indicators have been developed to measure the actual extent of financial integration.[4] Two are depicted in Figure 2.[5]

The left hand scale shows over time changes in the relationship between private domestic savings and private domestic investment for the fifteen countries in this study.[6] The right hand scale depicts changes in the average number of government restrictions imposed on cross-border capital flows, based on the International Monetary Fund's (IMF) categorization of capital controls.[7] These variables are obviously different. One examines economic activity in the private sector and can measure small changes in behavior; the other codifies government policies and is more "lumpy." Nonetheless, the two measures are highly correlated over time ($r = .77$). The constraints imposed on domestic investment by domestic savings declined substantially from the mid-1960s to 1990 – indicating a marked increase in the freedom of capital holders to move their money around the world to maximize rates of return. Over the same period, there was also a pronounced decline in the restrictions imposed by governments on cross-border financial flows.

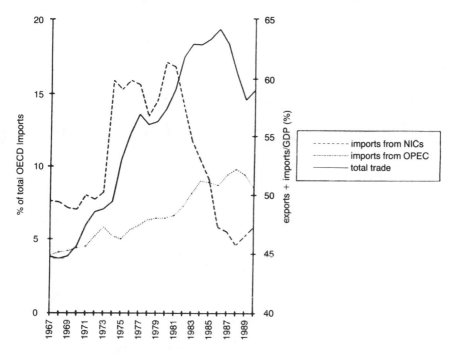

Figure 1. Trade. *Source*: OECD, Historical Statistics, various. Total trade data are annual fifteen country averages.

The purpose of this paper is not to discuss the sources of international economic integration, but instead to assess the domestic consequences of internationalization. Following recent studies, internationalization can be considered an exogenous development to which domestic actors must respond rather than the result of conscious policy choice. Even if policy liberalization invariably attends increases in trade and capital mobility, it is clear that other factors – such as changes in technology and transportation costs – are causally prior to changes in policy (Frieden and Rogowski 1996; Goodman and Pauly 1993).

Two arguments are commonly made with respect to the impact of economic internationalization on social democratic corporatism. First, some contend that market integration has weakened the domestic foundations of corporatism by reducing the power and cohesiveness of organized labor movements and by weakening political support for the left (Kitschelt 1994; Piven 1991). Second, others suggest that the globalization of goods, services, and capital markets has curtailed the ability of governments to pursue economic policies that are either more expansionary or more inter-

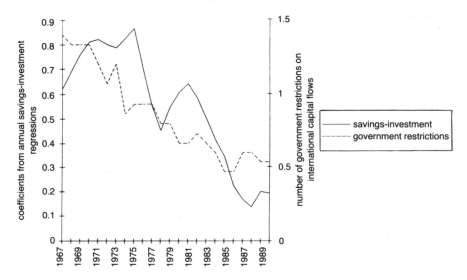

Figure 2. Capital mobility. *Sources*: OECD, Historical Statistics, various. IMF, Annual Report on Exchange Arrangements and Exchange Restrictions. Government restrictions are annual fifteen country averages.

ventionist than global trends, even if there remain domestic political incentives to do so (Kurzer 1991; Lee and McKenzie 1989; Notermans 1993; Scharpf 1991). Let us examine each claim in turn.

Internationalization generates new constellations of preferences that crosscut the traditional labor-capital cleavage (Frieden 1991b; Frieden and Rogowski 1996). In the increasingly international division of labor, workers, managers and owners in the same firms, sectors, or regions may have more interests in common with each other than those they share with their "class allies." The emergence of these crosscutting cleavages is potentially of great significance for the strength and structure of trade unions, and for the political support for leftist parties. The ability of powerful labor movements to generate voluntary wage restraint and to deliver strong political support for left parties is essential to social democratic corporatism (Alvarez et al. 1991). Changes in the structure of employment associated with the globalization of markets – the decline in manufacturing jobs, the expansion of the service sector, the growth in public sector employment and increasing part-time work – could be anticipated to have reduced the ranks of unionized workers, lessened the authority of central confederations, and diminished the left's core political constituencies.

The evidence, however, does not bear out these claims. Figure 3 presents annual fifteen country averages for the "partisan center of gravity" in cabi-

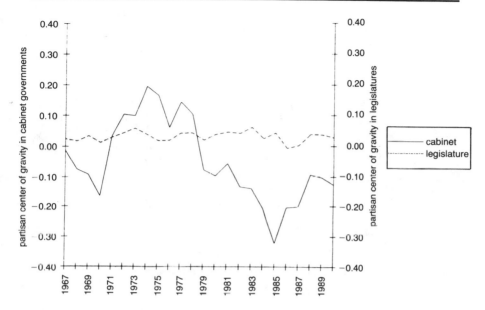

Figure 3. The balance of political power. *Source*: See footnote 20. Data are annual fifteen country averages.

net governments and in legislatures.[8] The cabinet measure delineates the direct control of different political parties over the instruments of economic policy. The legislative measure indicates the broader political constraints under which governments operate, regardless of their partisan stripe.[9] On both variables, "0" reflects a perfect balance of power between the left and right; positive (negative) scores denote the dominance of the left (right).

The cross-national balance of power in legislatures was remarkably stable at the center of the political spectrum throughout the period under investigation. However, the average partisan center of gravity for cabinet governments was more volatile. Left governments became more prevalent in the early 1970s, but the center of gravity in cabinet governments swung to the right in the late 1970s and early 1980s. The strength of the left then increased again at the end of the decade – returning to about the level of the late 1960s. These movements cannot be explained in terms of economic internationalization, which increased consistently throughout the period under investigation. Rather, the fate of governments seems to have been closely tied to the international business cycle. The fact that there were many incumbent leftist governments when the OPEC oil shocks hit made a swing to the right in the 1980s very likely. But this also made more probable the left's better performance in the late 1980s – as the latest international recession hit.

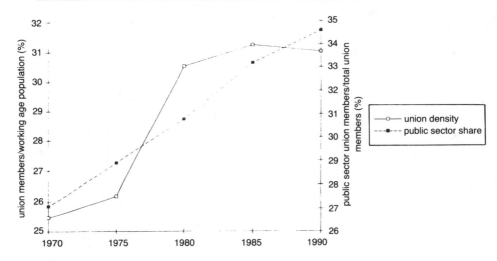

Figure 4. The density and composition of trade unions. *Source*: See footnote 22. Data are annual fifteen country averages.

Figures 4 and 5 present data on changes in the structure of trade unions since the mid-1960s.[10] The simplest measure of the strength of organized labor is union density, the sheer number of union members (relative to the eligible population), which grew from 1970 to 1985 and then stabilized in 1990 (Figure 4, left hand scale)[11] (Visser 1991). It would be unwise, however, to base conclusions about the power of trade unions simply on density. Most arguments about the consequences of union organization have tended to assume that the interests of all workers are the same. Recent case studies contend that if this assumption of undifferentiated workers were ever valid, it certainly has not been in recent years (Iversen 1995; Swenson 1992). Consistent with these studies, Figure 4 shows that the strength of public sector unions (right hand scale) grew appreciably from 1970 to 1990 (Visser 1991). This division between public sector unions and those in the tradables sector can be expected to have lessened the ability of labor movements to act collectively – in either the political or economic spheres (Garrett and Way 1995).[12]

The essence of most research on corporatism, however, is the notion that the concentration of union authority mitigates the centrifugal tendencies generated by differences in the interests of different types of workers (Golden 1993). Figure 5 presents data on two measures of union concentration – the percentage of all unionized workers who are members of the largest labor confederation in a country, and the number of unions affiliated with that confederation (Golden and Wallerstein 1994). These data

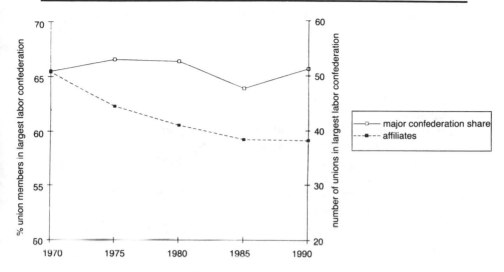

Figure 5. The internal structure of trade union movements. *Source*: See footnote 26. Data are annual fifteen country averages.

show that there has been no reduction in the organizational power of peak labor confederations. The portion of union members in the largest confederation averaged across the fifteen countries was quite stable from 1970 to 1990, while the average number of unions in the major confederation decreased somewhat (if anything, lessening the obstacles to collective action).

Taken together, the data in Figures 3 to 5 belie the common perception that the power of the left and organized labor have been undermined by economic internationalization. But this tells us nothing about the impact of market integration on economic policies. It could be the case, for example, that there was a marked decline in expansionary and interventionist macroeconomic policies across all the western countries – associated with the integration of markets – and that this was most apparent where left governments were allied with encompassing labor movements. The implicit hypothesis here would be that the only way the left could retain electoral competitiveness in this new economic environment was to mimic the policies of the right. This remainder of the paper scrutinizes this supposition.

II. THE POLICY CONSEQUENCES OF INTERNATIONALIZATION

How should we expect internationalization to have affected the course of economic policy in the industrial democracies? Let us begin by distinguishing the impact of capital mobility from that of trade, then introduce domestic political conditions, and finally analyze their interactive effects.

Capital mobility

The process by which capital mobility influences economic policy can be stated succinctly: the easier it is for asset holders to move their capital offshore, the stronger the incentives for governments to pursue policies that will increase rates of return on domestic investment. Given that it is more difficult for entrepreneurs with fixed investments in plant and equipment to redeploy their assets than it is those investing in stocks, bonds, or currencies, the expected reaction of the financial markets is likely to be the primary constraint on government policy in a world of mobile capital.

The clearest policy consequence of financial integration is the pressure it creates for cross-national convergence in monetary policy. In fixed exchange rate regimes with high levels of financial mobility, the prospect of capital flight creates powerful incentives for governments to keep domestic interest rates close to those in other countries (especially those that act as price setters, such as the United States). Interest rates will also converge where exchange rates float and there are no controls on capital flows, but expanding the domestic money supply will nonetheless have short term stimulative effects by lowering the exchange rate. However, these effects are liable to be quickly undermined by the higher price of imports. Moreover, foreign exchange markets are volatile and tend to react dramatically to small changes in economic fundamentals (such as interest rates, budgetary balances, and inflation). Thus, the prospect of speculative runs on currencies is a powerful disincentive against government attempts to run "managed depreciations" where capital is highly mobile[13] (McKinnon 1988).

Capital mobility can also be expected to be associated with cuts in government spending, smaller budget deficits, and lower rates of capital taxation. The case of capital taxation is the simplest. The more governments tax income derived from investment, the lower will be anticipated rates of return, and the stronger the incentives for capital to exit. Where there are few restrictions on cross-border capital flows, this specter should induce governments to cut capital taxes. With respect to fiscal policy, the removal of capital controls increases the pool of money available to governments for borrowing and hence might be considered to create incentives for governments to expand the public economy. However, these incentives are likely outweighed by the financial markets' skepticism about government spending. Today's expenditures must be paid for in the future either by increased taxation or by higher inflation. Either way, the markets can be expected to react to public sector expansion by demanding that higher interest rates be paid on loans. The anticipation of such interest rate premia, in turn, could be expected to induce governments to cut public spending and deficits.

Trade

The mechanism by which increasing trade influences economic policy is different from that for capital mobility. The time horizon of players in financial markets is notoriously short, and the long term ramifications of government policy are much less important than any immediate opportunities for arbitrage they present. In contrast, the constraints governments face from increasing trade are not day-to-day fluctuations in the financial markets but rather the longer run competitiveness of national producers in international markets. The prospects for open economies that do not compete well in international markets are grim. Unemployment will rise and economic growth will slow down. Running large trade deficits is infeasible in the long run because of the outflows of capital they necessarily entail. Governments that engage in widespread protection (much less autarky), face significant losses in aggregate welfare, and these increase the smaller the national economy (and hence the more important are achieving scale economies and exploiting national comparative advantages).

Does this competitiveness constraint create similar policy incentives to those for capital mobility? A neoclassical perspective would answer this question affirmatively. In order to boost competitiveness, governments must cut spending because it is an implicit tax on producers. They must balance the budget so as not to shackle future generations with the lodestone of a large public debt. Capital taxation should be reduced to foster entrepreneurial innovation.[14]

However, this view is not shared by all economists. The recent spate of research on endogenous sources of economic growth suggests – contra neoclassical theory – that government spending can increase productivity and competitiveness by generating collective goods that are undersupplied by the market. The basic argument underpinning new growth theory is that collective action problems and the logic of scale economies render it more efficient for governments than private actors to provide a wide array of goods and services – ranging from the training of workers to the provision of physical infrastructure such as roads and bridges – that contribute positively to growth (Aschauer 1990; Barro 1989; Lucas 1988; Romer 1990). This perspective does not advocate running deficits, nor taxing capital heavily. Nonetheless, new growth theory offers an economic rationale for "big government." One should therefore be reticent to claim that increased exposure to trade will inevitably result in a scaling back of the public economy.[15]

The interactive effects of internationalization and left-labor power

The basic arguments in the literature on social democratic corporatism are, first, that left parties prefer to pursue policies that redistribute wealth and social risk in favor of workers and the poor, and, second, that the existence of powerful and concentrated organized labor movements increases the macroeconomic efficacy of these policies by limiting their inflationary consequences (through voluntary wage restraint). As a result, one would expect that, *ceteris paribus*, greater left-labor power would be associated with higher public spending, larger deficits, higher capital taxation, and lower interest rates.

However, the more interesting issue in the global economy is how left governments allied with powerful labor movements will react to increased trade and capital mobility. Two distinct perspectives can be delineated. The first concentrates on the political incentives to pursue different economic policies. Increased integration into the international economy will inevitably create dislocations associated with the free play of market forces. If the global economy is in recession, for example, this will tend to increase unemployment in all countries. This relationship will strengthen the more tightly a national economy is linked to the international system. Thus, if the primary objective of governments dominated by strong left parties and allied with strong organized labor movements is to mitigate these market dislocations, one would expect the positive relationship between left-labor power and expansionary and interventionist economic policies to grow stronger with greater exposure to trade and integration into global financial markets. This can be considered the "compensation" hypothesis (Katzenstein 1985).

The alternative view – the "efficiency" hypothesis – concentrates on the macroeconomic consequences of internationalization (Kurzer 1991; Notermans 1993; Scharpf 1991). From a neoclassical perspective, the ability of the left and organized labor to increase government spending, tax capital heavily, and pursue expansionary fiscal and monetary policies would decrease with exposure to trade and capital mobility. According to this view, compensatory policies are always inefficient, and the macroeconomic costs of pursuing them would only increase with market integration. It should be remembered, however, that if endogenous growth theory is correct, there would not be a negative relationship between increased trade and public spending – even if governments were only concerned about efficiency. Rather, one would expect that the greater the power of the left and organized labor, the more likely that government would pursue the new growth path to competing in global markets – high public spending, highly skilled workers, high value-added and high quality production – because these policies also favor workers and the poor.

Hypotheses

The hypothesized effects of economic internationalization and domestic political conditions on economic policy are summarized in Table 1. The independent effects of increasing capital mobility and trade are the same – notwithstanding the different mechanisms by which the two facets of internationalization influence policy. *Ceteris paribus*, increasing internationalization can be expected to reduce government spending, deficits, and capital taxation. However, new growth theory suggests that the relationship between trade and public spending might be positive. Only capital mobility is expected to have a strong influence on interest rates, but the hypothesized effect is one of cross-national convergence, not higher or lower interest rates. The independent effects of left-labor power are likely to be the opposite of those for internationalization – in accordance with the basic thrust of the literature on social democratic corporatism. Increasing the power of the left and organized labor should be associated with higher public spending, bigger deficits, higher taxes on capital, and lower interest rates.

Finally, there are two distinct sets of expectations about the interactive effects of left-labor power and internationalization. The compensation hypothesis suggests that the positive relationship between left-labor power and expansionary and interventionist economic policies will increase with greater trade and capital mobility – as the political incentives to compensate for market dislocations grow (leading to positive coefficients on the internationalization left-labor power terms for spending, deficits, and capital taxation). In this case, the compensation hypothesis would also suggest that interest rates would be even lower under left governments at high levels of internationalization than in more closed economies (hence, negative coefficients for the interaction terms in the interest rate equations). In contrast, the efficiency hypothesis implies that the positive relationships between left-labor power and expansionary and interventionist policies will weaken with greater internationalization – as the macroeconomic costs of compensation increase (subject to the qualification of new growth theory with respect to government spending).

III. EMPIRICAL ESTIMATES OF THE RELATIONSHIPS BETWEEN INTERNATIONALIZATION, LEFT-LABOR POWER, AND ECONOMIC POLICY

Independent effects

The hypotheses formulated in the preceding section were tested using cross-sectionally heteroskedastic and time-wise autoregressive panel regres-

Table 1. *Hypothesized interactive effects of capital mobility and left-labor power*

	Capital mobility	Trade	Left-labor power	Capital mobility Left-labor		Trade Left-labor	
				Compensation	Efficiency	Compensation	Efficiency
Government spending	−	−/+	+	+	−	+	+/−
Budget deficits	−	−	+	+	−	+	−
Capital taxation	−	−	+	+	−	+	−
Interest rates	n/a	n/a	−	−	+	−	n/a

Note: "+, −" hypothesized directions of relationships; n/a – not applicable.

sion equations on data pooling annual observations for fifteen countries from 1967 to 1990.[16] The equations control for cross-sectional "fixed effects" by including country dummy variables. Instruments were substituted for the lagged dependent variables so as not to violate the regression assumption of a zero correlation between right hand side variables and the error terms (Alvarez et al., 1991). The general form of the estimated equations was:

$$POL_{it} = a + b_1 POLZ_{it-1} + b_2 CAPMOBILITY_{it} + b_3 TRADE_{it} +$$
$$b_4 LLPOWER_{it}$$
$$. + b_5 CAPMOBILIITY.LLPOWER_{it} + b_6 TRADE.LLPOWER_{it} \qquad (1)$$
$$+ \sum (b_j COUNTRY_{jit}) + \sum (b_k X_{kit}) + \mu_{it}$$

In this equation, *POL* represents the four elements of economic policy – government spending, budget deficits, capital taxation, and interest rates. The *a* is the intercept. The *b*'s are parameter estimates. The instrumental variables (*POLZ*) were generated by regressing the lagged dependent variable on its second lag and the lags of the economic controls. *CAPMOBILITY* is the measure of government restrictions on cross-border financial flows, multiplied by "−1" for easier interpretation (that is, higher scores indicate more capital mobility).[17] *TRADE* is exports plus imports as a percentage of gross domestic product. *LLPOWER* is an additive index of standardized scores for partisan center of gravity in cabinets and legislatures (left power) and for the density, composition, and concentration of labor movements (labor power). Higher scores indicate more left-labor power.[18] The $_j$ (that is, fourteen, with the U.S. as the reference category) country dummy variables are denoted by *COUNTRY*. The economic control variables (*X*) are economic growth and unemployment (and inflation and U.S. interest rates in the interest rate equation). The subscripts $_i$ and $_t$ denote, respectively, the country and year of the observations. μ is an error term.

The panel regression estimates are presented in Table 2. Almost all of country dummies were highly significant – suggesting that the fixed effects estimation used here is appropriate.[19] The large and significant parameter estimates for the instruments for the lagged dependent variables indicate considerable stickiness in all four facets of economic policy. The business cycle – proxied by economic growth and unemployment – also had large influences on government spending and budget deficits. In the case of interest rates, domestic inflation and interest rates in the United States had a great impact on national interest rates. We need not dwell on these relationships here. The primary purpose of including this battery of control variables was to increase confidence in the estimates of the relationships between economic internationalization, domestic politics, and economic policy. Let us now turn to these.

Geoffrey Garrett

Table 2. *Government spending, budget balances, and interest rates, 1967–1990*

	Government spending	Budget deficits	Capital taxation	Interest rates[a]
intercept	16.20[d]	−1.73[f]	−.07	.32
	(1.27)	(.93)	(.53)	(1.24)
dependent variable$_{t-1}$[b]	.51[d]	.84[d]	.26[d]	.26[d]
	(.04)	(.07)	(.02)	(.04)
economic growth	−.27[d]	−.27[d]	−.02	.01
	(.04)	(.04)	(.01)	(.025)
unemployment	.81[d]	.28[d]	−.01	−.09[f]
	(.07)	(.06)	(.02)	(.05)
inflation				.10[d]
				(.02)
U.S. interest rate				.55[d]
				(.04)
capital mobility[c]	−1.22[f]	−.88[f]	.04	−1.06[d]
	(.66)	(.55)	(.23)	(.38)
trade	−.0191	−.0516[f]	.0649[d]	.027
	(.0326)	(.0300)	(.0135)	(.023)
left-labor power	−.40	−.35	.45[d]	.52[e]
	(.27)	(.27)	(.11)	(.24)
left-labor power^f capital mobility	.53[d]	.30[d]	.03	.15[e]
left-labor power^f trade	.0227[d]	.0150[d]	−.0081[d]	−.002
	(.0054)	(.0047)	(.0021)	(.004)
observations	360	360	360	312
adjusted P^2	.933	.828	.964	.685

Note: Fixed effects (i.e. including $n=1$ country dummy variables) panel regression estimates using Kmenta's [1986: eqn 12.32] cross-sectionally heteroskedastic and time-wise autoregressive model. Figures in parentheses are standard errors.
[a]Excluding Finland and the United States.
[b]Instrumental variable with dependent variable$_{t-2}$, economic growth$_{t-1}$ and unemployment$_{t-1}$ (and inflation$_{t-1}$ and US interest rates$_{t-1}$ in the interest rates equation) as exogenous variables.
[c]Capital mobility is the number of capital controls multiplied by "−1."
[d]Significant at the .01 level.
[e]Significant at the .05 level.
[f]Significant at the .1 level.

Government spending. *Ceteris paribus*, greater capital mobility exerted downward pressure on government spending – but this coefficient was only significant at the .1 level. Increasing trade had no significant impact on public expenditure, supporting the expectations of neither neoclassical theory nor new growth theory. Contra the literature on social democratic corporatism, the parameter estimate for left-labor power was negative (but not significant) in the spending equation. However, both of the interaction terms between left-labor power and economic internationalization were highly significant and positive. The combination of left-labor power and high levels of internationalization resulted in more government spending – supporting the compensation hypothesis, rather than the efficiency perspective.

Budget Deficits.   The budget deficits equation is quite similar to that for public spending. Increasing trade and capital mobility, all else equal, were associated with smaller deficits (at the .1 level of significance), lending some support to the notion that internationalization constrains fiscal expansion. The parameter estimate for left-labor power again was the opposite of that expected by conventional understandings of social democratic corporatism – the greater the power of the left and organized labor, the tighter were fiscal policies – but this coefficient was insignificant. Most importantly, the parameter estimates for the two interaction terms were highly significant and negative. Again, this supports the compensation hypothesis: the greater the level of internationalization and left-labor power, the looser were fiscal policies.

Capital taxation.   The impact of increasing trade and capital mobility was to increase capital taxation. Although this relationship was only significant in the case of trade, these results are nonetheless interesting because they go against most understandings of taxation and competitiveness (which suggest that corporate taxes should decline with internationalization). In contrast with the spending and deficits equations, the parameter estimate for left-labor power was significant and positive – consistent with closed economy views of social democratic corporatism. However, the left-labor power-trade coefficient was negative and significant. This is completely consistent with the efficiency hypothesis: notwithstanding political incentives for the left and organized labor to push for higher capital taxes, there are very powerful constraints against this type of policy in the global economy.

Interest rates.   Trade had no significant impact on interest rates, but greater capital mobility was significantly associated with a lowering of rates. More importantly, the parameter estimate for left-labor power was positive and significant – implying that the financial markets always attached interest rate premia to the power of the left and organized labor. Moreover, the left-labor power-capital mobility coefficient was also positive and significant, suggesting that these interest rate premia increased with capital mobility. Presumably, these results reflect the market's skepticism about the willingness of governments consistently to pursue "prudent" macroeconomic policies where the left and organized labor are powerful.

Conditional effects

The primary objects of analysis in this paper are the interactive effects of left-labor power and internationalization on economic policy. It is impossible to delineate these relationships accurately from the results in Table 2. Specifically, the coefficients for the interaction terms only indicate the combined effects of trade, capital mobility, and left-labor "over and above" their independent effects (as represented by the noninteracted estimates for these variables) . Equation (1) must be rewritten directly to address questions such as "what happened to the relationship between left-labor power and spending as capital mobility increased?" or "did domestic political conditions affect the relationship between trade and deficits?":

$$POL_{it} = a + b_1 POLZ_{it-1} + b_2 CAPMOBILITY_{it} + b_3 TRADE_{it} +$$
$$(b_4 + b_5 CAPMOBILITY_{it} + b_6 TRADE_{it}).LLPOWER_{it} \qquad (2)$$
$$+\sum(b_j COUNTRY_{jit}) + \sum(b_k X_{kit}) + \mu_{it}$$

$$POL_{it} = a + b_1 POLZ_{it-1} + b_4 LLPOWER_{it} +$$
$$(b_2 + b_5 LLPOWER_{it}).CAPMOBILITY_{it} + (b_3 + b_6 LLPOWER_{it}).TRADE_{it} \quad (3)$$
$$+\sum(b_j COUNTRY_{jit}) + \sum(b_k X_{kit}) + \mu_{it}$$

In equation (2), $(b_4 + b_5 CAPMOBILITY_{it} + b_6 TRADE_{it})$ is the conditional parameter estimate for $LLPOWER_{it}$ (that is, the magnitude of the left-labor power coefficient at different levels of capital mobility and trade). Conversely, in equation (3), $(b_2 + b_5 LLPOWER_{it})$ and $(b_3 + b_6 LLPOWER_{it})$ are the conditional coefficients for capital mobility and trade, respectively, at different levels of left-labor power.

Left-labor power. The conditional coefficients for left-labor power are reported in Table 3. For simplicity, these are only presented for four exemplary cases drawn from the data set. The top and bottom rows present parameter estimates for the country–year observations with the most extreme combinations of exposure to trade and capital mobility (weighting the two dimensions equally). The case with the highest combined level of internationalization was Belgium in 1985, where trade constituted 146 percent of GDP and where there were no controls on cross-border capital movements (on IMF definitions). The lowest combined level of internationalization was Finland in 1976, where trade was 53 percent of GDP and all four types of capital control monitored by the IMF were in place.[20] The middle rows show conditional parameter estimates for the median (for the fifteen countries) levels of trade and capital mobility in the first year of the study, 1967 – trade 40 percent, capital controls on two of the IMF's categories[21] – and the last year, 1990 – trade 52 percent, 0 capital con-

Table 3. *The conditional impact of left-labor power on economic policy[a]*

Level of internationalization[b]	Government spending	Budget deficits	Capital taxation[c]	Interest rates[d]
highest	2.96[e]	1.84[e]	−.72[e]	.52[f]
(Belgium 1985)	(.76)	(.46)	(.23)	(.24)
median	.81[e]	.44[e]	.03	.52[f]
(1990)	(.25)	(.15)	(.06)	(.24)
median	−.54[f]	−.35[e]	−.13[f]	.22
(1967)	(.23)	(.11)	(.06)	(.23)
lowest	−1.30[e]	−.76[e]	.03	−.08
(Findland 1976)	(.43)	(.25)	(.06)	(.30)

[a]The conditional coefficients are derived from the parameter estimates in Table 2 for left-labor power, trade, capital mobility, and the interactions between them. The figures in parentheses are conditional standard errors.
[b]The trade and capital mobility scores used in this table are defined in the text.
[c]The coefficient for left-labor power capital mobility was not significant in the capital taxation equation and was excluded from the calculation of conditional coefficients and standard errors.
[d]The coefficient for left-labor power trade was not significant in the interest rate equation and was excluded from the calculation of conditional coefficients and standard errors.
[e]Significant at the .01 level.
[f]Significant at the .05 level.

trols.[22] These cases are representative of the general trend of ever greater internationalization across the OECD in the period under study.

The pattern of conditional coefficients graphically illustrates the impact of increasing trade and capital mobility on the politics of economic policy. At the highest combined level of trade and capital mobility in the data set, increasing left-labor power was significantly associated with higher government spending and larger deficits (consistent with the compensation thesis), but with lower capital taxation and higher interest rates (as anticipated in the efficiency hypothesis). These relationships were similar but somewhat weaker at the median level of internationalization in 1990 (and the capital taxation coefficient was not significant). In the median case in 1967, the conditional left-labor power coefficients were significant in the spending, budget deficits, and capital taxation equations – but in the opposite direction to that for the high internationalization cases. Finally, for the case with the lowest combined trade and capital mobility in the sample, the conditional parameter estimates for government spending and budget deficits were even larger. Thus, at low levels of internationalization, increasing left-labor power was associated with lower government spending and tighter budgetary policies, with higher capital taxation, but had little impact on interest rates.

One can gauge the substantive magnitude of these effects with the following simple counterfactual. What would have been the difference in economic policies – at a predetermined level of internationalization – had left-labor power been different by a given amount? To generate estimates that do not exaggerate the effects by using the tails of the left-labor power and internationalization distributions, let us base the counterfactual results on the case of median internationalization in 1967 and 1990, and consider the policy effects of moving from the twenty-fifth percentile in the left-labor power distribution (3.36, in Australia in 1977) to the seventy-fifth percentile (6.24, Germany in 1979) – a difference of 2.88 standard units.

At the median combined level of trade and capital mobility in 1967, increasing left-labor power by this amount would have cut public spending by 1.6 percent of GDP and the budget deficit by 1.0 percent of GDP, but increased capital taxation by 0.4 percent of GDP. Conversely in the case of the median level of internationalization in 1990, increasing left-labor power from the twenty-fifth to the seventy-fifth percentile would have increased public spending by 2.3 percent of GDP and increased the deficit by 1.3 percent of GDP, but it would also have increased interest rates by 1.5 percent. These counterfactual estimates are far from trivial.

Capital mobility. The conditional coefficients for capital mobility (at different levels of left-labor power) are reported in Table 4. Coefficients were not estimated for the capital taxation equation because neither the capital mobility nor the left-labor power-capital mobility term was significant (see Table 2). Again, only four scenarios are analyzed. The cases of the highest (8.42, Austria in 1970) and lowest (.94, France in 1968) left-labor power scores in the sample are included, as are two intermediate cases – the scores for the seventy-fifth and twenty-fifth percentiles in the distribution.

At the lowest level of left-labor power, increased capital mobility tended to reduce government spending, the deficit, and interest rates (although only the last conditional coefficient was significant at traditional levels). These relationships eroded where the power of the left and organized labor was greater. At the seventy-fifth percentile and above, the effects of increasing capital mobility were the exact opposite of those for the lowest level of left-labor power – higher government spending, larger deficits, and higher interest rates (although the last was not significant).

The substantive magnitude of these effects can be illustrated through a counterfactual analysis similar to that used in the preceding subsection. Here, let us consider the effects of moving – at the twenty-fifth and seventy-fifth percentile of the left-labor power distribution – from the me-

Table 4. *The conditional impact of capital mobility on economic policy*[a]

Left-labor power[b]	Government spending	Budget deficits	Interest rates
highest	3.24[c]	1.64[c]	.19
(Austria 1970)	(.46)	(.32)	(.19)
75th percentile	2.09[c]	.98[c]	−.13
(Germany 1979)	(.28)	(.20)	(.26)
25th percentile	.56[e]	.12	−.57
(Australia 1977)	(.33)	(.28)	(.35)
lowest	−.72	−.61	−.93[d]
(France 1968)	(.56)	(.47)	(.43)

[a]The conditional coefficients are derived from the parameter estimates in Table 2 for left-labor power, trade and capital mobility and the interaction between them. The capital taxation equation was omitted because the interaction term was not significant. The figures in parentheses are conditional standard errors.
[b]The left-labor power scores used in this table are defined in the text.
[c]Significant at the .01 level.
[d]Significant at the .05 level.
[e]Significant at the .1 level.

dian level of capital mobility in 1967 (2 categories of capital controls) to the 1990 median (no controls). At the twenty-fifth percentile, this increase in capital mobility would have resulted in 1.1 percent increase in government spending as a portion of GDP (using the only equation for which the conditional parameter estimate was significant). At the seventy-fifth percentile, however, the elimination of two capital controls would have resulted in an increase in spending of 4.2 percent of GDP and an increase in the budget deficit of 2.0 percent. These findings are supportive of the compensation hypothesis, rather than the efficiency hypothesis.

Trade. The trade coefficients at different levels of left-labor power are reported in Table 5. The structure of the table is the same as that for capital mobility, and the results are quite similar (although the interest rate equation is excluded because it was unaffected by the level of trade). At the lowest level of left-labor power, increasing trade had no significant impact on spending or the budget deficit but was significantly associated with an increase in capital taxation. Conversely, at the highest level of left-labor power, trade was associated with higher spending and bigger deficits (with no impact on capital taxation).

Let us again assess the substantive magnitude of these effects at the twenty-fifth and seventy-fifth percentile of left-labor power, assuming that

Table 5. *The conditional impact of trade on economic policy*[a]

Left-labor power	Government spending	Budget deficits	Capital taxation
highest	.172[b]	.074[b]	−.002
(Austria 1970)	(.019)	(.016)	(.008)
75th percentile	.123[b]	.042[b]	.015[c]
(Germany 1979)	(.012)	(.012)	(.006)
25th percentile	.057[b]	−.002	.038[b]
(Australia 1977)	(.016)	(.017)	(.008)
lowest	.002	−.038	.057[b]
(France 1968)	(.027)	(.026)	(.012)

[a]The conditional coefficients are derived from the parameter estimates in Table 2 for left-labor power, trade and the interaction between them. The interest rate equation was not reported because the interaction term was not significant. The figures in parentheses are conditional standard errors.
[b]Significant at the .01 level.
[c]Significant at the .05 level.
[d]Significant at the .1 level.

trade increased from its median level in 1967 (40 percent of GDP) to that in 1990 (52 percent). At the twenty-fifth percentile, this increase in trade would have led to a 0.7 percent increase in government spending and to a 0.5 percent increase in capital taxation (both as a portion of GDP). At the seventy-fifth percentile, a 12 percentage point increase in trade would have resulted in a spending increase of 2.1 percent of GDP and deterioration in the budget deficit of 0.9 percent of GDP.

Cross-national asymmetries in internationalization

Before summarizing the findings of this paper and its implications for the politics of economic policy in the contemporary advanced industrial countries, one more observation must be made – pertaining to the mix of trade and capital mobility in different countries. While there was a secular trend towards greater trade and capital mobility across the western countries between the mid-1960s and 1990, the combination of trade and financial integration varied systematically between countries on the basis of domestic political conditions (see Figures 6 and 7). Trade has always been higher in countries where the left and organized labor have been more powerful. The economic incentives to trade are greater in smaller economies (in terms of comparative advantage and scale economies), and at the same time small economies have proved fertile ground for the growth of trade

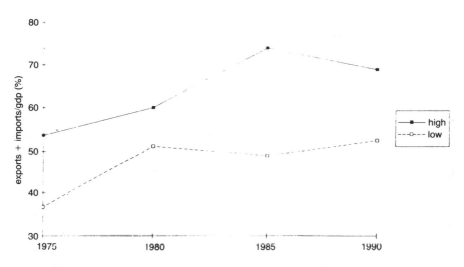

Figure 6. Trade by the power of the left and organized labor.*Source*: See Figure 1. Data are averages for the top seven and bottom eight countries on Left-Labor Power for the years 1967–74, 1975–9, 1980–4 and 1985–90.

unions and left parties (Cameron 1978). At the same time, however, these countries have also always imposed greater restrictions on cross-border capital flows than did countries where the right has been more powerful and trade unions have been weaker.

For present purposes, the most important implications of this asymmetry in trade and capital mobility concern how and when the effects of internationalization have been felt in different countries. Where the left and organized labor have long been powerful – the small economies of northern Europe – competing in global goods and services markets has been a reality for decades. But the effects of capital mobility have been felt much more recently in these countries. Even today, capital controls are still more prevalent in the strong left-labor cases. This suggests that the future political and economic developments in these countries will be more affected by the constraints of financial integration than by trade growth. Finland, for example, still had capital controls on three of the categories monitored by the IMF in 1990. Their subsequent removal to prepare for accession to the European Union had disastrous macroeconomic consequences during the currency crises of fall 1992.

Conversely, capital mobility has been a fact of life in the larger industrial economies for much of the postwar, whereas the significance of trade competition has only grown more recently.[23] It is thus not surprising that trade issues dominate contemporary economic relations between the two largest

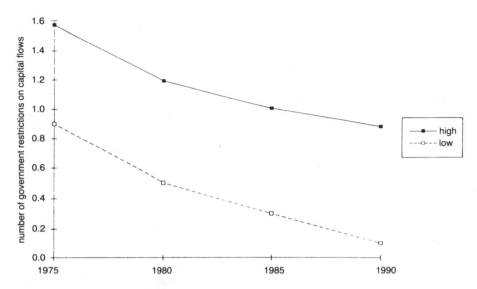

Figure 7. Capital controls by the power of the left and organized labor. *Source*: See Figure 2. Data are averages for the top seven and bottom eight countries on Left-Labor Power for the years 1967–74, 1975–9, 1980–4 and 1985–90.

(but smallest trading, as a percentage of GDP) western nations – Japan and the United States. The debate within these countries on how best to compete can only be expected to grow more heated as their trade exposure increases.

CONCLUSION

It is almost a cliché to claim that economic internationalization has undermined the traditional redistributive agenda of the left. The headline-grabbing events of the 1980s all seemed to concern the triumph of the market over the state – the Thatcher decade, the Reagan–Bush years, the rollback of social democracy in northern Europe, and even the demise of communism in the Soviet bloc. It didn't matter whether one listened to the self-congratulatory proclamations of conservatives or to the pessimistic grumblings of the left. The conclusion was the same: countries can only thrive (and governments can only survive) in the competitive global economy by heeding the prescriptions of neoclassical economics.

This paper demonstrates that the conventional wisdom is too simple and considerably overdrawn. The propensity to deficit-spend is the political economic sine qua non of social democracy. But rather than being constrained by increasing trade and capital mobility, the relationship between left-labor power and fiscal expansions has strengthened with greater internationalization. Without further analysis it is impossible to tell whether this has been the result of increased political incentives to ameliorate market dislocations or because certain types of government spending increased competitiveness (as new growth theorists claim). Either way, this finding stands in stark contrast to the received wisdom.

Nevertheless, internationalization has had adverse effects on the left and its traditional agenda. Increasing trade has cut capital taxation, but this effect was felt quite early in the bastions of social democratic corporatism. More importantly, financial markets have imposed significant interest rate premia on the power of the left and organized labor; and these increased with the removal of barriers to cross-border capital flows (presumably the result of market expectations of even more expansionary fiscal policies in the future). In time, one might anticipate that no government would be able to bear this burden. Given the proliferation of euromarkets and other financial processes that are virtually impossible for individual governments to control, the reimposition of barriers to capital mobility seems most unlikely (Goodman and Paully 1993). The integration of financial markets may yet be the death knell of social democracy. On the other hand, it is also possible that the expectations of new growth theory will be borne out. In turn, this might lead the financial markets to be more accepting of government spending (even if it is financed in the short term by deficits). If this were the case, the constraining effects of capital mobility on social democracy would decrease.

Finally, one can also speculate about the consequences of increased trade for the larger western economies. So long as the left and organized labor remain weak in these countries, the results of this paper suggest that governments will continue to respond to greater exposure to trade in the manner envisaged in neoclassical economics. However, higher trade will also increase political pressures to compensate those segments of society that are adversely affected by market forces. In this environment, the fortunes of the left and the popularity of interventionist economic policies might increase – as was the case in Germany in the 1960s and 1970s. Combined with the intellectual support of new growth theory, an increase in the power of the left in large economies might lead to cross-national convergence in economic policies. This convergence, however, would center on interventionist government.

At this point, it is impossible to assess which of these scenarios will transpire. Nonetheless, this paper has made clear that the conventional wisdom about the political economy of the past decade should be consumed with great caution.

Country	Political power			The structure of trade union movements					Left-labor power (rank)
	Legislature	Cabinet	Left (rank)	Union density	Public sector share	Major confederation share	Number of affiliates	Labor (rank)	
Austria	0.44	0.57	2	33	22	100	16	1	1
Sweden	0.43	1.00	1	45	23	66	29	2	2
Finland	0.31	0.59	3	22	26	69	31	7	3
Norway	0.30	0.06	4	30	29	80	35	4	4
Denmark	0.09	0.01	9	36	22	77	45	3	5
Germany	-0.04	0.52	6	21	29	83	17	5	6
Belgium	0.01	0.25	7	33	27	48	19	6	7
Italy	0.25	0.15	5	11	17	56	24	9	8
The Netherlands	0.18	-0.10	8	18	31	36	16	12	9
UK	0.04	-0.14	10	30	29	84	150	10	10
Australia	-0.10	-0.43	12	27	31	68	55	8	11
Canada	-0.29	0.00	11	18	20	51	85	11	12
Japan	-0.22	+1.00	13	16	18	37	63	13	13
U.S.	-0.43	-0.71	14	15	23	62	122	14	14
France	-0.51	-1.00	15	10	60	66	55	15	15

Appendix, continued
1975–1979

Country	Political power			The structure of trade union movements					Left-labor power (rank)
	Legislature	Cabinet	Left (rank)	Union density	Public sector share	Major confederation share	Number of affiliates	Labor (rank)	
Austria	0.45	1.00	1	34	24	100	16	1	1
Sweden	0.38	0.16	4	59	26	63	25	2	2
Norway	0.31	1.00	2	36	33	77	35	0	3
Finland	0.24	0.51	3	44	24	65	27	4	4
Denmark	0.11	0.56	5	45	22	74	40	3	5
Germany	-0.04	0.75	8	23	28	84	17	5	6
Italy	0.31	0.02	6	18	17	55	24	8	7
UK	0.02	0.67	7	35	30	85	111	10	8
Belgium	-0.10	-0.20	10	38	29	52	19	7	9
The Netherlands	0.19	0.09	9	18	34	39	15	11	10
Australia	-0.33	-0.67	15	31	35	64	45	9	11
Canada	-0.35	-0.17	11	20	24	43	78	13	12
Japan	-0.13	-1.00	12	16	19	36	64	12	13
U.S.	-0.35	-0.50	14	16	24	63	112	14	14
France	-0.25	-0.74	13	11	61	66	45	15	15

Appendix, continued
1980–1984

Country	Political power			The structure of trade union movements					Left-labor power (rank)
	Legislature	Cabinet	Left (rank)	Union density	Public sector share	Major confederation share	Number of affiliates	Labor (rank)	
Austria	0.45	0.80	1	34	26	100	15	1	1
Sweden	0.35	0.52	2	66	29	62	25	3	2
Finland	0.17	0.50	5	51	28	63	29	4	3
Denmark	0.14	−0.06	7	55	25	73	38	2	4
Italy	0.35	0.24	4	18	18	52	24	7	5
Norway	0.11	0.16	6	43	35	64	34	8	6
Germany	−0.03	−0.19	9	23	28	83	17	5	7
Belgium	−0.12	−0.38	11	40	30	57	19	6	8
The Netherlands	0.11	−0.25	8	17	36	60	17	11	9
Australia	−0.05	−0.20	10	30	37	65	42	15	10
France	0.25	0.64	3	10	55	57	42	15	11
UK	−0.19	−1.00	14	34	31	94	109	9	12
Japan	−0.17	−1.00	13	16	20	37	50	12	13
Canada	−0.33	−0.20	12	19	28	38	64	14	14
U.S.	−0.40	−0.80	15	13	25	65	104	13	15

Appendix, continued
1985–1990

Country	Political Power			The structure of trade union movements					Left-labor power (rank)
	Legislature	Cabinet	Left (rank)	Union density	Public sector share	Major confederation share	Number of affiliates	Labor (rank)	
Australia	0.38	0.50	2	33	31	100	15	1	1
Sweden	0.39	1.00	1	70	38	60	24	4	2
Italy	0.37	0.24	4	16	23	53	20	7	3
Finland	0.14	0.21	6	55	34	56	24	5	4
Australia	0.12	1.00	3	30	37	66	38	8	5
Norway	0.16	0.45	5	45	44	61	29	9	6
Belgium	0.03	-0.02	9	39	35	57	18	6	7
Denmark	0.00	-0.75	10	59	35	69	30	2	8
Germany	-0.02	-0;83	11	22	30	83	17	3	9
The Netherlands	0.11	-0.16	8	15	43	59	17	12	10
UK	-0.26	-1.00	13	28	32	82	76	10	11
Japan	-0.24	-1.00	12	15	17	62	81	11	12
France	0.03	0.08	7	7	51	26	38	15	13
U.S.	-0.40	-1.00	14	11	34	80	91	13	14
Canada	-0.52	-1.00	15	21	35	36	58	14	15

Source: See footnotes 20, 22 and 26. The data for major confederation share (public sector shares) in Australia (Belgium) are missing and were coded as the mean for the other 14 countries. The ranks for Left, Labor and Left-Labor Power were based on indexes of standardized scores for their constituent elements.

5

Economic Integration and the Politics of Monetary Policy in the United States

JEFFRY A. FRIEDEN

International economic integration has profound effects on monetary policy. In this chapter, I argue that it has equally important effects on the *politics* of monetary policy. It makes monetary policy more prominent politically, by heightening its impact on relative prices. Because high levels of capital mobility mean that national monetary policy implicates the exchange rate, it gives rise to clear-cut distributional effects that in turn lead to political divisions. At the same time, high levels of world trade make the exchange rate a critical price for much of the population. When the general effects of economic openness are compounded by international price shocks, there are strong incentives for affected groups to seek redress in the monetary arena. Economic internationalization leads to an increased politicization of monetary policy and a change in the sorts of socioeconomic and political divisions it implies.

The United States has in fact experienced the impact of economic integration on monetary politics. Both the country's integration into the world economy, and its monetary politics, have varied substantially over time. Indeed, monetary policy was once at the center of American politics. From the 1860s until the 1930s, "The Money Question" was, along with the tariff, the great constant of political debates in the United States. It brought forth messianic populist fervor, terrified defenses, two of the more successful third parties in the nation's history, and impassioned speechifying from the floor of Congress to the wheat fields of Kansas. However, after the mid-1930s, monetary policy seemed to drop off the political agenda, although it has resurfaced to some extent in recent years.

This chapter contends that changes in the level of American interna-

The author acknowledges support from the Center for International Business Education and Research and the Center for American Politics and Public Policy at UCLA; and useful comments and suggestions from Barry Eichengreen, Peter Kenen, Robert Keohane, David A. Lake, Nathaniel Leff, Lisa Martin, Kathleen McNamara, Helen Milner, Ronald Rogowski, Howard Rosenthal, Kenneth Shepsle, and Peter Temin.

tional economic integration help explain why monetary policy was high politics for over a half a century, then nearly disappeared from the political agenda. It asserts that a major cause of the political prominence of monetary policy before 1930 was the extensive ties of the United States with the rest of the world economy. Between about 1930 and 1970, the United States economy was quite closed, and monetary policy faded into popular oblivion and scholarly tedium. Since 1970, international financial and commercial integration have increased dramatically. This has made monetary policy more politically important and contentious, and is likely to change the political divisions and institutional settings in which monetary policy is made.

This analysis of the changing pattern of American monetary politics tends to support the proposition that international economic conditions have powerful effects on domestic politics. Changes both in the overall degree of integration of the United States into the world economy, and in specific relative prices, led to the mobilization of interest groups in ways that were both affected by and had an impact on the institutional structure of American monetary policy-making. International economic trends altered the environment within which monetary policy was made; they also had a differential distributional impact on socioeconomic groups, which led to substantial political conflict.

It is far beyond the scope of the present study to carry out a rounded evaluation of the sources of American monetary policy from the 1860s through the 1980s. Its purpose is to present a perspective on monetary politics that builds on the approach developed in this volume, and to apply it in a preliminary way to a vast swath of American monetary history. While systematic empirical evaluations of the approach are certainly possible, I believe that the historical evidence presented here helps at least establish the plausibility of my argument.[1]

This chapter, then, evaluates the impact of internationalization on the politics of American monetary policy over a 120-year period. In Section I, I summarize the expected effects of international financial and commercial integration on the politics of monetary policy. Section II surveys the American experience with monetary policy in an open economy between the Civil War and 1930, and in a relatively closed economy from the 1930s until the 1960s. In Section III, I look at how growing economic internationalization has affected American monetary politics since 1970. Section IV discusses implications of the study, and is followed by a conclusion.

I. MONETARY POLITICS IN CLOSED AND OPEN ECONOMIES

International goods and capital market integration have important effects on the economics and politics of monetary policy. These effects operate by way of two channels, on the effectiveness of particular policy instruments, and on the preferences and preference intensities of economic agents. The clearest way to see this is to look at two polar cases, of very low and very high levels of economic integration.[2]

In a closed economy, monetary policy has its primary impact by way of the nominal price level. A monetary stimulus raises prices, thus reducing real interest rates and encouraging spending.[3] By this channel, monetary policy may be able to affect such broad aggregates as growth and unemployment. As monetary policy in such circumstances lowers the real value of nominal contracts, political divisions are expected between borrowers and savers. A few specific industries favor "loose money," especially housing construction and some consumer durables, which depend heavily on the real cost of consumer credit; the financial sector and creditors usually want tight money. As closed-economy monetary policy affects the nominal price level but not relative prices among goods and services, it has broad but diffuse economic and political effects.

For these reasons, it is reasonable to expect monetary politics in a closed economy to involve relatively broad-gauged political divisions. A few narrow groups may have intense concerns – the housing construction industry, the financial sector – but it is the broad mass of producers and consumers that is affected by general macroeconomic trends.

Conditions are different in an economy open on current and capital account. Financial integration constrains domestic interest rates to world levels, while commercial integration binds the price of tradable goods.[4] In such an economy, monetary policy has a direct effect on the exchange rate: monetary expansion drives the currency down, makes locally produced goods cheaper relative to imports, and lowers their international (foreign-currency) price. Of course, monetary policy can also affect the nominal price level and interest rates, which adjust in line with real or expected movements in the exchange rate. But for our purposes the important point is that monetary policy in an open economy is intimately connected to the value of the national currency.

While closed-economy monetary policy has few effects on relative prices other than those of nominally denominated contracts, open-economy monetary policy directly affects a wide range of relative prices, especially between tradable and nontradable goods and services. Industries concerned about import and export competition are typically more clearly defined groups than net nominal debtors and creditors, and the impact of a depreciation or appreciation on them is typically more direct than the changes in the overall nominal price level for debtors or creditors. This leads me to anticipate that monetary policy will be more politically salient when it affects the exchange rate, more contentious in an open than in a closed economy.

The first implication of this analysis is that economic integration increases the sociopolitical prominence of monetary policy. It does so by giving monetary policy a more direct impact on relative prices of relevance to well-defined groups of producers and consumers than in a closed economy. In an open economy, the politics of monetary policy tend to be organized around the concentrated distributional effects of exchange rate movements, and thus are likely to resemble interest group politics involving such things as tariffs (for which, after all, a real depreciation can be a substitute).

The second implication is that economic internationalization alters political divisions over monetary policy. In a closed economy, the principal conflict is between those on either side of nominal debt contracts, along with a few industries strongly affected by the ease of borrowing. In an open economy, monetary policy's inevitable effect on the exchange rate brings into play quite different socioeconomic groups.[5]

Groups disagree over the desired currency value. Tradables producers favor depreciation of the currency to raise the (domestic-currency) price of goods they export, and of foreign goods imported in competition with them. Nontradables producers favor an appreciated currency to raise the price of their products relative to tradable goods. This is a different sort of division than that expected in a closed economy: the tradables–nontradables (open economy) division is quite distinct from the debtor–creditor (closed economy) division.

In addition, an open economy faces a choice about whether to fix or float the currency, which is typically much less significant in a closed economy. On this dimension, those heavily committed to cross-border trade and payments stand to lose from currency volatility, and are more inclined toward a fixed rate. The more attractive international economic opportunities are, the greater the incentive for those who can take advantage of them to press for a stable currency. In this context, the higher the level of international trade and payments, the more economic actors with existing or potential global activities want exchange rate stability.

However, those who operate on domestic markets alone have little interest in increasing the predictability of currency values. This includes most producers of nontraded goods and services, as well as tradables producers who are domestic in orientation, such as import-competers. Indeed, for them the surrender of monetary autonomy required by fixing the exchange rate is an unmitigated sacrifice – a price whose volatility they do not care about is stabilized at the cost of the government giving up the ability to affect domestic monetary conditions.

Economic integration, then, alters political divisions over monetary policy. Closed-economy monetary policy largely involves broad macroeconomic aggregates; its politics typically divide nominal debtors and creditors.

Open-economy monetary policy largely involves the relationship between tradables and nontradables prices, and the predictability of the exchange rate; its politics divide tradables and nontradables producers, as well as domestically and internationally oriented groups.

Commercial openness has analogous effects on the monetary policy views of economic actors. It makes the fortunes of larger segments of society dependent upon international relative price movements. This leads to stronger demands to use currency policies to counteract adverse international price trends.

Tradables producers are especially sensitive to the exchange rate; as more goods become tradable, more producers are more concerned about currency values.[6] Even nontradables producers care more about exchange rates as trade expands, for the import component of their inputs rises. Increased trade intensifies the interest of producers in moving exchange rates in their favor: in a closed economy the exchange rate is a weak tool to affect relative prices, but in an open economy it can be powerful.[7]

It is necessary to qualify virtually all of these observations.[8] For current purposes my point is simply that economic internationalization has two general effects on the domestic politics of monetary policy. First, monetary policy shifts from having its principal impact by way of the nominal price level to primarily affecting the relative prices of tradables and nontradables, thereby implicating more concentrated and defined economic interests. This makes monetary politics more contentious in an open than in a closed economy.

Second, the distributional effects of monetary policy change in line with the greater importance of the exchange rate, which in turn affects the political lineup. Conflict ensues between supporters of a higher and lower exchange rate, especially tradables and nontradables producers. Those with an interest in a stable currency square off against those primarily oriented to the domestic market. Political divisions develop over the level of the exchange rate and the degree of exchange-rate stability.

A third implication can be drawn from this analysis. When monetary policy is associated with currency values, it has effects similar to trade policy. Depreciation is functionally equivalent to an increase in trade protection or export subsidies, while appreciation has effects similar to a trade barrier reduction or export tax. However, a simple rise or fall of the nominal price level has no systematic impact on the relative price of traded goods, and therefore is unrelated to trade policy. In an open economy, trade protection can be used to mitigate pressure for monetary expansion (depreciation) and vice versa, but this is not true in a closed economy.

In an open economy, then, monetary and trade policies are potential substitutes, but this is not the case in a closed economy. This fact may have important ramifications. Producers are more likely to be able to organize for product-specific trade protection than for an economy-wide devaluation. However, it may be easier to organize a broad prodevaluation coalition than a protectionist logroll. Without exploring more detailed effects of this, I observe simply that in an open economy there is likely to be a strong connection between trade and monetary policies, while no such connection should be present in a closed economy.

A somewhat more speculative set of expectations has to do with how, in the American political setting, monetary politics find their institutional expression.[9] It is widely believed that members of Congress, with geographically defined electoral concerns, are especially susceptible to specific groups with relatively large numbers – such as labor unions or farmers. The executive with its national constituency, on the other hand, is especially focused on such issues of aggregate economic concern as growth and inflation. The reason commonly adduced is that members of Congress do not fully internalize the political benefits (or costs) of national policy, and have less incentive to worry about it than the President, who is held responsible (or credited) for national effects (Lohmann and O'Halloran 1994; for other treatments see, for example, McCubbins, Noll, and Weingast 1987; Weingast and Moran 1983).[10]

In a closed American economy, the diffuse concern of the broad electorate for national economic conditions gives the Executive branch the strongest incentive to attend to monetary policy. This should lead the President, with an eye to national electoral considerations, to play a more important part in formulating closed-economy monetary policy than Congress. Groups concerned with monetary policy, such as the housing and financial sectors, may focus on such agencies as the Federal Reserve System with particular responsibilities for money and finance. Monetary politics should involve primarily the Executive and the Fed in a closed economy, and we might best analyze it in terms of such aggregate political considerations as electoral cycles.

On the other hand, open-economy monetary policy draws well-defined producers into the political fray. This should lead Congress to want a major role in monetary policy, as large groups – manufacturing industries, farmers – are mobilized on the issue. Members of Congress from manufacturing or farming districts realize political benefits (or pay costs) for policies that affect relative prices crucial to their constituents. Economic openness should lead to more Congressional involvement in monetary policy.

These considerations can be brought to bear on the historical and contemporary American record. No detailed or rigorous evaluation of the argument is possible in this limited space, but I do find support for the plausibility of the approach. In what follows, I present two sets of such evidence. The first is a survey of the ebb and flow of American monetary politics from the 1860s through the 1960s, which covers periods of economic openness and closure. The second is a more detailed assessment of develop-

ments since 1970, undertaken in part because of the naturally greater interest in the implications of my argument for contemporary trends. In this
second discussion, I evaluate the degree to which gradually increasing economic openness has been associated with the effects I anticipate.

The United States in the last century has in fact gone through three
phases. From the Civil War through the early 1930s it was a relatively open
economy. Between the 1930s and the 1960s it was a relatively closed economy, while since about 1970 the U.S. economy has become increasingly
open to goods and capital movements. I expect these shifts to be accompanied by changes in the political prominence, political cleavages, and Congressional activity associated with the making of monetary policy in the
United States.

II. MONETARY POLITICS IN OPEN AND CLOSED ECONOMIES, 1870–1970

From the 1860s until World War One, and again in the 1920s, international
trade and investment were at extremely high levels. Between the 1930s and
the late 1960s, however, the U.S. economy was relatively closed on current
and capital account. The reflection of this in the United States was simple:
between the Civil War and the 1930s, the U.S. economy was closely integrated with the rest of the world, while in the later period the United States
was quite closed to international trade and payments.[11]

Table 1 presents some data meant only to be indicative, for measuring
capital and goods market integration is difficult.[12] However, trade flows
and investment stocks as shares of Gross National Product (GNP) are
reasonable measures for a preliminary assessment. The former show a
dramatic drop from the 11 to 15 percent range between 1869 and 1929, to
six or seven percent through the 1960s. The latter drop from the 24 to 28
percent range in the first period to 13 to 15 percent in the second. In both
instances, trade flows and cross-border investment stocks from the 1930s to
the 1960s are about half of what they were from the Civil War to the
Depression. It might also be noted that both trade and investment figures
have risen continually from 1970 to the present, to well above pre-1930
levels. Of course, aggregate figures mask very important details. This is
especially true as regards the concentration of American exports in primary
products in the early period: in the 1880s a fifth of the country's farm
output was exported, and in 1879 exports were 30 percent of American
wheat and 60 percent of cotton production.

The analytical discussion above has four implications for the differences
between monetary politics in these two periods, one with a generally open
world and U.S. economy, one in which both were far more closed. First, in
an open economy monetary policy should be closely related to the ex-

Table 1. *Indicators of the openness of the U.S. economy, 1869–1992*

A. Merchandise trade as a share of Gross National Product[a]

Period	Total trade, annual average Billion dollars	GNP, annual average Billion dollars	Trade/GNP in percent
1869–78	$1.1	$7.4	15.3%
1879–88	1.5	11.2	13.6%
1889–1900	1.9	14.4	13.1%
1901–13	3.3	29.5	11.1%
1920–9	10.7	88.6	12.0%
1930–9	5.0	76.5	6.5%
1946–59	23.9	345.1	6.9%
1960–9	48.8	683.0	7.1%
1970–9	205.2	1632.9	12.6%
1980–92	664.8	4355.6	15.3%

B. Cross-border investment stock as a share of Gross National Product[b]

Year	(A) Foreign private assets in US, Billion dollars	(B) US assets abroad, Billion dollars	(C) GNP, Billion dollars	(D) (A+B)/C, percent
1869	$1.5	$0.1	$6.6	24.2%
1897	3.4	0.7	14.6	28.1%
1914[c]	7.2	3.5	38.6	27.7%
1930	8.4	17.2	90.4	28.3%
1950	19.5	19.0	284.8	13.5%
1960	28.9	49.3	506.5	15.4%
1970	80.7	118.8	992.7	20.1%
1980	309.4	516.6	2633.1	31.4%
1992[d]	1380.7	1105.4	6045.8	41.1%

[a] = Total trade is equal to merchandise exports plus merchandise imports.
[b] = Includes only private assets, both short- and long-term.
[c] = Cross-border assets figures for 1914 are as of June 30, before the outbreak of World War One.
[d] = Based on the valuation of foreign direct investment at current cost. Valuation at market value would increase U.S. assets abroad by $110.0 billion and foreign assets in the United States by $200.1 billion, for a total of 5.1 percent of GNP. Excludes cross-border assets and liabilities of US banks not included elsewhere, which are largely intra-firm transfers that tend to cancel each other out. These are $666.9 billion and $700.7, respectively, for a total of 22.6 percent of GNP.
Sources: Historical Statistics of the United States, Colonial Times to 1970 (Washington: Government Printing Office, 1974): 224, 565, and 864–5. *Economic Report of the President*, various issues.

change rate, implicate clearly defined interests, and achieve political prominence. In a closed economy, on the other hand, monetary policy should be of interest primarily to broad macroeconomic aggregates, and clear distributional divisions should be uncommon.

Second, when world trade and investment are very large and the economy open, political divisions should be very different than in the closed-economy period. In the open economy I expect tradables producers to be especially desirous of a weak (depreciated) currency, nontradables producers of a strong (appreciated) currency; internationally oriented economic actors should be especially concerned to ensure currency stability, domestically oriented actors indifferent or opposed. In the closed economy, to the extent that political differences are clear they should be between net debtors and net creditors.

Third, there should be a strong connection between monetary and trade politics in an open economy, but not in a closed economy. Fourth, in an open U.S. economy the making of monetary policy should be of great concern to Congress, as it implicates the interests of well-defined groups of electoral importance. Closed-economy monetary policy should evince much less congressional interest. Unfortunately, simple measures to assess these contentions are not readily available. In what follows, I briefly present the historical record to indicate that the evidence does seem to bear out these expectations. I should note that this historical narrative contains little that is particularly novel or controversial; what is new is my attempt to understand it in a broader analytical context.

Monetary politics between 1865 and the early 1930s was always salient, but erupted with special vehemence in three periods: Greenback populism (1865–79), silver populism (1888–96), and price stability (1920–35).[13] The first episode stemmed from the fact that the dollar was taken off gold in 1862 amidst wartime inflation (the standard history is Unger 1964). After the Civil War "hard money" advocates wanted to go back to gold at the prewar parity, which implied a substantial real appreciation. Their principal base was in the international financial and commercial communities. Wall Street was heavily oriented toward marketing American securities in Europe, and this business depended on the reliability of the dollar. American international bankers and traders believed, probably correctly, that their international business would suffer unless the United States was on gold. The attempt to get back onto gold did indeed cause a major real appreciation: as indicated in Table 2, tradables prices dropped much more rapidly than nontradables prices.

Supporters of "soft money" wanted to stay on the depreciated paper currency (greenbacks) introduced during the war. The strongest original proponents of greenbacks were iron and steel manufacturers, who regarded a depreciated dollar as a complement to the tariffs they desired.

Table 2. *Relative price indices, 1869–1894 (1869=100, 1879=100)*

Product	1869	1879 / 1879	1894
Traded goods			
Agriculture	100	68 / 100	81
Manufacturing	100	66 / 100	66
Mining	100	56 / 100	75
Nontraded goods and services			
Construction	100	75 / 100	116

Sources: Calculated from Robert Gallman, "Commodity Output, 1839–1899." In *Trends in the American Economy in the Nineteenth Century*, Studies in Income and Wealth vol. 24 (Princeton: Princeton University Press, 1960): 13–43. Gallman's Variant *A* is used for construction.

Along with them were the railroad industry and associated nontradables producers, who had come to value the reflationary policies a floating currency allowed.

After 1873 international price movements brought two more important groups into the Greenback camp. In that year, prices of both silver and many agricultural products began to drop rapidly. Silver prices were driven down as European countries went onto a monometallic gold standard and sold off their silver stocks, and as rich new silver deposits were discovered. Grain prices declined largely as falling transport prices made possible the opening of the Great Plains, the pampas, and other areas.

Farmers swung over to the movement, recognizing that a depreciated currency meant higher dollar prices for their crops. Silver miners similarly joined as silver prices plummeted. The silver connection is complicated. Over the course of the 1870s, the Greenback movement modified its position to favor the free coinage of silver at a 16:1 ratio against gold. This would have kept the country off gold and on a depreciated silver standard. The economic implications were similar to those of a depreciated paper currency, except for the direct subsidy to silver producers (the government would have been obligated to purchase silver at well above the market rate). The tactical result of the turn from Greenbacks to silver was to ensure the support of silver miners, who had great influence in the sparsely populated Rocky Mountain West and thereby controlled many Senate seats.

Congress was favorable to Greenback and silver ideas, and the return to gold was only effected by President Ulysses Grant manipulating a lame-duck Congress in January 1875. The Resumption Act so passed was repealed by Congress repeatedly after that, but the two-thirds majority to override the presidential veto was not forthcoming. The country returned to gold on January 1, 1879.

Antigold sentiment grew again as world farm prices headed down in the late 1880s, and accelerated with the agricultural depression that began in 1888 (see Table 2). Farmers were well aware that reflation and devaluation under the silverite banner would raise agricultural prices. The silver miners, for obvious reasons, continued to support silver monetization. The Populists thus called for a paper money-silver standard, with a depreciated dollar fluctuating against gold (Hicks 1931 remains an excellent general survey).

Northeastern commercial and financial interests remained at the core of the hard-money camp. The bankers' position had, if anything, hardened. Not only had international trade and investment grown dramatically since the 1870s, Wall Street now hoped to become a leading international financial center, for which ironclad commitment to gold was a prerequisite. Manufacturers were less committed to soft money than they had been in the 1870s, for three reasons. First, declining prices of manufactured products were more than compensated by rapid productivity increases, so that few manufacturers felt substantially disadvantaged by the real appreciation. Second, by the 1890s some of American industry had become internationally oriented: manufactured exports had expanded and foreign direct investment was increasing (Lake 1988: 91–118 provides a survey of American trade policy in this period). Third and probably most important, import-competing manufacturers had been able to secure high tariffs. Trade protection accomplished much of what silver would have, and had (unlike silver) been obtained.

After nearly a decade of agitation, the issue came to a head in the 1896 presidential election, which was fought largely over the gold standard. Democrats and Populists jointly fielded William Jennings Bryan, who ran against the "cross of gold" upon which, Bryan thundered, the country was being crucified. The Republicans, in response, cobbled together a hard money-high tariff coalition. Presidential candidate William McKinley had impeccable protectionist credentials, having designed the tariff of 1890; despite long-standing support for silver, he switched to gold in 1896. The McKinley coalition of hard-money international trading and financial interests and high-tariff manufacturers narrowly defeated Bryan's farmer–miner coalition.

The third episode stretched from soon after the end of World War One until the middle 1930s.[14] Although the war had interrupted international trade and finance, these revived very rapidly after 1922. However, farm prices fell dramatically right after the war and remained depressed; between 1919 and 1928 they declined nearly twice as much as building materials, a typical nontradable (see Table 3). Internationally oriented firms re-

Table 3. *Representative relative price indices, 1919–1933 (1919=100, 1928=100)*

Product category	1919	1928 / 1928	1933
Traded goods			
Farm products	100	67 / 100	51
Metal products	100	75 / 100	83
Nontraded goods and services			
Building materials	100	82 / 100	82

Source: Calculated from George Warren and Frank Pearson, *Gold and Prices* (New York: John Wiley and Sons, 1935): 30–2.

mained adamant about the importance of currency stability, while farmers were concerned to engineer a devaluation. Farmers and many manufacturers indeed pressed for "price stability," government policy to reverse postwar price trends. They blamed much of the relative decline of tradables prices on the new Federal Reserve's commitment to gold. As before, support for gold came from international financial, commercial, and industrial interests, the core of the "internationalist" foreign policy bloc for whom the global role of the dollar was important. Once again, many manufacturers were indifferent, as they were largely shielded from import competition by high tariffs.

These debates involved both the content of monetary policy and the structure of the Federal Reserve. Hard-money supporters wanted to leave monetary policy in the hands of the New York Fed. Soft-money advocates wanted policy set by the Board in Washington, and wanted the Board to be controlled by Congress. Dozens of bills were introduced to force more reflationary monetary policy, devaluation, and Congressional control of the Fed. All of the bills were blocked by the Executive and the Senate, which was dominated by financial conservative Carter Glass of the Senate Banking and Commerce Committee.

Conflict over monetary policy increased during the Depression.[15] The hardest-hit victims of price trends in the early Depression were producers of traded goods and especially farmers (see Table 3). Between 1929 and 1933, as GNP fell 46 percent in nominal terms, output of durable goods fell 67 percent and that of farm products 53 percent; services output fell 28 percent. Meanwhile, the Fed was torn between domestic and international demands. Defense of the dollar exacerbated the domestic downturn, and provoked domestic protests.[16]

Congress made repeated attempts to force reflation and devaluation, but the Republican White House and Senate blocked these attempts

(Batchelder and Glasner 1992; Crawford 1940: 14ff.) Crawford and Glasner 1992). As the Depression dragged on and the world economy spiralled downward, sympathy for devaluation grew, especially after the British went off gold in 1931. Even many paragons of gold-standard orthodoxy came to regard easier money as temporarily necessary.[17] In the 1932 elections, in addition, the Democrats took control of the Senate and the presidency. In April 1933 the Roosevelt administration took the dollar off gold and, from October 1933 to January 1934, reduced the gold value of the dollar, depreciating it 44 percent from its March 1933 level against the pound.[18]

For over thirty years after the mid-1930s, the world economy was relatively weakly integrated, and the United States was largely closed to world trade and payments. Monetary politics in this period was quite subdued, especially relative to the roaring debates of the decades before 1935. The exchange rate was rarely called into question, and there was little political conflict over monetary issues. There is some evidence for the impact of broad national (especially presidential) electoral considerations on monetary policy. Although this is a hotly debated topic, many analysts believe that such factors as the approach of a national election affected monetary policy (examples include Alesina and Sachs 1988, Beck 1991, and Grier 1987).

While objective measures of the phenomenon are hard to imagine, few observers would question the assertion that monetary policy from the 1930s through the late 1960s was far less politically pronounced than it had been in the previous seventy years. Nor was there any clear connection between national trade policy and monetary policy in this period.

In addition to this reduction in the political prominence of monetary policy, there were important developments in the locus of monetary decision making. After 1930 monetary and exchange rate policies increasingly shifted away from Congress and toward the Federal Reserve and the Treasury, respectively.

This pattern of relative Congressional passivity began during the New Deal (Crawford 1940, Green 1981). The Banking Acts of 1933 and 1935 reorganized the Federal Reserve to increase the authority of the Board in Washington and expand the influence of the Executive on the Board. The Gold Reserve Act of 1934 vested control of the exchange rate in the Secretary of the Treasury.[19] This reassignment and division of monetary policy was deepened with the 1951 Treasury Accord, which gave the Federal Reserve formal authority to engage in monetary policy without regard for the Treasury's borrowing costs (Eichengreen 1985:66–81; for background, Kettl and Garber 1991). And in 1961, at the time of the creation of bilateral "swap" arrangements among major economic powers, the Treasury and the Fed agreed that the Fed would operate in currency markets with its own funds. This removed currency policy even further from the legislative arena.[20]

From the 1930s until the early 1970s, American monetary and exchange rate policy evolved in relative isolation from Congressional scrutiny. Exactly how and why this came to pass and endure are important questions which exceed the scope of this paper. Nor should the fact of delegation be taken to imply necessarily that Congress does not influence policy (McCubbins, Noll, and Weingast 1987). However, for whatever reasons and in whatever ways, Congressional activism on monetary policy declined substantially after 1930.[21]

This overview tends to bear out my expectations. When international economic activity was extremely important to the United States and the U.S. economy was quite open, monetary policy was closely related to exchange rate issues (the gold standard), pitted tradables against nontradables producers and internationally against domestically oriented sectors, was a focus of congressional attention, and was linked to trade policy. In the relatively closed American economy between the 1930s and the late 1960s, the politics of monetary policy in the United States looked very different indeed. There was no connection drawn between macroeconomic conditions and the exchange rate – no assault on the gold barricades. There was little attention to the issue by major interest groups – no return to the crackling politics of the 1890s or the 1920s. Congress paid little mind to the monetary arena, and trade and monetary policy evolved on separate tracks. I believe that the small scale of international economic activity, and the concomitant relative closure of the U.S. economy, go a long way toward explaining this trend.

If my argument is correct, changes in the world economy and America's position in it after the late 1960s should have altered the politics of monetary policy. It is to an evaluation of this expectation that I now turn.

III. MONETARY POLITICS IN AN INCREASINGLY OPEN ECONOMY, 1969 TO THE PRESENT

World trade and payments have grown at an extraordinary pace since the 1960s, and with them American integration into the world economy. The figures in Table 1 indicate that both trade and investment flows have grown at an extremely rapid rate since 1970; these measures now indicate an American economy at least as open as that of the late nineteenth century.

My argument implies that these changes should be leading to patterns of monetary politics similar to those observed before 1935. More Americans are interested in international economic activities, thus concerned about currency stability; and more Americans are exposed to adverse international price trends, thus prone to demand devaluation. I expect an increasing link between monetary policy and the exchange rate; greater interest group activity on the topic; more congressional interest in the issue; and ties between monetary and trade policy. In this section, I argue that there are many indications of a trend in this direction. The fact that economic internationalization has been growing gradually since the late 1960s means that I expect at most incremental change, and again it is hard to provide systematic evidence to this effect. However, I believe that such a trend is observable. Its operation can be seen, to differing degrees and in different ways, in the 1969–73 period during which the dollar went off gold, the late 1970s dollar depreciation, and the early and mid-1980s dollar appreciation. Without claiming that the following survey proves my point, I submit that it suggests that such changes in the politics of monetary policy are under way.

Devaluation and the end of Bretton Woods, 1969–1973

Over the course of the late 1960s, the dollar appreciated in real terms against the currencies of its principal trading partners.[22] This had its biggest impact on American import-competers: between 1967 and 1970 nontradables prices increased more than twice as rapidly as tradables prices, putting substantial price pressure on tradables producers (see Table 4).[23] Between 1967 and 1971 merchandise exports rose 24 percent in real terms, while merchandise imports rose 47 percent and durable goods imports 55 percent. The automotive trade balance, strongly positive throughout the postwar era, turned negative in 1968 and by 1971 it was $2.9 billion in deficit; total merchandise trade went into deficit in 1971 (*Economic Report of the President*, various issues).

Many American industries were concerned about the price pressure they faced as imports surged. Some argued that monetary policy was too tight and that the currencies of America's trading partners (especially Germany and Japan) were undervalued. However, most private-sector attention focused on trade policy. Manufacturers in such affected sectors as textiles, footwear, and steel, clamored for protection from imports. The AFL–CIO switched from general support for trade liberalization to pressure for trade protection, and protectionist political activity reached its highest point since World War Two.

The country's internationally oriented banks and corporations generally supported stable exchange rates, but there were two confounding realities. First, defending the dollar almost certainly meant maintaining capital controls, which international firms opposed.[24] Second, the real appreciation was exacerbating protectionist sentiment, which was worrisome to firms with important overseas activities. Global firms had strong reasons to counter growing protectionist pressures, and indeed more than sixty leading American corporations formed the Emergency Committee for American Trade (ECAT) to lobby against trade protection.[25]

As the dollar came under increasing attack, many free traders began to

Table 4. *Representative relative price indices, 1967–1973 (1967=100, 1970=100)*

Product category	1967	1970 / 1970	1973
Traded goods			
Industrial commodities	100	110 / 100	115
Finished goods	100	110 / 100	116
Motor vehicles	100	109 / 100	109
Farm products	100	111 / 100	143
Nontraded goods and services			
Shelter	100	124 / 100	114
All services	100	122 / 100	114
Public transportation	100	129 / 100	112
Medical care services	100	124 / 100	116

Source: Economic Report of the President, various issues. Constructed from producers' and consumers' price indices for the goods and services in question.

see a dollar devaluation as the lesser of two evils: better a depreciated dollar than either trade protection or capital controls, or both. As Peter Peterson, a Wall Street fixture who served as Commerce Secretary during the first Nixon administration, put it a couple of years after the events, "It was my view then that had we not taken that very vigorous action on the dollar, it was the sure road to protectionism" (Peterson 1973: 40).

The electoral cycle also exerted an influence. President Richard Nixon had, in his view, lost the 1960 presidential election due to tight monetary policy, and wanted to avoid a repeat of this experience. In the troubled conditions of 1970 and 1971, he was concerned to ensure recovery before the 1972 presidential election. Nixon may have come to regard the fixed-rate system (and the value of the dollar within it) as an impediment to his electoral aspirations. The commitment to gold appeared to restrict economic policy autonomy in the runup to an important election (Gowa 1983; Woolley 1984: 154–80; 1995).

As the dollar appreciated in real terms, there was some legislative pressure for easier money and for action on the exchange rate. In June 1971, Henry Reuss of the Congressional Subcommittee on International Exchange and Payments proposed legislation to float the dollar, and on August 6 a Subcommittee report called for devaluation – which may have helped push the Administration toward the eventual August 15 devaluation.

Although Congress appeared to want easier money and devaluation, it was certainly not as active in monetary politics in the early 1970s as it had been before 1935. Its most important role in foreign economic policy was in threatening protectionist legislation. In 1970 the protectionist "Mills Bill" was voted out of the House Ways and Means Committee, but did not pass the Senate. In 1971 Congressional action centered on the Foreign Trade and Investment Act, better known as the Burke–Hartke bill. This represented the most serious challenge to liberal American trade policy since the Depression. Although Burke–Hartke failed of passage, the battle over it revealed the depth and breadth of protectionist sentiment.

The early 1970s saw a general increase in Congressional monetary activism. After becoming chair of the House Banking Committee in 1975, Henry Reuss led attempts to reduce Fed independence. In March 1975 Congress passed House Concurrent Resolution 133 demanding more Fed reporting to Congress; in November 1977 the Federal Reserve Act was amended along these lines. This reflected the highest level of Congressional involvement in monetary policy since the mid-1930s.[26]

Eventually the Nixon adminstration devalued the dollar, defused most protectionist pressure, and removed capital controls. Over the course of 1970, the Administration took an increasingly aggressive stand against import competition, especially from the Japanese and the Germans. On August 15, 1971, President Nixon took the dollar off gold, as part of a package that included domestic wage and price controls and a ten percent surcharge on imports. By December 1971, the principal monetary powers had negotiated a revision of exchange rates that included an 8 percent dollar devaluation. In February 1973 Nixon devalued the dollar a further ten percent, as the Bretton Woods system collapsed definitively. As Table 4 shows, the dollar devaluations reversed adverse relative price trends for tradables producers: tradables prices rose at roughly the same pace as nontradables from 1970 to 1973.

The pattern revealed here is consonant with conditions midway between the polar open- and closed-economy circumstances central to my argument. On the one hand, many of the debates over monetary policy were tied to the value and fixing of the dollar, and much of the interest-group lineup was as expected. On the other hand, international monetary policy was largely subordinate to other issues. Import competing manufacturers focused more on trade policy than on the dollar; internationalist groups emphasized opposing protection and getting capital controls removed. While Congress was more active on monetary policy than it had been for over thirty years, it devoted most of its energy to trade policy. And broad electoral considerations were important to the policy outcomes. All in all, this case sits somewhere between the general disregard of exchange rates between 1935 and 1970, on the one hand, and the strong and explicit attention paid to exchange rates before 1935, on the other. This is perhaps not surprising, as the level of economic integration was substantially lower than it had been in earlier periods – or was to become.

Dollar depreciation and defense, 1977–1979

Jimmy Carter became president at a time of increasing vulnerability of American industry to imports. Given the influence of the labor movement in the Democratic Party of the 1970s, and organized labor's concentration in import-competing industries, it is not surprising that the Carter Administration oversaw a depreciation of the dollar. In this episode explicit links were drawn between domestic monetary conditions and the value of the dollar. Inasmuch as the dollar depreciation satisfied those groups most heavily represented in Congress, especially tradables producers, there was little need for Congressional activity on the topic. What political pressure was brought to bear on monetary policy largely came from internationally-oriented businesses wary of the administration's willingness to let the dollar drop on the foreign exchanges.

Almost immediately after taking office, the Carter Administration undertook to ease monetary policy. Policy was motivated by two interconnected goals: first, to stimulate the German, Japanese, and American economies to expand simultaneously (the "locomotive" approach), and second, to encourage a revaluation of the mark and the yen relative to the dollar. On the first front, the Administration pushed with limited success for coordinated reflation in the "trilateral" economies. On the second front, the administration engineered a depreciation in order both to help American tradables producers and to stimulate the economy more generally.

Through Carter's first year in office, Nixon appointee Arthur Burns was still Chairman of the Fed Board, but Treasury Secretary Michael Blumenthal was outspoken in expressing Administration opinion. The result was a depreciation of the dollar by 4 percent in real terms between the election and August 1977.[27] On world financial markets, the Administration was viewed as "talking down" the dollar – also labeled "malign neglect" or "open mouth operations."[28]

In October 1977 the dollar began to fall rapidly, and by January 1978 it had dropped by a further 10 percent against the mark and yen. The fall was not eased by the appointment of G. William Miller to succeed Burns in December 1977 – indeed, announcement of his nomination led the mark and the Swiss franc to rise two percent against the dollar in one day.

The dollar depreciation appeared in line with Congressional desires. In the late Ford Administration, Henry Reuss had called for a depreciation against the yen, and the Carter team in fact brought this about. The dollar's slide was, however, cause for concern on world financial markets and among internationally oriented American businesses. Representatives of the financial community especially argued against a weak dollar; cautionary notes were also sounded by the President of the Federal Reserve Board of New York, although Paul Volcker appeared to have little influence on

Fed policy. The dollar depreciation seemed to have the support of Congress and the Executive, especially as the currency stabilized over the summer of 1978.

Eventually the dollar began to drop again. A new anti-inflation package did little to slow the fall, and by now the Administration was under intense pressure from the international business community, and from other major OECD nations, to support the dollar. On November 1 Carter announced a dollar defense package that included tighter monetary policy and $30 billion to bolster the currency on the foreign exchanges, with only modest effect. In July 1979 Carter replaced Miller with Paul Volcker, which presaged more stringent monetary policy and an aggressive defense of the dollar.

This episode is not easy to analyze, for the politics of American monetary and exchange rate policy in the Carter Administration have never been thoroughly investigated. A few broad tendencies present themselves, however. Price trends in the late 1970s can be observed in Table 5. As the dollar depreciated, tradables producers did relatively well. Tradables prices indeed rose roughly in tandem with nontradables prices in the period. Some tradables sectors, notably autos and agriculture, faced difficulties – and indeed clamored for and obtained support in the early 1980s. However, between 1976 and 1980, relative prices of tradables moved quite favorably. By one reckoning the dollar depreciated 12 percent between the first quarter of 1977 and the second quarter of 1980, so that U.S. import prices rose by 9 percent more than the U.S. GNP deflator.[29] The rise in the relative price of imports had a positive impact on tradables producers, and manufacturing especially expanded. In fact, 1979 represents the high point of industrial employment in the United States.

In this context, soft-money interest groups represented in Congress had little reason to complain. As the Administration managed a dollar decline, especially relative to the yen, tradables producers faced favorable conditions. Trade policy disputes moderated, although a few sectors (notably steel) continued to lobby for protection. The major political pressure on the Administration's policies came from American international banks and corporations uneasy about or opposed to currency volatility. These were reinforced by assaults on the dollar on international currency markets, and by insistence from European and Japanese governments that the U.S. support the dollar.

The Carter experience diverges somewhat from traditional patterns, inasmuch as for a time the Executive pursued policies desired by soft-money interests. However, interest-group alignments tend to track my expectations. Tradables producers were pleased with the dollar depreciation, while internationally oriented firms – especially the international financial community – protested the dollar's decline. Tradables producers

Table 5. *Representative relative price indices, 1976–1985 (1976=100, 1980=100)*

Product	1976	1980 / 1980	1985
Traded goods			
Industrial commodities	100	152 / 100	118
Finished goods	100	145 / 100	119
Motor vehicles*a*	100	135 / 100	128
Farm products	100	130 / 100	92
Nontraded goods and services			
Shelter	100	156 / 100	136
All services	100	149 / 100	141
Public transportation	100	145 / 100	160
Medical care services	100	145 / 100	151

a Motor vehicles price trends in the early 1980s were distorted by the imposition of "voluntary" restraints on imports. Presumably, in the absence of these trade barriers motor vehicle prices would have risen more slowly.
Source: Economic Report of the President, various issues. Constructed from producers' and consumers' price indices for the goods and services in question.

got what they wanted, which explains their relative silence. Hard-money interests lobbied the Fed and the Administration but were unsuccessful until 1979. At the same time, broad popular concern with inflation was growing, and this may also have contributed to the shift in Administration policy.

Dollar appreciation, 1981–1985

The dollar rose continually from late 1980 through the middle of 1985. This appreciation had two sources. The first was the Federal Reserve's restrictive monetary policies initiated after the appointment of Paul Volcker as Fed chairman in July 1979, and tightened continually through the early 1980s. The second was the federal budget deficits caused largely by the Reagan Administration's tax reductions and increases in military spending. Both policies tended to raise interest rates in the United States, draw funds toward the dollar and boost the value of the American currency. Although figures vary according to how they are calculated, one series shows a real appreciation of the dollar of 64 percent between the inauguration of Ronald Reagan in January 1981 and its peak in March 1985, after which it declined 12 percent to September 1985, when the major financial powers agreed to coordinate attempts to bring down the dollar.[30]

Relative prices in the United States reflected the dollar appreciation, as tradables prices fell relative to nontradables (see Table 5). The index of finished goods prices rose 19 percent between 1980 and 1985, while the index of all services prices rose more than twice as much, by 41 percent. Specific goods and services show some variation, of course. With import quotas imposed, automobile prices rose more rapidly than other tradables, while farm prices actually dropped by 8 percent; public transportation and medical care prices rose even more rapidly than other nontradables.

Producers of tradable goods came under severe price pressure as the dollar appreciated. By one measure, between the second quarter of 1980 and the first quarter of 1985 U.S. import prices *dropped* by 29 percent relative to the American GNP deflator (Federal Reserve Bank of St. Louis 1986: 1). As a result manufactured imports went from 20 to 32 percent of total manufactured output, while manufactured exports dropped from 26 to 18 percent of output; manufacturing trade went from a surplus equal to 6 percent of output in 1980 to a deficit equal to 14 percent of output in 1985. During these years the American trade deficit went from $12 billion to $136 billion in 1982 dollars. Heightened foreign competition contributed to a 5 percent drop in tradables employment between 1980 and August 1985, at a time when nontradables employment grew 13 percent (Frankel 1985: 31).

Many of my analytical expectations were borne out in this period. American monetary and exchange-rate policy were linked in both markets and politics. Interest group activity on the dollar was fiercer than at any time since the 1930s, and found its outlet through major Congressional initiatives on the exchange rate. And trade policy was almost immediately drawn into the monetary and exchange-rate debate.[31]

As the dollar rose, American tradables producers demanded relief from the decline in the relative price of their products. Not only were American goods being priced out of third markets, they were losing major market share at home. The charge against the strong dollar was led by Lee Morgan, president of Caterpillar Tractors, beginning in late 1982. Calling the strong dollar "the single most important trade issue facing the U.S." (Destler and Henning 1989: 33), Morgan mobilized American industry around bringing the currency down. Agitation to weaken the dollar grew as the currency rose: in the middle of 1983 the Business Roundtable supported Morgan, and the National Association of Manufacturers followed suit in February 1984. By 1985 even those who had previously supported the Administration had become hostile or neutral (ibid: 35–7).

Congress was deeply involved at every step of the way. Indeed, congressional activism on monetary policy reached a high point in the early 1980s. Between 1979 and 1985, an annual average of 65 bills, resolutions, and proposals concerning monetary policy were introduced into Congress; after the dollar declined, between 1986 and 1989, the number went down to ten a year (Akhtar and Howe 1991: A–22). Perhaps the most striking instance was congressional debate over a 1983 Administration bill to increase the American quota in the International Monetary Fund, generally a pro forma procedure agreed upon by all member states. The IMF quota bill took on the character of a referendum on the Administration's international monetary policies, whose unpopularity very nearly led to the bill's failure.

Soon after, Republican Senator Charles Percy of Illinois, a major manufacturing state and Caterpillar's home base, introduced a resolution calling on the Administration to negotiate a coordinated reduction in the value of the dollar; the resolution passed the Senate unanimously. The Reagan Administration was unresponsive, and in May 1985 the Senate passed another resolution calling for any measures necessary, including unilateral exchange market intervention, to depreciate the dollar. By late 1985, there were seven bills before Congress that included specific reference to exchange rate issues (Destler and Henning 1989: 107–10).

Tradables producers frustrated by their apparent inability to affect exchange-rate policy soon turned their attention to trade policy. The connection was clearly perceived and widely remarked upon, as by Republican Senator John Danforth: "No trade agreements, however sound, no trade laws, however enforced, will give Americans a fair chance to compete in the international marketplace if an overvalued dollar has the same effect as a 25–50 percent [foreign] tariff" (ibid: 104).

Although a dollar depreciation would have had the desired effect, it seemed that no amount of private and Congressional pressure would induce Paul Volcker to loosen Fed policy, or the Reagan Administration to raise taxes and reduce spending, or the monetary authorities to intervene to drive the dollar down.[32] Congress could affect trade policy more directly, however, and import-competing manufacturers turned their attention to this arena. A flurry of trade bills was introduced, leading up to major protectionist legislation sponsored in 1985 by Democrats Lloyd Bentsen in the Senate, and Dan Rostenkowski and Richard Gephardt in the House. Affected manufacturers also used administrative means to obtain relief from import competition. They filed an unprecedented number of complaints with the International Trade Commission: antidumping cases, for example, rose from an annual average of 24 between 1977 and 1981, to an annual average of 61 between 1982 and 1984 (Deardorff and Stern 1987: 26, 23).

Internationally oriented sectors in the United States were threatened by the growth of American economic nationalism. Large segments of the American economy were increasingly tied into the world economy. As in the last years of Bretton Woods, American international banks and corporations were unconcerned by the strong dollar – and may have appreciated its impact on their businesses (Destler and Henning 1989: 131–6). But support for (or indifference to) the dollar appreciation was tempered by the realization that it was inflaming protectionist sentiment in the United States.

The preferred way to moderate the dollar's rise, in the view of the international business community, was to reduce the fiscal deficit. Looser monetary policy or exchange-market intervention raised the specter of a Carter-style dollar depreciation. The budget deficits, on the other hand, were not beneficial to global businesses and indeed came close to implying future monetary laxness. Better to increase taxes and reduce spending than to risk future inflation. Led by Peter Peterson, major internationally oriented corporate leaders began in early 1983 to lobby for a reduction in the budget deficit. This "Bipartisan Appeal" was signed by five former Treasury secretaries, along with representatives of the country's most important financial institutions and multinational firms.[33] Import-competing industries were conspicuously underrepresented. Although the effort did not meet with striking success, it is possible that its very visible nature contributed to legislative and executive attempts to control the deficit.

Nonetheless, the dollar remained strong through 1984 and into 1985, while pressure for policies to protect American tradables producers became increasingly intense. In a major shift, in early 1985 the Administration began to indicate that it regarded the dollar as "too strong." In January 1985 the Group of Five made some mild statements that were taken to imply general agreement on the desirability of a dollar depreciation. Whether in response to these changes in policy or to economic fundamentals, the American currency began declining in March 1985. By August it had gone down about 10 percent, but began moving upward again in the late summer. Finally, in September 1985, meeting at the Plaza Hotel in New York, the Group of Five finance ministers announced that they would undertake coordinated intervention to reduce the value of the dollar. Over the succeeding twelve months the dollar fell by over 20 percent, and by the end of 1987 it was back near the levels of 1980.

In this period, many developments were in line with my analytical expectations. The link between domestic macroeconomic policy and the exchange rate was drawn by all involved in the debate, and the topic was extremely visible. Both interest group and Congressional activity on monetary and exchange rate issues were more significant than at any time since the 1930s. Clear links were drawn to trade policy.

After the spectacular appreciation and depreciation of the early and middle 1980s, the dollar's movements were much less dramatic. Since 1987, the American currency has been relatively stable, and relatively weak. From 1987 to 1993, the dollar declined by 3.8 percent against a trade-weighted index (and by just 1.1 percent in real terms). Against the country's principal sources of import competition, the currency declined much more substantially: by 23.2 percent against the yen and by 8 percent against the Deutsche Mark (*Economic Report of the President*, various issues). It seems likely that the general weakness of the dollar gave tradables producers little to complain about, while its general stability gave those worried about currency volatility little cause for concern. Whatever the reason, political attention to exchange rates in the United States clearly subsided after 1987.

It would be a great exaggeration to argue that American monetary politics has come to look anything like what it did in the 1890s. However, the experiences of the 1980s do appear to diverge substantially from the subdued and diffuse discussions of monetary policy that prevailed between the 1930s and the 1960s; in the early and middle part of the decade, especially, there seemed some similarities to patterns of the era before 1935. This is not to insist on the repetition of history, only on recurrence of certain underlying economic conditions of potential political importance.

Complementary evidence is available concerning the economic developments I associate with my political argument. A study by de Kock and DeLeire (1994) indeed found a substantial increase in the importance of the exchange rate in American monetary policy in recent years. Most relevant to my purposes is that while the exchange rate accounted for nearly none of the transmission from monetary policy to output in the United States before 1982 (the researchers' dividing line), it has accounted for about one-third since then. This is consonant with my argument; if this change has taken place, it would be surprising if analogous political changes were *not* in train.

As world financial and commercial flows have grown rapidly, and American involvement in them has grown apace, American monetary policy has been changing. It has come to implicate the exchange rate, and in this process monetary politics in the United States are becoming more conflictual, more dominated by clear interest group pressures, more the stuff of Congressional activity, and more closely associated with trade policy.

IV. OBSERVATIONS AND IMPLICATIONS

I reiterate that the historical survey presented here does not constitute systematic empirical evidence for my argument. However, I do believe that this look at the historical evidence does tend to support the notion that changing levels of international economic integration are associated with changes in the making of American monetary policy. Economic integration changes the way in which monetary policy takes effect, making the exchange rate crucial. High levels of international trade and payments appear to increase the desire of American international businesses to reduce currency volatility. Commercial and financial openness heighten the vulnerability of many Americans to global price trends, and seem to increase the importance of the exchange rate as they try to counteract adverse price movements. In this way, the analysis in this paper is very much in line with the underlying argument of this volume that economic internationalization profoundly affects domestic politics.

None of this is meant as a full explanation of American monetary policy, or of the impact of international economic changes on American politics. It is meant to insist on the importance of introducing open-economy considerations into analysis of American monetary politics. However, the historical record also gives rise to some points that require clarification, to potential alternative explanations for the trends observed, and to some related observations.

Two preliminary clarifications are in order. First, my argument about the kinds of cleavages anticipated is not meant to imply that the relevant actors used the sorts of categories employed in my analysis. Indeed, many of the terms in question did not exist until recently. My argument is about the political cleavages I expect given a set of economic conditions. This depends on socioeconomic and political actors having a sense of what their interests are. It does *not* depend on their defining their interests as I do after the fact. My framework explains why farmers and manufacturers preferred certain monetary policies in the 1870s, 1890s, 1920s, and 1980s; it does not explain why these demands took different forms or met with different amounts of success. Mine is an *analytical* argument, not a claim to *describe* the way political actors thought or talked about the issues.

A second clarification is to make explicit my downplaying of a common insistence, in the historical literature, that monetary populism pitted indebted farmers against mortgage bankers. I do not dispute the division, but argue that it is inadequate to explain the debates. There are both analytical and empirical reasons to believe that political conflict in earlier eras was strongly affected by the tradables–nontradables divide.[34]

Several explanations that might be alternative to my own can be adduced. To do so is somewhat artificial, for to my knowledge the explanations have never been presented in the literature. While few scholars would disagree with my broad characterization of the ebb and flow of monetary politics in the past 120 years – especially in comparing the period before 1935 and that between 1935 and 1970 – there have been no scholarly attempts to explain this ebb and flow (so far as I know). Nonetheless, some potential arguments can be deduced.

One explanation for the quiescence of American debates over monetary policy before 1970 might have to do with America's international position. American monetary policy may rarely have been at issue because it was unconstrained: the United States so dominated the world economy that its policies determined global monetary conditions, so that there was no tradeoff between domestic and international concerns. This might be combined with the assertion that monetary consensus was due to the strictures of the Bretton Woods system within which the dollar's value was fixed at $35 per ounce of gold.

Both assertions point to potentially important international factors, but neither helps explain much variation across time. The United States was at least as large relative to the world economy, and world financial markets, in the 1920s as it was in the 1960s. This means that – even without any such intent on the part of American policymakers – monetary policy in the United States had substantial international effects in the 1920s and 1930s. However, domestic debates over American monetary policy were extremely heated in the earlier period and virtually nonexistent in the later one. As for the constraints of Bretton Woods, while the existence of the regime raised the costs of devaluation, in the early 1970s the U.S. did in fact devalue, international monetary regime or no. The point is that few political actors appear to have cared enough to make the exchange rate a policy issue until the 1970s.

Another potential explanatory rival might focus on the independent importance of the institutional changes discussed above. Some might argue that the decline in prominence of monetary politics was a *result* of Congressional delegation rather than a cause. This might be because Congress recognized the efficiency gains to be made by delegating responsibility to an independent agency. In this view the Fed was in fact implementing true Congressional preferences, just in a way that protected Congress from responsibility for unpopular policies.[35]

This view does not accord with two facts. First, the institutional structure of monetary policy making was hotly debated from 1907 until 1935, and interest group and Congressional preferences over institutions were well established. It was hardly the case that in the 1930s Congress sneaked institutional changes past unwitting constituents: for the previous fifty years constituents had been bombarding Congress with insistent institutional demands. In the 1930s these demands simply dissipated. Second, apparent Congressional willingness to give the Fed free rein in monetary policy declined precipitously after 1970. Congress ignored monetary and exchange rate policy so long as they did not implicate the interests of constituencies of electoral importance, as in the closed U.S. economy between 1935 and the late 1960s.

I do not mean to insist that there is no truth to these arguments, only that they do not clearly supplant my own. A fuller evaluation of the argument would require a more explicit formulation of alternative hypotheses, and more systematic empirical evidence. In the meantime, several observations can be made on the basis of the analysis and evidence presented here. Some follow directly from my argument; others point in somewhat different directions.

First, political activity on exchange rates appears asymmetrical. That is, while both real appreciations and depreciations have distributional effects, real appreciations give rise to a much more significant political response. As the dollar fell in real terms in the late 1890s, late 1970s, or late 1980s, there were few political repercussions. On the other hand, the real appreciations of the 1870s and early 1890s, late 1960s, and early 1970s, and again of the early 1980s, brought forth major reactions in both monetary and trade policies.

Relative price movements that hurt tradables producers thus appear more politically salient than those that hurt nontradables producers; a real appreciation seems more politically significant than a real depreciation. This may be because the costs of an appreciation are more concentrated than its benefits, or conversely that the benefits of a depreciation are more concentrated than its costs. A real depreciation (appreciation) helps (hurts) tradables producers in a direct and highly visible way. Inasmuch as the principal negative impact of a real depreciation is on consumers of tradables, the result may simply be a subset of the common phenomenon that producers tend to be better organized than consumers.

A related puzzle is why political demands appear much more strident when economic agents are faced with negative price trends. That is, demand for a depreciation appears to arise only when the currency appreciates or when tradables prices decline for other reasons. There is no reason why tradables producers should not try to benefit from depreciation at any time, but they seem to demand depreciation far more insistently in the wake of contrary price movements. Like the demand for trade protection, there is no obvious basis for this not to be constant. However, just as the demand for protection is countercyclical, so too does the demand for depreciation seem a function of past appreciation. Why this is so remains to be explained.

Second, there are important differences in the degree to which the relative price changes to which economic agents respond are truly exogenous. There is little question that the decline of grain prices in the late nineteenth century or the 1920s can be taken as given by broader trends in the world economy (although, of course, the actions of American farmers affected these, too). However, the real appreciation of the 1870s was the result of expectations that the dollar would return to gold, while the real appreciations of 1968–71 and 1980–5 were largely the result of American economic policy trends. A full explanation of these episodes would indeed have to uncover the reasons for the underlying trends that led to the real appreciations, while I have focused only on the political response to them.

Third, an important feature of exchange rate politics before 1935 and during the Bretton Woods period was the link generally drawn between the level of the exchange rate and its flexibility. There is no necessary tie between the two: one could prefer a depreciated fixed rate, or an appreciated floating rate. However, in practice interest groups divided into two broad camps. "Hard money" interests wanted a strong fixed rate; "soft money" interests wanted a devaluation and a floating rate. In other words, preferences about stabilizing the exchange rate were elided with views on whether to devalue the dollar.

How and why the elision of the two dimensions of currency policy took place is important to a full understanding of the interest-group and legislative politics of the era, as well as to policy outcomes. One possibility, which seems to accord with the evidence, is that the most intense preferences over exchange rates are in fact those for stability, on the one hand, and for depreciation, on the other. For reasons described above, preferences for flexibility and appreciation (such as those of nontradables producers for strong floating rates) may not be particularly intense and the groups may not be particularly concentrated. But this is only speculation.

Fourth, although I have addressed some institutional issues I have focused on interests. One thing appears clear from the historical record: Congress has typically been especially sensitive to the demands of tradables producers, while the Executive and the Fed have tended to be more responsive to the international business community. I presented some conjectures above as to why this might be the case, but they are not rigorously derived. Similarly, my discussion of how and why Congress delegated exchange-rate policy in the 1930s was superficial. For now the institutional characteristics of American monetary policy, and the evolution of these institutions over time, remain to be fully explained.

Fifth, especially in the more recent periods I have downplayed the importance of inflation aversion on the part of the general populace. This was typically not an issue before World War II, when deflation was perceived as more of a problem. But there is little doubt, for example, that during the late 1970s there was an increase in popular dissatisfaction with inflation, and that this sentiment contributed to the reversal of monetary policy in 1979–81. What remains to be explored is exactly how much these broad pressures mattered to policy.

Finally, I have said relatively little about the relationship among policy preferences, institutions, and outcomes. My argument is about the prominence, nature, and institutional representation of the political divisions expected over monetary policy in closed and open economies. This is of course a crucial building block for a broader analysis that can try to explain the *results* of these political debates, but it is not such an explanation. It is only a first step, albeit a necessary one, on the road to a much more complex analysis. The sorts of factors discussed in the contribution to this volume by Geoffrey Garrett and Peter Lange are undoubtedly crucial to understanding policy outcomes in this realm.

CONCLUSIONS

The politics of a nation's monetary policy are significantly affected by changes in the degree to which it is economically integrated with the rest of the world. Economic internationalization is associated with changes in domestic and international monetary politics.

In financially open economies monetary policy has powerful effects on the exchange rate. Commercial openness for its part makes more economic agents sensitive to currency values. Both together imply that financial and commercial integration will lead monetary politics to focus more on the exchange rate.

As exchange rates effect changes in relative prices while an overall change in the nominal price level does not, economic integration also implies that the politics of monetary policy will become more heavily influenced by concentrated interests rather than diffuse considerations. Inasmuch as Congress is especially responsive to electorally important interest groups, and the Executive to broad macropolitical trends, the increased importance of exchange rates and their impact on the relative prices facing powerful interest groups should tend to mobilize Congress more than in a closed economy. Finally, because the exchange rate is obviously related to import competition, it should be linked in political debates to trade policy.

In this context, I compared American monetary policy in three periods: one of high levels of global trade and investment before 1935, one with relatively low levels of financial and commercial flows between the 1930s and the late 1960s, and one of growing world economic activity after 1970. The changing pattern of global economic integration appeared to be associated with changes in American monetary politics. As monetary policy shifted toward the exchange rate, interest groups became increasingly mobilized, especially when the dollar appreciated in real terms. This was also connected to increasing Congressional attention to the issue area, and to growing ties between trade and exchange-rate policy in the public arena.

The conclusions drawn here about the future of American monetary policy are tentative. Current levels of international trade and investment, although high, may not be as high as those during the classical gold standard. Perhaps more important, these levels may not be stable, as macroeconomic and sectoral difficulties inflame the desire of many to impede the free movement of goods and capital across borders. Nonetheless, if links continue to grow between the American and world economies, it is at least plausible that the sorts of monetary policy trends discussed here will become increasingly important.

6

Internationalization and Electoral Politics in Japan

FRANCES McCALL ROSENBLUTH

INTRODUCTION AND OVERVIEW

Until its fall from power in the summer of 1993, Japan's Liberal Democratic Party (LDP) carried a near record among popularly elected one-party governments for longevity.[1] The feat is all the more remarkable because its reign extended through a period of profound change: recovery from a devastating war, reintegration into the world economy, and rapid urbanization. Throughout the postwar decades, despite mounting international pressures and domestic demographic shifts, the LDP presided over a sort of time warp, representing the same protectionist coalition of industry and agriculture.

At first cut, Japan's case is not a prize empirical specimen for the argument that international economic forces bear importantly on domestic politics. Given Japan's spectacular postwar success in the world economy, one would have expected a free-trade coalition to triumph, or at least to gain influence, long ago. Instead, Japan's markets, with the government's help, have been notoriously hard to crack. Round after round of multilateral and bilateral trade talks managed to reduce tariff barriers, only to expose higher and thicker nontariff walls of cartel regulation and "customary business practices." Despite the high fashion in Tokyo of just about anything associated with foreign cultures, the internationalization of the Japanese economy appears to have been a rather one-way affair.

In this paper, I evaluate the domestic effects of internationalization in the Japanese case. If, as the essays in this volume collectively suggest, globally competitive sectors should favor free trade, we need to be able to answer three questions. First, what accounts for the LDP's nearly forty years of protectionist policies? In this chapter, I argue that Japan's political institutions, and in particular its electoral laws, strengthened the hand of producer groups (of both competitive and noncompetitive firms) at the expense of consumers for many years.

Organizational and informational disadvantages beset consumers in any democratic society, but the political response to that handicap depends in part on the nature of political institutions. We need to explain how Japan's protectionism-oriented electoral rules survived Japan's intense involvement in the world economy in the postwar period. For that, we need to inject an element of international politics: even owners and managers of globally competitive firms preferred to gain monopoly rents in their closed domestic markets, as long as foreign governments tolerated it.[2] In fact, Japan's trading partners permitted its unilateral protectionism for decades, allowing proproducer electoral rules to persist. One could imagine a very different scenario – indeed, the one Rogowski (1987) presents for small European states – where electoral politics early on accommodate the internationally imposed requirement to open markets.

Second, how, if at all, did the international economy contribute to Japan's recent political reorganization? This, in a sense, is the flip side of the first question. If international forces contributed importantly to the collapse of the LDP's rule, we should expect to find that foreign governments' threats to retaliate drove a wedge between Japan's globally competitive producers and those who owned specific assets in noncompetitive sectors. We should also expect to find that the reformist politicians who brought down the LDP espouse market-opening measures. If, on the contrary, the issues of public debate are purely domestic ones, the case for international forces would be harder to make. Fortunately for the internationalization thesis, however, the debate over its world role does in fact figure prominently in the political arena in post-LDP Japan.

Third, what implications do recent changes in domestic political institutions have for Japan's future role in the world economy? As Milner and Keohane point out in their introduction to this volume, domestic sources of foreign policy have already been much studied compared to the impact of international forces on domestic politics. But if the domestic institutions themselves are established at least in part in response to international forces, we should be able to observe foreign policy decisions that are in line with those forces. Here, our conclusions are necessarily speculative, because the evidence is still preliminary. But recognizing the possibility of international effects allows us to deduce some hypotheses to be tested as events unfold.

In summary, Japan's case does not negate the importance of internationalization, but rather underscores the importance of domestic political institutions in channeling international forces in sometimes unexpected directions. It is not enough to understand domestic politics in isolation of the world environment, for much domestic change would remain mysterious. At the same time, evaluating international forces alone could lead observers far from the mark. In Japan today, as never before, one cannot understand one without the other.

The organization of this paper is as follows. First, the next section outlines Japan's political institutions that have mediated market forces, and attempts to explain their longevity. While not explicitly about internationalization, this is a crucial portion of the paper because these institutions have shaped Japan's responses to the outside world. Section II considers the international pressures for change, along with domestic demographic shifts. Section III examines three case studies of LDP policy-making in more depth, to show how international and domestic forces have combined in the past. Section IV reviews the domestic debate over electoral rules, and traces at least some of its impetus to international pressures. Section V defends my focus on electoral incentives in Japanese policy-making against the conventional notion of bureaucratic dominance. I conclude with some thoughts about how Japan's posture in the world economy might evolve.

I. LDP LONGEVITY AND JAPAN'S ELECTORAL RULES

Japan's multimember-district electoral system (1925–42; 1947–94) was distinctive in that it forced majority-seeking parties to field more than one candidate in most districts. In Lower House elections, Japanese voters had a single vote, despite district magnitudes ranging from one to six members.[3] Votes were not transferable to other candidates of the same party in the event that a voter's first choice had already made it past the post, as is the case in the single-transferable-vote systems in Ireland and Finland. In Japan, any party fielding more than a single candidate in any district confronted the problem of dividing the vote among its candidates in order to win as many seats as possible.

The LDP's method of dividing votes among its candidates was to allow the party's candidates access to government resources with which to compete for votes. Using what Cain, Ferejohn, and Fiorina (1987) have called the personal-vote strategy, each LDP candidate built a personal support group on the basis of policy favors for which he took credit. To be sure, all LDP Diet members shared the party label. But they also differentiated themselves from each other by specializing in particular types of constituency services. If one candidate developed strong ties with the agricultural community, for example, another focused on small retailers, and another on the construction industry. Each LDP politician's choice as to what types of services to provide was a niche-market decision; it was the membership in the LDP that gave the legislator goods to deliver.[4]

The LDP's need to divide the vote among its candidates placed a premium on organized, reliable votes. This enhanced the influence of groups that can deliver blocs of votes – as in the case of farmers and small business proprietors – and groups that could contribute large sums of money for use in coddling candidates' personal support networks.[5] Given the importance of constituency-specific investments that LDP members made in building up their support bases, it is no wonder that over forty percent of LDP Diet members "inherited" their electoral organizations from a father or mentor (Ichikawa 1990).

The personal-vote strategy was also expensive. Just the money LDP candidates collected from campaign contributors in election years, apart from the government resources they took credit for distributing, was of mind-boggling proportions. Political commentators estimated that Japan's five major political parties together spent about $3 billion leading up to the election of February 1990, over half of which the LDP alone spent (*The Economist* 1990).[6]

Where did the LDP get this money and why was the party able to raise so much of it? Corporate contributors were willing to bankroll the LDP because of what they got in return: policies that favored them at the expense of the median voter. Producers paid the LDP for favorable budgetary, tax, and regulatory treatment. Voters continued to vote for LDP candidates despite getting short shrift in many policies, because LDP candidates won their loyalty through small favors paid for by these corporate contributions. At least in Lower House elections, loyalty in exchange for personal favors made many voters less inclined to vote for members of other parties even if they were not entirely satisfied with the broader policies the LDP espoused.

Given their strong effect on policy, one might wonder where these electoral rules came from in the first place. In 1925 three parties, none of which commanded a legislative majority, landed upon the multimember-district system as the mutually least disagreeable compromise – each could reasonably expect to win one of the multiple seats in a district.[7] Before long, however, it became clear that the party in control of the cabinet could use government resources to help allocate votes among multiple candidates in each district (Ramseyer and Rosenbluth 1995).

In 1947, Prime Minister Shigeru Yoshida convinced Douglas MacArthur to abandon the Occupation-imposed proportional-representation (PR) rules in favor of the old multimember district system. He argued that the PR system was responsible for the sudden rise of the Socialist Party in the 1946 election – an argument that found a sympathetic ear in a MacArthur now as concerned about "the communist threat" as about political accountability in Japan. In the elections that followed, the conservative governments (the LDP formed in 1955) were able to use the multimember-district system to bolster their performance at the polls, using budgetary and other governmental resources to help divide their vote while leaving the opposition parties without such a solution.

It becomes clear, then, why the LDP did not jettison the multimember-district electoral rules long ago, despite the vote-division problem the rules generated. As long as the LDP had a legislative majority, and hence controlled the policy-making process, it could use the distribution of private goods to help divide the vote among its candidates. Meanwhile, the other parties' lack of comparable resources to dole out put them at a tremendous disadvantage relative to the LDP in solving their own vote-division problems. Note, however, that the LDP's use of private goods to carve up the vote efficiently in each district presumed that groups of voters were identifiable and targettable. As we will discuss in the next section, urbanization made this more difficult, and internationalization rendered it more costly.

II. THE LDP'S CHANGING CALCULUS: SHIFTS IN JAPAN'S INTERNATIONAL ENVIRONMENT AND DOMESTIC DEMOGRAPHICS

If the LDP managed to buy off Japanese voters with its personal-vote electoral strategy, Japan's postwar pro-producer economic policies were also premised on foreign tolerance for Japan's failure to reciprocate market access. It is not that Ministry of International Trade and Industry bureaucrats cooked up a plan for how best to prey on foreign goodwill for the sake of the country. As Section V argues in more detail, MITI bureaucrats necessarily operate within political constraints. Rather, Japanese firms – the very actors that MITI regulated – had "purchased" proproducer regulation in exchange for their financial support for the LDP. This proproducer regulation included barriers to entry from would-be domestic as well as foreign challengers. The LDP, through various forms of statutory aid and administrative guidance, did the same for the agricultural, small business, and financial sectors.

Though Japan's growth-oriented policy environment seemed to be a stable pattern for many years, several parts of the arrangement began to shift. First, internationally oriented firms with large and growing stakes in their trade and investments abroad grew increasingly concerned about the threat of foreign trade retaliation. To deflect foreign criticism from themselves, these firms advocated the dismantling of the protective barriers surrounding Japan's least competitive sectors, agriculture and small business.[8]

A second pressure for change also came by way of the business community's perception of changes in the international economic opportunity structure facing Japan. Domestic cartel regulation was less valuable than in the past to the many Japanese corporations that already had to compete in noncartelized markets abroad. These firms were less willing to pay the huge sums required to oil the Liberal Democratic Party's electoral machine that generated proproducer regulation. In their cost-benefit calculations, exporters and investors abroad had to weigh the gains from high domestic barriers to entry against the expected costs of trade retaliation as well as the amount they had to contribute to the LDP's electoral success.

The third factor undermining Japan's political commitment to its traditional protectionist policies was demographic change. In 1960, according to government census data, 80 percent of all electoral districts were basically rural. By 1975, only 35 percent of electoral districts were still rural (Jichishō gyōsei kyoku [Ministry of Home Affairs Administrative Bureau], 1988). This change, too, was internationally driven, to the extent that Japan's export success brought relatively greater returns to urban industrial areas than to the countryside.

Urban dwellers in Japan tended to be better educated and more mobile. Urban workers also tended to earn a greater percentage of their income in fixed wages, in contrast to rural farmers and small-scale manufacturers whose income varied more closely with their sectors' profitability. Urban voters therefore tended to have more diffuse interests – many of which were tied up in their role as consumers – than farmers and proprietors whose producer interests dominated.[9] The steady migration into cities forced the LDP to shift its policies at the margins toward consumer interests.[10]

III. EXAMPLES OF POLICY CHANGES

In recent years, the combination of domestic demographic change and foreign pressure on the business community forced the LDP to begin reducing support to some of the party's traditional supporters, farmers and small businesses. The LDP shifted policy direction only slowly, over the objections of many, especially rural, backbenchers. On the other hand, party members representing the interests of competitive businesses or of urban districts pushed the party to move faster. Ultimately, however, this was not a tightrope the party could safely walk. As the interests of the LDP's divergent constituents pulled even farther apart, the party's leadership faltered, as we see in the next section.

Farmers

Japanese farmers have been among the most protected in the world. Thanks to a ban on rice imports and rice price supports, the price Japanese farmers got for their rice was typically about eight times the world's price of rice (Calder 1988). In exchange for this protection from market forces, the nationwide network of agricultural cooperatives (*Nōkyō*) mobilized the farm vote at elections on behalf of the LDP. Although farmers made up less than twelve percent of the Japanese population, including part-time farmers who made up about 8 or 9 of the 12 percent, the LDP valued disproportionately the agricultural vote as long as the electoral system required vote division among LDP candidates. It was the predictability of the agricultural vote that gave farmers their clout.

Magnifying even further the importance of the agricultural vote to the LDP was the well-known malapportionment of electoral districts in favor of rural areas. The Japanese government had not undertaken a thoroughgoing reapportionment of its electoral districts since 1947, when Japan was substantially more rural than it is now. A few seats were added over the years in some of the more populous districts, and occasionally a seat was removed from the most sparsely populated. But this tinkering at the margins left a gap in per capita representation of nearly four-to-one between districts at the two extremes.

In 1983, the Japanese Supreme Court ruled that any representation ratio exceeding four-to-one would be unconstitutional. This left the LDP a bit of breathing space in dealing with the apportionment issue, and it is easy to see why the LDP was loathe to take drastic action. As long as the electoral rules required the LDP to divide the vote among multiple candidates in most districts, the well-organized farmers were valuable, targettable voters. But alas for the LDP, foreign governments trying to pry open Japan's agricultural market were not as easy to mollify as Japan's Supreme Court.

The United States, as a major exporter of farm products, grew increasingly impatient with Japan's virtually impenetrable agricultural market. In the face of this pressure, the LDP budged a little. In the 1970s, the Japanese government eased somewhat the quotas on beef and citrus imports, two product lines of particular interest to the United States. In 1990 the Japanese government finally agreed to "tariffize" beef and citrus quotas, with an eye towards gradual import liberalization. But the Japanese government made each concession only after the greatest resistance, and was careful to avoid altogether discussion of the Japanese agricultural industry's staple, rice.

In June 1991 the leadership of the LDP began speaking obliquely about the possibility of lifting the import ban on rice. Leadership was cheered on by the Keidanren, the nation's most influential business association, which had adopted a resolution asking the administration to open the agriculture market as soon as possible. The Ad Hoc Administrative Reform Promotion Council, an advisory body to the prime minister made up of businessmen, academics, and media representatives, endorsed the partial opening of the rice market in its July 1991 interim report.

The LDP set a course of agricultural liberalization. But the pace of change was exceedingly slow because the LDP had to face the farmers under the multimember-district electoral rules. Absent more substantial changes in LDP members' electoral incentives – which would include a change in electoral rules or a more drastic demographic shift – the most Japan's trading partners could hope for were tiny import quotas for rice and rather stiff tariffs on other agricultural products.[11]

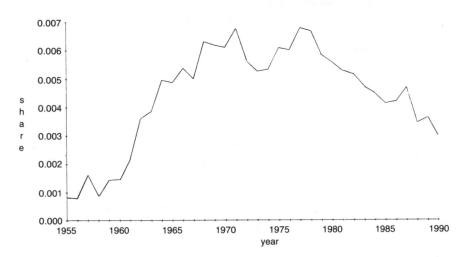

Figure 1. Funds for Small- and Medium-Sized Businesses: Share of General Account Budget, 1955–90. *Notes:* The vertical axis indicates, in percentage terms, the share of General Account Budget allocated to the Program for Small- and Medium-Sized Businesses (Chuso kigyo taisakuhi). Most of the allocations are funneled through the Ministry of Trade and Industry's Small- and Medium-Sized Enterprise Agency (Chuso kigyo cho), but some funds are also distributed through other ministries as well, including Health and Welfare, and Labor. *Source: Kuni no yosan* (The Government Budget), Tokyo: Ministry of Finance. Various years.

Figures 1–3 that follow compare the budgetary shares of the Ministry of Agriculture, Forestry and Fisheries, and of the Ministry of Health and Welfare. The comparison underscores, if somewhat crudely, the LDP's gradual reorientation of its electoral strategy in response to demographic changes and changes in the international opportunity structure. For quite some time, the Japanese government was phasing back subsidies to farmers, while it increased allocations to health and welfare programs aimed largely at the urban dweller. As the shifting budget shares suggest, the LDP was unable to ignore the growth in the nation's urban electorate. But the adjustments were only at the margin, for the LDP could not survive without the backing of the agricultural sector under Japan's multimember-district electoral rules.

The distribution sector

Another issue that pit the interests of uncompetitive firms against those of more competitive firms was the protection of the distribution sector. At the heart of many LDP Dietmembers' personal support networks, small shop-

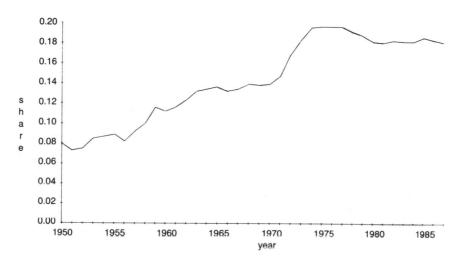

Figure 2. Ministry of Health and Welfare: Share of General Account Budget, 1952–89. *Note:* Vertical axis indicates the share of the General Account Budget allocated to the Ministry of health and Welfare. *Source: Kuni no yosan* (The Government Budget), Tokyo: Ministry of Finance. Various years.

keepers have been extraordinarily well represented in Japan. The Large Scale Store Law, with roots in 1937 but resurrected in 1957, has protected neighborhood Mom-and-Pop stores from "excessive competition" from larger, more efficient stores by limiting floor space of stores and by giving smaller stores a veto in store-siting decisions (Upham 1993).

Since the early 1980s, the LDP began lessening gradually the protection in response to complaints by foreign governments that Japan's multi-layered distribution system was slowing the flow of imports into Japan. Budgetary allocations, regulation, and tax policy changed subtly, but the changes had begun to accumulate into an identifiable pattern of reduced support. The government lowered budget allocations as well as subsidized loans from the Fiscal Investment and Loan Program to small businesses since about 1982.

These measures did little, and in 1989 the Large Scale Store Act found its way on to the priority list of U.S. trade negotiators. The Japanese government amended the law in 1989, somewhat weakening both the large retailers' cartel as well as the veto power of small retailers over the establishment of new stores in their neighborhoods. But this change, too, was an incremental one, and small firms did not lose their recourse to limit the expansion of large stores.

At the prompting of larger firms, the LDP also began to reduce the tax

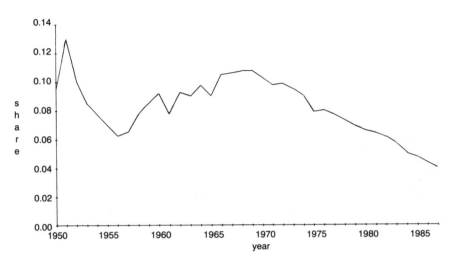

Figure 3. Ministry of agriculture: Share of general account budget, 1952–89. *Note:* The vertical axis indicates the share of the General Account Budget allocated to the Ministry of Agriculture, Forests and Fisheries. *Source: Kuni no yosan* (The Government Budget), Tokyo: Ministry of Finance. Various years.

breaks small store owners traditionally enjoyed. The introduction of a sales tax, effective April 1989, was a move by the LDP to take some of the tax burden from corporate and individual income taxes, even if that meant reducing tax advantages to small businesses. The Japanese government allowed small firm proprietors to underreport their earnings, resulting in the so-called 9-6-4 street wisdom that urban salaried workers paid taxes on ninety percent of their income while small businesses paid taxes on sixty percent (and farmers on forty percent of their income).[12] Once the government budget deficits reached enormous heights in the mid- and late 1970s the corporate sector, fearful of inflation or higher income taxes, pushed for an indirect tax (Mabuchi 1989; Shindō 1989). The final version of the law bought small firm proprietors some time. Rather than a value-added tax, which would have generated records of costs and sales of each stage of production and distribution, the sales tax was a simple final-goods levy. Initially, small firms did remain relatively free to underreport their profits. But since the passage of the bill, the LDP began to tighten the reporting requirements on these firms.[13]

　　Figure 1 shows that small- and medium-sized businesses received, in the late 1980s, a gradually shrinking slice of the government budget. The budgetary shifts paralleled the regulatory story: the LDP was phasing down its support of the small business sector for years. But so long as, at election time, the LDP had to apportion the vote in most electoral districts among multiple candidates, the party could not afford to alienate a group so ubiquitous and well-organized as small business. Short of electoral reform, any government changes in small business policy continued to be incremental.

Banks and interest rate deregulation

During its nearly forty year rule, the LDP rewarded banks' generous campaign support with profit-padding regulation. One pillar of the protective regulatory scheme was the Interest Rate Control Act of 1947, which capped interest payments on deposits at below-market rates. Lending cartels enabled banks to keep some of the cheap money as profits rather than passing all of it along to corporate borrowers.

At the wholesale end of the banking business, competition from the Euromarket largely destroyed the financial cartels. Deregulation was the banks' best choice, given that large Japanese firms could circumvent domestic banks' high fees by raising their funds in London and elsewhere. But in retail banking, where customers had no close substitutes for domestic bank or postal savings deposits, deregulation was slower in coming. The primary impetus for deregulation was from the U.S. government, which threatened to limit business opportunities for Japanese banks in the U.S. if Japan did not open up opportunities to American banks in Japan (Rosenbluth 1989).

Note that financial deregulation in the wholesale market, unlike agricultural liberalization or deregulation of the distribution sector, did not create a crisis within the LDP because it did not particularly hurt small, less efficient banks. This was because these small banks tend to specialize in the retail business, or in loans to firms too small to access profitably the Euromarket. Not surprisingly, the LDP moved at a snail's pace in deregulating retail, or small-scale bank deposit rates, even in the face of American threats. The LDP was concerned not so much to protect the large banks, which were already globally competitive and in any case would be the first to lose in the event of U.S. retaliation. Rather, the LDP was worried about the hundreds of small financial institutions – in every electoral district – that would collapse if prices for banking services were market-determined.

Eventually, threats of foreign retaliation raised the costs of coddling the small banks, and the LDP was gradually retreating from its blanket protection. By the late 1980s, the Ministry of Finance had begun to allow interest rates on even small deposits to creep towards market levels. But the measures were not enough to quell the sense of foreign banks and their governments that the Japanese banking sector was still unfairly rigged.

IV. PRESSURES FOR INSTITUTIONAL ADJUSTMENT

The LDP became increasingly uncomfortable with its heavy electoral dependence on less efficient sectors of the economy, such as agriculture and the small firm sector. As outlined briefly in Section III, the costs to the LDP of protecting these sectors were rising for three reasons. First, efficient exporters faced trade retaliation on account of Japan's closed markets and were pressing the LDP to change its policies. Japan's largest business organization, the Keidanren, spearheaded the push both for agricultural liberalization, for example, and for electoral reform. Keidanren Chairman Gaishi Hiraiwa, in fact, presided over the fundraising organization (*koenkai*) of the Ozawa/Hata proreform group within the LDP described below (Inoue 1993: 79). Second, competitive firms were less willing to bankroll the LDP's expensive electoral machine in exchange for cartel regulation. The business community had increased its pressure on the LDP to abandon the multi-member district system, arguing that other electoral rules would allow the party to compete for power more economically by reducing fierce intra-party competition.[14]

Third, apart from the pressure for change from the business community, the LDP's "personal vote" electoral strategy was both more expensive and less effective in urban and suburban areas. Most concerned about the consequences of not reforming the electoral system were young Diet-members in urban districts whose votes came in substantial part from white collar workers and consumers. Their constituents were hard to snare in traditional personal support networks because they were not already organized into producer groups or neighborhood associations. In addition to the costs of the favors themselves – help with loans or school applications, for example – politicians also had to bear the costs of identifying and organizing these voters in the first place, and build personal support networks largely from scratch (Iseri 1991: 77–8; Takahashi 1988: 58–9).

As serious as these problems may sound, long-term observers of Japanese politics wondered if they really added up to sufficient pressure for changing electoral rules. After all, the LDP owed its long-lived reign to this very system. The LDP had seemed to be in electoral trouble before, such as in the mid-1970s, but managed to adjust to the problems and resuscitate itself rather well. In any case, as late as spring 1993 there appeared to be no serious competition. The largest opposition party, the Socialists, managed to keep itself tied up in ideological knots that a majority of voters found irrelevant at best.

Given these factors in the LDP's favor – its own adaptability juxtaposed against the opposition's apparent incompetence – why change anything? Electoral reform would be especially risky, because it is impossible to predict perfectly the consequences of a different system. So the arguments went.

The case for institutional conservatism was not without merit. Although it is always unwise to count on the incompetence of the opposition, the electoral rules themselves disadvantaged any party but the majority party. As I have argued, a private-goods strategy trumped any public goods strategy in a single nontransferable vote (SNTV), multimember-district system because private goods divided the vote more efficiently than public goods or appeals to public goods could.

The danger for the LDP was not that some opposition party would overtake it. But the LDP needed only to lose a few seats to forfeit its legislative majority and its attendant monopoly on its private goods strategy. Second, there was a growing number of LDP members, many from urban districts, who found that the LDP party label was a liability for which private goods from the LDP barely compensated. For them, it was electorally costly to be associated with proproducer policies. It was these LDP members, recalculating their electoral prospects, who broke away from the party in May 1993 and, in so doing, destroyed the LDP majority.

The LDP leadership had contemplated for several years a drastic overhaul of Japan's electoral system precisely because it took the threat to its majority status seriously. But the party waited too long, for in 1989 the LDP lost its majority in the Upper House. The LDP leadership would now have to steer clear of the dual shoals of LDP backbencher concern on the one hand, and defensiveness by the opposition parties, on the other. The party's first plan, announced in April 1990, was for a double-ballot system combining single member districts and proportional representation. Three hundred single-member districts, which favor large parties, would give the LDP (and to a lesser extent, the Socialists) an electoral advantage over the more proportional multimember district system currently in place. The remaining 171 seats would be allocated by proportional representation to party lists, giving the smaller opposition parties a chance to survive. This, clearly, was a bill designed to get through the opposition-controlled Upper House.[15]

This plan ran aground in September 1991, however, when a large number of incumbent LDP members questioned their ability to get reelected under the new redistricting blueprint. Many would have to run in new districts, where there would be little or no overlap with the personal support networks they had come to rely on for a substantial portion of their votes. After several stormy battles in the LDP's Policy Affairs Research Council and the Executive Committee, the party leadership abandoned the double-ballot plan and agreed to return to the drawing board (Takahashi 1991).

In the fall of 1992, the party unveiled a new electoral reform plan which called for a simple single-member district system. The clear advantage over the earlier plan was that this formula satisfied the backbenchers. By insuring that at least the overwhelming majority of incumbents were assigned to districts within their current "bailiwicks," the party's single-member-district plan laid to rest concerns that incumbents would be starting from scratch in appealing to their constituents. LDP incumbents, after all, rightly attributed their electoral success to their competence in doling out favors and organizing voters into personal support networks. Many were understandably insecure about their ability to win under new rules that would weaken their personalistic ties to their voters, or that put them at the mercy of the party leadership in ranking them on the party's list. The disadvantage for the LDP compared to its earlier draft, however, was that this would be a harder sell in the Upper House.

Note that incumbents' interests are not always, as they were not here, synonymous with the party's longer-term interests. The personal endowments that made LDP incumbents successful politicians under multi-member-district rules are not necessarily those that would be best suited to championing the party label in single-member districts or on proportional-representation ballots. Vote-organization skills, for example, would likely be overshadowed by rhetorical skills.

This disjuncture of requisite talents under different electoral rules is precisely what makes any kind of electoral reform such a tricky calculation. On the one hand, LDP incumbents wanted their party to retain a legislative majority. To the extent that the LDP's electoral base was eroding, many incumbents were willing to take measures – even drastic ones – to hold onto that majority. On the other hand, they most assuredly wanted to be ongoing members of that majority, and not to be replaced by someone with different, perhaps more appropriate talents.

Incumbents ultimately hold their leaders accountable to their interests, and LDP incumbents dragged out the process of electoral reform even at the cost of the party's viability. From the standpoint of incumbents, after all, losing is losing. For an incumbent, it is as deplorable to lose a political career on account of the party's reforming too fast – even if the party thereby renegotiates its lease on life – as it is to lose because changing demographics pulled one's constituency rug out from under him.

The clash of interests between LDP backbenchers in the Lower House and the opposition parties controlling the Upper House ultimately destroyed the LDP's electoral reform plans. Prime Minister Miyazawa, caught between a brewing mutiny within the LDP's ranks and staunch opposition in the Upper House, gambled in favor of taking more time to work things out. In the best scenario, the LDP could regain control of the Upper House in 1995. With a majority in both houses, then, the LDP could draft whatever reform rules it pleased.

Unfortunately for the LDP, Miyazawa lost his gamble. In December 1993 a proreform group, led by mavericks Ichiro Ozawa and Tsutomu Hata, had established a new faction in protest of the party's slow pace in implementing electoral reform. Contrary to Miyazawa's (and most other observers') expectations, this group, some 45-strong, helped the opposition parties in the Lower House pass a no-confidence vote against Miyazawa in June 1993 (*Nihon keizai shimbun*, June 19, 1993). The LDP lost its majority in the elections that followed a month later. In so doing, for the first time in thirty-eight years, it lost its grip on the government as well.

The motley assemblage of parties that replaced the LDP was poorly suited to govern for long. The defectors from the LDP as well as members of Hosokawa's New Japan Party favored deregulating the economy and opening closed markets. Ichiro Ozawa's book, published just before the election, stressed the need for Japan to embrace free trade and become a "normal nation" (Ozawa 1993). Without a majority, however, these defectors were forced to join with the Socialist Party, which over the years had actually become more rurally based than the LDP (Curtis 1988). But the one thing the parties agreed on – and the single pledge common to all their campaign platforms – was that the old electoral rules would have to go. They blamed the rules for corruption, single-party dominance, trade friction, and a host of other political and social ills.

For months, various parties struggled to dominate the governing coalition and haggled over how precisely to combine single-member districts and proportional representation. On January 29, 1994, the Diet passed an electoral reform bill similar to Kaifu's original plan – 300 seats in single member districts, and an additional 200 to be elected in regional proportional representation districts. That the bill so resembled the LDP's first reform proposal is not surprising given that the anti-LDP government lacked a Diet majority and therefore still needed LDP votes to get the bill through the Diet.

The LDP–Socialist combination that took control of the government in the summer of 1994 was more rurally based than the anti-LDP coalition it replaced (*Asahi shimbun*, July 7, 1994: p. 2). Now in a position to preside over the details of electoral districting, this government did its best to gerrymander the districts to shore up its rural representation. On the policy front, the government stalled on agricultural liberalization – much to the dismay of Japan's business community (*Asahi shimbun*, July 5, 1994: p. 5; July 6, 1994: p. 3).

Regardless of which party or coalition of parties controlled the government, however, the most important development from the standpoint of

Japan's long-term role in the world economy was eliminating the multi-member districts that engendered intraparty competition. It was this intra-party competition, and the vote-division strategy it put into play, that gave Japanese politicians a strongly protectionist bias. Instead, under the new rules, politicians would compete on the basis of party platforms. They would have a greater incentive to address issues that many voters care about than to coddle small groups of voters with expensive private favors.

This is not to say that electoral reform alone will eliminate trade protectionism. Depending on how the district lines are finally drawn, rural areas may retain some advantage. Moreover, even without the vote-division problem, organized groups typically are more effective politically than the unorganized voter-on-the-street in any representative democracy. Nonetheless, important barriers to political entry were eliminated, and political entrepreneurs will have an easier time shifting the debate to issues that more voters care about. In some ways, the institutional changes underway in Japan may resemble nineteenth-century England's. There, some years after the elimination of multimember districts in 1832, the parties reorganized and the once-protectionist Conservative party began championing free trade.[16]

IV. DO ELECTORAL INSTITUTIONS MATTER?
POLITICAL VERSUS BUREAUCRATIC CONTROL OF POLICY-MAKING

So far, we have discussed Japan's policy direction in terms of politicians' electoral incentives. The conventional wisdom, however, stresses the central role of bureaucrats in shaping the country's policy choices. To the extent that Japan's bureaucracy is insulated from the turmoil of elections and changing cabinets, electoral rules should matter very little indeed. In the next section, I argue that history is at least as consistent with the electorally driven as with the bureaucratic-control argument.

Recent academic writing acknowledges the growing influence of politicians over the policy-making process in Japan since the early- to mid-1970s (Krauss and Muramatsu 1987; Pempel 1987).[17] Implicitly, they suggest that, because LDP members seldom interfered in the bureaucrats' policy-making in the first two decades of LDP rule, LDP members would have wanted, but were unable, to intervene. These authors speak of numerous handicaps LDP politicians faced in competing with bureaucrats for policy-making control, such as inferior information, expertise, and prestige. This, if true, bodes ill for the political novices in non-LDP coalition governments.

Overt intervention in the policy making process by LDP backbenchers did indeed become extensive only from the mid-1970s, as the bureaucratic-dominance school argue. But this can be explained as easily by backbencher

Table. 1 *Prefectural legislature seats by party, 1963–1987*
(Percentages)

	LDP	JSP	DSP	KOM	JCP	Other
1963	67.9	19.8	3.2	1.6	0.8	6.7
1967	60.3	21.8	3.8	3.9	1.7	8.5
1971	60.6	18.5	3.5	4.4	4.5	8.5
1975	53.4	16.1	3.9	6.4	3.6	16.7
1979	53.1	14.3	4.0	6.8	4.6	17.6
1983	55.9	14.0	3.8	6.8	3.2	16.3
1987	51.8	16.6	3.9	7.0	4.4	16.4

Notes: The "Other" category comprises primarily independent candidates, many of whom were loosely affiliated with one or more of the large parties. The 1968 *Chiho jichi nenkan* breaks the independents into "convervatives" and "progressives" but does not in subsequent volumes, presumably because a growing number of candidates began to forge ties to both the LDP and the opposition parties.
Source: Chiho jichi nenkan [*Local Government Annual*]. *Tokyo: Jichi kenshu kyokai, various years.*

satisfaction with cabinet-led policy as by party ineptitude in the face of clever bureaucrats. LDP incumbents became less satisfied, however, as LDP leaders began to respond to the urbanization of the electorate. In its effort to win back its electoral ground lost to opposition parties in the 1970s (see Table 1 on Prefectural Legislative Seats by Party), the LDP began allocating a growing percentage of budgetary resources to the public goods sucessfully championed by opposition parties. The LDP undertook unprecedented environmental regulation, allocated more funds to social welfare expenditures, and underwrote an expensive national health insurance system (Anderson 1987; Campbell 1991; Krauss and Simcock 1980; McKean 1981).

While this shift away from private goods may have been politically necessary, it left in its wake scores of disgruntled LDP backbenchers. Incumbents had already made large, constituency-specific investments in building up their personal bases of support, and relied on the continual flow of private goods to protect those investments. Even though the LDP leadership calculated that a more generous provision of public goods would stave off electoral desertion of the party as a whole, the provision of private goods was still the most effective means individual members had of dividing the vote, and thereby of securing their own reelection. What *appeared* as greater LDP control over policy, therefore, was nothing of the sort. It was merely the grudging permission by the party leadership to allow greater backbench "cheating" on party policy and the continued provision of private goods.

I have argued in this chapter that these ad hoc adjustments in the balance between public and private goods faced certain limits. The problem for the LDP with a public-goods strategy was that they provided no way to divide the vote. The problem with a more purely private-goods strategy, on the other hand, was that urbanization made it increasingly costly precisely at a time when business supporters were eager to cut their contributions. Unable to undertake electoral reform, the LDP continued to tinker with policy change only at the margins.

In the post-LDP era, coalition governments will find it harder to steer the bureaucracy than did the LDP. But their difficulties will stem not from the bureaucracy's clever subterfuges and superior information; given the probability of being found out and punished, risk averse bureaucrats are not likely to gamble away their careers.[18] Rather, coalitions may simply have a hard time formulating unified goals in the first place. Bureaucrats, who still have to try to anticipate what the politicians want, find themselves with a job that is harder, not easier. Their room for maneuver is as constrained by politics as it was before.[19]

CONCLUSIONS

In assessing the impact of internationalization on Japanese politics, we have addressed three questions:

1 What accounts for the lag time in Japan's market opening?
2 What, if any, international forces are driving institutional changes underway in Japan?
3 What consequences do those changes have for Japan's future role in the world economy?

Although we identified important international pressures, we have found not a unilateral effect from international forces, but an interaction with existing institutions and electoral calculations.

Our answer to the first question pointed to both international and domestic factors. At the international level, there is little wonder that Japan did not behave as a "free trade hegemon," throwing open the doors of its markets to induce others to do the same. Japan enjoyed an even better fate in the wings of its free-trade patron, the United States. For most of the postwar period, the U.S. gave Japan access to its markets virtually free of charge and sponsored Japan's access to other markets. The U.S. began attaching conditions to Japan's access to U.S. markets only as Japan's success in world markets has become conspicuous over the last two decades. But for Japan, these conditions were still cheap compared to the costs of any conceivable alternative.

Domestically, the configuration of interests supporting the LDP had been changing for some time, suggesting that, all else equal, policies should have changed in tandem. The case of Japan shows, however, the importance of political institutions that structure and channel the incentives of policymakers. When institutions take on an independent force of their own – by, for example, creating barriers to entry into the political marketplace – they may generate policies that no longer directly reflect the balance of social forces.

In Japan, as in other democracies, the process of weighing the costs and benefits of alternative policy choices is essentially an electoral calculation. But it is also important how the electoral rules shape politicians' incentives. The LDP made domestic and foreign policy decisions on the basis of what its most important constituents wanted. Under Japan's multimember-district electoral rules, it was the campaign contributors and organized blocs of votes – most often producers of goods and services – whose interests were best served.

That brings us to the second question of how, if at all, international forces contributed to Japan's domestic political reorganization. Japan's case suggests that at some threshold, pressure for change – filtered through domestic interests – becomes sufficiently great to force substantial changes in the institutions themselves. But, as Haggard and Maxfield point out elsewhere in this volume, "it is difficult to assess ex ante when the accumulated weight of new sectoral interests will tip in the direction of policy reform" (p. 234). We do not fault the Frieden–Rogowski model for failing where no one else has succeeded. Absent many more cases to control for the myriad intervening variables, precise measurement will continue to elude us all.

Apart from Frieden and Rogowski's emphasis on international economic forces, we noted the importance of international political pressures. Japan's export sector, feeling increasingly vulnerable to the possibility of trade retaliation, urged the LDP to reduce protection of the least efficient sectors of the economy. The LDP obliged, if only at a painfully slow pace aimed at holding together a winning electoral coalition. Ultimately, the producer interests backing the LDP – the inefficient on the one hand and the globally competitive on the other – had become too divergent to stay together.

Along with the changing interests of the business community, the expansion of the urban "floating vote" in Japan added pressure on the LDP to adjust its agriculture and small business policies. Yet under Japan's old electoral rules, the LDP calculated the less predictable urban votes at a substantial discount. While the LDP shifted some policies at the margin, a wholesale embrace of consumers' interests was not a winning electoral strategy. In the final analysis, the LDP's steady pace of small adjustments got itself nowhere. The LDP's rickety coalition of farmers, small business, and big business crumbled altogether in July 1993.

The third question of what comes next is, of course, the hardest to answer. As Milner and Keohane remind us, it may be difficult to recognize fundamental changes for what they are until well after the event. Japanese politics will likely remain in transition for several elections. It will take parties some time to adjust to the new electoral incentives, and to assemble themselves into workable coalitions. What is significant for Japan's international economic relations, however, is that Japan is no longer governed by a majority party that uses a private-goods strategy to divide the vote. New electoral rules will pit political parties and broad platforms against one another, rather than reward individual candidates bearing gifts.

In the short run, Japanese politics may remain adrift as politicians and parties seek out their best coalition partners. The first pivot to emerge was a weak rural–urban divide. But this would be short-lived, because the new electoral rules substantially redressed the malapportionment problem. The LDP temporarily allied with the Socialists, its Cold War era foe, in a vain attempt to hold on to majority status. But both parties were destined to weaken, as the July 1995 Upper House elections showed, unless and until they could correct their rural bias and could forge platforms with broader popular appeal.

Whether or not the LDP manages to restore its electoral fortunes, the revamped electoral system will likely have significant consequences for Japanese voters, and for Japan's trading partners as well. For under the new electoral rules, parties must cater more to voters' interests, not because of any conversion to new moral principles, but because that is what will get them elected. Japan may sooner or later put lie to what journalists have flagged as Japan's "enduring culture of cronyism," its "tenacious xenophobia," and its "fundamental allergy to open markets."

Foreign governments should not jump to the conclusion, however, that Japan will soon become a pliant partner. In the first place, Japan's political parties will take some time to reorganize themselves around new, coherent policy platforms, as with nineteenth-century British parties or postreform Italian parties today. Secondly, the day Japan throws open its doors to free trade is also the day Japan unburdens itself of a debt of gratitude to the United States. Japan will no longer have to purchase American tolerance of its protectionism with cooperation in other spheres, such as financial backing for American security operations. The "normal nation" of which Ozawa writes is a more self-confident, self-directed country than we have seen in Japan for many decades.

PART III

Internationalization and Socialism

Stalin's Revenge: Institutional Barriers to Internationalization in the Soviet Union

MATTHEW EVANGELISTA

Our economy is supercentralized, overcentralized, and the outcome is a paradox. The whole world is striving to push borders outward. Thus, Europe is planning to open everything up in 1992 and create a single economic system. That is fundamentally correct. Why then are we here in the Soviet Union seeking to divide up into regional economies?
– Adviser to striking coal miners in the Kuzbass region of western Siberia, February 1990 (Mandel 1989–91: 7)

Western Marxists have long argued that the central paradox of unions is that they arise to defend workers' interests as defined by the capitalist system. It has proven extraordinarily difficult to persuade workers to define their interests in terms other than those set by capitalism – that is, to adopt a revolutionary rather than a reformist strategy. The same paradox holds true for workers under socialism: their interests are defined by and within the structure of the old economic system.
– Peter Rutland (1990: 322)

Among the major economies, the Soviet Union in the last decades of its existence was by any measure the least "internationalized." Even taking into account the problematic nature of Soviet economic statistics, the general picture is striking. In 1988 – at the high point of its international economic activity – the USSR's foreign trade represented a mere 1.7 percent of total world trade, even though, as the world's second or third largest economy, it produced 13.6 percent of world Gross National Product. At that time, the value of Soviet exports, as a share of GNP, was 1.6 percent. By contrast, the People's Republic of China, with an economy about one-seventh the size of the Soviet one, constituted a larger proportion of world

I would like to thank the following institutions for support during the research and writing of this chapter: the Michigan Memorial–Phoenix Fund at the University of Michigan, the United States Institute of Peace, the National Council for Soviet and East European Research, and the Center for Science and International Affairs at Harvard. I am grateful for comments on earlier presentations of this material received from participants in the Internationalization project, the PIPES seminar at the University of Chicago, and the Olin seminar at Harvard's Russian Research Center. I especially thank Sharon Werning for her outstanding research assistance.

Table 1. *USSR foreign trade by country group, 1955–1989*
(Billion Rubles)

	Exports to:				Imports from:			
	World	CMEA	OECD	LDC	World	CMEA	OECD	LDC
1955–9	3.8	2.9	0.6	0.3	3.6	2.7	0.6	0.3
1960–4	6.0	4.3	1.0	0.7	5.9	4.1	1.2	0.5
1965–9	8.8	5.9	1.7	1.2	8.0	5.4	1.8	0.8
1970–4	14.6	8.8	3.4	2.4	13.9	8.5	3.8	1.6
1975–9	32.7	19.0	8.8	4.9	31.6	17.6	11.0	3.0
1980–4	62.4	34.4	18.6	9.4	55.7	30.6	18.2	6.9
1985–9	69.0	43.9	15.4	9.7	66.0	42.9	17.2	5.9

Source: OECD 1991, from *Vneshniaia torgovlia SSSR* annual.

trade (1.9 percent). Exports accounted for 13.6 percent of Chinese GNP in 1988 (Feinberg, et al. 1990: 5–8). Foreign investment in the Soviet economy, even after Mikhail Gorbachev's reforms were well under way, was negligible by international standards.[1]

Yet the USSR had always been involved, albeit at a low level, in the world economy, and that involvement increased substantially during the 1970s as the country exported energy products and imported machinery and grain (see Table 1). Indeed the increase in Soviet trade from the early 1970s through the late 1980s is comparable to that of the OECD countries and the developing world (as, for example, reported in the Milner–Keohane and Frieden–Rogowski Chapters). The growth in Soviet foreign trade far outpaced the growth in its GNP (Tables 1 and 2). In that respect the USSR participated in the expansion of trade that constitutes the starting point for the analyses in this volume.

Three major qualifications are in order, however. First, the contribution of trade to Soviet GNP was so miniscule by the end of the 1960s that even a major expansion from such a small base still left the USSR, relatively speaking, a closed economy. According to one ranking of countries by the contribution of exports to their national income, out of a field of 126 states the USSR finished last (Samuelson 1990: 154–5). Second, the expansion of trade did not have the salutary effect on the Soviet economy that international trade theory or the example of other countries would anticipate.[2] The Soviet economy continued to experience long-term secular decline in all major economic indices, particularly in overall economic growth and growth in labor productivity (Table 2), despite the partial opening to the world economy. Third, the peculiar structure of Soviet trade isolated the country from the most significant changes in the world economy, particu-

Table 2. *Soviet economic growth, 1961–1990*

	GNP (%)[a]	Labor productivity growth (%)
1961–5	4.8	3.4
1966–70	5.0	3.2
1971–5	3.1	2.0
1976–80	2.2	1.4
1981–5	1.8	1.3
1986–90	1.3	n.a.

[a]CIA estimates Gross National Product, in keeping with Soviet practice, to exclude services that do not contribute directly to material output.
Sources: CIA 1988b: 9; Gregory and Stuart 1986: 331, 335; Ofer 1988: 15; Noren and Kurtzweg 1993.

larly the internationalization of production and finance. It was, in the words of two Soviet reform economists writing in the late 1980s, a "colonial" structure, whereby the Soviet Union exported raw materials and imported advanced-technology machinery (and grain). Thus, "despite the quantitative growth – both absolute and relative – of the foreign trade turnover in the 1970s and early 1980s, the Soviet economy remained basically closed, shut tight, since it was hardly involved in those profound qualitative shifts that characterized the development of international economic ties" (Shmelev and Popov 1989: 223–4).

These economists, and many other reformers, recognized that isolation from the world economy posed substantial opportunity costs for the USSR, particularly in the productivity and technological level of Soviet industry – as the theories of political economy outlined by Frieden and Rogowski would anticipate. Part of the impetus for *perestroika,* the economic reforms launched by Gorbachev in the mid-1980s, was the desire to integrate the USSR more fully into the world economy and to benefit from the dramatic international economic changes underway.

The institutional legacy of Soviet isolation posed substantial barriers to such integration into the world economy. Isolation constituted a form of "protectionism" that – while deleterious to the economy as a whole – benefitted particular interests, especially workers in industries incapable of competing on the world market, not to mention government officials whose very raison d'être was administering the closed economy (Hough 1986: 489–503). This observation is consistent with Frieden and Rogowski's analysis. Yet the institutions that insulated the Soviet economy from the outside world made it difficult for those domestic economic actors who might prosper in an open economy even to *recognize* that fact, let alone act upon it. This finding confounds the expectations of the political-economy approaches and suggests a more prominent role for domestic institutions than even the Garrett–Lange institutionalist framework envisages.

Described in these terms the Soviet example might seem an easy case for an institutionalist account of the relationship between internationalization and domestic politics. By contrast, it would appear very difficult for the Soviet case to validate the political-economy claim made by Frieden and Rogowski (Chapter 2) that "changes in relative prices have predictable effects on the policy preferences of socioeconomic actors" (p. 29), and, particularly, their behavior.

On the other hand, popular impressions about how the Soviet Union ended highlight the effect of economic competition with the West and the debilitating consequences of isolation. In the last years of Mikhail Gorbachev's USSR, and even more so in the first years of Boris Yeltsin's Russia, there was a clear trend toward increasing trade and financial liberalization. This would seem *prima facie* evidence that the political mechanism that Frieden and Rogowski postulate does explain what really happened. They argue that "exogenous easing" of trade should "increase the pressure for trade liberalization from individuals, firms, and industries that could compete globally – even in highly insulated developing and Communist countries." Moreover, "specific price shocks create pressures from particular potential beneficiaries and losers, even where governments have typically tried to shield domestic economies from such global price trends" (p. 42). Frieden and Rogowski repeatedly insist that their "expectations hold even, and indeed especially, in *very closed economies*" (Frieden and Rogowski, p. 34, original emphasis). Such strong claims merit investigation.

Before joining the dialogue between political-economy and institutionalist approaches to internationalization as they apply to the Soviet case, we must review the basics of the Soviet economic system. The first part of this chapter identifies the actors who controlled the main economic assets of the USSR and how they perceived and pursued their interests. It then discusses the institutional barriers established in the first dozen years of Soviet power to control the impact of international economic influences on the Soviet economy. I focus in particular on the foreign trade monopoly with its price-equalization mechanism, on the "administrative-command" system of central planning, and on a key political institution: democratic centralism. If this discussion has something of the quality of a primer about it, it is nevertheless necessary. Although the details of the Soviet economic system are well known to students of the moribund field of comparative economics, they are far less familiar to those schooled in international and comparative political economy, with its assumptions of market institutions, and, often, democratic polities. My discussion of the actors and institutions of the Soviet economy makes it appear highly unlikely that the politics of economic policy could have worked in anything like the manner Frieden and Rogowski posit.

Still, the international economy was hardly irrelevant to Soviet politics, even if it did not act in the direct fashion that some of the political-economy literature would expect. The next section of the chapter examines three alternative, but not mutually exclusive, interpretations of the role of internationalization as an impetus to liberalizing reform and ultimately as a stimulus to the breakup of the Soviet Union. These interpretations, drawn from various scholarly and popular accounts, resemble in some respects the Frieden–Rogowski model. The first argues that Western price increases in the 1970s gradually and indirectly infiltrated the Soviet economy and ultimately helped undermine it. The second describes how the "semiopening" of the Soviet economy in the postwar period created a "new, new class," which provided the possibility for a coalition in support of the kind of economic and political reforms that Gorbachev then attempted. The third summarizes an analysis of how international economic involvement of the Soviet bloc influenced the USSR's relations with its East European allies and helped determine the fate of the Soviet Union itself.

Ideally, a test of the Frieden–Rogowski hypotheses as applied to the USSR would draw on detailed information about the preferences and behavior of Soviet economic actors. Unfortunately, such information remains largely unavailable, despite the demise of the Soviet Union.[3] Thus, my critical analysis of the plausibility of these three interpretations of the effects of internationalization – which bear at least superficial resemblance to the Frieden–Rogowski model – must serve as an alternative quasi-test of their approach.

The concluding sections of the chapter focus on the energy sector – the main source of Soviet hard-currency revenue and the primary route by which the USSR increased its involvement in the world economy. First, by examining the regional politics of energy production I show how Soviet institutions hindered the direct translation of international economic stimuli into the kind of incentives for domestic political behavior that the political-economy literature would anticipate. Then I present a brief case study of the coal industry to provide a tentative discussion of the politics of class, sectoral, and regional conflict at a time of great economic upheaval, as the old institutions were dismantled and nothing much took their place. Here we glimpse some of the dynamics that the political-economy approaches would expect to see, but even so the institutional legacy of the Stalinist system maintained a strong influence on the politics of the coal workers' movement (as elsewhere in the former Soviet economy) well past the demise of the Soviet Union itself.

The chapter concludes with a summary of how Soviet institutions shaped the interests of domestic economic actors vis-à-vis the international economy and how changes in the international economy were refracted through Soviet institutions to affect domestic politics.

ASSETS, INTERESTS, AND INSTITUTIONS

Virtually all productive assets in the Soviet Union were controlled by the state.[4] This basic fact – the complete absence of private owners of capital – contrasts sharply with the situation in even the most closed economies, ruled by the most authoritarian regimes, elsewhere in the world. The "owners" of Soviet assets were those who held state power and monopolized economic transactions.

The Soviet "ruling class"

The "ultimate repository" of monopoly power was the Communist Party's Politburo (Hewett and Gaddy 1992: 20; Pejovich 1990). Responsibility for implementing its decisions was held by the Party's Central Committee, the government's Council of Ministers, and most directly, the State Planning Commission or Gosplan. Below the level of the Central Committee and the Council of Ministers an army of bureaucrats administered the Soviet economy. That these people stood the most to gain from the Stalinist administrative-command system and the autarkic pursuit of "socialism in one country" was apparent to observers at the very genesis of the system. Whichever term they employed – the cadres, the bureaucracy, the *apparat,* the *nomenklatura* – most analysts referred to essentially the same socioeconomic stratum. For Leon Trotsky, the cadres were "in their very essence the organs of domination and command. A cult of 'cadres' means above all a cult of bureaucracy, of officialdom, an aristocracy of technique" (Trotsky 1937: 238).

Although Trotsky chose not to identify the bureaucracy as a class, subsequent analyses explicitly did so. For Djilas, "the new class may be said to be made up of those who have special privileges and economic preference because of the administrative monopoly they hold" (Djilas 1957: 39; Winiecki 1989). In Voslensky's assessment (1984: 11), "these administrators completely comply with Lenin's definition of a class. And because this class plays the leading role in Soviet production and all other fields of social life, it is the ruling class, and the one by which all other classes are oppressed – whence comes our class antagonism."

Although Soviet society encompassed a broader range of diverse and conflicting socioeconomic interests than these characterizations imply,[5] we should not simply dismiss them as the hyperbole of embittered émigrés (Voslensky) or losers of élite power struggles (Trotsky, Djilas). Understanding the dominant role of the *nomenklatura* in the Soviet economy is essential to any analysis of how particular groups pursued their economic interests, vis-à-vis the international economy or anything else.

In the language of the new institutional economics, the ruling stratum of party functionaries (*apparatchiki*) and economic administrators set up a structure of property rights intended to maximize their rent from monopoly control of the economy (Winiecki 1989). In an extremely hierarchical system, their salaries and other perquisites (especially access to goods and services in short supply) were directly tied to their place in the *nomenklatura* – the list of positions requiring approval by Party organizations at a given level (Voslensky 1984). The *nomenklatura* structure operated throughout the Soviet Union so that even in a nominally federal system ultimate control of assets resided in Moscow.

A plausible case can be made that the ruling strata of Soviet society maintained their power by both insulation from and selective access to the international economy. For a time the approach also served as a strategy of economic development, with tightly regulated international trade compensating for shortcomings in a system aptly characterized as "bureaucratic centralism" (Arato 1978; Luke and Boggs 1982). These shortcomings included, most notably, lack of technological innovation (Amann and Cooper 1982; Amann, Cooper, and Davies 1977). Both as development strategy and as a means for maintaining political power, the Soviet approach sowed the seeds of its own destruction.[6]

Central planning and the foreign-trade monopoly

The two main institutions that sought to insulate the Soviet economy from the international economic environment were the state monopoly on foreign trade and the "administrative-command system" of central planning. The foreign-trade monopoly antedates the establishment of the command economy by many years. It was established by Lenin himself over the objections of Nikolai Bukharin and others. Lenin argued (quoted in Hough 1988: 11–12):

Our border is maintained not so much by customs or border guards as by the monopoly of foreign trade . . . no tariff policy can be effective in the epoch of imperialism and of the monstrous difference between poor countries and incredibly wealthy ones . . . Any of the rich industrial countries can completely break this protection . . . Russia can be made an industrial power not by any tariff policy, but exclusively by a monopoly on foreign trade. Any other protectionism is in Russia's contemporary condition completely fictitious – a paper protectionism.

As Jerry Hough (1988: 12) points out, "Lenin's policy was continued by his successors, but was really institutionalized and strengthened not by the monopoly of foreign trade, but by the planning system that was established in the 1930s." Particularly important was the fact that *prices were centrally*

*determined and used as accounting devices rather than as signals for alloca-
tion of resources.* Thus, the USSR was able to insulate its development
process from major international disturbances, such as the Great Depression. It certainly helped that, as the world's largest country, enormously
rich in natural resources, the USSR was in an especially favorable position
to attempt a policy of economic autarky.

Even when the USSR began to move away from autarky by expanding
its international trade after Stalin's death, it was still able to blunt the
effect of world economic changes. Unlike the case for open, market
economies, changes in the international economy did not affect the Soviet economy directly through the medium of prices. The central planning system was deliberately designed to cushion and delay, if not nullify,
the impact of world prices, and in many respects it succeeded. The so-
called price equalization system kept domestic and foreign prices separate by offsetting changes in the foreign currency price of exports or
imports through taxes and subsidies. Consequently, changes in external
prices affected the Soviet state budget, but had "no impact on domestic
prices, production or consumption," as a major international study recently concluded (International Monetary Fund 1991, 1: 363). Contrary
to its role in market economies, the exchange rate in the USSR before
1987 was used, like domestic prices, as an accounting unit and played no
part in the allocation of resources (International Monetary Fund, 1991,
1: 363).

The foreign trade monopoly was deliberately designed to separate Soviet
producers of exported goods and consumers of imported goods from their
foreign customers and suppliers. Soviet enterprises were subordinate to the
central planning organizations and ministries and were constrained to follow directives from the center rather than market signals from abroad. Ed
Hewett (1984: 13) explains how the Soviet system operated into the second
half of the 1980s:

Central control of foreign trade is an integral element of the entire system. No
Soviet enterprise of any importance has the right to export or import on its behalf.
It must go through its ministry to gain permission to import, or it is told by its
ministry what to export. The actual transactions are handled through a foreign
trade organization (FTO) that specializes in the products involved and is supervised
by the Ministry of Foreign Trade. The domestic enterprise that ships a product to
an FTO for export receives the industrial wholesale price, irrespective of whether
the product involved has a relatively high or low price on world markets.

Under the old system, prices played no role as signals for enterprises to
alter their production. If a particular enterprise produced a product for
export whose international price was increasing, the enterprise would see
no change in its own receipts. The additional profits would be transferred
to the state budget.

Two consequences flowed from these institutional arrangements. The bureaucratic structures intervening between foreign and Soviet parties to some international exchange often increased transaction costs and led to suboptimal outcomes – for example, Soviet firms receiving western technology unsuited to the task for which they had requested it. *As a consequence of the price-equalization system, Soviet enterprises had no incentive to export.* Material incentives – in the form, for example, of worker and management bonuses – were tied to plan fulfillment and standards for domestic goods were typically lower than those for exports. As Shmelev and Popov (1989: 221) point out, "export deliveries were paid for in the same rubles and at the same prices as deliveries for the domestic market, but they were far more bothersome than products earmarked for a local consumer who was not very demanding." Thus, Soviet enterprises preferred to fulfill the plan in products for the domestic market (Bykov 1988: 14; Ryzhkov 1992: 252–3).

Democratic centralism

Soviet economic institutions such as central planning and the foreign-trade monopoly clearly shaped the economic incentives facing enterprises and workers dealing with international markets. Soviet groups and individuals were further constrained by a key political institution – democratic centralism – according to which the Communist Party leadership enforced discipline through the *nomenklatura* system of appointments at all levels of the economic and political administration. Thus, *even if groups and individuals could clearly recognize their interests vis-à-vis the international economy, they could not always act upon them.*

II. INDIRECT EFFECTS OF INTERNATIONALIZATION

Despite the institutions deliberately created to attenuate the influence of international economic changes on the Soviet economy, several observers have identified indirect ways that internationalization might have influenced Soviet politics and economics. Here I discuss three. The first is mainly economic, the second mainly political, and the third both economic and political.

Internationalization, inflation, and the budget deficit

The barriers posed by the Soviet economic system to influence from the international economy have persuaded some observers that "the performance of the Soviet economy was affected little, if at all, by the international economic disturbances of the seventies . . . The principles of Soviet

economic regulation . . . effectively preclude the transformation of external disturbances into automatic, self-propagating internal disequilibria by
sacrificing microeconomic efficiency for the sake of full employment,
steady growth, and price stability" (Rosefielde 1980).

It is evidently an exaggeration to state that external economic changes
had no impact on the Soviet economy. Indeed some analysts argue that
despite the best efforts of Soviet central planners to insulate the USSR's
economy from the vagaries of the international market, in one respect they
failed quite dramatically. Even though domestic prices never reflected the
vast increases in the prices of key traded goods, the Soviet economy nevertheless suffered the same consequences as in the West – namely, inflation.
Although it did not always show up in prices, some inflation was –
according to this argument – imported into the Soviet system from the
West and eventually made its presence known in rather insidious ways –
most notably, through "hidden inflation," repressed inflation, and an enormous budget deficit.[7]

The basic argument goes as follows: Because it was a major exporter, the
Soviet Union enjoyed a substantial windfall of hard currency when the
price of oil skyrocketed in the 1970s. As a leading gold producer and
exporter, it also benefitted when the Bretton Woods signatories went off
the gold standard in 1970 and gold prices took off.[8] The Soviets used their
new supply of petrodollars to make up for shortfalls in agricultural production, resulting from a string of poor harvests, by importing wheat. They
also bought western machine tools and equipment intended, among other
things, to upgrade their oil fields and refineries.

Partly by design, and partly, it seems, by inadvertence, Soviet planners
did not allow the increasing prices of their imports to affect domestic
prices. One Soviet economist explained the psychology behind this practice: "In the Soviet planned economy, based on the balance method, an
approach took root toward foreign economic relations as towards some
residual sector, when imports served as a means of covering internal
shortages and exports were viewed as a necessary evil, seemingly just the
payment for imports" (Bykov 1988; also Shmelev and Popov 1989: 221).
As a consequence, there was no mechanism for bringing domestic prices
into line with world market prices. As Vladimir Treml (Treml 1980: 185)
points out,

The transmission of external disturbances is, needless to say, related to and dependent upon the internal planning and administration of foreign trade flows expressed
in domestic values. Strange as it may seem, the Soviet planning system operate[d]
without an explicitly recognized or separately prepared and executed national plan
of commodity exports and imports in domestic prices . . . there [was] no comprehensive plan showing the integration of foreign trade flows in domestic values with
the rest of the economy.

To the extent that the policy of isolating the domestic economy from external price disturbances was intentional it had strong ideological and pragmatic motives. At the most mundane level, the Soviet authorities were unwilling to raise the price of bread. Even though the price of U.S. Hard Red Winter Wheat – the main variety the USSR imported – rose from $1.54 a bushel in 1970 to $4.45 in 1980, the price of a kilo of bread remained at twenty kopecks from 1955 until 1991 (Moody 1991: 23). The planners covered the shortfall by introducing subsidies to make up the difference between procurement and retail prices.[9] They amounted to 29.9 billion rubles in 1982, and grew to 54.7 billion rubles two years later. The 1984 figure amounted to 14.2 percent of that year's state budget (Hewett 1987: 133).

The growth of the subsidies coincided with a major and prolonged decline in the price of oil on world markets. Curiously, the Soviet authorities chose to increase the price of oil for domestic industrial consumers – more than doubling it – just as the world price began to drop in the early 1980s (see Table 3). If the enterprises could not afford the increase, they simply passed it on to the government as a demand for further subsidies – they were not allowed to go bankrupt. The result was a central budget deficit. The government "financed" the deficit by printing rubles. Soviet citizens found themselves with more disposable income at a time when shortages of consumer goods were at their worst in recent memory. Even the black market – which, unlike the state sector, did reflect inflation in its prices – was unable to compensate for the excess consumer demand. Corruption became intolerable. The implicit social contract between the Brezhnev leadership and the Soviet people broke down (Millar 1985), and many of them were clearly ready for change long before Gorbachev came into office in 1985.

Yet, as Hewett and Gaddy (1992: 13) point out, the international economy was not good to Gorbachev:

Between 1985 and 1989 oil prices fell 40 percent – with virtually all of the decline occurring in 1986 – drawing down the average price of all Soviet exports to developed countries by 25 percent. Since import prices were stable (indeed, grain prices even rose somewhat), Soviet terms of trade with nonsocialist countries declined 20 percent during those years. The rapid reduction in the purchasing power of Soviet exports amounted to a windfall loss of approximately $5 billion a year during 1986–89.

Soviet planners financed the shortfall mainly by borrowing abroad, doubling Soviet net dollar debt in four years (Hewett and Gaddy 1992: 13; Ryzhkov 1992: 229–30).

The story seems consistent with the Frieden-Rogowski model, especially its hypothesis that "exogenous easing [of trade] leads to the 'import' of global economic trends into domestic politics" (p. 31). But how plausible is

Table 3. *Soviet internal-use versus world market oil prices, 1973–1987 (in dollars per barrel)*

Year	Soviet internal-use price[a]	World market price[b]
1973	4.63	3.39
1974	4.53	11.29
1975	4.77	11.02
1976	4.56	11.77
1977	4.60	12.88
1978	5.01	12.93
1979	5.21	18.67
1980	5.28	30.87
1981	4.77	34.50
1982	10.87	33.63
1983	10.64	29.31
1984	9.69	28.70
1985	9.46	23.49
1986	11.19	17.90
1987	12.45	17.82

Note: All prices are best approximations, intended only to demonstrate trends.
[a]The prices that Soviet oil-consuming enterprises paid for their oil (as opposed to the prices oil producers received, as in Table 4), converted from rubles at the official exchange rate for the given year.
[b]Official sales price, OPEC average (except 1973: posted price).
Sources: Hewett 1984; CIA 1986, 1988a.

it? Was internationalization responsible for Soviet inflation and the budget deficit? Inflation had important domestic causes, many of them inherent in the centrally administered "shortage economy," and exacerbated by the enormous amount of resources devoted to the military sector.[10] One need not appeal to the international economy to understand why the Soviet Union experienced inflation (Kornai 1992: 278–86). Likewise, the budget deficit had many sources besides the decline in terms of trade (Birman 1990). In fact, contrary to popular wisdom about the Soviet Union's perennially balanced budgets, the country's leaders deliberately ran deficits on several occasions long before *perestroika* – most notably in 1953–4 and again in the middle to late 1960s. These budget deficits were evidently not responses to international developments, but to domestic political exigencies – part of the coalition-building strategies of certain Soviet leaders (Roeder 1993: 151–3). Finally, in an economy the size of the Soviet one, with such a small portion of its GNP accounted for by trade, one would not expect external shocks – mainly sharp changes in prices – to have dramatic economy-wide impact.[11]

In support of the Frieden-Rogowski hypothesis, one might argue that the peculiar structure of Soviet trade made it more vulnerable to imported inflation than one might otherwise expect. In 1986, for example, Soviet imports were dominated by agricultural products (17.1 percent) and machinery (40.7 percent), much of the latter consisting of advanced technology machine tools unavailable in the USSR. The effects of increased prices in both of these sectors could have spread throughout the economy. On the export side, in 1986 energy products and raw materials accounted for 64 percent of Soviet exports (fuel and electric power alone represented 47.3 percent). Even though the authorities tried to protect domestic industries from paying the higher world market prices for energy inputs, the opportunity costs of subsidizing domestic energy use should have been considerable.

Thus, a quasi test of the "import of global trends" hypothesis yields mixed results. The story seems plausible in many respects, yet competing explanations based on domestic determinants of poor economic performance cannot be excluded.

Internationalization and the reformist coalition

Once Gorbachev launched his campaign to reform the Soviet economy he was undoubtedly hampered by adverse international economic developments (mainly, declining terms of trade). These, in combination with his own egregious domestic policy mistakes, ultimately undermined the reforms. Yet, according to some accounts, it was the international economy itself – or, more accurately, the Soviet Union's partial opening to it starting in the mid-1950s – that provided the original basis for the reformist coalition that brought Gorbachev to power. Alexander Yanov (1977) offers a particularly intriguing argument about how that came about – or, rather, how it would come about, since he wrote his analysis almost a decade before *perestroika*. I use his discussion as representative of the many accounts that associate the emergence of Soviet reformist politics with an economic decline attributed largely to isolation from the world economy, combined with a partial opening to the West during periods of détente. Such accounts would at first glance appear to lend credence to the more formal Frieden–Rogowski model of international–domestic linkages.

Yanov argued that the best possibility for reform of the Soviet system was provided by a potential alliance between the intelligentsia, the competent, well-trained enterprise managers, and the Soviet "aristocracy" – the privileged élite who would like to make their advantages more secure, even "hereditary." Yanov (1977: 3) maintains that "it was possible for these [latter] strata to appear only when the USSR became a 'semiopen' system, and when commercial, scientific, cultural, and technical contacts with the West began to expand rapidly." At that point they "acquired a monopoly on travel to the West," and became accustomed to Western consumer goods and a bourgeois lifestyle. This *"new,* new class," as Yanov calls it, perceived a need for economic reform in order "to pay the people for its privileges" by providing them "with at least a minimum European standard of living."

The new, new class should find common cause with the "techno-structure" – the talented managers and engineers who feel hobbled by the petty tutelage of the local Party bosses (the "little Stalins") and their allies in the Central Committee and state planning agencies, who are "caught up by the idea of the technological revolution . . . are ashamed of Soviet backwardness, its dependence on foreign technology, its humiliation" (Yanov 1977: 29).[12] These two groups would join with the Westernizing intelligentsia, many of whom were already by the 1970s expressing concern that the USSR was isolating itself from the global "scientific-technological revolution," and would fall behind economically if it did not integrate itself into the world market (Arbatov 1991; Burlatskii 1991; Hoffmann and Laird 1982; Parrott 1983, 1985). Yanov (1977: 15) identifies a common program of these three groups "that would provide for guarantees of privileges (for the positive segment of the élite), guarantees of the reconstruction[13] of the economy (for the managerial class), and guarantees of elementary human rights (for the intelligentsia); and that would make it obvious that there is an indissoluble connection among all these elements of a positive social system."

Yanov's analysis fared remarkably well in anticipating the reformist coalition that initially backed Gorbachev as well as the groups that opposed and ultimately sought to overthrow him.[14] Most of the evidence coming out of Russia in the wake of the USSR's demise – particularly memoir accounts of politicians, intellectuals, military officers, and managers in the civilian and military economies – seems consistent with Yanov's account. Individuals appear to have identified their interests much as Yanov surmised and tried to forge the appropriate political coalitions (Adzhubei 1989; Akhromeev and Kornienko 1992; Arbatov 1991; Burlatskii 1991; Cherniaev 1993; Falin 1993; Ligachev 1993; Mikhailov 1993; Ryzhkov 1992; Shevardnadze 1991; Shmelev and Popov 1989; Zaslavskaya 1990). Moreover, Yanov's identification of the international environment as a stimulus to domestic change seems plausible and fits the emerging memoir evidence.[15]

Yanov's account apparently shares many points in common with the

Frieden–Rogowski model: isolation from international competition producing technological stagnation; proponents of greater openness and liberalization forging coalitions against the advocates of continued isolation and protection; partial opening ("exogenous easing") leading to further demands for openness. Yet, in fact, some of the resemblances are rather superficial and possibly spurious. Whereas Frieden and Rogowski, for example, identify supporters of liberalization as *owners* of assets whose world market price is rising, Yanov identifies them as *managers* – of any sector, as long as they are competent and frustrated with the arbitrary control and "micromanagement" of Party *apparatchiki* and the Plan. Technological stagnation is certainly part of both Yanov's story and the Frieden–Rogowski model, but in fact it is part of any account of the failures of central planning, from various theoretical (and atheoretical) approaches. Finally, so much of Yanov's story is dependent on noneconomic factors – the lure of bourgeois lifestyles, of Western culture and travel, the value of human rights and individual liberty, the desire of managers to work in a rational, meritocratic environment. In seeking an explanation for *perestroika* from such accounts it is hard to give pride of place to the international economy, to disentangle the impetus for economic liberalization from pressures for cultural, ideological, and political reform – and that is probably how it seemed to the actors themselves.[16]

Internationalization and the end of empire

The third type of analysis that relates Soviet involvement in the international economy to internal political change concerns economic relations with Eastern Europe. Here again oil price changes play a key role. The basic argument holds that despite the dramatic increase in world oil prices after 1973, the Soviet Union continued to sell oil to its East European allies at concessionary prices – through the mechanism of a five-year moving average (Bunce 1985; Marrese and Vanous 1983). Thus, the USSR endured some opportunity costs for not selling the oil at the full world market value and for not selling it for hard currency (see Table 4).[17] Moreover, the East European communist regimes became dependent on the subsidized energy imports as a means of maintaining economic growth rates adequate to keep their populations quiescent. The recession of the early 1980s, following a period of extensive loans by western banks to the East European regimes, left the USSR's allies in precarious economic circumstances. The situation in Poland suggested that economic growth was a necessary, but perhaps not even sufficient, condition for maintaining stable, pro-Moscow regimes in the region.

With economic growth rates declining at home, and energy production stagnating, the Soviet leaders began to seek alternatives to the heavy subsidies they were providing to their allies. When Mikhail Gorbachev came

Table 4. *World oil prices versus Soviet producer and export prices,*
1971–1982 (in dollars per barrel)

| Year | Soviet prices | | | World prices[b] |
	Paid to oil producers[a]	Export to West	Export to CMEA	
1971	3.33	2.42	2.28	1.75
1972	3.63	2.42	2.73	1.90
1973	4.05	4.58	2.96	3.39
1974	3.96	11.23	3.29	11.29
1975	4.17	11.45	6.40	11.02
1976	3.99	12.31	6.68	11.77
1977	4.02	13.88	8.61	12.88
1978	4.38	13.41	11.15	12.93
1979	4.56	25.52	13.01	18.67
1980	4.62	34.76	14.59	30.87
1981	4.17	35.81	17.20	34.50
1982	4.14	33.00	n.a.	33.63

Note: All prices are best approximations, intended only to demonstrate trends.
[a]The prices paid to Soviet energy producers (as opposed to the prices Soviet industrial firms had to pay for oil, as in Table 3), converted from rubles at the official
exchange rate for the given year.
[b]Mideast Light Crude.
Sources: Hewett 1984: 135, 155, 163; CIA 1986.

into office, the possibility for a rethinking of Soviet policy became reality.
It is still not clear what exactly Gorbachev had in mind for Eastern Europe.
At first he seemed to favor a greater integration of the CMEA economies
as a way of boosting Soviet economic prospects; later he seemed to think
that allowing more economic contact with Western Europe, and especially
inter-German relations, would permit the CMEA to benefit from the transfer of Western technology and investment (Gorbachev 1987: 164–9). Whatever his intentions, the result of Gorbachev's policies of *glasnost'* in domestic politics and "new thinking" in foreign affairs was to take the lid off long
smoldering political and economic discontent among the citizens of the
Soviet client states. As communist regimes were first weakened – as with
the establishment of a "roundtable" coalition government between the
communists and Solidarity in Poland – and later overthrown, it seemed
only a matter of time before the demonstration effect would begin to work
in the other direction: from Eastern Europe back into the Soviet Union. In
that way, one might argue, internationalization of the Soviet bloc contributed to the disintegration of the USSR.

Clearly this case, as with the other two, illustrates some of the key points of the Frieden–Rogowski model, particularly concerning the economic distortions caused by maintaining artificially low prices as the world market value of a country's exports increases. One former Soviet official involved in relations with eastern Europe estimates that price discrepancies cost the Soviet Union the equivalent of six to eight billion dollars a year and that the effort to eliminate them and switch directly to a relationship based on hard currency was quite destabilizing for Soviet client states (Falin 1993: 451–2).

Yet Frieden and Rogowski's discussion of the political implications of such a situation bears little resemblance to the Soviet case. Whereas they would expect an increase in "pressure for trade liberalization from individuals, firms, and industries that could compete globally" (p. 42) – in this case, the Soviet oil industry – we find the impetus to change, the plan to reduce subsidies on oil exported to Eastern Europe, did not come from the lobbying efforts of officials in the energy sector. Relations with Eastern Europe, including economic ones, held major foreign policy implications. Decisions were taken at the highest level by the Politburo (Akhromeev and Kornienko 1991: 67–9; Cherniaev 1993: 81–2; Falin 1993: 451–2; Gorbachev 1987: 164–9). Pressure from regional or sectoral economic interests played no role. Indeed, as the next section argues, the nature of Soviet institutions constrained economic actors from pursuing – or even recognizing – their interests vis-à-vis the international economy, as theories of political economy might define them.

III. INSTITUTIONAL CONSTRAINTS AND THE PERCEPTION OF INTERESTS

Neoclassical trade theory, and the political models derived from it (such as Frieden and Rogowski's), would argue that the opportunity costs of Soviet isolation from the international economy grew as world trade expanded: "The easier are international economic transactions in general, the greater the social cost of sustaining economic closure for any one country, and the greater the social impact of global economic trends on any one country – no matter how economically closed the country in question" (p. 34). Even if they could not fully protect the Soviet economy from the vagaries of the world market, however, Soviet economic and political institutions continued to the end (and even beyond) to distort the influence of the international economic changes on Soviet domestic actors.

The distorting impact of Soviet institutions is particularly striking in the case of Soviet regional politics. Here a model that posits a direct relationship, not mediated by institutions, between the international economic environment and domestic politics would anticipate certain regional responses to changing international opportunities, as represented, for exam-

ple, by price fluctuations. Those regions that had the most to gain from
direct access to world markets would, according to this logic, be the most
likely to seek liberalization. In Frieden and Rogowski's discussion, this
expectation is qualified somewhat, when they admit that "in very closed
economies . . . massive distortions obscure the identity of potential gainers
and losers from liberalization." Yet they expect these distortions to matter
least in the case of regions that are rich in natural resources: "oil- and
uranium-producing areas of the former Soviet Union, for example" (p. 36).
Thus, the regional politics of Soviet foreign economic policy should constitute a fair test of their hypotheses.

Regional politics and the energy sector

The energy sector is where we would most expect to see the influence of the
international economy on Soviet regional politics. Energy accounted for 57
percent of Soviet exports to nonsocialist countries in 1985 (arms exports
accounted for a further 16 percent). Oil alone represented 44 percent
(Hewett and Gaddy 1992: 11). Within the framework outlined by Frieden
and Rogowski one would anticipate that as world market prices for energy
products skyrocketed in the 1970s holders of assets such as oil reserves
would seek to reap the benefits of the price increases. But who held the
assets? In the Soviet system, those who controlled economic assets in any
region of the USSR were the relevant ministers in Moscow, the administrators of Gosplan, and, ultimately, the Politburo. These officials did act to get
the best return on "their" assets – oil, for example – but within the limits
of their other objectives, such as maintaining stability in eastern Europe
and keeping inefficient domestic enterprises afloat by providing subsidized
energy.

Within the Frieden–Rogowski framework one might alternatively hypothesize that the regional economic authorities and enterprises would
consider themselves the rightful owners of local assets and seek to enhance
control over them in order to profit from changes in world prices. The
power of the central institutions was such, however, that regional and other
actors were largely unable to perceive their interests vis-à-vis the international economy – even leaving aside the formidable ideological taboo
against endorsing the market mechanisms of the world capitalist economy.
The central-planning system in effect set the agenda and terms of debate
about economic reform itself by its inefficient management of the domestic
economy. The first item on the agenda of any reformer – including regional
economic authorities – was weakening the power of the central planners,
reducing hypercentralization and bureaucratic arbitrariness. In short, those
whose interests might have been affected by changes in the international
market had first to fight against the institutions of the administrative-

command economy that prevented them from clearly perceiving their interests, let alone acting upon them.

The institutions of "socialist federalism" and the administrative-command economy constrained the pursuit of local interests but did not eliminate all manifestations of them. Nevertheless, it is difficult to argue that the behavior of regional actors in energy-rich areas came in response to external economic trends (changes in the world market prices for oil, for example) rather than as a function of the shortcomings of Soviet economic and political institutions. On the contrary, as Bahry (1987: 87–8) argues, "energy, fuels, and natural resources were a major regional preoccupation long before the energy crisis of the 1970s pushed them higher on the national government's agenda." Scholars have found evidence of competition between coal-producing territories and gas- and oil-producing territories for priority in the allocation of central investment funds, but such competition would exist in a centrally planned, shortage economy regardless of the international situation (Biddulph 1983: 41).

The Soviet authorities deliberately sought to limit the domestic impact of internationalization in the energy sector, as elsewhere, by relying on manipulation of relative prices. While the world price for oil rose manyfold in the 1970s, for example, domestic prices remained almost constant for the Soviet oil-producing enterprises from 1967 to 1982 (see Table 4). Although the artificial domestic price stability probably reduced the potential for regional conflict in the short to medium term, it had economic conse quences that weakened the system in the long run. As Hewett, Gustafson, and others describe, attempts at insulation from foreign market pressures undermined important regime goals in the energy sector and in the economy at large. Maintaining constant domestic oil prices gave no incentives to enterprises to conserve energy, for example, eliminated the potential payoffs to oil exploration teams for finding new oil, and stifled any initiative to improve energy efficiency through technological innovation (Gustafson 1989; Hewett 1984: 14). These consequences are precisely what Frieden and Rogowski would predict and identify as static and dynamic efficiency costs of closure.

From a political standpoint, the institutional constraints represented by the price-equalization system, government censorship, and other limitations on information about world energy prices combined to prevent potentially affected groups from pursuing or even recognizing their interests vis-à-vis the international economy in ways that comparable groups in an open economy would do. Note how this characterization of Soviet institutional constraints differs from the way Garrett and Lange propose to assess the impact of institutions. They focus only "on the mediating role of institutions between raw preferences and government behavior" (p. 52), and consider particularly the relative degrees of government responsiveness to changes in domestic preferences and the impact of independent bureaucratic agencies such as central banks. My argument about the impact of Soviet political and economic institutions is stronger. Central planning, the foreign trade monopoly, and democratic centralism distorted the actual *perception* of group and individual interests as well as the translation of preferences into state policy.

The Stalinist economic system, which persisted in its essentials up to the end of the Soviet period, may have been functional in its early years as a strategy for rapid industrial development and the buildup of military power and as a buffer against the pernicious effects of the Great Depression in the 1930s. By the 1950s, however, the institutions were widely understood (at least among the intelligentsia) to have outlived their usefulness and become a brake on Soviet economic development, even though high level acknowledgment of the fact came only in the Gorbachev period (Arbatov 1991; Burlatskii 1991; Medvedev 1974). In Schumpeter's terms, Soviet political and economic institutions had become atavistic and counterproductive.[18] Only when those outdated institutions came under attack did regional and other interests have an opportunity to express themselves in ways that one would expect, given the change in the world economy in areas such as energy.

IV. INSTITUTIONAL LEGACIES AND NEW OPPORTUNITIES

So far we have seen that changes in the international economy and the degree of Soviet involvement in it coincided with certain changes in the Soviet economy and polity – particularly a rise in inflation and the budget deficit, a decline in living standards, and advent of a reformist coalition. But it was not always easy empirically to distinguish international from domestic causes. I argued that international economic changes did not have a *direct* impact on holders of assets in the Soviet Union for two main reasons: because control of those assets was so highly concentrated in the political élite and because institutions mediated and buffered international transactions.

One way of evaluating the role of institutional factors as variables intervening between the international environment and domestic politics is to change them and see what happens. Happily, for social scientists, the Soviet case provides just such an "experiment." The elimination of the Communist Party's political monopoly, the initiation of competitive elections, and the prospect of privatization and deconcentration of economic assets should have had some impact on how the international economy affected domestic interests – even if the USSR itself had remained intact.

Some evidence suggests that the change in the Soviet domestic structure from the late 1980s did have an impact on the relationship between international, transnational, and domestic politics in other issue areas, such as environmental and security policy (Checkel 1993; Darst 1994; Evangelista 1995). In the economic domain we should anticipate the changes to be less pronounced. Privatization, especially of large industrial enterprises, proceeded slowly and many of the institutions of state control and direction of the economy continued to operate in the absence of feasible alternatives and as a result of political and bureaucratic resistance. Nevertheless, one should be able to detect some influence of the changes that have taken place and to anticipate the direction of future changes – if the transition to an open, market economy continues.

The coal industry

The coal industry in the former Soviet Union provides a useful case study for exploring the impact of changes in domestic structures. In its position vis-à-vis the international economy, it resembles the oil industry (see the discussion by Frieden and Rogowski of substitutive goods): during the 1970s prices for coal increased on world markets while remaining stagnant on domestic ones (see Table 5). Compared to the oil sector, however, much more is known about the coal industry in respect to how the relevant actors perceived their interests – for a simple reason: the wave of miners' strikes that began in June 1989. The strike wave and subsequent mobilization of workers' movements provide ample evidence – albeit mainly anecdotal rather than systematic – about the interests of those involved in the coal industry.

The case of the Soviet coal miners offers an opportunity to illustrate in some detail the interplay between the external economic environment and internal institutional legacies. The case provides evidence of sectoral, regional, and class conflict, and suggests some tentative support for the kinds of relationships that the Frieden–Rogowski approach would anticipate. It provides a particularly strong endorsement, however, for their acknowledgment that in very closed economies "massive distortions obscure the identity of potential gainers and losers from liberalization" (p. 36).

Regional differences. What makes the coal industry especially interesting is its regional variation.[19] Three of the major coal-producing areas – the Kuznetsk basin (Kuzbass) in western Siberia, the Donetsk basin (Donbass) in eastern Ukraine, and Karaganda in Kazakhstan – accounted for more than half of total Soviet coal production (Hewett 1984: 86). They differ in several respects. The Kuzbass has generally high quality coal in relatively accessible deposits. Worker productivity was high by Soviet standards, owing in part to substantial bonuses for working in Siberia. The Kuzbass

Table 5. *Soviet and U.S. coal prices,* 1970–1989 (*in dollars per metric ton*)

Year	Soviet prices[a]	U.S. prices[b]
1970–3	14.26	8.13
1974–85	16.35	25.17
1986–9	23.58	24.93

Note: All prices are best approximations, intended only to demonstrate trends.
[a]Steam coal.
[b]Bituminous coal and lignite; free on board, mines.
Sources: OECD and IEA 1992.

miners seemed confident that their mines could be run profitably. Already in 1990 they had signed export contracts with Japan and were agitating for self-management of their mines (Mandel 1991: 111). The Donbass miners were more pessimistic – with good reason. Their mines are, in Rutland's description, "old and near exhaustion, marked by deep shafts (in excess of one kilometer), high temperatures, narrow seams (less than one meter on average), high accident rates, and low pay" (Friedgut and Siegelbaum 1990: 6–8; also Hewett 1984: 88–9; Mandel 1991: 112–13; Rutland 1990: 293). The profitability of the Karaganda mines was also open to question. Moreover the quality of its coal – its caloric content – is too low for world market standards (Mandel 1989–91: 26). A fourth area – the Vorkuta and Inta mines of the Pechora Basin – is unusual in several respects. Located north of the Arctic Circle in the Komi Autonomous Republic (part of Russia), Vorkuta's climate is harsh and work conditions are severe. As a former "island" in the Gulag archipelago of prison work camps it has remained under the influence of the institutional legacy of Stalinism (Burawoy and Krotov 1992).

The economic policies promoted by the strike committees in the four regions appeared to correspond to their situations – as Frieden and Rogowski might predict – with the Kuzbass workers most enthusiastic about economic autonomy and regional self-management, the Donbass and Karaganda regional committees less willing to risk loss of central government subsidies, and the Vorkuta workers exhibiting the most militant and hostile attitudes towards Moscow and its local representatives.

Class conflict. Perhaps most revealing, though, is that all of the miners expressed the same criticisms and frustrations about the hypercentralized planning system and the inefficiencies and irrationalities it introduced into their work. Thus, in all cases demands for regional economic autonomy and control over local resources seemed overshadowed by, or at least conflated with, demands for less interference from the planners of the Party bureaucracy or *apparat*. The miners were less concerned about earning world market prices for their coal than about making their work situation tolerable by doing away with the absurdities of Soviet central planning. The point is that the influence of Soviet economic institutions was so strong – and pernicious, in the miners' view – that the miners directed their actions against the domestic economic system rather than in response to changes in the international economic environment.

Thus, if we accept the terminology of Djilas, Voslensky, and others, the initial conflicts were of a *class*-based nature: the workers against the *nomenklatura* class of Party bureaucrats. As the chair of one of the Donbass strike committees put it in describing the early protests in the summer of 1989: "These rallies were not directed against the Communist Party, as many are trying to label them, but against the apparat . . . not [against] the rank-and-file Communists . . . the ordinary Communists, but [against] the Communists with briefcases" (Mandel 1989–91: 16).

The opposition of workers to the *nomenklatura* seems compatible with the Frieden–Rogowski discussion of asset specificity. Many mines are located in isolated villages which function, in effect, as "company towns." The miners, by their skills, are very much tied to their profession (consequently, if they are located in one of the uncompetitive branches of the industry, their demands to the government usually include appeals for job retraining). The *nomenklatura* by contrast, has considerable flexibility in deciding where to invest "its" (the state's) resources – in this case, subsidies from the state budget. Under these circumstances Frieden and Rogowski would predict more class conflict, between the miners and the Party élite, than sectoral conflict between the coal industry and other industries, and this seemed to fit the Soviet case.

Sectoral and regional conflict and collaboration. Many of the miners recognized the potential for sectoral conflict and deliberately sought to foster good relations with workers from other branches of the economy. At the same time they accused the central authorities of pursuing a strategy of divide and conquer by portraying the miners as selfishly seeking advantages over other socioeconomic groups, telling "everybody that we were demanding specific consumer goods of which there are shortages" (Kuzbass miner, February 1990, in Mandel 1989–91: 8).

A natural reaction to conflict with the Party apparat and the central authorities was to pursue solidarity with other workers on a regional basis. Thus, in the Kuzbass the Regional Council of Workers' Committees that emerged from the July 1989 strikes eventually came to include not only miners, "but chemical industry workers, railwaymen, steel workers,

power generation workers, agricultural workers – the whole economy"
(Chair of the Kuzbass Coal Miners Strike Committee, February 1990, in
Mandel 1989–91: 8). A similar situation developed in the Donbass and in
Kazakhstan. Building coalitions between the coal miners and other economic groups had practical benefits beyond the expression of regional
solidarity. New, horizontal networks of trade and production were established to replace the previous, Moscow-dominated, vertical ones (Mandel
1991: 108–9; CIA/DIA 1991: 3–4).

Despite the efforts at intersectoral solidarity, some of the interests of
workers in related sectors were clearly at odds and probably irreconcilable
under the Soviet system. Higher wholesale prices for energy products
would benefit workers in the coal and oil industries, for example, but
would hurt workers in energy-intensive industries because profitability
would decline under the new system of cost accounting (*khozraschet*) and
workers' wages would suffer. In early 1990, threats of strikes from workers
in steel mills and pulp plants forced the Soviet government to retreat after
it had proposed to increase fuel costs to enterprises as part of a supposed
move to a market economy. At the same time, oil and mine workers were
demanding higher prices for their commodities (Rutland 1990: 314–15).
Such "ripple" effects (as Frieden and Rogowski describe them) on one
sector from price increases in another have become even more prevalent
under post-Soviet market conditions.

Given the unpredictable economic and political conditions in the coal
mining regions of the former Soviet Union, it is difficult to draw any firm
conclusions about the main locus of conflict or its determinants. Contradictions abound during a period of uncertain transition. As one observer put
it: "The miners are for marketization if it means they can get a higher price
for their coal. But they are against marketization if it means mine closures,
free rein for speculators, increased food prices, or the selling of state industries to private citizens or foreigners" (Rutland 1990: 318). Thus, while
much of the politics of the coal sector resonates with aspects of the
Frieden–Rogowski model, things are still too much in flux to provide any
reliable test of its validity. Developments since the break-up of the Soviet
Union suggest, however, that theories that highlight the effect of domestic
institutional arrangements may still be more valuable in accounting for the
behavior of post-Soviet economic actors than ones that focus exclusively on
international determinants.

After the fall: The post-Soviet energy sector

The end of the Soviet Union and the advent in Russia and the other former
union republics of leaders who espouse promarket economic policies
changed little in the energy sector. In Russia, two years after the demise of

the USSR, the "free market" for coal, for example, was hardly in evidence. The Vorkuta coal conglomerate (Vorkuta Ugol'), which consisted of fifty enterprises, including a dozen mines, received "state orders" (*goszakazy*) that required each mine to provide 83 percent of its output to the government. Only the remaining 17 percent could be sold through market mechanisms, such as they were. Coal required to fulfill *goszakazy* had to be sold at artificially low prices that did not cover the mines' costs. The difference was made up by government subsidies (Burawoy and Krotov 1992: 5–6).

Well into 1993 the Russian oil and gas sectors were still run as government monopolies. When Russian and foreign press reports indicated in mid-May of that year that the industry might be broken up and privatized in order to spur competition and increase output, the Minister of Fuel and Energy objected with the argument that "there is no more efficient industry in Russia than the fuel and energy complex" (Whitlock 1993). He particularly opposed plans to divide the industry up on regional lines. Eventually the Russian oil sector was transformed into an oligopoly dominated by a few gigantic firms, the most prominent of which is LUKoil. The state natural gas monopoly became a private company controlling 95 percent of production as well as the network of export gas pipelines throughout the former Soviet Union (Mursaliyev 1995).

Rather than break up the state energy monopolies, the Yeltsin government "privatized" them in a way that gave government ministers greater personal control over the energy sector than they had enjoyed even under the old regime. The key figure in the privatization scheme was Viktor S. Chernomyrdin, the former minister of the Soviet Gas Industry (Gazprom) under Gorbachev, and, since December 1992, the prime minister of Russia. Chernomyrdin, who installed a direct telephone line to Gazprom from his Kremlin office, engineered the privatization of the state natural gas monopoly in order to maintain direct control over its shares (Aslund 1995; Bush 1993; Erlanger 1995; Kiselev 1995; Mursaliyev 1995).[20] He helped insure that the domestic price of oil and gas remained well below the world-market price, so that he and his allies could profit from the difference when selling Russian energy products abroad (Aslund 1995). Chernomyrdin secured a controlling interest in Imperial Bank, one of Russia's most powerful, on behalf of Gazprom and LUKoil, the bank's founders (Mursaliyev 1995).

The economics literature on rent-seeking behavior, from which Frieden and Rogowski draw, has much to say about how political leaders with such close ties to the post-Soviet energy monopolies might act to further their economic interests. But some knowledge of the institutional legacy of the Soviet system would be necessary for understanding how the politicians came to achieve their dominant economic and political positions and what use they make of them. Chernomyrdin, for example, has used control of the network of gas pipelines to enlist support for his new political party (nicknamed the "party of bosses") among regional governors. If the governors refused voluntarily to join, "they received information from the Gazprom company or one of its branches about a reduction of gas delivery to the region due to debts" (Kiselev 1995). Such coercive behavior led Yegor Gaidar, the reform economist whom Chernomyrdin succeeded as prime minister, to claim that "the well-being of the regions depends on the corridors of power in Moscow rather than on common sense in economic policies" (Morvant 1995) – as it did during the Soviet period.

Concern that the Soviet legacy could derail transition to a market economy is not limited to domestic political rivals of the Russian prime minister. In July 1995, for example, Jacques de Larosiere, the president of the European Bank for Reconstruction and Development (EBRD), predicted that "Russia could become a distorted market economy centered on a limited group of powerful lobbies" if it did not address the corruption engulfing the former state monopolies and government ministries (Parrish 1995). Likewise, Anders Aslund, the Swedish economist and adviser to Boris Yeltsin, warned that "corruption in Russia's energy sector is so deep that without action it can threaten democracy and stability" (Aslund 1995). Clearly, much of the centralized, bureaucratic management of the Soviet era, with its attendant inefficiencies and corruption, remains. The behavior of relevant economic and political actors will undoubtedly continue to be shaped by that institutional environment.

V. THE SOVIET CASE IN THEORETICAL PERSPECTIVE

The evidence presented here offers some support for the "second image reversed" – that the international economic environment influenced Soviet domestic politics and may even have contributed to the disintegration of the USSR. Yet the strongest statements of the internationalization hypothesis find little supporting evidence in the Soviet case. Soviet socioeconomic groups did not react directly to changes in the relative prices of tradeable and nontradeable goods by organizing to pursue their interests; Soviet regional actors did not respond to increased prices for their exports by seeking greater control over them any more than they would have done in the absence of such price increases; Soviet republics did not break away from Moscow primarily in order to take advantage of world market prices and eliminate the opportunity costs of isolation. Indeed many of them are now clamoring for a return to the formerly subsidized energy that Moscow prefers to sell for dollars.

Another set of expectations does, however, seem quite strongly supported by the evidence. These concern the role of preexisting institutions in shaping the domestic consequences of internationalization. Such institutions were clearly present in the Soviet case; indeed, they were specifically designed with that purpose in mind – to limit the impact of international contacts by equalizing domestic and international prices, by monopolizing the conduct of trade in centralized, state organizations, and by allocating resources and making production decisions (including production for export) on the basis of plan targets rather than market signals. The institutions did for the most part what they were intended to do – up to a point. Ultimately, however, the strategy of selective access to the world economy backfired. In political terms the opening to the international economy fostered both mass and élite expectations that could not be fulfilled within the context of the old system. In the economic sphere, the fall in Soviet export revenues (owing mainly to decline in energy prices from the early 1980s), combined with increases in the cost of many imports, contributed to a largely hidden budget deficit. The decline in the terms of trade apparently exacerbated the otherwise domestically induced inflation that helped undermine Gorbachev's economic reforms and still plagues the Russian economy. Finally, in its relations with its east European allies, the Soviet Union's attempt to mix elements of the administrative-command system with the capitalist world's conventions of trade and finance offered no panacea and probably hastened the demise of the Soviet bloc.

The Soviet case reinforces the impression that, despite their theoretical elegance, political models derived directly from neoclassical trade theory are an inadequate guide to understanding the domestic politics of economic policy. Moreover, the evidence from the USSR suggests a need to go beyond the call for "supplementing an analysis of preferences and preference change with attention to the institutional context of politics" (Garrett and Lange). At undoubted risk to the parsimony of our explanations – but with a potential pay-off in validity – we must focus more attention on the sources of the preferences themselves.[21] Not only actors' strategies and behavior but their very goals are influenced by the institutional context. Institutions shape actors' perceptions of their interests, and, therefore, their behavior, sometimes even after the demise of the institutions themselves. The legacy even of such defunct and discredited institutions as Soviet central planning and the foreign-trade monopoly can continue to exert influence on actors' perceptions and behavior.[22] The subject of institutional legacies and the origins of preferences has implications beyond the study of political economy and certainly merits further inquiry.

Internationalization and China's Economic Reforms

SUSAN L. SHIRK

Foreign trade and investment policies have made a very significant contribution to the success of China's economic reform drive begun in December 1978. The momentous decision of Chinese Communist Party (CCP) leaders to abandon autarky and open up to the world economy came early in the reform drive, in 1979. The so-called opening policies, that is, to welcome foreign investment and expand and decentralize foreign trade, were not only extraordinarily successful in economic terms, thereby stimulating the growth of the domestic economy, but also evoked crucial political support for the reform drive from key sectors and regions and thereby helped sustain it despite serious obstacles for a decade and a half.

The question addressed in this paper is what role, if any, did the internationalization of the world economy over the past four decades have on Chinese foreign economic policies in the pre-reform era, on the initiation of reforms, and on the economic and political success of reforms.

Chapter 7 on the Soviet Union, by Matthew Evangelista, suggests that Leninist regimes are a "tough case" for demonstrating the impact of internationalization on domestic policy outcomes because the thick institutions of the Communist Party state prevent information about the international economy from reaching domestic actors. As a result of this self-isolation, the coalition of groups that gain most from protection against international competition, that is, capital intensive heavy industries, inland provinces, and Communist Party and military control organizations, are able to maintain themselves in power. The rapid growth of economic linkages among other countries raises the cost of autarky to the Leninist states who have adopted it, but almost no one in these states is aware of this cost. The history of Chinese economic policies during 1949–78 confirms the effectiveness of communist domestic institutions in blocking out the influence of international economic developments on policy-making.

Internationalization cannot explain why Deng Xiaoping and his allies decided to initiate economic reforms in 1978; discrete events defy definitive explanations. Although the trends in the international economy had over time increased the *probability* that China would initiate policies to open its economy, this increase was unobservable because groups were prevented by communist institutions from perceiving international opportunities for gain or from organizing to gain access to them. The immediate context of the Chinese decision to transform its foreign trade and investment policies was the competition for leadership structured by communist political institutions. The death of China's founding leader Mao Zedong in 1976 launched a contest to succeed him and motivated aspiring leaders to seek bureaucratic support by proposing policy innovations. Yet internationalization shaped the coalitional possibilities open to political entrepreneurs. Although an internationalist coalition was unable to mobilize on its own given the constraints of communist institutions, intelligent leaders, motivated by ambition, could mobilize one. Deng Xiaoping, along with his lieutenants competing to succeed him, took advantage of the coalitional possibilities created by internationalization. They appealed to the groups who would benefit the most from participating in the world economy, namely light industry, agriculture, and coastal provinces, who had an international comparative advantage offered by China's most abundant factor, labor.

Once the wall between China and the international economy was lowered, internationalization exerted a powerful influence on the reform process during the 1980s and '90s. China's comparative advantage as an exporter of labor-intensive products stimulated its economic growth and generated political momentum behind the reform drive. Predictably, opposition to the opening policies and domestic reforms arose from the capital-intensive heavy industries and the inland provinces which had been protected and subsidized by the closed system. The challenge of international competition increased the value to them of government protection. The government won over these "losers" with policy sidepayments distributed on a particularistic basis and by continued subsidies and protection of the domestic market which expanded rapidly thanks to the reforms. And before long, envy of the remarkable success of the labor-intensive manufacturers in coastal regions who attracted foreign capital and exported, motivated heavy industries and inland provinces to join the reform bandwagon and to demand greater access to foreign investment and the world market for themselves.

While China before 1978 tells a story of domestic political institutions prevailing over international economic forces, China after 1978 tells a story of how international economic forces made the reforms politically as well as economically successful.

I. AUTARKY AND THE COMMUNIST PARTY-STATE IN CHINA

Under communism, China's economic system was an extreme form of import substitution (Lardy 1992: 16). Communist institutions formed a thick wall isolating the domestic economy from trends in the world economy. The central foreign trade monopoly, administratively set prices, and a near ban on contacts with foreigners maintained autarky and effectively screened out information about changes in relative international prices and their implications for various groups within China. Extensive Communist Party control of society and a ban on the formation of interest groups would have made it impossible for groups to make political demands even if they could have known they were disadvantaged by communist policies.

For many years Mao Zedong's rhetoric of revolutionary agrarian populism disguised the true identity of Chinese and Soviet economic development strategies. Both communist parties were committed to rapid capital-intensive industrialization centered on steel and machinery, and both established economic and political institutions that reinforced a proindustry and antiagriculture bias. Once China's domestic development strategy was set, an import substitution trade regime naturally followed (Lardy 1992; Perkins 1968). Imports, largely of industrial equipment and material inputs, were targeted on building a self-reliant industrial economy.[1] Under central planning by material balances, industrial demand that could not be satisfied domestically (under rapid growth policies, excess demand was common) was satisfied by imports. The need to finance a particular level of imports determined the level of exports. A nonconvertible and overvalued local currency discouraged exporting and built a wall between the domestic and international economies. The only organization empowered to transverse the wall was the government foreign trade monopoly whose trade corporations handled all trade transactions and which subsidized exports with profits earned from imports.[2]

The big winners under the Chinese extreme version of import substitution were heavy industry (including workers as well as managers), inland provinces, the military,[3] and the central agencies of political and economic control, a set of groups we can call the "communist coalition."[4] The eighty percent of China's population who worked in agriculture were penalized by being cut off from world export markets which would have pushed the prices of their products above the low levels maintained by administrative fiat in China. Light industry and the more advanced coastal provinces were unable to benefit from their international comparative advantage offered by abundant, well-educated labor because they also were held back from world export markets. Consumers, in both city and countryside, were harmed by the administrative suppression of consumption levels and the denial of access to foreign consumer goods, as well as by the nonavailability of high quality domestic consumer goods.

Chinese political institutions reinforced the policy bias toward those who controlled capital. In the 1950s, Chinese Communist Party (CCP) leaders modeled China's economic and political institutions on those of the Soviet Union. These institutions embodied the developmental priorities also adopted from the Soviet Union, namely heavy industry over light industry, industry over agriculture, and production over consumption. The lack of democratic elections meant that citizen–consumers and the agricultural majority were disenfranchised. The Communist Party, and not the people, held ultimate authority. Within the Communist Party, industrial interests were overrepresented and agricultural ones underrepresented both in the general membership and the Central Committee. Politicians were accountable only to an elite selectorate of Communist Party and government officials that chose CCP leaders (Shirk 1993). The CCP Central Committee that was the core of this selectorate consisted of three main blocs: Central CCP and government officials, provincial CCP and government officials, and military officers. The top Communist Party leaders appointed subordinate party, government, and military officials, and these officials, through their representation on the Central Committee, chose top leaders, creating the distinctive pattern of institutional authority characteristic of authoritarian regimes that I call "reciprocal accountability" (Roeder 1994; Shirk 1993).

The Communist Party delegated the work of making and implementing economic policy to the government State Council and the commissions and ministries under it.[5] The voice of industrial producers was amplified in these government institutions. The State Council had approximately fifteen heavy industrial ministries, but only a few ministries concerned with agriculture and only two (the Ministry of Light Industry and Ministry of Textiles) for light industry. The clout of heavy industry was enhanced by its intimate ties to the People's Liberation Army; all but one of the six (later eight) of the machine building ministries produced military equipment and were administered by the PLA. The absence of genuine legislative institutions representing regional interests robbed the economically stronger, more populous coastal provinces of a political voice and reinforced a redistributive development strategy favoring inland China. The distribution of power created by these political institutions tilted policy outcomes toward the extensive growth import substitution strategy that China had adopted from the Soviet Union. In pre-1978 China, specific interest groups with privileged access had influence that was disproportionate to their economic capabilities.

The institutional arrangements for economic ownership and public finance also favored industry, particularly heavy industry. Heavy industrial ministries "owned" many of their factories and ran them directly from Beijing, while light industrial and textile factories were under local governments, and farms were collectively owned and managed. Without enterprises directly under their control, officials in the light industry, textiles, and agriculture ministries were treated as political lightweights and were discriminated against in the allocation of central investment funds. A pub-

lic finance system based on revenues from the profits of state-owned factories reinforced a system of administratively set prices that made industry
"rich" (that is, profitable) and agriculture "poor" (that is, not profitable).
China's institutional arrangements tilted policy-making toward rapid industrialization and import substitution, policy outcomes that worked to the
detriment of China's powerless consumers and peasants and benefited the
communist coalition of heavy industry, inland provinces, the military, and
central agencies of control.

Institutions shaped policies, but policies also had institutional consequences. The self-reliance import substitution policy put a premium on
administrative control and thereby strengthened the role of the Communist Party and government central authorities, an outcome that undoubtedly pleased CCP leaders. As the "owners" of capital, which was scarce
in China, party and state officials benefited from high levels of protection
and collected administrative rents from their authority to ration and allocate capital. The planners in the State Planning Commission controlled
all capital investment funds and determined which ministries and localities would be allowed to expand by purchasing domestic or imported
equipment. The separation of domestic and world prices gave the Ministry of Foreign Trade stringent foreign exchange controls to reclaim all
hard currency to pay for imports and subsidize exports.[6] To prevent massive urban unemployment under policies biased toward capital-intensive
urban industry, the central government enforced strict restrictions on
rural–urban migration. Import substitution may have resulted in economic irrationalities, but it enhanced the state's political control over the
economy and society. The bureaucratic organizations responsible for en-
forcing this control, such as the State Planning Commission, the Ministry
of Foreign Trade, the Ministry of Public Security, and the central depart-
ments of the Communist Party, naturally had a particularly strong interest
in its perpetuation.

II. INTERNATIONALIZATION WITHOUT POLICY CHANGE IN THE 1970

Trends in the international economic opportunity structure, that is, the
liberalization of international product and factor markets and the increasing volume of world trade that began in the 1970s, raised the opportunity
costs to China of its autarkic policies. Communist institutions, however, by
freezing in power the communist coalition and by preventing information
about world markets from penetrating China, thoroughly blocked these
trends from influencing Chinese policy-making until Mao Zedong died and
a contest to succeed him ensued.

As Frieden and Rogowski show, economic internationalization commencing from the 1970s increased the opportunity costs of autarky to all countries. Groups associated with a country's comparative advantage were particularly harmed by the deprivation of trading opportunities. China's comparative advantage clearly lies in its abundant and relatively well-educated labor. The opportunity costs of its closed economy therefore fell most heavily on labor and on labor-intensive firms, sectors, and regions as internationalization increased the shadow prices of their products.

Changes in the Asia-Pacific regional economy presented particularly attractive opportunities that were costly to resist for labor-intensive industries, labor-rich coastal provinces, and for China as a whole. Beginning as early as the 1960s, a number of developments within the Asia-Pacific region made economic participation in the region more attractive. In addition to a commitment to relatively free trade, United States grand strategy in Asia had long focused on tying Japan, South Korea, Taiwan, and to a lesser extent Southeast Asia to a growing U.S. market (Cumings 1984). Japan was the first to exploit this opportunity, but in the early 1960s, the East Asian Newly Industrialized Countries (NICs) followed suit: Taiwan undertook its outward oriented reforms in 1958–60, Korea over the early 1960s, and Singapore following its separation from Malaysia in 1965 (Haggard 1990). Competition from the NICs in turn spurred a wave of foreign investment from the United States into the region, oriented both to serving the local market and for export in sectors such as electronics. By the 1970s, Japan had begun to invest in the region as well, particularly after the rise of the yen in the second half of the 1980s. Japanese investment became a major force in integrating the region and in creating the "flying geese" pattern of economic development. Japan, as its currency and labor costs rose, transferred its labor intensive manufacturing offshore to Korea and Taiwan, so that it could move up to higher technology knowledge-intensive industries; a decade or so later, Korea and Taiwan, were ready to do the same, moving up the product cycle by transferring labor-intensive manufacturing to the next tier of countries, which included Southeast Asia and could include China. Japan, Korea, and Taiwan were ready to facilitate this upgrading process by investing capital and transferring technology to neighboring countries, especially one like China with a large domestic market as well as low-cost labor.

Despite the appeal of these nearby temptations, there was no perceptible pressure from agriculture, light industry, coastal provinces, or consumers to open China's economy to the region or the world. In communist systems like China, the authoritarian institutions of social and economic control block information about international economic trends from the groups who would potentially benefit from them. Further, the political disenfranchisement of such groups in communist institutions would have prevented them from demanding opening policies even if they had been aware of the high opportunity costs they were paying from closure.

So long as Mao Zedong ruled the country the possibilities for political change remained extremely limited. In communist states, political leadership roles have no fixed terms of office and the contest for power is constant. The "campaign" heats up, however, when an elderly incumbent appears likely to soon depart the scene. When Mao Zedong's health deteriorated after 1971 (Li 1994), the competition to succeed him intensified. Yet Mao's personal authority as the preeminent leader and his institutional authority as CCP Chairman were so dominant that competition among other leaders was oriented upward toward Mao rather than downward toward groups of second-tier officials. The best way to promote oneself was to bandwagon on Mao's policy positions, that is, to show oneself a loyal disciple, and not to differentiate one's policy positions from Mao's. During the 1970s, although according to Avery Goldstein (1991), the structure of Chinese politics was transformed from "bandwagoning" to "balance of power," aspiring leaders still tended to play up to Mao rather than proposing policy change. Sticking one's neck out with a new idea was too dangerous in Mao's China.

Mao Zedong himself was the only one who could safely initiate a new policy. In 1971, when the ultra-Leftism of the Cultural Revolution was in its heyday, Mao stunned everyone, in China and abroad, by opening a diplomatic dialogue with the United States. The motive for the foreign policy realignment was strategic rather than economic.[7] China's security was endangered by the military threat from the Soviet Union, which erupted into overt conflict at the border in 1969 and 1971 and by the war with the United States in Indochina.[8] For twenty years the ideological divide of the Cold War had prevented China from exploiting the leverage inherent in its position between the Soviet Union and the United States within the strategic triangle. With one bold stroke, Mao broke through this inhibition to enlist potential military support from Washington against Moscow by helping the U.S. find a face-saving route for withdrawal from Indochina.

Although Mao's reorientation of China's diplomatic and strategic relations had little short-term effect on the country's autarkic economic policies, it opened the way for their eventual demise. When the ban on contacts with foreigners fell, China's political and academic elites began to travel abroad and discovered with their own eyes the disparity between China's technological and economic backwardness and modern life in foreign countries. They were not surprised by the gap between China and the United States and Europe, but they were shocked and humiliated by the gap with Japan and other Asian countries to which they had traditionally felt superior. By the time of Mao's death in 1976, members of China's elite were agreed that national pride and the restoration of the Communist Party's prestige after the Cultural Revolution debacle required improving economic performance and raising living standards. Despite an elite consensus on the political necessity of economic progress and a narrowing of the gap with foreign countries, there was no agreement on the means to achieve them.

Deng Xiaoping expressed an opinion in the mid-1970s that economic isolation was detrimental to China's welfare and national security, a view that under the bandwagon politics of that time was lambasted by the radicals as typical of "lackeys and compradors in the service of foreign bosses."[9] Deng argued that China's economic backwardness put it at risk of military defeat by the Soviet Union. The way to accelerate economic modernization was to import technology, equipment, and managerial skills from the West; Mao's initiative to improve political ties between China and the Western countries, including Japan, had created a favorable international environment for such imports (Huan 1987). Deng's proposals for expanding trade (nothing was said about foreign investment) were blocked by his radical rivals, and he was purged again, not to return until after Mao Zedong's death in 1976. As a result of the backlash, foreign trade stagnated during 1974–7.

Mao's chosen successor, a politically weak and relatively unknown figure named Hua Guofeng, picked up on some of Deng's ideas about increasing exports and importing more technology, but colored them with Mao's ideological rhetoric of mass mobilization and tilted them squarely in the direction of the old communist coalition. The increase in world oil prices was a major factor in Hua's policy to base China's "great leap outward" on petroleum exports. The leaders of China's energy and heavy industrial sectors (which are concentrated in inland regions), the so-called petroleum faction, formed the core of Hua Guofeng's support. There was not an iota of market reform suggested in Hua's development strategy. To the contrary, Hua's vision was of a highly centralized stepped-up import substitution drive directed toward heavy industries and led by oil exports. The 1976–8 Hua Guofeng line can be interpreted as a reactionary response of heavy industries not just to high world oil prices but also to newly available information about the decline in the international shadow prices of their capital-intensive manufactured products during the decade. As a result of Mao's diplomatic opening, these industries came to recognize that the value to them of government protection had increased, and they therefore intensified their efforts to perpetuate protectionist policies by entrenching their privileged position in communist institutions.

III. LEADERSHIP COMPETITION AND POLICY INNOVATION

It was in this context that Deng Xiaoping sought to regain national political power and replace Hua as China's top leader. He developed an alternative policy vision that would help him build a coalition of supporters within the bureaucratic selectorate. Hua appeared to have the traditional communist coalition (heavy industry, inland provinces, military, central bureaucracies) in his corner. To create a reform coalition, Deng turned to light industry and agriculture, coastal provinces, and provincial officials. He appealed to these groups with a platform of decentralization, marketization, and economic opening.

The introduction of domestic market reforms and the opening to the international market thus can be understood as Deng Xiaoping's strategy to depose Hua and win the contest for leadership succession, although like any politician in any country, Deng no doubt also believed that the policies he espoused were in the national interest. Reform initiatives in communist countries must come from above, from the first tier of elites trying to build constituencies among the second tier who constitute the selectorate. Communist institutions preclude overt demands for policy innovation from below by disenfranchising society and by prohibiting bureaucrats from ministries, provinces, and so on at the second tier and lower from forming blocs to press for change.[10,11] Because there is no separate sphere of open political competition such as elections, the contest for power is piggybacked on the policy process within the bureaucracy. Power and policy are completely intertwined in a style of politics that T. H. Rigby has described as "crypto-politics" (Rigby 1964).

Deng Xiaoping's challenge to Hua Guofeng received an unexpected boost at the end of 1978 when estimates of Chinese oil reserves were revised downward and commitments to import plants and expand heavy industry could not be sustained (Cumings 1989: 210). The 1978 annual plan, which had been based on overly optimistic projections of oil production, essentially collapsed. Having made the decision to open the door to technology imports, the Chinese leaders suddenly realized that they had almost nothing other than oil to export for hard currency. A sense of economic crisis pervaded meetings of party leaders.

Deng Xiaoping took advantage of the economic crisis to discredit Hua Guofeng and weaken the heavy industry czars from the petroleum faction who dominated the central government. His platform, introduced at the Third Plenum of the Eleventh Central Committee in December 1978, consisted of (1) decentralization and gradual marketization of the domestic economy and (2) foreign economic policies that welcomed foreign investment and promoted exports of light industrial manufactured goods. Deng Xiaoping and his advisers may have understood from their recent travels abroad that the foreign economic plank of the platform would generate momentum behind the domestic reforms because the rapid economic growth in Hong Kong, Japan, and the East Asian NICs had enlarged regional markets for labor-intensive light industrial goods[12] and these countries were willing to transfer capital and technology to China.

The new foreign economic approach made excellent political sense from

Deng's perspective. It allowed Deng to tap the support of the natural beneficiaries of the open policy, namely light industry and agriculture, coastal provinces, and provincial officials and make an end run around the central planners and industrial bureaucrats who had perpetuated import substituting self-reliance. While Deng's reform initiatives may not have represented a self-conscious strategy, in the context of Chinese political institutions and the pressures exerted by the world economy, they were the route that worked politically – for consolidation of his own rule and for building a coalition behind the reform drive. The core components of Deng's open policy,[13] introduced in a series of policy initiatives over the decade after 1978, were the following:

- The expansion of exports, particularly of light industrial manufactured goods, by decentralizing and making more incentive compatible foreign trade administration. The monopoly of the central foreign trade ministry (called MOFTEC, or the Ministry of Foreign Trade and Economic Cooperation, in its current incarnation) was smashed and trading authority dispersed among various ministries and provinces, who also were allowed to retain a proportion of their foreign exchange earnings. Collective township and village enterprises (TVEs) located in the countryside were encouraged to export.
- The acquisition of foreign technology, investment, and managerial and international marketing know-how through joint ventures. To attract foreign investment, approval authority was decentralized to ministry and provincial officials.
- The creation of Special Economic Zones in the coastal provinces of Guangdong and Fujian authorized to offer concessionary terms to foreign investors.

IV. DOMESTIC POLITICAL INSTITUTIONS AND REFORM STRATEGIES

Succession competition may have created the opening for Deng Xiaoping to initiate foreign economic reforms, but why wasn't their implementation blocked by communist bureaucrats? How could China carry out foreign economic reforms without altering the political institutions that empowered the communist coalition, not the potential beneficiaries of reform? The answer is that the Chinese version of communism proved to be more flexible than the Soviet version because in China, political and economic authority was more decentralized and less institutionalized than in the Soviet Union. In the context of Chinese political institutions, it was possible to break down reforms into particularistic benefits for Chinese officials and thereby give them new vested interests in reform.

Under Mao Zedong, Chinese central control over economic life was never as extensive or effective as in the USSR itself, and the role of local government was stronger. Mao pioneered the political strategy of "playing to the provinces" later adopted by Deng Xiaoping to promote economic reform. In the Great Leap Forward (1958) and the Cultural Revolution (1966–9), Mao sought to overcome the resistance of stodgy central bureaucrats to his vision of accelerated growth and revolutionary collectivism and egalitarianism by promising provincial officials more authority and resources and by expanding the bloc of provincial officials in the Central Committee. In China, as a result of Mao's initiatives, a substantial share of economic activity went on outside the national plan and much of it was administered at the provincial level. The central party-state bureaucracies were a less formidable obstacle to market reforms, and previous waves of administrative decentralization created the possibility that provincial politicians could become a reformist counterweight to the more conservative center. Although these provincial politicians are appointed by the central Communist Party organization, under reciprocal accountability they also have the leverage of a key constituency in the selectorate.

China also was way behind the Soviet Union in giving institutions and not personalities the authority to make decisions.[14] The Central Committee of the Soviet Communist Party definitively established its authority to choose party leaders in 1957; although the CCP Central Committee has the same constitutional powers, its actual authority is still shared with other party elites, some of whom are retired elders who do not even hold official posts. The locus of authority is ambiguous because it is actually moving from an informal group of revolutionary elders to the collective institutions of the Communist Party. In the Soviet Union, the preeminent leader's authority to dispense patronage and determine the membership of the Central Committee was highly constrained by the collective norms of the party; in China, Deng Xiaoping had much more latitude to dispense patronage and shape the Central Committee, and he used it to build support for himself and reform.

The looser, less institutionalized character of Chinese communist institutions made it more feasible for China than for the Soviet Union to introduce economic reforms without radical changes in the political rules of the game. Because reform policies had to be processed through the communist party-state bureaucracy, however, they emerged in a distinctive form.

As noted below, once the wall between China and the world economy was partially dismantled, international economic forces evoked positive domestic responses to China's reform drive. These responses were channeled in distinct ways, however, by China's communist political organizations that were left in place. The trajectory of reform policies that was the result of this confluence of international economic forces and domestic political institutions sets China apart from other communist countries. Chinese-style economic reform was characterized by gradualism, administrative decentralization, and particularistic contracting.

Gradualism

To avoid antagonizing the powerful communist coalition, reforms were introduced gradually. Instead of attacking the perquisites and powers of the central planning and trade agencies and industrial ministries head-on, reformist leaders encircled the government bureaucracies by creating new forms of business exempt from normal state rules, such as private, collective, and joint venture firms and the Special Economic Zones. A two-track system was created, and producers were drawn away from the plan by the higher prices and foreign exchange earnings in the market track. The plan continued to exist, but the economy was allowed to outgrow the plan (Naughton 1995). State enterprises were permitted to participate in the market track after they met their plan quotas. Officials who served as gatekeepers to the more lucrative market track were able to reap personal political and economic rewards.

Reformist leaders were also careful to coopt key individuals and groups in the communist coalition with sidepayments to obtain their acquiescence to reform. Heavy industries continued to receive priority in allocations of central state investment, and inland provinces still received their fiscal subsidies. The energy industries were pleased by the continued promotion of oil exports (international oil prices didn't drop until the mid-1980s), by offshore exploration financed by foreign oil companies, and by large foreign investments in coal. Central authorities made special efforts to attract foreign investment to modernize China's manufacturers of aircraft, automotive vehicles, and other heavy equipment.[15] When preferential foreign exchange retention rights were granted to coastal provinces, they were extended to several poor inland provinces at the same time. The exports of military industries were highly subsidized by preferential foreign exchange retention rights. The children of senior leaders, including conservative leaders who were potential opponents of the opening policies, were allowed and even encouraged to pursue careers in foreign trade companies where they made fortunes trading on their high level influence.

The strategy of gradualism also involved protecting the domestic market from being flooded by foreign products and destroying China's dinosaur heavy industries. Only when Deng and other proreform leaders decided in 1992 that entrance to GATT was essential to realize their economic goals, did they agree to open the domestic market to a substantial flow of imports. (Implementation of market opening agreements remained problematic.) Despite continued protection against international competition, over time Chinese industry became more competitive due to new challenges from domestic private, collective, and joint venture enterprises.

Administrative decentralization

China's foreign economic reforms primarily involved administrative decentralization to local governments, with little economic decentralization down to the firm level. Authority to manage foreign trade, approve foreign investment projects, and control hard currency were devolved to lower level officials, not to managers themselves. China's open policy involved ending the central foreign trade monopoly and dispersing authority to various bureaucratic actors, but it was by no means true trade liberalization. The provincial officials who were a key constituency in the selectorate were the prime beneficiaries.

Previous waves of devolution of economic administration down to provinces and cities had left them with planning and financial authority over all of the light industrial plants located within their territory. Although some heavy industrial factories were also sent down to local administration, the largest and most capital-intensive heavy industrial factories were administered directly by central ministries. Even before the recent reforms, therefore, local officials and light industrial managers had worked closely together. The reforms served to strengthen the identity of interests between them.

The decentralization of fiscal revenues early in the reform drive (1980) gave provincial and lower level officials new incentives to develop their local industries; and the devolution of foreign exchange retention rights gave these officials incentives to increase exports. Building on their close ties to local enterprises, these officials turned into bureaucratic entrepreneurs who promoted the outward orientation, technological upgrading, and expansion of local industries.[16] As the central plan and the center's share of total investment shrunk gradually, local governments became less dependent on Beijing and turned outside of China for capital, material inputs, and markets. The natural beneficiaries of this process were the coastal provinces where China's labor force is concentrated; where labor is better educated; where most of the prior light industry was located; and where memories of precommunist era commercial ties with the world still exist.

Particularistic contracting

A key feature of China's approach to economic reform, both in the domestic and foreign sectors, was what I call "particularistic contracting." New arrangements for foreign trade and investment, like those for domestic industrial management and finance, were negotiated for each unit (province, locality, or firm). First, a small number of units were chosen to be reform "experiments" that were not only allowed new freedoms but also were blessed with other preferential treatment to guarantee that the "experiment" was successful.[17] Naturally, other units demanded the same deal. As the scope of reforms expanded, party and government officials at every level from the center down to the county gave out generous reform contracts to build factions of grateful clients. Reform proposals that applied standardization formulas to each unit were consistently rejected in favor of proposals that applied different rules to each. The particularistic contracting model of economic reform was politically successful in the context of Chinese political institutions because it mimicked the familiar pattern by which production, supply, and trade quotas were bargained out and political support networks built under traditional central planning. Moreover, particularistic contracting reforms were embraced because they were a way to make inherently redistributive reforms non-(or less-) redistributive; enterprises and localities could make sure they were no worse off by implementing reforms. The patrimonial style of Chinese communist politics (which was caused as much by the absence of institutional checks on patronage within the CCP as by the persistence of Chinese cultural tradition) proved to be an advantage in building bureaucratic support for the reform drive. Chinese style economic reform was successful in large part because its particularistic contracting form generated political resources for communist politicians from Deng on down.

Gradualism, decentralization, and particularism were the means by which reformist politicians, operating in Chinese communist institutions, took advantage of the positive responses to economic opening from the groups linked to China's abundant labor and appeased the groups linked to capital who were hurt by it. Moving forward on economic reform before political reform had some real advantages. Authoritarian politicians were able to credibly commit sidepayments to previously favored and protected groups like inland provinces and heavy industrial ministries to help ease the costs of transition; a system of particularistic contracting was better for the losers under the open policy than would have been the anarchy of the market. By the time the pressures for political reform build to the point that China expands the political arena to include elected representatives who might push for protection and reregulation, the rigors of domestic and intellectual competition will have further enhanced the competitiveness of Chinese industry so that the demand for protection will be weaker.

V. INTERNATIONALIZATION AND THE REFORM BANDWAGON

Once Deng Xiaoping and his allies laid out the general orientation of the reforms, the domestic response was rapid and largely positive. By combining economic opening with marketization of the domestic economy, reformist leaders tapped a tremendous reservoir of economic dynamism and political support. Once the wall dividing China from the world economy came down, the Frieden–Rogowski model describes very well what happened. The groups whose interests were linked with labor (light industry, agriculture, coastal provinces, and local officials) rushed to take advantage of foreign business opportunities. Foreign investors, most notably Chinese businesspeople from Hong Kong, Singapore, Taiwan, and Southeast Asia, but Americans, Japanese, Europeans, and South Koreans as well, swarmed into China to establish joint ventures, attracted by the size of China's domestic market and its abundant labor. Total foreign investment went from almost nothing in 1978 to approximately $60 billion in 1993 (Lardy 1994: 632). Labor intensive manufactured exports took off, growing from 33 percent of China's total exports in 1965 to 74 percent in 1990 (China: Foreign Trade Reform 1994). China between 1979 and 1993 increased its exports at an average annual rate of 16.1 percent and became the tenth largest exporter in the world (Lardy 1994: 30–7).

Labor-intensive light industry and coastal areas made so much money by selling abroad and drawing in foreign capital that everyone wanted to follow them, even the heavy industries and inland provinces that had begun as opponents of the open policies. Compared with coastal China, inland China is disadvantaged vis-à-vis the international economy by its less abundant labor; compared with other countries, however, inland China may still have a comparative advantage. Strategic business alliances with coastal regions, moreover, have enabled inland provinces to share in the benefits of the open policies. Although sniping by conservative opponents of reform within the Communist Party agencies of control never entirely disappeared,[18] the bureaucratic support for reforms snowballed over the decade. By the 1990s, the bureaucratic coalition for the open policy had grown beyond the core groups of light industry and agriculture, local officials, and coastal provinces to include even many inland provinces and heavy industries. Foreign firms and governments were also an important element in the domestic political coalition promoting opening. The political momentum was to extend the deregulation and marketization of foreign economic relations, not to restore central control and self-reliance. The open policy had become irreversible, locked in by strong bureaucratic support.

The dramatic economic success of the Chinese economic reforms was stimulated by the advantages of backwardness in international competition. China's low-tech industries with their abundant supplies of unskilled labor and simple forms of organization were able to respond immediately and efficiently to international demand and capture large shares of export markets. Soviet industries, on the other hand, are more technologically sophisticated, organizationally complex, and depend on more highly educated manpower; therefore, they respond more slowly and with greater adjustment costs to new international opportunities. The comparatively easy, rapid adjustment of China's labor-intensive industries to global competition may not explain the timing of China's reform drive or its choice of reform policies, but it does help us understand why once these policies were enacted, China's economy took off.[19] Economic success, of course, translates into political support for reforms by generating resources to reduce the costs of transition and by vindicating the policy choices of reformist leaders.

The creation of special economic zones illustrates the way domestic demand for access to the international economy built a reform bandwagon in China. In 1979, the CCP authorized special trade and investment measures for two coastal provinces, Guangdong and Fujian, and allowed the provinces to create special zones to attract foreign investors. The zones were allowed to offer concessionary tax, rents, and so on to potential investors. The zones also were allowed to escape almost completely from the old planning system and come close to establishing a market economy. At first, only four special economic zones (SEZs) were established, three in Guangdong (Shenzhen, Zhuhai, and Shantou) and one in Fujian (Xiamen).[20]

The economic rationale for the establishment of export-processing zones, resembling those previously created in Korea, Taiwan, and other developing countries in the 1960s and 70s, in labor-rich coastal China was obvious. As noted earlier, the industrialized East Asian nations were ready to transfer investment funds and technology to China as part of their effort to shift offshore their labor intensive production of light manufactures. They were eager, moreover, to penetrate the massive China market which had for so long been closed to them. Another potential asset for China was the capital in the hands of the Chinese living outside of the Mainland, the so-called overseas Chinese. The special economic zones were located in South China, near Hong Kong, Taiwan, and Singapore, and the original home of most of the overseas Chinese. The zones enabled China to take advantage of these sources of international capital to spur its development efforts.

The creation of the SEZs also had a political logic in the context of communist leadership succession. Deng Xiaoping was just beginning to consolidate his power after supplanting Hua Guofeng as national leader. Drastic reforms which would not have been acceptable to the conservative elders and members of the communist coalition if implemented on a wide scale, could be sold if they were limited to a small number of experimental points (Crane 1990: 28–9). Deng also could argue to the conservatives that locating special zones in direct proximity to Hong Kong and Taiwan would help reassure these two areas about reunification (Crane 1991: 37).[21]

By limiting special zone status to only four locations, Deng Xiaoping and other communist leaders were also able to exploit the political advantages of particularism for building support for the reforms and themselves. Deng Xiaoping may not have initiated the SEZ policy, but he soon became personally associated with it (Naughton 1993: 509). Special zone status involved generous fiscal and foreign exchange revenue contracts for the provinces of Guangdong and Fujian. Extending special privileges to these geographic areas earned Deng political credit with the provincial authorities.

Geographic particularism proved to be a potent strategy for reorienting local officials away from self-reliance and toward the world economy. The economic dynamism stimulated in the SEZs by the special subsidies and freedoms they were granted naturally sparked envy among other less fortunate regions. Shanghai, which had always considered itself China's economic capital, fiercely resented the preferential treatment given to the zones.[22] (Deng Xiaoping later admitted that he had erred in not making Shanghai a special zone.[23]) At the outset, inland provinces objected to the widening of the economic gap between themselves and the SEZs on the coast. The regions who felt left behind responded in three different ways. At first, they tried to sabotage the SEZs and the open policy with ideological attacks on them for selling out the country to the foreigners and tolerating corruption and cultural decadence (Crane 1990: 36).

Over time, however, the other regions tried to get some benefit from the open zones, even if it was a trickle compared to what the coastal areas got. Inland provinces tried to win a piece of the action by setting up businesses in the zones, mainly in Shenzhen. With its market economy and access to foreign funds and markets, Shenzhen became an important domestic trade entrepot where firms could buy and sell steel, cars, consumer goods, and almost anything else. Shenzhen even established its own shipping companies to transport the goods. (Shenzhen benefited from the tremendous demand for interregional trade that had been pent-up by administrative blockades erected by local officials responding rationally to fiscal and industrial decentralization.) The inward domestic orientation of the SEZs was viewed as a problem by many people who believed that the zones were supposed to be primarily outward oriented (Tossing 1991: 274–5). In fact, the economic ties between the SEZs and the inland areas created economic benefits for both and widened the base of political support for the open policy.[24]

Another benefit for the inland areas was the increased demand from coastal regions for raw materials and labor. The dynamic growth of export-oriented processing industries in the SEZs and coastal China as a whole raised the domestic shadow price of primary materials produced largely in inland China. Inland industries that extracted such materials gradually weakened their resistance to reforms and began to demand to be freed from the plan to reap the rewards of the market. As the demand for labor in the export-oriented coastal areas grew, restrictions on internal migration were lowered and millions of inland laborers took advantage of the new opportunities on the coast. The remittances from these migrants have become a significant income source for inland regions.

Finally, the creation of specially privileged foreign trade and investment zones spurred inland regions and other coastal regions to demand similar privileges for themselves. Economic envy is a powerful motivation. Provincial officials, some of whom were initially hostile to the open policy, soon began to advocate extending the policy throughout China. Such pressure was responsible for extending zone-like freedoms to fourteen coastal cities in 1984 and to three larger delta areas (the Pearl River delta, the Yangtze delta, and southern Fujian) in 1985. In 1987–8, then CCP general secretary Zhao Ziyang sought to outflank his more conservative political rival Premier Li Peng by launching a new "coastal development strategy" and won Deng Xiaoping's support for the strategy (Yang 1991). Officials from the interior remained dissatisfied and in 1988 organized a series of meetings arguing for the benefits of the open door to be spread beyond the coastal areas. In response, the center expanded the foreign trade and investment autonomy of a number of inland provinces and localities. After 1989, when the Tiananmen demonstrations provided an opening for Li Peng and his conservative allies to defeat Zhao Ziyang, Li continued to appeal for support by extending foreign trade and investment privileges selectively to subordinate officials. He supported the creation of a massive new open zone of Pudong in Shanghai, a city which had felt neglected by previous special zone policies. Li Peng also led the State Council to allow localities, in the interior as well as the coast, to set up their own foreign trade and investment development zones, an attractive form of patronage that produced an explosion of development zones (150 were set up by localities in the first four months of 1992; Shi Jian 1992: 28).[25] By selectively authorizing particular places as privileged open zones, beginning with a small number and gradually adding more, Chinese leaders broadened the support of regional officials for the reform drive.[26]

Another example of the positive impact of internationalization on China's reform bandwagon was the process of foreign trade decentralization. The decision to smash the MOFTEC monopoly over foreign trade management was essentially a choice to reduce central control in order to increase the volume of trade and build bureaucratic vested interests in the open policy. Under the MOFTEC monopoly, a dozen of the ministry's trading companies had handled all foreign trade transactions; by 1990 there were more than 5000 trading companies established by ministries, provinces, and cities. By the end of 1987, there were nearly 900 foreign trade companies in Guangdong province alone (Lardy 1992: 39).

Deng Xiaoping and his allies chose a path of gradual decentralization of trade rather than moving rapidly to its full liberalization. This choice involved maintaining the nonconvertibility of Chinese currency during the transition and distributing differential rights to retain foreign exchange earned from exports (that is, import entitlements) to provinces, ministries, cities, and, to a much lesser extent, to enterprises as an export incentive. Because domestic economic reform released a tremendous hunger for imports of both assembly lines and consumer goods, the system of foreign exchange retention rights generated a valuable selective benefit that officials could distribute to their friends and supporters or keep for themselves.[27]

Over the decade, central authorities distributed an increasingly large share of foreign exchange earnings to local governments and, less so, to enterprises.[28] As a favor to provincial and municipal officials, the first foreign exchange retention rules introduced in 1979 allowed locally managed firms to retain 40 percent of their export earnings over the 1978 level, while ministry-managed firms could keep only 20 percent. Beginning in the early 1980s, especially generous retention deals were given to certain regions (the coastal provinces of Guangdong and Fujian and the remote inland province of Xinjiang) and sectors (petroleum, machinery and electronics, military industries, and science and education). In 1982, the State Council set fixed retention rates for each province; the rates ranged from 3 to 25 percent (the average provincial rate was 8 percent). In 1985, the provincial foreign exchange retention rates were raised to a minimum of 25 percent; the rates for Guangdong and Fujian were lifted to 30 percent, and seven inland provincial-level regions (Inner Mongolia, Xinjiang, Guangxi, Ningxia, Yunnan, Guizhou, and Qinghai) were allowed to retain half their foreign exchange earnings. Producers of machinery and electronic product exports had their retention rate raised to 65 percent. Also in 1985, a new system was established that gave most provinces 25 percent of the earnings of planned exports, and 70, 80, or 100 percent of above-plan earnings. By 1986, the four Special Economic Zones and four development zones (including both coastal and inland) in Hainan, Huangpu, Guangzhou, and Xijiang were allowed to keep all their export earnings. A 1987 policy encouraged the export of light industry, arts and crafts, and garments by raising their retention rates (information in this paragraph is drawn from Lardy 1992: 53–7).

Each of these foreign exchange retention schemes was extended by Beijing officials to promote exports and generate bureaucratic support for the reform drive. Although all provinces have lobbying operations in the capital and industries and well-represented through their ministries, there is no evidence that demands from below drove the policies.[29]

Under the dual track system, the national budget continued to take domestic currency losses on foreign trade and export incentives remained inadequate to compensate for the pull of domestic demand generated by rapid economic growth. The central government's solution was another form of particularistic contracting called foreign trade contracts. All provinces and national foreign trade corporations signed contracts with MOFTEC specifying the quantity of export earnings (in foreign exchange), the quantity of foreign exchange to be remitted to the central government, and the level of domestic currency profits and losses in foreign trade transactions. The contracts, negotiated individually for each province, perpetuated the practice of granting provinces different rates of foreign exchange retention (Lardy 1992: 102–3).

The Chinese gradual, decentralized, particularistic approach to reforming foreign trade administration and encouraging exports was extraordinarily successful in both political and economic terms. The perpetuation of a two-track system won bureaucratic (especially local) support for the open policy by creating a system of selective access to foreign exchange and imports. Local governments, whose interests were closely aligned to those of light industry, avidly promoted exports.

The decentralization of foreign trade administration was accompanied by decentralization of authority to approve foreign investment projects. With both types of decentralization, local officials were happy to be unleashed to gain access to foreign technology, equipment, and capital. Fiscal reforms had given them a direct stake in the profits of local industry, and an imported color television assembly line or a joint venture with a foreign firm could mean a windfall. Once central controls were lifted, local officials hustled up foreign business like seasoned merchants by offering tax breaks and other inducements, and the volume of trade and foreign investment grew dramatically.[30] On the negative side, an inevitable consequence of decentralization was an intensification of competition for foreign business among provinces and a resulting loss of bargaining power for China as a whole vis-à-vis foreign corporations (Shirk 1990).[31]

CONCLUSION: INTERNATIONALIZATION AND ECONOMIC POLICIES IN CHINA

The case of China presents a complex picture of the impact of internationalization on economic policies. On the one hand, China's pre-1978 experience confirms findings from other communist countries that Leninist political and economic institutions block the influence of internationalization on domestic outcomes. The foreign trade monopoly and administratively set prices of the command economy kept domestic groups ignorant of international price signals so that neither the preferences nor the behavior of these groups reflected internationalization. Economic interests, moreover, were not permitted to organize to influence policy-making. These interests were articulated only through the Communist Party and government ministries and agencies, which were structured since the mid-1950s to enhance the power of the holders of capital, which is scarce in China, and thereby to perpetuate policies of rapid industrialization and autarky. The communist coalition of heavy industries, inland provinces, the military, and central agencies of political and economic control was frozen in place by Leninist institutions, while sectors and regions in which labor was most abundant, that is, agriculture, light industries, and coastal provinces, were effectively disenfranchised. Pre-1978 China provides evidence that Leninist institutions prevail over international economic factors in shaping economic policies. Yet the coercive nature of these institutions that served to protect the groups with the weakest position vis-à-vis the world economy, testifies to the strong pressure of international economic factors; it takes a major political effort to keep the world economy at bay.

Before 1978, the internationalization of the world economy, and in particular of the Asia-Pacific region, by raising the opportunity costs of autarkic policies to China, increased the probability that policy change would occur. The international opportunity structure created a latent coalition in favor of opening among labor-intensive light industries and agriculture and the labor rich coastal provinces. Yet Leninist institutions sustained China's self-isolation and blocked any possibility of opening. In this institutional environment, the initiative for altering China's stance to the world economy could come only from above, from a political entrepreneur like Deng Xiaoping who sought support within the official selectorate by proposing innovative policies.

On the other hand, once Deng took the initiative to open China's economy, the strong positive domestic response confirms the powerful influence of internationalization on the preferences and behavior of local groups. The core of the coalition that formed behind the reforms was as Frieden and Rogowski would predict: the groups associated with labor-intensive sectors with a comparative advantage in international competition: that is, agriculture, light industries, and coastal provinces. The attraction of the international economy generated tremendous domestic economic and political momentum behind the reform drive; and foreign investors tripped over one another to commit funds and show support. Yet international factors did not determine the specific content and style of reform policies; the domestic institutional setting did. The Leninist political institutions that remained in place did not prevent reforms and proved to be surprisingly flexible once the preeminent leader came down on the side of reform. Chinese reforms, forged in this institutional arena, were extremely effective at sustaining the support of the groups associated with labor, and even more remarkable, at buying off the groups controlling capital and drawing them into the reform bandwagon.

PART IV

International Economic Crisis and Developing Countries

The Political Economy of Financial Internationalization in the Developing World

STEPHAN HAGGARD AND SYLVIA MAXFIELD

Developing country governments have historically imposed controls on capital movements, the international activities of domestic financial institutions, and the entry of foreign ones. In the last decade, however, a growing number of developing countries have opened their financial systems by liberalizing capital flows and the rules governing the international operations of financial intermediaries; Table 1 provides a typology of these liberalization efforts.[1] This chapter seeks to explain both the general trend toward what we call "financial internationalization" as well as variations in the pace and scope of these reform efforts across countries.

The rush to liberalize capital movements and open domestic financial systems to foreign competition is puzzling on several accounts. A growing economic literature on the sequencing of economic reforms has underlined a number of preconditions required to make capital account liberalization an optimal policy. There are well-documented cases of premature and ill-conceived liberalization efforts that had extremely high costs, including the Southern Cone experiments of the late 1970s in Chile, Argentina, and Uruguay and, more recently, Mexico (Bisat, Johnston and Sundarajan 1992; Corbo and de Melo 1985, 1987; Edwards 1984, 1995; McKinnon 1991). It is revealing that the advanced industrial states are only now completing the internationalization of their own financial markets (Goodman and Pauly 1993; Pauly 1988; Rosenbluth 1989).

Even if there were a strong economic case for the liberalization of capital flows, a number of *political* questions would remain. As with trade liberalization, there is the question of why sectoral interests favored by controls would concede to a change of policy. Governments, in addition to pro-

We would like to thank Peter Beck, Benjamin Cohen, David Cole, Jeffry Frieden, Robert Kaufman, Robert Keohane, Andrew MacIntyre, Helen Milner, John Odell, Manuel Pastor, Ben Schneider, and Jeffrey Winters for comments on earlier drafts. This paper first appeared in slightly different form in *International Organization*.

Table 1. *A typology of financial market internationalization*

	Direction of liberalization	
	Inward	Outward
Liberalization of:		
I. Capital movements	1. Liberalization of rules governing foreign direct investment, including sectoral restrictions, screening practices, and performance requirements 2. Liberalization of foreign access to domestic equities and real estate 3. Liberalization of rules governing foreign borrowing by domestic firms and the international operations of domestic banks 4. Deregulation of sale and purchase of short-term domestic securities by foreigners	1. Deregulation of outward direct and portfolio investment by nationals 2. Liberalization of restrictions on repatriation of capital and disinvestment by foreign nationals and firms 3. Liberalization of restrictions on payments for invisibles, including profits and dividends 4. Deregulation of domestic foreign currency accounts, for residents and nonresidents 5. Deregulation of sale and purchase of short-term foreign securities by domestic residents
II. Entry	Liberalize entry of foreign banks securities firms and other nonbank financial intermediaries	Permit or encourage domestic banks, securities firms and nonbank financial institutions to establish foreign branches and networks

Sources: Derived from Organization for Economic Co-operation and Development, *Liberalisation of Capital Movements and Financial Services,* (Paris: OECD, 1990), pp. 11–12; and International Monetary Fund, *Developments in International Exchange and Payments Systems* (Washington D.C.: International Monetary Fund, 1992), pp. 29–31. See note 2.

tected financial sectors, can also have a strong stake in capital controls. Increased financial integration holds governments hostage to foreign exchange and capital markets, forcing greater fiscal and monetary discipline than they might otherwise choose (Andrews 1994; Frieden 1991b; Goodman and Pauly 1993; Kurzer 1991; 1993; Winters 1994). To the extent that capital account liberalization erodes domestic financial controls, it eliminates a tool of both industrial policy and patronage and reduces the opportunity for governments to finance themselves through the sale of government bonds at lower-than-world interest rates (Alesina and Tabellini 1989; Giovannini and de Melo 1993; Roubini and Sala-i-Martin 1992).

Given the common trend in policy across a large number of developing countries, there are good reasons to think that international systemic pressures are at work and that the developing countries' growing integration with the world economy has constrained government choices with respect to the world economy has constrained government choices with respect to international financial policy. There are two distinct mechanisms through which these pressures have operated.

The first are the effects of increased trade and financial interdependence on the preferences and capabilities of policy-relevant economic interests (see Frieden and Rogowski). Increasing interdependence expands the weight of domestic actors with foreign ties, increases the array of interests likely to benefit from, and demand, greater openness of financial markets, and thus tilts the balance of political forces in a more internationalist direction. Interdependence also implies a greater political voice for foreign investors in the domestic policy process. Financial firms from advanced industrial countries have become more active lobbyists for market opening and have enlisted their governments to maintain both multilateral and bilateral pressure for liberalization. Moreover, the growing magnitude and complexity of trade and investment relations make capital controls more difficult to enforce because of the myriad opportunities for evasion and arbitrage.

These changes in the configuration of interests have been used to explain capital account opening in developed countries and constitute an important backdrop to recent policy developments in developing countries as well. We argue, however, that the proximate cause for financial market opening in the developing countries is more frequently found in a second source of international pressure: balance of payments crises. At first blush, this argument appears counterintuitive; we might expect, rather, that international shocks would be associated with a movement towards closure. Yet the International Monetary Fund (IMF) reports that from 1985–90 – a period of profound balance of payments difficulties for much of the Third World – the number of liberalizing measures taken by all developing countries with respect to the capital account not only consistently exceeded the number of tightening measures, but it increased dramatically over the period: from 22 in 1985, to a peak of 62 in 1988 before falling to 49 in 1990.[2]

The reasons for this tendency have to do with the high costs that countries pay for inward-oriented responses to crises under conditions of increased financial integration. Maintaining or increasing financial openness in the face of crisis signals foreign investors that they will be able to liquidate their investments, indicates government intentions to maintain fiscal and monetary discipline, and thus ultimately increases capital inflows (Bartolini and Drazen 1994; Laba and Larrain 1993).

In the first two sections of this chapter, we explore the theoretical arguments linking economic interdependence and balance of payments crises to policy reform. In the remainder of the paper, we explore the plausibility of these arguments by examining reform efforts in four middle-income countries: Indonesia, Chile, Mexico, and South Korea.

I. ECONOMIC INTERDEPENDENCE AND POLITICAL PRESSURES FOR FINANCIAL INTERNATIONALIZATION

In the Hecksher–Ohlin model, liberalization of trade and capital movements are substitutes (Alesina, Grilli, and Milesi-Feretti 1993a; Edwards and van Wijnbergen 1986: 141–8; Hanson 1992: 2). Standard welfare analysis can thus be used as a starting point for identifying competing interests and constructing a political economy of the capital account. In a closed, labor-abundant developing economy, the rate of return to capital in the domestic market exceeds the rate in the rest of the world. Lifting capital controls leads to a capital inflow from which labor gains.

Frieden (1991b) has argued, however, that in a more plausible specific-factors model, the distributional consequences are quite different. Specific factors in capital-poor countries do well, since they can now borrow at lower interest rates, while liquid asset holders face lower returns. Politically privileged clients may benefit from government control over preferential credit, but as international financial markets expand, the major corporate consumers of financial services will find protected, inefficient domestic financial markets and restricted access to international opportunities increasingly costly (Frieden 1991b: 437; Haggard and Maxfield 1993: 313–16).

While identifying a politically important source of support for capital account liberalization, Frieden's spare model misses important features of the politics of finance in developing countries and as a result, overstates the likely resistance to capital account liberalization. In many developing countries, returns to savers can be *lower* than world interest rates because financial intermediation is taxed through restrictions on deposit rates, high inflation, and the lack of opportunities to acquire foreign assets. Though liquid asset holders have recourse to parallel markets where returns are higher, the informal nature of these markets is associated with corresponding risks. To these considerations must be added the substantial political risk that characterizes financial markets in a number of developing countries. As Williamson (1992) argues, liquid asset holders in a capital-poor country can profit from liberalization of both inflows and outflows. Local investors gain security, albeit at lower yields, by gaining the freedom to invest abroad; foreign investors gain a greater expected yield for a modest cost in terms of security.

Frieden's analysis also needs to be extended to comprehend the interests of financial intermediaries, both domestic and foreign, since they are likely to have a substantial political voice in the liberalization process. These interests cannot be understood unless a distinction is drawn between the liberalization of capital flows and the liberalization of exit and entry. Domestic financial intermediaries stand to gain from liberalizing capital inflows and outflows, since it opens opportunities to intermediate foreign purchases of domestic securities and to manage pent-up domestic demand for foreign assets. Given the structure of the financial system in most developing countries, opening the capital account will also provide arbitrage opportunities, since domestic and international interest rates are unlikely to converge quickly if financial markets are organized as oligopolies (Galbis 1986). Domestic financial institutions are also likely to be a source of pressure for capital account liberalization as their clients' international operations expand. Rosenbluth, for example, concludes that decontrol in Japan was "propelled by financial institutions, acting in cooperation with the Ministry of Finance and sometimes politicians, to construct a new set of rules they need[ed] to compete in a changing economic environment" (Rosenbluth 1989: 5).[3]

Yet if liberalization of flows is accompanied by liberalization of entry, these gains may accrue to foreign financial intermediaries, which have access to large pools of foreign funds, superior technology, and a sophisticated knowledge of foreign market opportunities. Thus the financial sector may support a liberalization of capital movements, but take a protectionist stance with reference to the entry of foreign firms.

The pent-up demand for financial services in protected markets will increase the interest of foreign financial institutions in lowering barriers to entry, however. As "emerging markets" have grown, the opportunity costs of being closed out of them grow accordingly and foreign firms have become active lobbyists for liberalization. American financial firms have been particularly aggressive in securing diplomatic support for their interests. These political pressures have played out at a number of different levels, from the formulation of the services agenda at the GATT, to regional negotiations such as the NAFTA, to bilateral consultations, such as those between the United States and Japan, Korea, and Taiwan.

Increasing international economic integration not only changes the distribution of preferences; it is also likely to erode the effectiveness of governments in maintaining controls (Mathieson and Rojas-Suarez 1993). Governments have a variety of motives for restricting capital account transactions, including an interest in maintaining policy autonomy, access to low-cost finance, and the ability to distribute rents. Evasion of controls has always existed, but growing interdependence increases both the motivation and opportunity for it. The expansion of the tradable goods sector increases the opportunities for firms to get around capital controls through under- and overinvoicing, as does the growth of illicit trade. As firms from the developing countries have begun to invest more extensively abroad, governments face increasing difficulties in monitoring foreign financial operations and the transactions between headquarters and subsidiaries. The increase in travel and the deepening of telecommunications ties have also made it easier for individual citizens to circumvent capital controls, even where controls over the international transactions of financial institutions remain in place.

In sum, increases in international trade and investment ties and the opportunities opened by the deepening of international financial markets should increase interest group pressures for financial internationalization, including from foreign firms, while decreasing the effectiveness of government controls. Yet such broad changes are of more use in explaining general trends than they are in accounting for why specific countries liberalize when they do. Crises play an important role in this regard.

II. PAYMENTS CRISES AND FINANCIAL INTERNATIONALIZATION

The traditional wisdom is that payments crises generate pressure for capital controls in order to limit capital flight and for increased trade protection to manage short-term balance of payments constraints. There are a number of countries that appear to conform to this pattern; the initial responses of Mexico, Argentina, and Venezuela to the debt crisis of 1982–3 constitute examples (Reinhart and Smith 1995). However, as the IMF data cited in the introduction suggests, this pattern was not a general one in the 1980s and early 1990s. Even in the three countries just mentioned, brief episodes of closure were quickly followed by liberalization efforts.

To understand why, consider a simple account of a balance of payments crisis.[4] Prior to the crisis, the country is running a current account deficit, financed by public and private capital inflows. External creditors judge that the growth of external debt is on an unsustainable path, and they are unwilling to continue to provide financing at previous levels. This might occur because domestic macroeconomic policies are unsustainable, or because of adverse developments in the world economy such as a change in the terms of trade. Though the reduction of external finance might in principle be negotiated and gradual, it is more typically made manifest in speculative attacks on the exchange rate, rapid capital flight, and a sudden collapse in the availability of external lending.

Under what conditions will governments respond to such crises with liberalizing policy changes? Where the dependence on foreign finance has been low, where international liquidity is abundant, or where the government is confident in its ability to generate foreign exchange through exports, the cost of a more closed policy response to crisis is low. However, in most middle-income countries, these conditions have not pertained. Dependence on foreign finance grew rapidly in the 1970s when capital was abundant, but lenders retreated en masse from the developing world in the wake of the debt crisis. Moreover, with the exception of the East Asian NICs, the development strategies of most middle-income developing countries have been notoriously weak in generating a level of exports adequate to avoid recurrent balance of payments difficulties.

Under these conditions, crises are likely to have an important political consequence: they will strengthen the political position of those sectors that are holders or generators of foreign exchange. These include liquid asset holders, the export sector, private foreign creditors and investors, foreign financial intermediaries, and the multilateral financial institutions. This "coalition" does not need to organize or mobilize politically to press its case, though it typically does. Its power also resides in the politically compelling threat of exit or continued unwillingness to lend or invest. The collective action problems that typically plague decentralized political actors are overcome by the fact that coordinated action is generated spontaneously by private responses to market signals.

The holders and generators of foreign exchange favor capital account liberalization, particularly in the wake of a crisis, because it provides an exit option; an open capital account constitutes protection against future government action. From the government's perspective, capital account liberalization helps resolve both short and long-term foreign exchange problems by increasing the credibility of the government's economic policy stance in the eyes of creditors and earners of foreign exchange (Bartolini and Bondar 1992; Perez-Campanero and Leone 1992; Reinhart and Smith 1995; Vinals n.d.). Liberalizing the capital account is a form of signaling aimed at inducing the resumption of capital inflows (Rodrik 1989).

Such signaling is not limited to changes in discrete policies, but is likely to extend to *institutional* changes that increase the cost of policy reversal, particularly by delegating authority over those policies to agencies, typically central banks, that are likely to pursue them in the future. An increase in the relative scarcity of foreign exchange can therefore change not only the coalitional balance in the economy as a whole, but the balance of power among government ministries and even decision-making structures (Garret and Lange; Maxfield 1995; North and Weingast 1989).

To summarize, secular changes related to growing international economic integration have increased the incentives for capital account liberalization on the part of both economic interests and the government itself. However, crises are likely to substantially increase the power of those forces that favor liberalization, both within and outside the government. The proximate causal mechanism is politicians' perception that liberalization of the capital account will reassure investors and thus ultimately induce capital inflows. By contrast, we would expect the pressures for liberalization to be least in countries with a low degree of openness that have avoided crises. Easy access to credit and foreign exchange, whether through borrowing or commodity booms, also permits governments the luxury of maintaining controls and exercising selectivity towards foreign investors and financial firms.

The remainder of this paper is dedicated to an evaluation of this argument through an examination of the history of capital account policy in four countries: Indonesia, Mexico, Chile, and Korea. Though not a random sample, these four countries were chosen independently of the number or magnitude of balance of payments crises or significant change in capital account policy. They are broadly representative of the larger, middle-income developing countries that have become identified as "emerging markets."

III. FINANCIAL INTERNATIONALIZATION IN FOUR COUNTRIES: A COMPARATIVE OVERVIEW

Devising measures or proxies for the balance of payments position of a country or its international financial policy is not straightforward. Quantitative indicators of the balance of payments can be highly misleading; large current account deficits may be voluntarily financed in one country, while small deficits signal a loss of confidence and crisis in another. The annual percent change in international reserves provides a reasonable first approximation of the balance of payments situation; a sharp deterioration in reserves is likely to be a good measure of balance of payments difficulties. Nonetheless, this indicator must be supplemented by a qualitative assessment of the country's ability to manage these constraints: its stock of credibility with creditors and investors; the extent of international liquidity; and the capacity to adjust through an expansion of exports.

Combining both quantitative indicators and qualitative judgments, we find eleven periods during which the countries in our sample faced serious balance of payments constraints: Indonesia in 1965–6 (which predates our quantitative series on capital account openness), briefly in 1975, in 1981–2, and again in 1986–8; Mexico in 1976 and more or less continuously from the 1982 debt crisis through the late 1980s; Chile in 1971–5 and again in 1981–2; and Korea in 1971, and in conjunction with the two oil shocks in 1974 and 1980–2.

The overall policy stance of governments is also difficult to assess; it must be derived from a complex of policy actions in different areas, not all of which necessarily covary. Moreover, liberalization programs typically unfold across a number of years, and thus an action taken in a given year may have its origins in an earlier period. Nonetheless, to provide a comparative context for our case studies we devised a coding scheme on the level of financial policy openness in each country for the 1970–90 period based on information contained in the International Monetary Fund's annual report on exchange arrangements and restrictions (Table 2). The measure sums our coding of the rules governing transactions in four areas: the international operations of domestic and foreign commercial banks; payments for financial services and repatriation of capital; portfolio investment and borrowing; and direct investment. The indicator varies from the least open score of zero (zero in all four policy areas) to twelve (three in all four areas). A full explanation of the coding is contained in the Appendix.

The data reveal eleven episodes of significant changes in financial market policy, defined as a change in the level of openness. We find evidence of liberalization in eight instances: Indonesia in 1970 and 1987–8; in Mexico in 1978, 1983, and 1988; in Chile in 1974 and 1976–80; and in Korea in 1990. We find three episodes of a move toward greater closure: in Indonesia in 1974, Mexico in 1982, and Chile in 1971.

Of the eight episodes of liberalization, all except one had its origin in a balance of payments crisis. Indonesia (1971) and Chile (1974) came in the aftermath of crises that toppled governments and led to fundamental policy changes.[5] The 1976–80 reforms in Chile were at one level a continuation of Pinochet's initial reform moves, but were initiated in the wake of the severe balance of payments problems Chile experienced *after* the military coup in conjunction with the oil crisis of 1974–5. Mexico's 1978 liberalization came in the aftermath of the 1976 crisis. The 1983 liberalization effort was clearly a response to crisis, quickly reversing the initial move toward a more closed policy stance in 1982. The 1988 reforms must also be seen as an effort to regain access to international capital markets following five years of financial drought and the mid-decade collapse of oil prices. The change in oil prices also helps explain Indonesian policy at the end of the 1980s.

The one exception to the rule is Korea in 1990, when U.S. pressure appears to play a dominant role. However, our case study shows that this liberalization was the culmination of a decade-long liberalization effort that had its origins in the balance of payments problems the country experienced in the early 1980s. Moreover, the very gradualness of the program can itself be explained by Korea's strong balance of payments position throughout the decade.

The reform efforts in our sample may be spurred by crises, but do balance of payments difficulties always lead to financial opening? One case can justifiably be removed from consideration. The severe balance of payments crisis in Chile in 1981–2 was not followed by a further opening of the capital account, but this was due to the fact that the crises of the mid-1970s had already generated a substantial opening; indeed, what is striking is the fact that the Chilean government did not retreat from its commitment to an open capital account.

Table 2. *Internationalization, crises, and financial policy in Indonesia, Mexico, Chile and Korea*

	Level of financial openness	Exports + imports/GNP	Percent change in reserves
Indonesia			
1970	8	21.7	24.4
1971	9	21.3	15.7
1972	9	30.2	66.7
1973	9	39.7	28.9
1974	8	57.9	46.0
1975	8	42.6	−155.1
1976	8	38.8	70.0
1977	8	38.3	40.3
1978	8	34.8	4.5
1979	8	39.3	35.4
1980	8	47.1	24.7
1981	8	42.5	−7.5
1982	8	41.3	−59.5
1983	8	39.2	15.5
1984	8	37.9	22.1
1985	8	32.2	4.0
1986	8	29.0	−22.8
1987	9	34.6	27.6
1988	10	38.2	−10.8
1989	10	42.7	7.4
1990	10	46.7	19.4
Mexico			
1970	6	8.5	13.2
1971	6	8.5	24.5
1972	6	10.3	23.0
1973	6	12.4	15.9
1974	6	13.4	6.3
1975	6	11.4	10.5
1976	6	10.0	−16.4
1977	6	10.1	28.0
1978	7	13.5	10.5
1979	7	17.2	11.1
1980	7	21.4	30.0
1981	7	20.8	27.3
1982	4	17.7	−388.5
1983	7	20.5	78.7
1984	7	25.1	46.2
1985	7	23.7	−48.2
1986	7	14.6	13.5
1987	7	22.3	54.5
1988	8	27.2	−136.1
1989	8	26.0	16.6
1990	8	25.5	35.8
Chile			
1970	4	27.1	15.4
1971	0	20.3	−50.2

Table 2. *(cont.)*

	Level of financial openness	Exports + imports/GNP	Percent change in reserves
1972	0	16.9	−43.0
1973	0	21.5	25.6
1974	5	37.8	−66.2
1975	5	35.8	36.0
1976	7	41.7	624.7
1977	7	36.8	5.3
1978	8	34.9	155.6
1979	8	45.6	77.8
1980	9	41.5	319.1
1981	9	33.9	−60.4
1982	9	26.0	−43.5
1983	9	28.2	12.2
1984	9	33.3	13.1
1985	9	37.2	6.4
1986	9	43.4	−4.0
1987	9	50.7	6.5
1988	9	59.4	26.1
1989	9	63.7	14.8
1990	9	61.0	67.2
Korea			
1970	5	32.6	9.4
1971	5	34.2	−39.9
1972	5	37.7	17.1
1973	5	56.3	40.9
1974	5	68.0	−219.2
1975	5	60.3	64.5
1976	5	62.0	60.3
1977	5	62.7	33.6
1978	5	62.8	−7.4
1979	5	61.8	6.6
1980	5	64.2	−1.1
1981	5	66.7	−9.1
1982	5	60.7	4.5
1983	5	60.1	−19.7
1984	5	66.1	14.8
1985	5	64.9	4.0
1986	5	62.6	13.6
1987	5	71.8	7.4
1988	5	74.5	71.0
1989	5	66.3	18.8
1990	6	57.9	−2.8

Sources: Changes in reserves from International Monetary Fund, *International Financial Statistics*, various issues. Changes in reserves is change in total reserves minus gold, measured as U.S. dollar value of SDRs, reserve position and foreign exchange. Trade share is from World Bank, *World Tables*, various issues. Exports and imports are on a customs basis. Level of financial openness is coded by the authors from information contained in International Monetary Fund, *Annual Report on Exchange Arrangements and Restrictions*, various issues. For a full explanation of coding, see Appendix.

Our expectations with respect to the remainder of the cases depend heavily on the extent to which the government is capable of generating finance through other means. The apparent anomalies – Indonesia in 1975 and 1981–2 and Korea in 1971, 1974, and 1981–2 – are precisely the countries in which either abundant international liquidity and ability to borrow (in the 1970s) or strong export performance (in all four episodes) quickly alleviated short-term balance of payments problems. In contrast to the other crisis cases, these developments limited the extent to which government leaders saw the fall in international reserves as requiring increased effort to induce capital inflows through an opening of the capital account; in Indonesia, the oil boom even led to a partial reversal of its open stance toward foreign investors.

III. FINANCIAL INTERNATIONALIZATION IN FOUR COUNTRIES: CASE STUDIES

Indonesia

From independence in 1949 until the second half of the 1960s, Indonesia had a relatively restrictive policy regarding capital account transactions.[6] The government subjected payments for invisibles to licensing and controlled foreign investors' remittances. During the first half of the 1960s, Indonesia suffered recurring balance of payments crises, related directly to incoherent monetary and particularly fiscal policies. The response to these was a complex system of multiple exchange rates that left the rupiah increasingly overvalued. As inflation accelerated, the financial system, dominated by deposit banks, suffered severe financial disintermediation. The balance of payments and financial crises came to a head in 1965, adding to the tensions within Sukarno's fragile coalition between the Communist Party and the military and contributing to the bloody collapse of the regime in the fall of 1965. By December 1965, "the only thing left in the national till were some bureaucratic fingers groping for any remaining dollars" (Palmer 1978: 7).

There can be little doubt that the series of reforms of the late 1960s, which culminated in a commitment to full currency convertibility in 1971, were the response of the new government to the crisis of 1965–6. They grew directly out of the interest in attracting foreign capital, including particularly from the multilateral institutions, and to a lesser extent in maintaining the confidence of domestic holders of liquid assets, particularly Chinese businessmen. As Palmer concludes, "Because of lack of foreign exchange and external creditworthiness . . . the first hurdle that had to be cleared . . . was to regain a measure of credibility in the eyes of foreign governments" (Palmer 1978: 15). Numerous foreign advisers were involved in the design of stabilization policies. But on the issue of establishing a regime which would facilitate capital inflow and halt speculative outflows their views were in accord with those of the Indonesian technocrats, and more importantly, of the president himself (Cole and Slade 1994; MacIntyre 1993: 135–41; Palmer 1978: 15).

The reforms unfolded in stages. In 1966 a debt moratorium was put in place and a stabilization plan was initiated by Suharto's "New Order" government with support from the IMF. 1966 also saw the first steps in liberalization of foreign exchange markets, devaluation of the rupiah, and a commitment to fully eliminate the multiple exchange rate system. Important legislation liberalizing foreign direct investment followed in 1967, including increased freedom to remit profits and dividends and to repatriate capital. The ability to attain loans or open accounts denominated in dollars and to convert these into rupiah and back dates to 1968 (Arndt and Suwidjana 1982). In the context of other legislation designed to help banks attract and keep deposits, the banks themselves began to offer loans and accounts denominated in dollars. When multiple exchange rates were abolished in April 1970 the government temporarily closed these facilities by decree but they were restored with a new decree of full currency convertibility in 1971.

The government also sought to encourage the entry of foreign financial intermediaries as a way of attracting foreign capital, even though state banks continued to dominate the financial landscape. Restrictions on foreign bank entry were eased and between 1968 and 1971 there was a major expansion of foreign bank presence in Indonesia, including First National City, Bank of Tokyo, Bank of America, and Chase Manhattan (Grenville 1981: 104; Economist Intelligence Unit, *Quarterly Economic Report,* 1971, 2: 9). The government also authorized, for the first time, the operation of non-bank financial institutions (NBFIs) both domestic and foreign. Prior restrictions on the transfer of most stocks and shares were also lifted in 1970 allowing shares to be denominated in dollars or rupiah, though the stock exchange remained a sleepy institution until the reforms of the 1980s.

Despite this wave of liberalization and institutional change, important restrictions remained that reflected the interests of the government in maintaining political control over the allocation of credit. Even though foreign banks gained entry into Indonesia in the late 1960s, the government blocked foreign bank branching outside of Jakarta in order to prevent international banks from challenging the relatively uncompetitive state deposit banks operating under government protection throughout the archipelago (Economist Intelligence Unit, *Quarterly Economic Report for Indonesia,* 1971, 1: 9). In particular, the government was unwilling to allow competition which would threaten the discretionary allocation of credit to rural Indonesia, one instrument for maintaining the patron–client networks which underlay much of Soharto's power (MacIntyre 1993; Winters 1992).

The international operations of Indonesian banks were also restricted through the 1970s and into the 1980s. In 1985, the growth of international opportunities led local banks to lobby for permission to expand overseas through establishment of more agency and representative offices. They argued that international expansion would foster trade and investment with Indonesia, particularly in nonoil goods (Economist Intelligence Unit, *Quarterly Economic Report,* 1985, 1: 12). Bank Indonesia rebuffed these demands, in part fearing the possibility that the international expansion of Indonesian banks would lead to demands for reciprocity, which in turn would require lifting restrictions on foreign bank operations in Indonesia.

A third area of continued restriction on international capital movements was the prohibition of foreign participation in the Jakarta Stock Exchange (JSE). Following the liberalization of the early 1970s, foreign banks began to take business from local banks because they could raise funds at relatively low cost outside the Indonesian market (Economist Intelligence Unit, *Quarterly Economic Report,* 1973, 1: 6–7; Palmer 1978: 43). Promotion of the JSE throughout the 1970s and 1980s was sold as a way to provide capital to businesses not favored by the foreign banks or by the government-controlled system of subsidized credit distribution (Economist Intelligence Unit, *Quarterly Economic Report,* 1977, 1: 6 and 1977. 4: 6).

Not only were these restrictions retained, but new ones emerged in the mid-1970s. The implementation of credit ceilings and interest rate controls in 1973 was initially a stabilization measure designed to control the inflationary pressures associated with rising oil revenues and balance of payments surpluses (Cole and Slade 1994). However, the controls also garnered support from interventionists in the government who were responsible for dispensing state largesse to a growing network of corporate clients within both the state-owned and private sectors.

Despite the debt problems faced by the state-owned oil firm Pertamina in 1975, the resurgence of oil revenues and renewed lending permitted a more selective and interventionist stance towards foreign investment; this change in policy accounts for our more restrictive coding beginning in 1974. In contrast to the late 1960s and 1980s, government leaders did not view the 1975 balance of payments crisis as warranting a change in capital account policy. Indonesia quickly rescheduled its debts; Indonesia was the first country to use the so-called Paris Club rescheduling facility. The combination of oil and the availability of capital through the Eurodollar markets made it easy for government leaders to avoid liberalizing reforms.

The 1980s ushered in a new period of concern with the balance of payments as opportunities for international borrowing dried up. 1983 saw an important deregulation of the domestic financial system, but it was in the second half of the 1980s as world oil prices began to drop that external pressures mounted. There were several episodes of moderate capital flight in 1984 and 1985 followed by two bouts of serious capital flight: one in late 1986 and a second in mid-1987. Capital flight not only triggered exchange rate adjustments, but led to further financial opening.

A broad package of liberalization measures was announced in October 1988 (Cole and Slade, 1994; McKendrick 1989; MacIntyre 1993: 157–9; Winters 1992). One of these measures, foreign participation in the JSE, was hotly debated because it implied the possibility of increased foreign ownership of Indonesian companies, already a sensitive issue (Economist Intelligence Unit, *Quarterly Economic Report,* 1985, 4: 8 and 1987, 4: 12–13). The concerns of economic policy makers and the prospects for tremendous gains dominated nationalist sentiment, however, and foreign participation was permitted. In 1989 the JSE began to boom, fueled primarily by overseas demand. In the fourth quarter of 1989 estimates put foreign holdings of total shares listed on the JSE at roughly one-third (Economist Intelligence Unit, *Quarterly Economic Report,* 1989, 4: 10–11).

The October 1988 package also affected banking. In addition to domestic reforms, restrictions were eased on the operations of foreign banks in an effort to increase the inflow of foreign funds. The government lifted the prohibition on branching outside Jakarta.[7] Domestic banks, leasing and factoring operations, securities trading firms, insurance companies and credit and consumer finance companies were also permitted to engage in joint ventures with foreign banks with minimum domestic ownership of 15 percent. As a result, seven Japanese banks and Credit Lyonnais launched joint venture negotiations with local partners. Lifting these barriers to entry naturally implied further liberalization of capital flows: limits on offshore borrowing by banks and NBFIs were removed as part of the 1988 bank reform.

The timing of major policy changes in Indonesia suggests that the balance of payments position has been a major determinant of capital account politics. The first wave of liberalization occurred in the five years following the combined political and economic crisis of 1965–6 and culminated in a dramatic opening of the capital account in 1971. These changes were sustained through 1974, when the government *tightened* the rules governing capital account transactions, particularly by instituting new restrictions on foreign direct investment. The model of crisis-induced policy change would predict a policy shift in the direction of greater openness at the time of the Pertamina crisis in 1975. This crisis was addressed quickly through devaluation and Paris Club debt rescheduling, however; it was seen as a short-term liquidity problem. The need to undertake significant policy reform was quickly mitigated by abundant liquidity in international financial markets and more importantly, by the massive inflow of oil revenues. A second wave of liberalization, centered primarily on the opening of the financial sector and the lifting of restrictions on foreign investment, did not come until the 1980s when the country experienced declining oil prices and new balance of payments difficulties.

Chile

Chile had placed some restrictions on capital account transactions from the 1940s until the 1960s, when there was some liberalization. The election of Salvador Allende reversed this trend, and at the beginning of the 1970s, capital account restrictions increased sharply. Initially, these changes were related to the political program of the government, which included among other things the nationalization of the copper industry and greater restrictions on multinationals. By the end of Allende administration, however, controls reflected the desperate efforts of the government to conserve foreign exchange in the face of hyperinflation, a complete loss of both external and internal confidence, and severe balance of payments difficulties (Griffith-Jones 1981).

The crisis contributed directly to the military coup of 1973. The initial focus of the Pinochet government's financial market policy was on domestic deregulation, which had the effect of creating new private sector actors (Arellano 1983: 7; Dahse 1979; Hastings 1993: 210–18; Silva 1991, 1993). The liberalization of interest rates on short-term transactions provided a boost to the creation of new nonbank financial intermediaries, the *financieras*. Financieras mushroomed because the government did not lift controls on commercial bank deposits until later in the year, and deregulation was not fully effective until after the banks were privatized in 1975. A second pillar of the new financial regime dates to May 1974 when all but one of the nationalized commercial banks were offered for sale, a measure obviously supported by private sector organizations. The banks were bought by a small number of entrepreneurs who constituted a new generation of economic groups or "grupos" that combined traditional import-substituting activities with greater participation in the export sector and in finance. The abolition of distinctions among different types of banks (commercial, investment, mortgage) encouraged aggressive entry by the new group-based banks into a variety of financial services. With only minimal regulatory oversight, banks favored lending to related companies within their grupos, leading to a sharp increase in the degree of concentration in both the manufacturing and the financial sectors.

However, the government's financial market policy was not limited to the domestic market. As we would expect in the wake of crisis, the liberalization of external controls that did take place centered on courting foreign investors. The government lifted restrictions on capital outflows by foreign investors in 1974, making Chile's investment laws the most liberal in Latin America in that regard. Foreign banks were also encouraged to enter Chilean financial markets.

Eduardo Silva provides evidence suggesting that these early domestic reforms strengthened a set of financial players – financieras, the new more internationally oriented grupos, and foreign banks – at the expense of more traditional import-substituting groups (Silva 1991; 1993). These new actors stood to gain from greater access to international financial markets because they were more heavily engaged in financial activities, and because despite deregulation, domestic interest rates remained extremely high, opening tremendous arbitrage opportunities (Vylder 1989: 61). Those firms lacking access to credit through their membership in a group were critical of capital controls on the grounds that they contributed to the maintenance of high interest rates. In a curious alignment, critics on the left held similar views, arguing that the gradual pace of capital account liberalization and the continuing use of quantitative controls on borrowing provided rents to those groups in the private sector with preferential access to foreign finance (Vergara 1986: 95). Silva (1991: 243–8) shows that the portion of the economic team in charge of financial market reforms had strong ties to the internationalized segments of the private sector, including in the financial sector. As Wisecarver (1985: 194) concludes, "the capital account was finally opened due to pressures from the financial community."

However, these sectoral pressures overlapped with a balance of payments crisis which also had a significant influence on government policy toward the liberalization of controls. In response to the near hyperinflation of the last months of the Allende regime, and to manage the new inflationary and balance of payments pressures generated by the oil crisis and a downturn in copper prices, the new Pinochet government experimented with an orthodox stabilization program in 1974–5. The failure of this orthodox shock approach, reflected in continued triple-digit inflation, resulted in a crucial shift in stabilization policy by a new economic team, the infamous "Chicago boys," toward an emphasis on the exchange rate.[8]

The new team designed stabilization policy to influence expectations about government policy and increase foreign and domestic creditor confidence. The assumption was that an exchange-rate led stabilization, first through a crawling peg and then through a fixing of the exchange rate, would serve to integrate domestic and international capital markets and reduce domestic interest rates by reducing the anticipated rate of devaluation. Liberalizing capital inflows was crucial to achieving these technical objectives. But Central Bank officials also saw an open capital account as providing a check on future fiscal and monetary policy and a way of signaling government intentions. Though this policy collapsed disastrously in 1982, it is worth quoting Sergio de Castro's conception of the plan: "What these programmed revaluations and devaluations had in common was that they gave a signal to the country since certain objective facts (the substantial drop in the fiscal deficit and the surplus in the balance of payments) had not been assimilated rapidly enough by the public" (cited in Douglas 1985: 61).

In September 1977, commercial banks gained authorization to borrow abroad for the first time, though with various limits in terms of aggregate quantities, term structure, and a prohibition on direct arbitrage. After 1977, the central bank made numerous small changes in capital account regulations. Edwards and Edwards (1987: 55) argue that capital could not move completely freely until just prior to the crisis of 1982. Nonetheless, June 1979 marked a substantial change in policy: the limits to external borrowings by banks were increased markedly. The only limit retained was the overall borrowing limit, including both internal and external borrowing, of twenty times capital and reserves (Corbo 1983; French-Davis and Arellano 1981). The government eliminated monthly restrictions on capital inflows in April 1980, granted commercial banks permission to lend their own resources abroad in June 1980, and authorized commercial banks to invest in foreign financial assets in September 1980.

The crisis that followed in the wake of this global monetarist experiment has been dealt with extensively elsewhere, and need not be detailed here (Corbo 1983; Foxley 1983; Hastings 1993; Ramos 1986). Under extreme pressure from international creditors, the Chilean government reluctantly assumed the external obligations of private financial creditors, and effectively renationalized a number of financial institutions. In the short run, the management of the debt crisis demanded controls on external financial transactions, but these did not last. In the early 1980s a more pragmatic economic team with broader private sector links came to power; it was under this team that export performance begins to boom and talk of the "Chilean miracle" began. Yet despite the pragmatism of the new team, it remained strongly committed to liberal ideas, and the fundamental posture of the government toward capital account openness remained unchanged.

To summarize the Chilean story, the election of Salvador Allende ushered in a three-year period of tight controls which mushroomed as balance of payments difficulties mounted. Liberalization came in the wake of a regime change which could itself be traced in no small measure to severe economic crisis. The new military government of Augusto Pinochet undertook a substantial liberalization effort immediately on coming to office, and then initiated a second round of opening following the balance of payments problems of 1974–5. By 1981, the capital account was highly open with regard to both capital flows and entry and exit.

In contrast to Indonesia and Mexico, Chile dismantled domestic financial controls prior to the liberalization of international capital movements; as a result, there were important new domestic financial interests which stood to gain from the lifting of foreign controls as well. This helps explain why the profound crisis of the early 1980s did not fundamentally alter the government's commitment to an open capital account.

Mexico

Compared with the other three countries examined here, Mexican commitment to currency convertibility, including freedom for foreign investors to remit profits and capital, is of long standing. The Mexican case must therefore be treated in a somewhat longer historical perspective, beginning with the intractable problems with capital flight and financial instability that accompanied and followed the revolution. In the 1920s, gold, silver pesos, paper pesos, and dollars all circulated within the Mexican financial system. Gold and dollars were the preferred store of value and, with the aid of Mexican banks, hemorrhaged from the national financial system at any sign of a renewal of political or policy instability.

Convinced that the proximity of the United States made it impossible to arrest capital outflows through legal or administrative actions, the government decided in 1930 that speculative capital flows could only be limited through a government guarantee of convertibility. Mexico was heavily indebted to international (mostly New York) banks in the 1920s and struggled to make the minimal debt service payments necessary to maintain access to international credit markets. Negotiations with international creditors led to the establishment of a fund which would backstop the transition to convertibility. This mechanism "linked foreign debt with the exchange problem . . . It was a way of arresting lack of confidence . . . and lack of foreign capital" (Diaz 1982; Gaytan 1980: 184).

In response to the severe balance of payments crisis of the 1930s, the government considered, and rejected, the implementation of capital controls. The populist economic program of President Cardenas (1934–40) induced growing dollarization of the financial system, since there was no official prohibition on opening fully convertible dollar-denominated accounts with Mexican banks. Between 1934 and 1937 dollar deposits relative to total demand deposits reached levels not seen again until the 1982 financial crisis. Cardenas did not seek to limit convertibility; his central bank director argued that exchange controls would hurt international trade and could never be enforced (Martinez 1980; Maxfield 1990: 72). Through the 1960s there were no exchange controls applied to incoming or outgoing capital account transactions by Mexican residents or nonresidents. Nor were payments for invisibles restricted; foreign investors remittances amounted to close to 10 percent of all foreign exchange outflows in this period.

Commitment to free currency convertibility did not mean a liberal policy on foreign entry into the domestic financial market or freedom of Mexican financial institutions to operate abroad. From 1924 until 1941 the government allowed branches of foreign banks to conduct banking and credit services in Mexico with permission of the Finance Ministry, though they were prohibited from engaging in bond issues. In 1941 the government further curtailed foreign bank activities. From then until the imposition of yet further restrictions in the 1970s, the combination of operational limitations and Ministry of Finance refusal to grant new entry authorizations significantly reduced the foreign bank presence in Mexico. Legislation enacted in 1973 expressly forbade the establishment of foreign bank branches, and though it permitted the operation of foreign bank representative offices these were prohibited from engaging in domestic financial intermediation (Martinez 1991; Quijano 1985).[9]

This protectionist stance reflected the preferences of Mexican banks; uncompetitive by international standards, they enjoyed a regulatory environment which made their operations highly profitable. However, closure also reflected the motivations of the Mexican government. Protection facilitated efforts to control a portion of domestic bank lending for industrial and agricultural policy reasons. Perhaps more importantly, the Mexican government financed its industrial policy in the 1950s and 1960s, including the expansion of the state-owned enterprise sector, in part through reserve requirements on domestic banks. Banks accepted these reserve requirements in return for a government financial policy regime which compensated them for the costs of high reserve requirements, in part through protection from foreign competition.

Mexico experienced its first balance of payments crisis in over two decades in 1976. The sharp decline in international reserves and subsequent devaluation were quickly overtaken by euphoria as oil export revenues and commercial banking lending exploded, but the crisis did provide the occasion for some financial liberalization. Legislation passed in 1977 and implemented in 1978 permitted Mexican banks to open foreign branches, in part to service their increasingly internationalized clientele, in part to tap the Eurocurrency markets more effectively.

In 1982, Mexico became the first large Latin American country to experience a debt crisis. In a syndrome that was to become all too common, growing current account deficits were followed by the withdrawal of foreign financial support and massive capital flight. When the government declared dollar-denominated accounts inconvertible, instituted broader exchange controls, and nationalized Mexico's banks in 1982, indignant Mexicans referred to the transformation of Mexdollars into "ex-dollars" (Tello 1984).

This nationalistic response appears to suggest that crises are just as likely to lead to foreign exchange and capital controls as they are to liberalization. However the controls proved surprisingly short-lived; both domestic politics and foreign pressures played a role. First, the controls were wildly unpopular (Maxfield 1990: 146–53). The incoming president, Miguel de la Madrid, openly opposed the policy and publicly expressed his interest in removing the controls as rapidly as possible. However, the policy stance of the incoming administration was hardly populist; rather, it marked a sharp shift toward the technocratic end of the Mexican political spectrum (Centeno and Maxfield 1990: 57–86). This move to the right was, in turn, closely tied to external considerations. The IMF expected Mexico to end exchange controls as part of its standby agreement, and the standby was central to the successful renegotiation of Mexico's debt to private international creditors (Tello 1984).

The effects of the crisis were not limited to the short-run reversal of controls; rather, it ushered in a period of intense economic reform, accelerated following further balance of payments difficulties in 1988. The NAFTA-related reforms have been outlined elsewhere (Hufbauer and Schott 1993: 61–5; Maxfield 1993: 253–7); here it is only important to note that reforms included substantial deregulation of the domestic financial market, reprivatization of the banks that had been nationalized in the wake of the crisis, and the opening of the financial sector to foreign competition. U.S. banks had long sought freer entry into the Mexican market and the negotiation of the North American Free Trade Agreement provided them an entry point. Despite the strong external pressure and the Salinas' administrations interest in seeing the NAFTA succeed, the newly privatized banks were able to win a gradual phase-in of the entry provisions and certain market-share restrictions. However, the crisis of 1994–5 resulted in an acceleration of the NAFTA liberalization timetable (Maxfield 1995b).

How do we explain changes in the Mexican government's commitment to free currency convertibility and capital movements? Certainly, close proximity to the United States limited the potential effectiveness of government currency controls from an early date. However, the government was able to devise a system which maintained convertibility while simultaneously placing limits on the behavior of foreign investors and protecting the domestic financial system. The initial response to the debt crisis was closure, but this policy was reversed in a matter of months, giving way to a renewed commitment to an open capital account. Decline in international reserves in 1988 overlapped with the process of negotiating the NAFTA, and led to a final step in Mexico's financial internationalization: the beginning of the end of the restrictions on foreign banks. Interestingly, the government's international financial policy was not reversed in 1995, despite a wrenching domestic adjustment.

South Korea

When Korea's international financial policy is placed in comparative perspective, two facts are striking. First, when compared with other middle-income developing countries, Korea has been relatively immune to balance of payments trouble. Second, the country exhibits a surprisingly low level of policy openness, particularly given the country's strong export orientation. The crises of 1971 and particularly 1974 prompted debate over domestic financial market reform, but a plan for liberalization of the capital account or greater entry for foreign banks was not advanced until the balance of payments difficulties the country experienced beginning in 1979. The implementation of the plan was prolonged, gradual and partial. The reasons have to do precisely with Korea's ability to borrow its way out of the oil crises and the sustained ability to generate exports. These conditions limited the influence of those within the government in favor of greater financial internationalization. The shift in policy reflected in our coding for 1990 did not come in response to balance of payments difficulties; rather, strong diplomatic pressure from the U.S. and ultimately a change of government in 1993 appeared to play the central role. But as throughout the decade, the Korean response was cautious and gradual.

The Korean government has consistently intervened in financial markets.[10] The motive for this intervention has been related to the conduct of industrial policy. Following the military's seizure of power in 1961, the banking system was nationalized and preferential credit to exporters became a central element of Korea's export-led growth strategy. In the early 1960s, the government turned to foreign borrowing to finance the import of capital goods, but all foreign borrowing was intermediated by state-owned banks and required government approval and guarantee. With the exception of the few export-processing zones, the regime governing foreign direct investment was surprisingly restrictive and the rules governing individuals' access to foreign exchange were even more draconian than those facing firms.[11]

The balance of payments problems the country faced in 1971 resulted in some important domestic financial reforms, but balance of payments equilibrium was quickly restored and there was no fundamental change in foreign financial policy. Following the oil crisis of 1973–4, the government relied even more heavily on both financial subsidies and foreign borrowing in an effort to engineer a "big push" into heavy and chemical industries;

this first crisis pushed Korea toward greater state intervention. After contentious intrabureaucratic conflicts between those committed to the heavy industry drive and a growing group of technocrats who opposed its excesses, Park Chung Hee acquiesced to a wide-ranging adjustment plan in early 1979 (Haggard, et. al. 1994: ch. 3). Among other things, the plan called for the liberalization and internationalization of the financial market.[12] Implementation of the plan was interrupted by the assassination of President Park in 1979 and an economic and political crisis in 1980, but following the seizure of power by Chun Doo Hwan in May 1980, the technocratic reformers, led by Kim Jae Ik, regained their position and initiated a series of important financial reforms, both domestic and foreign.

In January 1981, the government announced its plan to internationalize Korea's capital markets by allowing foreigners to invest in domestic stocks indirectly through investment trust funds (Euh and Baker 1990: 44–7; Mahler 1988: 10–11). One motive for this move was the effort to diversify sources of foreign capital away from bank borrowing. Korea managed to maintain access to foreign capital through the early 1980s because of its dynamic export performance; in no sense did Korea experience a crisis comparable to the large Latin American debtors. Nonetheless, the country did run high current account deficits following the second oil shock, banks were more wary of lending to Korea than they had been in the past, and liberalization was seen as a way of improving access to new sources of foreign financing.

The early stages of the program emphasized liberalizing capital inflows, rather than outflows, but the strategy was highly gradual and the complete liberalization of the capital account was not envisioned until the early 1990s. Domestic firms were not allowed to raise funds abroad until the second half of the 1980s. Only fourteen of the largest companies were allowed to borrow directly through the issue of convertible bonds, and then only with Ministry of Finance approval, a pattern that conformed with the government's preferential treatment of the *chaebol*.

The government also maintained a highly protectionist stance toward the entry of foreign financial intermediaries, a stance which can be explained in part by the politics of a closed and heavily regulated financial system (Euh and Baker 1990: 19–43). Domestic banks were just being privatized, capital markets were relatively undeveloped, and important portions of the economic bureaucracy remained wedded to interest rate controls. Moreover, the banks were saddled with nonperforming assets, many of them policy loans associated with the heavy industry drive of the late 1970s (Choi 1993: 40–54). Foreign entry would only compound the adjustment problems in the financial sector, not only among banks but in the heavily protected insurance and securities industries as well.

Despite the internationalization of Korean industry, the large conglomerates, or *chaebol,* had a number of concerns about both domestic deregulation and internationalization. First, though they welcomed the opportunity to enter the financial sector and to gain independent access to foreign financial markets, they remained heavily dependent on preferential finance from state-owned banks. Second, despite efforts to diversify ownership, many of the largest groups remained family-dominated enterprises; this was even more true among smaller and medium-sized firms. These firms feared that foreign entry into the capital markets would dilute control. Finally, the export dependence of the *chaebol* actually acted as a brake to rapid opening to external capital movements because of the fear that capital inflows would put upward pressure on the exchange rate, precisely as had happened in Chile after 1979; this remained an important concern well into the 1990s.[13]

In the absence of pressing balance of payments constraints, the government was under little pressure to liberalize. In fact, from 1985 through 1988, Korea experienced large current account *surpluses,* peaking at over eight percent of GNP in 1987. These surpluses generated pressures that were exactly the opposite of those experienced in the crisis cases. On the one hand, the government relaxed its controls on capital export in 1987 and 1988, encouraged firms to prepay their external debt, and promoted outward foreign investment. On the other hand, the rapid accumulation of surpluses created daunting problems of macroeconomic management and strong incentives to slow down the initial timetable for the liberalization of capital inflows. When the current account turned to deficit in 1989, the government returned to its traditional practice of controlling capital export as well.

The main source of pressure on Korea came not from the balance of payments, but from the U.S. government. Under the 1988 Trade Bill, the U.S. Treasury was authorized to determine whether countries manipulated their exchange rates to prevent effective adjustment or to gain competitive advantage. The Treasury found that Korea was manipulating its exchange rate, and in February 1990, Financial Policy Talks were launched. The premise of these talks was that the Korean currency, the *won,* had failed to appreciate adequately because the continued use of capital controls limited demand for it (Balassa and Williamson 1990). These complaints coincided with an array of complaints from American banks that they experienced discrimination in their Korean operations, and from American securities firms which began to develop an interest in gaining access to the lucrative Korean market.

After 1988, concessions to the United States were balanced by efforts to maintain policy autonomy and to tailor foreign entry to limit the competitive pressure on domestic financial firms. In March of 1990, the government introduced a more flexible exchange rate system. The problem of foreign banks' access to domestic funds – a recurrent complaint – was addressed by increasing the limit on CD issues. In June 1991, the government revised the Foreign Capital Control Act and moved toward a negative list system approach, under which all transactions not explicitly prohibited would be permitted.

Yet liberalizing moves were counterbalanced by the government's continuing interest in control. The opening of the capital market to direct portfolio investment and foreign entry into the securities business provides a clear example. Direct purchase of Korean securities was open to foreigners in January 1992, though the government limited foreign ownership of the total shares of a single company to 10 percent, and ownership by a single firm to 3 percent. Given that some of the largest firms had been allowed to issue convertible bonds, these limits were quickly reached (*Business Korea,* February 1992: 27). At the March 1992 Financial Policy Talks with the United States, the Ministry of Finance presented a document outlining a new blueprint for the "comprehensive" liberalization of the financial sector. The first phase included a variety of small measures, such as a marginal increase in CD issuance limits for foreign banks, permitting some bond trading by foreign financial institutions, and an expansion of the daily foreign exchange fluctuation band. But the plan stipulated that future stages of liberalization would be contingent on the balance of payments, lower inflation, and a narrowing of domestic and international interest rate differentials, a condition the U.S. argued would only occur if the domestic market were opened (U.S. Department of Treasury, May 1992: 20).

Similar efforts at balancing foreign and domestic pressures are visible in the controversy over opening the domestic financial sector to foreign entry. When the government announced the criteria for those foreign securities firms that would be allowed to enter the domestic market, the considerations included the extent to which the entering firm contributed to the development of the *domestic* industry, implying that joint ventures would be favored over wholly owned ventures. Moreover, the capital requirements were so high and the exact scope of allowed business so vague, that a number of foreign firms refused to even apply. All of the Japanese applicants were excluded on the grounds that Korean entry into the Tokyo market was closed, yet the interpretation given by financial analysts was that Korean firms were fearful of the cash-rich Japanese companies and that the list had been tailored to respond to American and British trade pressures (*Business Korea,* January 1991: 28–9 and April 1991: 49–50).

In the absence of a severe foreign exchange constraint Korean liberalization was extremely gradual. The oil crisis was managed through increased borrowing and aggressive promotion of exports. Portions of the economic bureaucracy saw shortcomings in the control-oriented policy style of the late Park years, but the government was constrained by its close relations with the *chaebol.* The largest firms continued to enjoy access to preferential credit and the domestic financial sector managed to retain a substantial degree of protection. Moreover, the government maintained the political advantage of being able to use the financial system as an instrument both of macroeconomic management and for allocating resources to favored uses.

CONCLUSION

Our analysis suggests two sources of external pressure on the financial policies of developing country governments. First, in line with Frieden and Rogowski we found evidence that increased interdependence and the opportunities provided by deepening financial market integration led to changes in the domestic "preference map" with respect to issues of financial internationalization; these changes also heightened the interests of foreign actors in gaining market access. These changing configurations of interests provided an important background condition for the liberalization episodes we have traced.

However, we placed particular emphasis on similar consequences wrought by a country's balance of payments position. Crises strengthened internationalist forces both within the government and in the economy. Episodes of capital account opening appeared to be motivated by the efforts of political leaders to reassure creditors and investors, both domestic and foreign. By contrast, periods of easy access to finance, commodity booms, or successful export-led growth strategies increase the bargaining power of governments vis-à-vis investors and allow politicians to continue to use controls for political ends.

Despite these findings, it is important to underline several empirical and theoretical weaknesses in the approach that focuses on the policy and political consequences of international factors. First, since the extent of economic openness and the opportunity costs of remaining closed change only gradually, it is difficult to assess ex ante when the accumulated weight of sectoral interests will tip in the direction of policy reform. In the absence of crisis, both government and sectoral interests in controls remained strong or "sticky" in all cases.

Two further problems pose more profound challenges to the internationalization hypothesis and return us to the important institutional and political issues raised in this volume by Garrett and Lange. First, we found that the motives for government intervention and liberalization are not fully captured by a model of policy in which the international position of different sectors is the driving causal mechanism. Governments had political motives for controls and liberalization which went beyond the factor and sectoral stories that are at the heart of the Frieden–Rogowski approach. These included both the advantages in terms of seignorage and government finances and the ability to use the financial system for industrial policy and patronage purposes.

A second problem resides in the fact that the "international" variables which are at the center of this project – external shocks, the openness of the economy, the opportunity costs of closure – are themselves partly a function of past government policy. When we probe the origins of balance of payments crises in our four countries, for example, we find, first, that domestic political factors were deeply implicated in each case, and second that changes of policy only occurred following changes of government or even regime.

In Mexico, the renewed commitment to free currency convertibility in the 1920s and 1930s followed a history of chaotic financial policies associated with the revolution. Subsequent financial reform did constitute an effort to assuage foreign creditors, but its precise form was tailored to the interests of the new PRI elite in consolidating their hold on power. Mexican political leaders used financial market policies in ways which were not inconsistent with a sectoral story, but which also reflected much broader political motivations. For example, the government used financial controls to fund *itself*, as well as import-substituting industry and agriculture. Subsequent changes in the rules governing the capital account were but one component of much larger policy shifts and political realignments. The restrictions on foreign investors instituted under Echeverria in the early 1970s was but one component of a broader political reaction against the conservatism and growing inequality of the "stabilizing development" period. Conversely, the liberalization of the 1980s marked a reaction against the failures of the Echeverria and Lopez Portillo years.

In both Indonesia and Chile, the balance of payments problems which provided the context for later capital account liberalization can be traced to a tumultuous history of macroeconomic instability and unsustainable exchange rates under the populist governments of Sukarno and Allende respectively. The resolution of these balance of payments crises was not simply the result of an existing government changing course. Rather, the crises contributed to regime changes that marked fundamental realignments in the economic-cum-political coalitions supporting the government, in leadership and in the basic institutional arrangements of politics as well. In Chile, Pinochet exploited his power to undertake a dramatic restructuring of the economy on new lines; financial market policy was but one component of a neoliberal strategy aimed at rooting out the conditions that had given rise to Allende in the first place. In Indonesia, by contrast, the government liberalized the capital account, but continued to exploit the segmentation of markets and financial controls in order to dispense patronage and secure bases of political support.

Finally, the strong control over both fiscal and monetary policy and the long-standing push to promote exports help explain how Korea managed to avoid the kind of balance of payments difficulties which provoked capital account opening in the other cases. But this growth path, in turn, cannot be understood without reference to the intervention of the military in politics in 1961, an intervention which fundamentally altered the nature of state–society relations in Korea. As in the other countries, financial controls, both domestic and foreign, were a component of a broader political strategy for maintaining power. These instruments of intervention and political control proved surprisingly resistant to change, despite substantial "internationalization."

It is beyond the scope of this paper to explore the nature of these domestic factors in detail; we have pursued this line of research elsewhere (Haggard and Kaufman 1995: ch. 5; Haggard and Maxfield 1993; Maxfield 1990) and our purpose here was to focus on the important effects of internationalization. It is clear, however, that domestic politics plays a significant role in the way internationalization has shaped decisions concerning the capital account in the cases we have examined, and that these domestic political constraints cannot be wholly reduced to shocks or the interests of social groups.

However, we close by noting that the role of such domestic political variables may well decline in the future. As the integration of financial markets deepens, accelerated by the very policy changes that we have analyzed here, international constraints will play an increasing role in future policy decisions, not only with regard to the capital account but with reference to economic policy more generally.

Appendix

The index of the openness of international financial policy is the sum of four separate indices on particular policy areas. The codings are based on a four point scale from zero to three, thus permitting a total range of the index of zero to twelve. The coding rules for the four policy areas are as follows:

I. THE INTERNATIONAL OPERATIONS OF COMMERCIAL BANKS

0 No or minimal international operations by private domestic banks; foreign banks either prohibited from entry or subject to substantial controls on all foreign transactions. Most foreign financial transactions managed by government-owned banks.

1 All international transactions of domestic banks subject to government approval with limits on terms and on the net foreign currency position of the bank. International operations of foreign banks subject to government approval and limits.

2 International transactions of domestic and foreign banks subject to some statutory limits, but with substantial freedom within those limits.

3 Substantial freedom for outward and inward transactions by domestic banks. Substantial freedom of operation for foreign banks and a generally nondiscriminatory environment.

II. PAYMENTS FOR FINANCIAL SERVICES, INCLUDING PROFITS AND DIVIDENDS, AND REPATRIATION OF CAPITAL

0 All payments for financial services, including repatriation of profits and dividends, subject to limits and government approval. Limits on repatriation of capital.

1 Limits on payments for financial services and repatriation of capital, but guarantees on the repatriation of profits and dividends.

2 Substantial freedom to secure foreign exchange for financial services. Guarantees on the repatriation of profits, dividends, and capital.

3 Complete freedom to secure foreign exchange for all financial services. Guarantees on the repatriation of profits, dividends, and capital.

III. PORTFOLIO INVESTMENT AND PRIVATE BORROWING

0 No inward or outward portfolio investment; all foreign borrowing intermediated by the state.

1 No or very limited access by domestic residents to foreign securities; no or limited rights for domestic firms to issue securities abroad. Substantial limits on foreign holdings of domestic securities. Substantial limits on the foreign operations of domestic securities firms and on the domestic operations of foreign securities firms. Strict government controls on all foreign borrowing.

2 Mechanisms for domestic residents to purchase securities and for domestic firms to issue securities abroad, though with restrictions. Some limits on the operations of both domestic and foreign securities firms, typically with continuing discrimination in favor of domestic firms. Freedom to borrow abroad, typically with government approval.

3 Substantial freedom for domestic residents to purchase securities, for domestic firms to issue securities abroad, and for foreigners to acquire local securities. Generally open and nondiscriminatory regime toward foreign securities firms. Substantial freedom to borrow abroad.

IV. FOREIGN DIRECT INVESTMENT

0 Substantial sectoral restrictions, all investment subject to screening and extensive requirements with regard to trade behavior, employment, domestic equity, domestic content, etc.

1 Sectoral restrictions, but some sectors and/or projects open without, or with only nominal, screening. Some requirements with regard to trade behavior, employment, domestic equity, domestic content, etc.

2 Sectoral restrictions, but primarily in post and communication, energy, utilities, and extractive industries; most remaining areas open without government screening, with nominal screening, or screening only for very large projects. Limited requirements with regard to trade behavior, employment, domestic equity, domestic content, et cetera.

3 Very limited sectoral restrictions, freedom to invest outside of those areas with no or minimal screening. No requirements with regard to trade behavior, employment, domestic equity, domestic content, etc.

All data are coded from information contained in the International Monetary Fund, *Annual Reports on Exchange Arrangements and Exchange Restrictions,* various issues. See also *Developments in International Trade* and *Exchange Systems* (Washington, D.C.: International Monetary Fund, September 1989) and *Developments in International Exchange and Payments Systems* (Washington, D.C.: International Monetary Fund, June 1992).

PART V

Conclusion

10

Internationalization and Domestic Politics:
A Conclusion

HELEN V. MILNER AND ROBERT O. KEOHANE

In this conclusion we seek to answer the questions raised in our introduction in light of the evidence in the empirical chapters. We proceed by elaborating the causal mechanisms, or pathways, linking internationalization to domestic politics that were suggested in the introduction, then assessing the hypotheses put forward there. Our intention is systematically to summarize what we have learned about the impact of internationalization on group interests, government policy and domestic institutions, as well as to explore some of the impacts of such institutions on internationalization itself.

We first explicate three specific pathways by which changes in the world economy can alter domestic politics: by creating new policy preferences and coalitions, by triggering domestic economic and political crises, and by undermining government control over macroeconomic policy. This discussion refers directly to Section III of the introduction, focusing on the broad coalitional processes discussed there and on propositions 1 and 2. The second part of this conclusion seeks to answer the questions put forth in corollaries 1 and 2 of the introduction: Are autarchic countries also affected? Who wins and who loses from internationalization? Our third section assesses the three effects of domestic institutions that were identified in Section IV of the introduction: blocking international price signals, freezing domestic coalitions, and channeling political responses to price changes. In few cases were domestic institutions able completely to block international price signals, but they have often mediated those signals and have slowed down the process of change. In our concluding section we offer some observations about connections between the world political economy and the institutions of domestic politics.

I. INTERNATIONALIZATION AND POLITICAL CHANGE:
THREE PATHWAYS

In the introduction we distinguished three ways in which internationalization could exert effects on domestic politics: by affecting actors' policy preferences and the resulting political coalitions; by creating crises; and by undermining governmental autonomy and policy efficacy. We return to these "pathways" here.

Policy preferences and coalitions

Frieden and Rogowski argue that internationalization can be expected to lead to changes in actors' policy preferences, as suggested by economic theory. For instance, we expect that internationalization will cause a rise in the relative price of some goods and that groups involved in the production of these goods will thus press for greater liberalization. Or internationalization may lead to capital inflows in response to rapidly increased raw materials' exports; in turn, this will lead to an appreciation of the real exchange rate and difficulties for producers of tradable goods ("Dutch disease"), who should oppose such exchange rate changes. These sorts of changes will affect the incentives for political action by asset holders; internationalization will enhance or threaten the returns (profits or wages) that groups receive. In reaction, they may be induced to act politically: for instance, they may lobby to protect rents through increasing protectionist policies or conversely to acquire the ability to employ valuable assets more profitably through further liberalization. The general point is that relative price changes alter the returns to owners of the assets whose prices have changed, leading to predictable shifts in their policy preferences.

Internationalization will affect not only the preferences of domestic actors but also their influence at home. For instance, removing capital controls and trade barriers means that owners of mobile factors of production such as financial capital, and firms that can shift their production abroad, gain bargaining advantages over immobile factors of production (such as most blue-collar labor in advanced industrialized countries) and firms relying on locally specific assets. The newly empowered actors may then be able to threaten "exit" in order to increase their influence ("voice") in domestic politics (Hirschman 1970). By affecting both preferences and power, internationalization should affect state policy.

Internationalization should, according to this argument, also affect political institutions. In this view, institutions reflect the preferences of powerful actors: when actors' preferences change and new policies are pursued, institutional change is likely to follow.

There is much evidence of changes in preferences and coalitions in this volume. Among the developed countries, both Japan and the U.S. show evidence of this. Frances Rosenbluth describes how the growth of export and multinational ties has changed the preferences of business in Japan. No longer are large, internationally oriented firms willing to tolerate high levels of protection for other domestic actors and no longer do they see the benefits of paying huge campaign contributions to the once dominant Liberal Democratic Party (LDP). The preferences and political behavior of firms in Japan have changed due in part to their increased international competitiveness. For Frieden, changing coalitions are an integral part of the story of U.S. monetary policy. Internationalization makes monetary policy contentious, as it draws sectors into direct opposition with one another and directly involves the Congress.

Interestingly, the ex-socialist countries also manifest this effect of internationalization. Evangelista points out that one of the effects of the internationalization of the Soviet economy beginning in the 1950s was the creation of a "new, new class." This class, which benefited from internationalization, became the basis for the reform movement that swept the Soviet Union after Brezhnev's death. He notes that "according to some accounts, it was the international economy itself – or more accurately, the Soviet Union's partial opening to it starting in the mid-1950s – that provided the original basis for the reformist coalition that brought Gorbachev to power." (p. 171). However, he stresses that internationalization was only one of several factors that explained the initiation of perestroika.

In China, a similar process seems to have occurred. As Shirk relates, internationalization helped create a group of actors with whom Deng Xiaoping could develop an alliance to oppose the "communist coalition." This group of agricultural producers, light industry, coastal provinces, and consumers benefited from the opening of China's economy and became the political linchpins in Deng's strategy to unseat the ruling communist coalition and begin economic reforms.

Hence, the Frieden–Rogowski relative price model may help us to anticipate which groups governments are likely to try to attract to their coalitions in response to international economic change. Shirk, for example, even suggests that Deng had such a model in mind when planning his strategy of reform: "Deng Xiaoping and his advisors may have understood from their recent travels abroad that the foreign economic plank of the platform would generate momentum behind the domestic reforms" (p. 194).

New interests and coalitions were also created by internationalization in the less developed countries. Haggard and Maxfield show that internationalization created new pressures for the liberalization of capital markets in the LDCs, as banks and other financial asset holders grew increasingly interested in such policies. As the exit option of mobile capital asset owners grew, governments had to take these interests more seriously and hence pressures for reform mounted.

Triggering domestic economic and political crises

Proposition 1 claimed that internationalization meant an expansion of the tradables sector, increased sensitivity to world price trends and shocks, and therefore greater likelihood that external pressures could generate economic crises that could erupt into major political reforms. It also anticipated that domestic political debate about issues associated with the international economy would rise. This proposition seems to be supported in most of our cases.

Increasing political as well as economic sensitivity to the world economy is a major theme in the chapters on the United States and other developed countries. Effects of the world economy become clearest when currencies are under pressure. Pressures on a country's currency signal governments that asset holders have lost confidence in, or otherwise dislike, their policies. As domestic markets grow more international, this constraint grows. Hence, when countries adopt policies that generate large and persistent budget deficits or inflation, relative price changes in international markets may wreak havoc on the country's currency. The crisis that ensues often forces policy change. The experience of the French socialist government in the early 1980s is a prime example. But many European governments, including Britain, Italy, Spain, and Sweden, have experienced such pressures, as the European currency crises of September 1992 and August 1993 showed. One reason why European governments have tried to fix their exchange rates (that is, the European Monetary System and ERM) is to alleviate such currency fluctuations and their deleterious consequences. Even more extensive coordination in a monetary union (EMU) is now foreseen as a way to allow European states to avoid national currency fluctuations and the political pressures they generate.

Governments are, however, caught in a dilemma. If they want fixed exchange rates in an environment of mobile capital, then they sacrifice their independent monetary policy capability and bring pressure to bear on their fiscal policies. Large fiscal imbalances, especially deficits, put pressure on interest rates and hence on exchange rates. A central issue today for most European governments is how to maintain their extensive welfare systems in the face of these strong international pressures for monetary and fiscal discipline. As Garrett shows, financial markets have imposed significant interest rate premia on countries run by left-labor governments, and these premia have increased as barriers to cross-border capital flows have been removed. Hence, he argues, "the integration of financial markets may yet be the death knell of social democracy" (p. 103). Balance of payments or fiscal crises generated by the loss of confidence of international financial markets in a country can lead to major policy and institutional reforms.

Chapter 9 by Haggard and Maxfield points out that balance of payments crises have constituted critical political turning points for many less developed countries. Being small and more exposed, these countries cannot sustain persistent international pressures against their currencies; and confidence in their institutions may be more easily shaken than in the institutions of rich, long-term democracies. During the 1980s, the prevailing policy changes were liberalizing, promoting the interests of internationally oriented groups and winning applause from dominant financial elites in the rich countries. But as the Mexican crisis of winter, 1994–5 showed, openness can make a developing country extremely vulnerable to loss of confidence and capital flight.

In eastern Europe and the Soviet Union the consequences of internationalization were starkly evident: state-socialist institutions resisted adaptation, but when change took place, it was radical indeed. So far, China has been able to avoid crisis induced by internationalization, but as its dependence on international markets and capital grows, the likelihood of external shocks will also increase.

Undermining the efficacy of government macroeconomic policy

As Richard Cooper (1968) suggested many years ago, internationalization can undermine the efficacy of macroeconomic policies and trade and capital controls that governments maintain vis-à-vis transactions in their markets. In terms of the Frieden-Rogowski framework, what this means is that relative price changes generated by internationalization alter the behavior of economic agents such as firms in the face of existing policies, and that this new behavior alters the impact of the policies, undermining their value to the government. Hence, the government may change its policies even without direct pressure from social groups.

Evidence from the chapters suggests that the efficacy of certain policy instruments (such as capital controls and Keynesian macroeconomic policies) has been eroded by internationalization: well-established domestic practices and entitlements conflict directly with policies that promote external economic balance. In the United States, the recent internationalization of capital and goods markets has reduced the efficacy of interest rate policy and shifted attention toward exchange rate policy, as Frieden argues in Chapter 5. As Garrett shows for a larger set of industrialized democracies, the increasing openness of the economy to trade may undermine the ability of governments to use capital taxation and monetary policy. High levels of capital mobility combined with increasing left-labor power resulted in lower capital taxation and higher interest rates. But for these social democratic governments, fiscal policy was not constrained by either high levels of trade or capital mobility; they tended to have higher government spending and deficits. Moreover, certain forms of internationalization may be less constraining on domestic actors than others. Garrett adds nuance to the world economy argument by providing evidence from Europe, between 1960 and 1990, that differentiates between the effects of trade and financial integration. Garrett's cross-national quantitative analysis leads him to argue that financial market integration seems likely to impose more stringent constraints on left-labor governments in Europe than trade integration. Garrett's and Frieden's chapters provide the strongest evidence for our fourth hypothesis: that internationalization, especially in the form of capital mobility, reduces the autonomy and efficacy of governments' macroeconomic policy choices.[1] But Garrett's chapter does show that social democratic governments still do have choices; they are much less constrained in the fiscal area than in monetary policy. As he notes, "But rather than being constrained by increasing trade and capital mobility, the relationship between left-labor power and fiscal expansions has strengthened with greater internationalization" (p. 102–3). Despite the pressures of internationalization, governments still have policy choices, and fiscal policy may be the most important instrument for choice.

For the developing countries, the utility of various economic policies seems especially vulnerable to the pressures of the world economy. This is not surprising given that these countries tend to be small players in the international economy and to depend heavily on international markets. In their discussion of Indonesia, Mexico, Chile, and South Korea, Haggard and Maxfield point out that one cause of decisions to end capital controls was the diminished utility of these tools given the internationalization of these economies. Controls discouraged investment, but at the same time, the internationalization of firms in these countries made them increasingly ineffective. Recognition of altered conditions combined with balance of payments crises led these governments, in different degrees and in different ways, to alter their calculations of the costs and benefits of policies, and to engage in at least partial liberalization of markets.

Finally, even in the socialist countries relative price signals made their impact felt on government preferences. Matthew Evangelista finds some evidence that autarchic Soviet policies were rendered ineffective and counterproductive by the hidden inflation they generated. As he notes, "despite the best efforts of Soviet planners to insulate the USSR's economy from the vagaries of the international market, in one respect they failed quite dramatically. Even though domestic prices never reflected the vast increases in the prices of key traded goods, the Soviet economy nevertheless suffered the same consequences as in the West – namely, inflation" (p. 168). In turn this inflation led to enormous budget deficits and other problems that helped undermine the legitimacy of the Soviet government. While stressing that this inflation might have occurred without any international changes, Evangelista notes that these relative price changes in the world economy helped make traditional policy instruments increasingly costly and led to a search for new policies that might be more effective. Price signals also had an impact on Chinese policy. Susan Shirk argues that the reformist Chinese leadership of the late 1970s believed that continued economic closure would inhibit growth and that opening China to the world economy could both increase Chinese state power and enhance the prestige of the Communist Party.

In effect, internationalization has called into question the "embedded liberalism" compromise, in which extensive state involvement in the economy helped to generate support for openness in many advanced industrial countries (Ruggie 1982). At the moment, the prevailing view seems to be that less intervention is desirable, and that economic growth will thrive in a less regulatory environment. In time resistance to the costs of rapid adjustment could increase, and new forms of government intervention – many of which seek to regulate and condition this openness – may be chosen. The declining policy autonomy of states as they cede control to markets may only be a temporary phase, until new forms of intervention are demanded and discovered.

II. TESTING THE COROLLARIES

The first corollary in the introduction claims that internationalization should have significant effects in autarchic countries, given the rising opportunity costs associated with it. However, Evangelista's discussion of the Soviet Union throws considerable doubt on this proposition. Evangelista shows that perestroika had little to do with the international economy and that many groups in the Soviet Union did not perceive their preferences as a function of their potential relative prices. Likewise, in China before 1978 domestic political institutions blocked information about the rising opportunity costs of autarchy. Reform was not inevitable; it required leaders to mobilize actors to realize their preferences and to choose the direction of policy.

Corollary 1 must then be strongly qualified. Autarchic countries with nondemocratic political systems can survive a long time even as internationalization proceeds. However, in the longer run, as discussed below, internationalization may affect the domestic politics of autarchic economies by imposing rising opportunity costs. As inefficiencies grow, public dissatisfaction may rise and the government's legitimacy may suffer.

Our second corollary contends that internationalization increases the power of internationally mobile capital, whether firms or financial intermediaries. According to this argument, internationalization offers international capital greater opportunities for exit, and hence greater leverage over the government, than less-mobile firms or labor. Since democratic governments benefit electorally from prosperity and lose from deteriorating economic conditions, governments will have to be concerned about threats of exit and hence noninvestment by mobile capital. Having more credible threats to exit will give these groups greater leverage over policy-making. As Bates and Lien conclude, "Those sectors that possess more mobile factors will have greater control over public policy." Since capital will generally be more mobile than labor, this means that it should be advantaged by internationalization. "In the context of the world economy, the most effective market response [to unfavorable government policies] would be to move assets to other, more favorable, jurisdictions. And an implication of [this] is that it is therefore possible for international capital, as opposed to national capital, farming, or labor, to gain control of public policy" (Bates and Lien 1985: 59, 63).

While the chapters in this volume were not specifically intended to address this issue, they support the generalization that internationalization tends to favor mobile capital over immobile firms or labor. Increasing capital mobility especially enhances the power of financial asset holders. In the industrialized countries, one reflection of the increased power of capital versus unskilled labor may be reflected either in lower relative wages for unskilled labor or higher unemployment, although the magnitudes of the effect are controversial (Cooper 1994; Wood 1994). Governments may not only alter their policies to promote investment; they may even change their institutions to reassure investors and make their new policies credible. Chapter 9 by Haggard and Maxfield provides illustrations of such measures by governments of less developed countries.

However, two qualifications to this generalization are important. First, there is great variation across countries and across issue areas. Haggard and Maxfield point out that in less developed countries where capital is scarce and labor abundant, openness favors labor at the expense of national capital. Furthermore, once capital has been invested, the assets acquired become less mobile and more specific to sectors; thus, the chapters suggest the importance of looking at sectoral as well as factoral interests.

Second, domestic institutions may give advantages to organized groups, affording them access and voice, and thus prevent international capital from taking full advantage of its mobility. The losers from internationalization may be able to use entrenched institutions to block or channel change to the detriment of internationally oriented capital. If the society is sufficiently attractive to its affluent residents that they wish to remain there, with their businesses, such "defensive strategies," as Albert Hirschman once called them, may be effective (Hirschman 1978). For example, despite Japan's growing insertion into the international economy, its international business leaders have been unable to push through all the political reforms they desire, and the ones they have achieved have taken a long time. Hence, even in an open, market-oriented economy, the anticipated effects of internationalization may be muted. Certainly in the short- to medium-term, change can be blocked by preexisting coalitions and institutions. Hence, our proposition about the advantages of internationalization to mobile capital must be qualified.

III. THREE IMPACTS OF DOMESTIC INSTITUTIONS

The nature of domestic institutions is not simply dictated by considerations of economic efficiency, but reflects social values and the preferences of the major actors in a society. As outlined in Section IV of the introduction and supported by the chapters in this volume, domestic institutions seem to exert three different types of effects on the processes linking internationalization to domestic politics: they can block price signals, freeze existing domestic coalitions and policies into place, and channel political responses to changes in relative prices. As Garrett and Lange argue, the formal political institutions that help to organize socioeconomic interests are too important to ignore.

Blocking price signals

Domestic institutions can block price signals emanating from the international environment. In countries with heavy state intervention, such as the Soviet Union and China, government policies and institutions can act as a "wall" between the domestic economy and the international one, muting the impact of changes in relative prices on international markets. As Evangelista maintains, "Even if they could not fully protect the Soviet economy from the vagaries of the world market, Soviet economic and political institutions continued to the end (and even beyond) to distort the influence of the international economic changes on Soviet domestic actors" (p. 175). To a lesser extent the import substitution policies (ISI) pursued by Mexico, Chile, and other less developed countries not studied here, along with South Korea's policies of industrial intervention and capital controls, were also attempts to block, or at least reshape, international price signals.

Very strong domestic institutions may shape the preferences of domestic actors even in the presence of internationalization. Evangelista argues that in such countries as the Soviet Union before the late 1980s, "not only actors' strategies and behavior but their very goals are influenced by the institutional context. Institutions shape actors' perceptions of their interests, and, therefore, their behavior, sometimes even after the demise of the institutions themselves." (p. 185)

While the Soviet case may be extreme, Haggard and Maxfield also show that in the less developed countries they studied, internationalization either did not evoke the policy preferences expected from domestic actors by the relative price changes they faced or failed to elicit active pressure from these groups on the state. As in the Soviet case, domestic actors may either be unaffected by world price changes or be unable to overcome the collective action problems involved in translating their potential gains into political action. Hence, as noted above, the evidence from our case studies severely qualifies the second proposition put forward in the introduction: that internationalization will have significant effects in autarkic economies.

However, the long-term ability of domestic institutions to block price signals is more questionable. The debt crisis of the same period propelled several countries, including Chile, Indonesia, and Mexico, toward economic liberalization. Most dramatically, during the 1970s and early 1980s socialist countries that had been autarkic for thirty to sixty years began to have increasing difficulties. The Soviet Union responded by a strategy of "selective access" to the world economy, seeking the benefits of international exchange without having to change the essentials of a planned economy. However, as Evangelista notes, "ultimately, the strategy of selective access to the world economy backfired. In political terms the opening to the international economy fostered both mass and elite expectations that could not be fulfilled within the context of the old system" (p. 185). The institutions of the Soviet Union are now in Trotsky's famous "ash can of history." Internationalization may be one factor helping to account for this outcome.

Unlike the rulers of the Soviet Union (and of other East European countries), the new, previously persecuted leaders who came into power in China during the late 1970s were able and willing to change policy. Shirk argues that when members of the Chinese elite were able again to travel abroad during the 1970s, they were shocked by China's backwardness relative to Japan and other Asian countries, and were therefore motivated to promote major economic changes. International pressures thus induced domestic policy change: "the Leninist political institutions that remained in place did not prevent reforms and proved to be surprisingly flexible once the preeminent leader came down on the side of reform" (p. 206).

What generalization can we offer about the ability of domestic institutions to block responsiveness to price signals? In the short term, domestic institutions can impose barriers between the world economy and domestic policy outcomes; but over the longer-term and in the face of the massive changes in the world economy during the last fifteen years, they have proven unable to withstand these pressures. Eventually the blocking price signals leads to overwhelming inefficiencies, which in turn reduce the standard of living and hence slowly but surely erode the legitimacy of the government. As Garrett and Lange note, however, this process is likely to be much slower in more authoritarian systems. Wherever governments can afford to channel benefits to their core supporters and ignore or suppress broader opposition, then resistance to change can persist longer. But ironically the more resistance domestic institutions put up, the more costly and dangerous is the process of change likely to be.

Freezing coalitions and policies

Even if price signals are not blocked effectively – and in industrialized capitalist countries it is difficult to do this successfully – preexisting institutions may negate or modify the influence of the world economy by "freezing" coalitions and policies into place. International price signals may enter the domestic economy, but politics will remain frozen in time-worn patterns. Similar to Lipset and Rokkan's (1967) claims about the "freezing" of party systems into place in European countries, this argument maintains that coalitions supporting existing policies are also locked into place. The notion of "path dependence" also evokes this sense of resistance to change (Arthur 1994; David 1985; North 1990, ch. 11). What Peter Katzenstein has described as strategies of "domestic compensation" may be developed in order to render maintenance of an established political structure consistent with national competitiveness (Katzenstein 1984, 1985). Garrett shows that social democratic countries have been able, despite internationalization (and perhaps because of it), to pursue expansionary fiscal policies. This evidence qualifies Frieden and Rogowski's argument in Chapter 2 about how changes in the world economy tend to create new interests and coalitions. It may not be so easy for new coalitions and interests to form; there may be high costs to entry into the political system.

Some of the empirical chapters lend support to this argument. Strong testimony is provided by recent Japanese history: the resistance of the LDP to political reform, the fissures in the LDP over this issue, and eventually its loss of power because of this resistance. As Rosenbluth points out, "Domestically, the configuration of interests supporting the LDP had been changing for some time, suggesting that, all else equal, policies should have changed in tandem. The case of Japan shows, however, the importance of political institutions that structure and channel the incentives of policymakers. When institutions take on an independent force of their own – by, for example, creating barriers to entry into the political marketplace – they may generate policies that no longer directly reflect the balance of social forces" (p. 155). Resistance to change from dominant coalitions is also evident in the Soviet Union, South Korea, and Western Europe. Evidence that preexisting institutions can deflect and mediate international price signals is thus widespread.

Yet these preexisting institutions and coalitions seem unable indefinitely to resist change in the face of major and continuing changes in relative prices. The difficulties encountered by northern European corporatist states during the 1980s, particularly in Sweden, indicate that even successful, highly legitimate political institutions cannot forever resist adapting to dramatic changes in the world economy (Kurzer 1993; Thelan 1993). Although as Garrett emphasizes, substantial policy variations persist, internationalization has put severe constraints on social democratic governments' tax and macroeconomic policies and the coalitions supporting such policies. In a statement that could hold more generally, Rosenbluth's analysis of the decline of Liberal Democratic Party dominance in Japan shows that "at some threshold, pressure for change – filtered through domestic interests – becomes sufficiently great to force substantial changes in the institutions themselves." (p. 153). For almost all of the countries examined here, such substantial changes have occurred.

Once policies shift to permit price signals to affect the domestic economy, institutions may have to be altered as well. Haggard and Maxfield demonstrate this effect clearly in three of their four cases. They note that internationalization combined with balance of payments crises often leads to "institutional changes that increase the costs of policy reversal, particularly by delegating authority over those policies to agencies, typically central banks, that are likely to pursue them in the future" (p. 215). In Japan, as Rosenbluth suggests, fundamental changes in electoral institutions were precipitated, in part, by pressures arising from internationalization.

The evidence is therefore strong not only that established institutions have a major impact on policy, but that internationalization has even put into question well-established institutions – from the Japanese electoral system to social democracy in Sweden and communist rule in the Soviet Union. Yet there is substantial variation by country, both in degree of adaptation and success in maintaining basic structures of power while changing economic policy. For instance, as Haggard and Maxfield point out, financial policy reform lagged in South Korea.

Channeling responses to change

Domestic institutions also mediate the impact of the world economy by channeling responses to international-level changes. The country studies make clear that while all have made reforms in a neoliberal direction, they have not done so in exactly the same way. Not only different institutions but different patterns of trade and finance make a difference. For instance, if Garrett's argument is generally correct, high levels of internationalization via trade should have different effects than high levels of international financial integration. Preexisting institutions may make a difference in these choices, but so should different patterns of trade and financial integration.

The cases show evidence of the variegated pathways that countries may take in response to the pressures of increasing internationalization. China's choice of economic reform without political reform contrasts with the Soviet case. Korea's slow moves to liberalize capital markets contrast with the earlier, rapid movements by Chile, Indonesia, and Mexico. The maintenance of different spending patterns among the West European countries suggests their ability to choose diverse strategies when confronted with similar international economic pressures. Preexisting institutions filter the international pressures, and countries make different choices about their responses to the world economy.

No social science theory successfully predicts these choices, or the success or failure to adapt to change. There seems to be enough leeway for action that leadership can make a difference. International price signals do not automatically dictate outcomes: the entrepreneurship of a Deng Xiaoping, Gorbachev, or Salinas may be needed to galvanize the potential beneficiaries of reform into a winning coalition.

Institutions, strategies, and policies

All three of these mechanisms suggest that there is nothing automatic about the definition of policy preferences or the path of policy and institutional change as internationalization grows. Preexisting domestic institutions can block price signals in the short term, modify and refract them over the medium term, and shape the policy preferences of political leaders and domestic groups. As internationalization increases, however, and especially as capital market integration grows, pressures for changes in policies and institutions that block or distort price signals often become irresistible. Political leaders may have some leeway as to how they respond, but the pressures for policy convergence can be extremely powerful, as the global trend toward neoliberal policies seems to indicate.

In addition, pressures from the international economy are not the only source of external pressure that matters for domestic politics. *Political* pressures emanating from the international system may also play a significant role. In case after case such political pressures affected the outcomes. In the less developed countries examined by Haggard and Maxfield, the impact of the IMF and its stabilization plans was a critical factor. In exchange for new loans these countries agreed to follow the plans of the IMF, including capital market liberalization. In many other cases throughout Latin America and Africa the pressure of the U.S., the World Bank, and the IMF have combined to bring about neo-liberal policy changes (Haggard and Kaufman 1992; Little, et al. 1993, esp. ch. 12; Nelson 1990). In these cases exogenous *political* pressures may have acted simultaneously with the economic pressures generated by internationalization. The exercise of power by international forces is also apparent in the Japanese and Korean cases. There American political pressure induced both countries to alter their policies; threats of American "retaliation" have prompted this. Finally, the strategic embargo imposed by the West on the Soviet Union and to some extent on China helped produce change in those countries, as the opportunity costs of socialist policies were heightened by the embargo. Powerful actors within the international system – whether states like the U.S. or institutions like the IMF – can also affect domestic politics, and can probably do so even more as internationalization progresses.

CONCLUSION

This volume demonstrates that internationalization of the world economy has had important effects on domestic politics. The clearest effect of internationalization has been to undermine governments' autonomy in the domain of macroeconomic policy, and this has resulted largely from rising capital mobility, rather than trade. A second notable effect has been to create the "political space" necessary for leaders to embark on major domestic political reforms. Rising internationalization has increased the portion of the economy susceptible to external economic shocks. It has thus triggered domestic economic crises – usually either in the balance of payments or in currency values – which in turn have sparked major political changes.

Internationalization has also created new policy preferences and coalitions through the relative price changes it has wrought. In response, governments have often worked hard to erect barriers to prevent shifts in relative prices from affecting the domestic economy. Over time the costs of such policies have grown, but depending on the political system these costs have been withstood for long periods. Hence, there is an ongoing interaction between pressures from internationalization and resistance by entrenched interests and institutions.

The blocking and freezing effects of domestic institutions are most powerful in the short run. However, in the long run they seem unable to persist: even institutions change under the pressure of constraints and the lure of opportunities. Hence, the third effect of institutions – that they shape the strategies that leaders devise to adapt to internationalization – may be the most important. Especially for political-economic systems that entered the 1980s insulated from international economic transactions, it was "adapt or die." But how adaptation occurred was fundamentally conditioned by preexisting political institutions, as well as by the character of national leadership at critical moments of transition.

For social scientists, internationalization of the world economy should sound the death-knell to the anachronistic divisions, institutionalized in universities, between "comparative politics" and "international relations." Cross-national comparisons are meaningless without placing the countries being compared in the context of a common world political economy within which they operate. Likewise, theories of international relations that treat all countries as fundamentally similar provide only limited insight into the variations in policy and institutional change. Neither comparative politics nor international relations can be coherently understood without aid from the other.

In addition, internationalization has implications for international relations theory. David Andrews (1994) has argued that capital mobility should be considered as a structural characteristic of the international system, similar to anarchy. Our study of internationalization reinforces his point. These external flows have become so significant for most economies that they can only opt out of such a system by paying enormous costs. Like anarchy, exposure to the international capitalist economy has become a fact that individual states confront and can only ignore or seek to change by paying such high costs that no state can afford it. Hence, again like anarchy, states face similar pressures from the international economy, and they can respond differently to the extent that they are willing and able to pay the costs to do so. As in international politics, this willingness and ability depends on their domestic environment – the leaders, political and social institutions, and preferences of domestic groups. If the impact of anarchy is to create a situation where self-help and balancing behavior by states dominates, then the implication of internationalization is to create a new audience – international financial markets – that political leaders must satisfy.

Governments have some options in the face of extensive internationalization. As we saw above, insulation from such external pressures is possible but is costly and affords only a short- to medium-run strategy. Manipulating international markets is a similarly short-run tactic, as Mexico discovered in late 1994; even though these markets lack perfect information about governments and their behavior, fundamental imbalances cannot be sustained without impressive costs. Coordinating with other states is also a possibility (see also Helleiner 1994). This is the strategy that Western Europe in the form of the European Union has chosen in the postwar period; the recent EMU agreement is another step in this direction. Given the difficulties of international cooperation, however, this strategy too has limits.

Finally, states may concede to international market pressures. This tends to imply the adoption of policies that impose financial "discipline" and promote competitiveness, or the elimination of policies that hinder these two goals. The problem for states is that such a strategy requires credible commitments; indeed the more undisciplined and uncompetitive the domestic economy originally, the more credibility required. Attaining such credibility often requires the redesign or creation of new political and economic institutions. For example, in Europe and increasingly elsewhere, an independent central bank is seen as an indicator of the credibility of a government's neoliberal policies. This example suggests that domestic institutions may be strongly affected by the international pressures generated by internationalization. For instance, small, open nations in Europe found corporatism a congenial institutional design for the four decades after World War II (Katzenstein 1985). In the future we may see new institutional innovations that respond to the need for international markets' demand for credible neoliberal policies.

Nothing in this book's analysis of the recent past provides the basis for easy predictions about the future. Indeed, since few political scientists anticipated the radical changes of the 1980s – the collapse of communism, global adoption of neoliberal policies, and the remarkable "Third Wave" of democratization – we must be humble now. The safest prediction is that change in the next century is unlikely to follow a linear pattern. Liberalization and democratization are not necessarily the wave of the future, and history has not come to an end.

Modern capitalism has always developed unevenly, and its gale-force winds of "creative destruction," in Joseph Schumpeter's phrase, have always generated political resistance. "The bourgeoisie," said Karl Marx and Friedrich Engels, "cannot exist without constantly revolutionizing the instruments of production, and therefore the relations of production, and with them the whole relations of society" (Marx and Engels 1848/1959: 10). Both Marx and one of his greatest critics thought that, in Schumpeter's words, the "very success" of the capitalist system "undermines the social institutions which protect it, and 'inevitably' creates conditions in which it will not be able to live" (Schumpeter 1942/1950: 61). Capitalism may be more resilient than Marx and Schumpeter thought, but recent experience in the former Soviet Union suggests that its ability to destroy established social institutions has not diminished over time.

Notes

CHAPTER 1

1 Since labor moves much less readily across national borders than goods or capital, we have not considered migration as part of internationalization. In some areas, such as parts of Europe and the southwestern part of the United States, this assumption is already problematic; and in future work, serious attention should be given to including migration in the analysis of internationalization. We are indebted to Ashutosh Varshney for making this observation to us. We also note here that the focus of this volume is on internationalization, not democratization. Democratization and internationalization may be related to one another, but they are by no means the same. East Asian countries such as South Korea and Taiwan until recently, and Singapore and China now, demonstrate that countries can become successfully integrated into the world economy without democratization. We view economic internationalization as an explanatory variable and seek to explore its effects on domestic politics in a variety of countries – some of which have long been democratic, some of which have shifted toward democracy, and some of which remain authoritarian. Some of the chapters in this volume may shed light on processes of democratization in particular countries or regions, but our systematic analysis focuses on internationalization. For a fascinating analysis of democratization, see Huntington (1991).
2 Internationalization need not necessarily imply greater sensitivity to prices elsewhere; for instance, if increases in international flows of short-term capital are accompanied by a move to floating exchange rates, certain countries may experience increased monetary independence (Bryant 1980; Zevin 1992).
3 The *locus classicus* of strategic analysis is found in the work of Machiavelli. For a clear recent statement of the institutional implications of a strategic point of view, see Shepsle (1986).
4 For instance, the radical changes in the Italian constitution, while they are likely to be consequential for Italy's role in the world economy, were affected both by the end of the Cold War and by corruption scandals.
5 Cooper argued that rising interdependence undermined decision makers' capabilities to control their own economies. "Increased economic interdependence, by joining national markets, erodes the effectiveness of [domestic] policies and hence threatens national autonomy in the determination and pursuit of economic

objectives." In this formulation, interdependence is seen as having a similar effect on countries as did the presence of transnational corporations. In their volume on *Transnational Relations and World Politics,* Keohane and Nye followed Cooper in discussing "loss of control" by governments. But the research on this topic did not go sufficiently deeply into domestic politics to substantiate the claim; responses of states to interdependence were not closely examined.

The one literature that did focus more on the domestic implications of the international economy was the dependency and world-systems literature. Immanuel Wallerstein (1974) makes the most explicit argument. He claims that the international capitalist economy segregates countries into three roles: core, semiperiphery, and periphery. Countries in the periphery are consigned to having a "weak" state; that is, one unable to resist the pressures of the international economy in order to overcome their dependence. There is a long literature in these traditions that argues that less developed countries are disadvantaged by their international economic position and that many of their domestic ills spring from this external dependence; see, for example, Cardoso and Faletto (1979), Dos Santos (1970), and Evans (1979).

 6 In the three-factor model presented by Rogowski, shifts in the level of trade, given endowments of countries in land, labor and capital, generate predictable shifts in the domestic political cleavages within countries. More differentiated models with more factors, based on specific sectors, or relying on distinctions between national and multinational corporations, could predict different patterns of cleavages.

 7 Gourevitch's findings for more recent periods of "hard times" – the Great Depression of the 1930s and the "crisis" of the 1970s and early 1980s – provide less clear support for the production profile explanation.

 8 Trade in services, rather than goods, has been less well documented, although there is strong evidence that it has grown very rapidly in recent years. We focus on trade due to data availability.

 9 It should be noted that these capital flows reflected current account imbalances, which as a percentage of GNP were larger before 1914 than they were in the 1980s. The nature of these capital flows, however, has greatly changed in the past century. See Turner (1991: 12–13) for the differences.

10 Goodman and Pauly 1993, cited, table 1, p. 54.

11 Between 1965 and 1990, inflation-adjusted merchandise exports grew by 439 percent, while world production rose only 136 percent. *Economic Report of the President* 1993: 280. For the 1980s as a whole, world trade growth exceeded the growth in output by 50 percent. International Monetary Fund (IMF 1992: 8).

12 David Andrews (1994) puts this issue well: "Capital mobility refers to the capacity of capital to cross borders rather than to actual flows of money. It is essential to recognize that this *capacity* of capital to cross international boundaries may not manifest itself at any given moment, due to the (relative) absence of profit incentives deriving from differential rates of expected return in different states." Italics in original.

13 Bryant 1980: 181. Note that this means that foreign countries' policy actions have more impact on other countries than before. Also it implies that shocks originating at home have *less* impact than before since they dissipate abroad, while shocks originating abroad have greater impacts at home under higher levels of internationalization.

14 Under these latter circumstances, if fiscal expansion either induces inflationary expectations or government budget deficits, pressures on the exchange rate will

increase; ultimately the government will be constrained by the degree of its commitment to exchange rate stability, its foreign exchange reserves, and its tolerance for monetary contraction.

CHAPTER 2

1 A third theoretically possible cause of increased returns to international exchange would be (along the lines of the Rybczinski theorem) an increasing disparity in countries' or regions' factor endowments. As Wood (1994: 174–80) notes, there is little empirical support for this possibility.

2 We should note that by "preferences" we mean *policy* preferences, that is desired methods by which the government can achieve desired goals. The goals themselves we would call "interests." In this sense the relationship between interests and preferences is analogous to that between ends and means or between target and instrument.

3 Inflation is widely regarded as a problem precisely because *not* all prices increase in lockstep at a perfectly anticipated rate. Rather, prices typically increase in varied and unpredictable ways. This means that some economic agents win and some lose; and that all are subjected to uncertainty about their future fortunes. By way of contrast, well-executed currency changes (for example, deGaulle's 1958 substitution of a "new" franc, worth precisely 100 "old" francs) have virtually no distributional effects.

4 Where such barriers are erected, the "shadow" prices nonetheless converge, with important consequences. See Section III.

5 In theory, forward markets and insurance can completely smooth out such shocks and eliminate the attendant risks to economic agents; in practice, manifestly, this does not happen.

6 We discuss this point in greater detail, and with reference to standard trade theory, later.

7 Consider, for simplicity, the case of an exogenous decrease in the costs of trade. The cost of moving a good between two regions defines the maximum disparity in their domestic prices; hence every reduction in that cost will bring prices in the two regions closer together, converging at the limit on a single "world" price. The plummeting transport costs of the late nineteenth century, as Kindleberger (1951) trenchantly observed, indeed brought European and American grain prices closer together, to the serious disadvantage of European farmers.

8 This ignores the potential impact of demand elasticities on particular products, but the essential point is unaffected.

9 Most important in this vein is what has come to be called "endogenous growth theory." Seminal papers are Lucas 1988, Murphy, Shleifer, and Vishny 1989, and Romer 1986. A useful survey is Krugman 1993a and attendant commentary.

10 Particularly illuminating are the examples of telecommunications and informational networks, in which European firms have been stunted by national and EU protectionism. See, respectively, *The Economist,* August 13, 1994, pp. 55–7, and the *Wall Street Journal,* September 9, 1994, p. 1.

11 In standard Cobb–Douglas notation, production Y is determined by capital (K) and labor (L) according to the formula

$$Y = AK^{\alpha}L^{\beta}, \text{ equivalent to } \ln Y = \ln A + \alpha\ln K + \beta\ln L;$$

where α and β are both assumed to lie in the interval $(0,1)$; and returns to scale are decreasing, constant, or increasing, according to whether $\alpha + \beta$ is less than, equal to, or greater than unity. The coefficient A, in this formula, represents total factor productivity.

12 For evidence that TFP rises consistently with the level of economic development, see (among many other sources) Dowrick and Nguyen 1989.

13 A particularly illuminating example of the importance of organization, and of the goad of world competition, is provided by the spectacularly successful microchip firm Intel. In order to stay ahead of its rivals, "Intel has halved the time it takes to develop each new generation by replacing a single design team with four – three in America, one in Israel – working in parallel on two successive generations of the chip. . . . The teams liaise [sic] constantly with each other; after work on Pentium was finished, its design team gave a three-day seminar for 200 of Intel's other chip designers." *The Economist,* July 3–9, 1993, p. 22. Similar success has been achieved by strikingly similar means in the area of databases and computer networks by Electronic Data Systems (EDS): the *Wall Street Journal,* September 9, 1994, p. 1.

14 For an argument along these lines see Casella 1992.

15 At the same time, we note that the relative backwardness and the extreme closure of some societies with a great deal of trade potential, including high levels of TFP, engenders intense opposition to liberalization in many sectors. The former East Germany provides a concrete illustration.

16 On the effects of the franchise and of district size, see Garrett and Lange, this volume.

17 We do not mean to imply that external shocks are the most important source of economic dislocation even in extremely trade-exposed societies. Domestic perturbations may still outweigh them. We do say that exogenous easing increases the impact of external shocks.

18 The domestic compensation schemes of the most trade-exposed industrial economies, as examined most notably by Cameron (1978) and Katzenstein (1985), can be understood in large part as social insurance, or at least as smoothing mechanisms, against such terms-of-trade declines.

19 In interwar Europe, for example, the drastic fall in world grain prices made agricultural protectionism ever more costly.

20 This discussion, like the one immediately preceding, abstracts from dynamic considerations. For example, some analysts would argue that economic openness increases the ability of a country to respond flexibly to price changes.

21 By this we mean simply that the ratio of acres of land to hours of labor required to produce a unit of grain will always exceed the similar ratio for a unit of steel.

22 This raises a common confusion, having to do with the sometimes interchangeable use of the terms "asset" and "factor." In some settings it is assumed that factors are inherently defined as such broad aggregates as land, labor, and capital. But this is often arbitrary. Factors of production can be defined as broadly as "all land," or as narrowly as "land suitable for the growing of nutmeg." In this context the major distinction between the usual interpretations of Heckscher–Ohlin (Stolper–Samuelson) and Ricardo–Viner (specific-factors) views of the world is in their *definitions* of the factors of relevance. For the former, labor and capital are relevant factors; for the latter, factors need to be defined much more narrowly, such as "capital used in the production of steel." The different political predictions of the two approaches flow from this quasi-definitional distinction.

23 On the other hand, because in the long run no assets are specific, it is often said

that the Ricardo–Viner perspective applies to the short run, the Stolper–Samuelson one to the long run. In this (limited) sense, the two perspectives are complementary.

24 Formally, a production process is characterized by increasing returns to scale (and, equivalently, its cost function exhibits economies of scale) if doubling all inputs more than doubles total output; or, more precisely, if multiplying all inputs by any factor $t > 1$ multiplies output by some factor greater than t. See again, n. 11, 23.

25 This argument tacitly assumes some specificity of the relevant capital.

26 Operationally, sectors that exhibit either high levels of intraindustry cross-border trade or a high degree of regional concentration are usually assumed to be EOS.

27 On the latter, see Forsyth and Nicholas 1983. A similar phenomenon has been associated with the inflow of capital to Latin America in the late 1970s and to the United States in the early 1980s, both of which led to similar real appreciations and "deindustrialization" episodes.

28 A related issue is the extent to which social and political assets transfer among economic activities. In the later nineteenth century, for example, British elites supposedly could move almost costlessly from landowning into commerce or manufacturing; Continental (and particularly German) landowners lost prestige and power by doing so. Hence, in conventional accounts, British elites better internalized aggregate social (as opposed to class) costs and benefits. See, for example, Mansfield and Snyder 1995: 27–8.

29 Self-evidently, some early democracies, notably Australia, Canada, and the U.S., were highly protectionist, probably because in them unskilled labor was both economically scarce and politically powerful. On average, however, a more participatory regime guarantees greater attention to aggregate welfare.

30 Rae's index of partisan fragmentation is simply a Herfindahl index of party shares, i.e. where f_i is the i-th party's share of the total vote (or, alternatively, of the total seats), the index is $1 - \Sigma f_i^2$. Thus if one party captures the entire vote, fragmentation is zero; if two divide it equally, fragmentation is .5; if ten each receive ten percent of the vote, fragmentation is .9; and so on.

CHAPTER 3

1 There are exceptions to this rule, but they are rare. See, for example, Bawn (1993) and Lohmann (1995).

2 The seminal work on the relationships between economic outcomes and government tenure pertains to the stable democracies. See Hibbs (1987) and Kramer (1971). However, recent research shows that economic outcomes significantly affect the probability of less orderly transfers of power (such as coups and revolutions). See Londregan and Poole (1990).

3 In this paper, we do not explore collective attempts among governments to change the structure of the international economy, which has been the subject of much scholarly attention in the past decade. See, for example, Keohane (1984) and Krasner (1983).

4 This assumption is tenable for all modern economies with the possible exceptions of the U.S. and Japan. There may, of course, be some domestic producers who have marginal price advantages over international competitors due to location, local knowledge and networks, and the like. In general, however, the price taker assumption is appropriate.

5 Less competitive producers in the tradables sector may, of course, be sheltered from international competition by protectionist barriers. Nonetheless,
their welfare is still ultimately constrained by their ability to compete in global
markets.

6 What is and what is not tradable is difficult to determine precisely. The specific
composition of these sectors, however, is not relevant to our analysis. We are
only concerned with the mediating effects of institutions on a given economy,
rather than with its specific make-up.

7 For detailed analyses of these variables, see Golden and Wallerstein (1994).

8 In so doing, they can gain the short-term benefits from maintaining overall
employment levels while putting off until the future paying the costs (through
borrowing).

9 For detailed analyses of this wage setting regime, see Flanagan, Soskice, and
Ulman (1983).

10 For analyses of corporatist political economies that emphasize the importance
of reconciling competitiveness pressures with compensatory needs, see Garrett
and Lange (1991) and Katzenstein (1985).

11 Permutations on the pace of policy change under different electoral rules are
discussed in the next subsection.

12 The seminal analysis remains Rae (1971).

13 We will not discuss other forms of proportional representation, such as the
single transferable vote (used in Ireland) and the single nontransferable vote
(used in Japan). Voting outcomes under these electoral formulae are more
complex to analyze, but nonetheless all multimember electoral district formulae
will yield more proportionate distributions of seats than will first-past-the-post
in single member districts.

14 For an excellent analysis of the implications of the geographic distribution of
votes for electoral outcomes, see Gudgin and Taylor (1976).

15 The population of Montana could shrink to one person, but under the U.S.
constitution it would still be represented by two senators in Washington.

16 For the state of the art on central bank independence – in terms both of theory
and empirical testing – see Cukierman (1992).

17 Under different institutions, this tension could be mitigated. For example, the
existence of strong and centralized trade unions renders the KWS compatible
with good economic performance, even in our open economy at t_1.

CHAPTER 4

1 Reliable cross-national data on all the variables of interest were not available
for a wider range of OECD countries nor for a longer time series.

2 The capital taxation variable combines taxes on corporate income with employers' social security contributions, which operate as a de facto tax on corporate
income. I thank Deborah Mitchell for suggesting this operationalization.

3 However, trade has always been much higher in countries where the left and
organized labor are powerful. Thus, the decision to cut capital taxes to promote
competitiveness in international markets was made long ago in these countries,
not in the 1980s.

4 For a discussion of alternative measures of financial integration, see Frankel
(1991).

5 It was not possible to use the indicator preferred by Frankel – cross-national
variations in "covered" interest rates (the interest rate minus expected inflation

and the forward exchange rate) – because the data on forward exchange rates do not cover all the countries nor all the years in this analysis.

6 The reported figures are parameter estimates for the impact of private domestic savings on private domestic investment for annual cross-national (fifteen country) regression equations for each year from 1967 to 1990. The seminal paper on this approach is Feldstein and Horioka (1980). The measure used in this paper is taken from the modification of the Feldstein–Horioka approach suggested in Bayoumi (1990).

7 The data are from International Monetary Fund, *Annual Report on Exchange Arrangements and Exchange Restrictions* (various). The categories are restrictions on the capital account, bilateral payments with IMF members, bilateral payments with nonmembers and foreign deposits. Recent papers that have used these data include Alesina (1993), Eichengreen (1994), and Epstein and Schor (1992).

8 The partisan centers of gravity scores reflect the share of cabinet portfolios and legislative seats (in the primary chamber) held by different parties in each year, based on the classification provided by Castles and Mair (1984). The data on legislative seats are from Mackie and Rose (1991). The data on cabinet portfolios are from *Keesings's Contemporary Archives* (various).

9 The correlation between these measures is far from perfect ($r = .69$). In separation of powers systems, elections to the executive and legislative branches are distinct. In proportional representation systems, the composition of governments often changes without any alteration in the balance of power in the legislature. Finally, in Westminster systems, holding 50 percent + 1 of seats in the legislature is sufficient to dominate cabinet government.

10 With the exception of union density, these data are only available at five-year intervals beginning in 1970.

11 Some argue that the portion of wage contracts covered by collective bargaining agreements is a better measure than union density (Traxler 1994). However, "coverage" data are only available for the 1980s.

12 The strategic calculus of workers in the public sector is very different from that in the exposed sector. Wage growth has great and immediate consequences for the welfare of workers in the exposed sector. The price of goods and services is determined by international market conditions. Thus, changes in output and employment are directly affected by changes in labor costs (relative to productivity). This relationship is much weaker in the public sector. The proximate determinant of employment is government preference rather than the competitiveness of public goods and services. There is nothing akin to a "world market price" for public sector products. Moreover, governments are likely to use public sector jobs to prop up employment in hard times because in so doing can gain the short-term benefits from employment creation while putting off until the future paying the costs (through borrowing).

13 Exchange rate parities at a given point in time reflect the currency markets' beliefs about future economic conditions. These are highly sensitive to any "signals" sent by governments. If, for example, a government announces a new fiscal or monetary stimulus, or even allows others to believe that it might so act in the future, reactions in the currency markets will likely be very swift and often "overshoot" with respect to the actual economic impact of the policy change.

14 Neoclassical theory would yield no clear expectations about interest rates since competitiveness pressures would decrease reliance on Keynesian demand man-

agement (all else equal, higher interest rates), but higher rates would tend to depress investment and hence lessen competitiveness.

15 This is not to say that new growth theory pertains to all types of government spending. For example, it would be hard to argue that family allowances or industrial subsidies constitute productivity-enhancing collective goods.

16 The full Kmenta model was not used because this procedure exerts a downward bias on standard errors when applied to panel data sets with relatively short time series (as is the case here; Beck and Katz 1995).

17 Coefficients from annual savings-investment regressions only characterize capital mobility across all the countries in a given year. Hence these are not suitable for analyzing the effects of cross-national – as well as intertemporal – variations in capital mobility.

18 These data are described in more detail in the Appendix.

19 These coefficients are not reported to simplify the presentation, but they may be obtained from the author.

20 Trade constituted a lower portion of GDP in many other cases, but in all of these there were simultaneously very few controls on capital flows (as in the United States), and the combined internationalization scores (based on the sum of standardized scores for trade and capital mobility) were higher than for Finland in 1976.

21 The median level of trade in 1967 was in Canada, while the median number of capital controls existed in Austria, Belgium, Japan, The Netherlands, Norway, and Sweden.

22 The median level of trade in 1990 was that for the United Kingdom. The median number of capital controls occurred in Australia, Belgium, Canada, Denmark, Germany, The Netherlands, the United Kingdom, and the United States.

23 Indeed, Krugman argues that the effects of trade competitiveness on the U.S. economy are still trivial.

CHAPTER 5

1 Indeed I am developing more systematic evaluations. In the American context, this involves detailed analysis of the politics of a series of episodes of monetary politics. A survey similar to that presented here is in Frieden (1994b); quantitative evidence on a crucial period is in my "Monetary Populism in Nineteenth-Century America: A New Interpretation," (unpublished manuscript). Applications to contemporary European monetary politics include Frieden (1994a).

2 It should be clear that in the framework of this volume, the relative price changes in question referred to here primarily have to do with those affecting the overall attractiveness of international economic activities. Analysis might also focus on the impact of specific international price movements on domestic monetary politics. I discuss this in the evaluation of individual cases. For reasons of space, I emphasize the effects of increased international economic integration. The impact of particular international price changes is relatively straightforward, in any event – producers whose product prices decline want monetary policies to reverse this decline.

3 In most of what follows, I ignore the inevitable objections of those who, in line with the rational expectations revolution, might downplay the real impact of nominal variables. Whatever the mechanism – labor market rigidities, incomplete information, signalling a change in regime, and so forth – it seems well

established that monetary surprises, whether by way of the nominal price level or by way of the exchange rate, have had a substantial real impact. For an interesting summary of current controversies and conundrums in international monetary economics see Krugman (1993).

4 To be precise, it is covered (exchange rate-adjusted) interest rates that are constrained to be equal. The insight is that of the famous Mundell–Fleming approach, which originated with Mundell (1962, 1963). The model implicit in this discussion is one in which asset prices adjust more rapidly than goods prices, and prices of tradables more rapidly than prices of nontradables. These characteristics cause the "overshooting" and real depreciation/appreciation discussed here. While controversies rage over these and other features of modern monetary economics, this perspective is as close to consensual as feasible. Its exposition can be found in any good textbook discussion of open-economy macroeconomics; a useful survey is Corden 1986.

5 For a more detailed discussion of these issues, see Frieden (1991b, 1994b).

6 Again, I take the tradability of goods and services as exogenous. In the terms of this volume, the cause of an increase in the share of tradables in the local economy might be an exogenous change in international transportation costs, or in the stability of the international payments system, or in other countries' policies. In some treatments of this sort of issue, the home country's trade policy is taken to make certain goods nontradable. Since this can confound cause and effect, I reserve my discussion of nontradability to those goods and services generally recognized to be difficult to trade across borders for technical reasons, not due to (endogenous) policy.

7 Unfortunately, there is only a small empirical literature on these issues. Akhtar and Harris (1987) found that output fluctuations in the consumer and producers' durables industries were two-thirds due to exchange rate changes and one-third to interest rate changes, while fluctuations in residential construction were entirely due to interest rate changes; see also Ceglowski and Hilton (1987: 403–500). Branson and Love (1988) focus on the differential impact of exchange rate movements, and suggestive results along similar lines are reported in Goldberg (1990).

8 For example, preferences about the level of the exchange rate may well vary in intensity: the sensitivity of tradables producers to exchange rate movements is a function of the price elasticities of demand for their products. And whatever positive impact price increases may have on profitability have to be measured against the negative effects of higher prices on demand and the entry of new competitors.

Other peculiarities are also important. For example, intensive consumers of imports will be hostile to depreciation; these consumers may be concentrated industrial users of imported inputs. Overseas investors appreciate the added purchasing power that an appreciated currency gives them, but this appreciation also erodes the home-currency value of their overseas earnings.

Perhaps most important, the two dimensions are often elided, a point to which I return. A fixed rate may imply a strong currency, while a floating rate may imply a weak one. In this case, exporters would have to weigh their desire for exchange rate stability against their desire for a weak exchange rate, and determine which of the two was more important to them.

9 It should be noted that I claim no general applicability of this schema to other national institutional settings. While the general logic may well apply – those policymakers most likely to be held accountable for a policy's impact have the

greatest incentive to be concerned about it – the implications will vary widely from setting to setting.

10 The burgeoning and important literature which applies modern political economy to American politics tends to assume institutional preferences in different ways. The variety assumed here is meant to be illustrative rather than rigorously deduced; whether it holds in practice will be seen in the historical narrative.

11 As mentioned above, I ignore here the fact that to some extent the gradual revival of international trade and payments in the postwar period was a result of American policy, as indeed to some degree economic closure in the 1930s also reflected U.S. government actions. For the purposes of this analysis, the overall level of international trade and investment is taken as given; a fuller analysis would have to account for reciprocal effects between American policy and the environment within which that policy was made.

12 This is especially because there is no necessary correlation between levels of integration and flows of goods and capital. However, scholars have attempted to test for the links between American capital markets and those on the other side of the Atlantic, especially in London. Typical studies, such as Neal (1985) and Officer (1986), focus on the covariation of interest rates in London and New York, and find the two markets very closely linked.

Other studies indicate that American capital markets were not particularly integrated into world capital markets before 1980, after which they became increasingly so. Feldstein and Horioka (1980) demonstrated relatively low levels of international capital mobility in the postwar era; Frankel (1991) brought the data up to date and showed significant increases in American financial integration after 1979.

13 It should be emphasized that in what follows there is little disagreement among historians about the evidence. Virtually every scholar of the period knows who supported and opposed gold, silver, and related policy proposals. My presentation differs in ways described below from most *analyses,* that is I *explain* the political differences with different tools. However, the general contours of the facts are not in any appreciable dispute.

14 I ignore the 1907–13 debates over the founding of the Federal Reserve. These debates focused on the central bank's lender of last resort and international bargaining functions, on which see Broz (1993). The monetary policy aspects of the debate are relevant, but they do not differ significantly from those carried out in the 1920s, so I omit discussion of them in the interest of brevity. The outstanding source on this period is D'Arista (1971); other sources include Kettl (1986: 18–44) and Woolley (1984: 30–47).

15 The literature on this period is of course enormous. Analyses of events leading up to, and through, the first stage of the Great Depression include Barber (1985); Batchelder and Glasner (1992); D'Arista (1971: 117–31); Freidel (1990: 88–91, 100–5, 133–4); Friedman and Schwartz (1963: 299–419); Kettl (1986: 29–44); and Wigmore (1985).

Much of the sentiment for reflation and devaluation coalesced around the ideas of George Warren, a Cornell economist who believed devaluation would raise commodity prices. "Rubber-dollar Warren," as his detractors called him, has received something of an undeservedly bad press. As Eichengreen (1992: 340–1) notes, there were two sources of slippage in Warren's mechanism – between the gold price and the exchange rate, and between the exchange rate and commodity prices – so that the relationship was not unproblematic. Nonetheless, devaluation did in fact serve to raise commodity (and, more generally, tradables) prices. In some ways Warren's ideas were closer to modern real exchange rate analysis than those of his more orthodox contemporaries. For a flavor of his views, see Warren and Pearson (1935).

16 On which there is a small political-economy literature, which tends to argue that Fed policy responded to the needs of its member banks rather than the macroeconomy. See Anderson, Shughart, and Tollison (1988) and Epstein and Ferguson (1984).

17 In March 1933, the Chairman of the Clearing House Association and President of Central Hanover Bank and Trust recognized that the gold standard could not be sustained: "in the face of today's figures we are already off the gold standard whether the fact is legally recorded or not" (Wigmore 1987: 748). After the crisis had receded, the bankers desired stabilization – and they got it, culminating in the Tripartite Agreement of 1936. An interesting incident was the involvement of Walter Lippman (Steel 1980: 302–9). Lippman was prevailed upon by Morgan's two leading partners to write a column about the need to go off gold; the column appeared on April 18, 1933, and was referred to repeatedly by Roosevelt in his justifications of his decision.

18 Temin and Wigmore (1990) indeed argue that the devaluation was the crucial policy shift underlying the New Deal recovery.

19 Todd (1992) presents an interesting discussion, while Sylla (1988) provides a more detached survey.

20 Auerbach (1990) in fact argues that this arrangement was devised explicitly to avoid Congressional influence on exchange-rate policy. For a summary of the generally accepted legal situation, see Destler and Henning (1989: 86–8).

21 Students of American foreign economic policy will recognize strong parallels between Congressional action in delegating trade and monetary policy in the New Deal. Indeed, the trade-policy equivalent of the monetary and exchange-rate policy initiatives discussed here, the Reciprocal Trade Agreements Act, was passed within a few weeks of the Gold Reserve Act (Haggard 1988).

22 Classic sources for this episode are Calleo (1982: 62–117), Eckes (1975: 237–71), Gowa (1983), Odell (1982), and Solomon (1977: 176–234).

23 The tradables–nontradables relationship is unambiguous, while measures of the real exchange rate are mixed: most estimates show the dollar's real appreciation in this period as about three or four percent. The principal reason for the difference is trade weights, especially the overwhelming role of Canada in U.S. trade. The issue is beyond the scope of this study; for now it is enough to note that disaggregated price trends indicate very significant pressure on tradables producers.

24 Aronson (1977:137–50) discusses these developments. On the tradeoff between capital controls and fixed rates, see Maxfield 1992. It should be noted that the choices available inherently ruled out domestic macroeconomic adjustment, which would have involved substantial austerity and was generally perceived as politically infeasible.

25 ECAT members had average overseas assets equal to 42 percent of total assets and foreign sales equal to 44 percent of total sales. On the general role of such groups see Destler and Odell (1987) and Milner (1988).

26 Congressional intent was to get looser monetary policy and more Fed responsiveness, but the Fed's supporters were able to make the requirements as enacted relatively lax. On this episode and related developments see *Journal of Monetary Economics* (1978), Kettl (1986: 140–66), and Woolley (1984: 144–53).

27 All real effective exchange rate figures in this and the next section are from a
    series calculated by Allan Meltzer and graciously supplied by him to the
    author. Exchange rate statistics for the late 1970s are a bit confused, especially
    as the dollar moved differently against different currencies – appreciating
    against the Canadian dollar and depreciating against most major currencies.
    Given the great weight of Canada in American trade, this reduces the dollar's
    depreciation in calculations of the effective exchange rate. Where this appears
    relevant, I indicate both the effective exchange rate trend and movements
    against the mark and the yen. For monthly trends, I use the real effective
    exchange rate; this makes little difference in the short run as nominal and real
    rates moved quite closely together. Over the longer run, of course, they
    diverged somewhat.

28 The literature on this period includes Cohen and Meltzer (1982: 15–64), Destler
    and Mitsuyu (1982), Golub (1986), Greene (1984), and Kettl (1986: 167–79).
    On the macroeconomic diplomacy of the period see Putnam and Bayne (1984:
    67–136).

29 Federal Reserve Bank of St. Louis 1986. To give an example of the statistical
    difficulties, measures of the real effective depreciation between 1976 and 1980
    range from 13 percent (*Economic Report of the President*, various issues) to 2
    percent (Morgan Guaranty Trust Company, various issues), passing through
    figures of 7 percent (Meltzer's series, mentioned above fn. 27), 8 percent (Inter-
    national Monetary Fund, various issues, based on wholesale price indices), and
    9 percent (same source, based on relative unit labor costs). In some sense, then,
    the tradables–nontradables figures reported in Table 4 may be the most mean-
    ingful available, as they represent the relative price trends experienced by
    American producers in the American market.

30 Figures from the Meltzer series, described in fn. 27. The Fed series indicates a
    64 percent nominal effective appreciation, and a 56 percent real effective appre-
    ciation, between 1980 and 1985; see Federal Reserve System, various issues.
    Over the same period Morgan Guaranty's figures indicate a 40 percent nominal
    and 36 percent real appreciation. The IMF's figures based on relative unit labor
    costs show a 38 percent real appreciation, while those based on relative whole-
    sale prices show a real appreciation of 36 percent.

31 The outstanding work on this episode is Destler and Henning (1989), which
    presents a detailed history and expert analysis of the 1980–5 period. With a few
    exceptions, the analysis presented here parallels theirs. Also useful are Frankel
    (1994) and Funabashi (1988: 65–86).

32 I do not mean to take a position here on which of these policy measures, if any,
    would indeed have led to a depreciation. Whatever economists may decide
    about the matter, at the time tradables producers believed that monetary policy,
    fiscal policy, and intervention would have, respectively, certain, likely, and
    conceivable effects on the value of the dollar.

33 The original appeal, with the list of initial signers, appeared in national newspa-
    pers on January 25, 1983.

34 Indirect support for my argument can in fact be gleaned from the slender
    modern literature on the Populist era, especially as it finds farm prices (rather
    than debt) the principal determinant of monetary populist protest. For exam-
    ple, McGuire (1981) found Populist fervor closely related to price instability,
    while Bowman and Keehn (1974) found agrarian political unrest rose during
    periods of farm price declines.

35 On this aspect of the RTAA, see Haggard (1988). For examples and evalua-

tions of the enormous literature on central bank independence see Grilli, Masciandaro, and Tabellini (1991).

CHAPTER 6

1 The LDP ruled virtually uninterruptedly from 1955 to 1993, with the minor exception of a brief coalition with the New Liberal Club in 1976. Sweden's Labor Party holds the record for political longevity by a smidgen, having governed from 1932 to 1976.

2 This point echoes arguments Milner (1988) makes about which French firms were likely to favor freer trade.

3 In the last election under the old rules, Japan had 1 single-member district, 4 two-member districts, 42 three-member districts, 37 four-member districts, 41 five-member districts, and one six-member district.

4 Though one might consider ideological spacing of LDP candidates to be a cheaper, alternative way to divide the votes, this would have posed several problems that the personal vote strategy did not. The first would be unpredictability. It would be extremely difficult to know, on the basis of platforms alone, who would vote for whom. Second, the party would have jeopardized both its party label *and* the personal vote. If LDP candidates attacked each other's platforms, voters would get little sense of the party's goals and intentions. Sufficiently negative campaigns could even lose rather than gain votes for the party. I am indebted to Gary Cox for this point. For a fuller explication of the interaction of Japan's electoral rules and the LDP's electoral strategy, see McCubbins and Rosenbluth (1995).

5 Because for decades Taiwan and Japan were the only two countries in the world to have multimember-district SNTV electoral rules, it is difficult to test empirically the particularism argument. But it is worth noting that in prereform Italy, where voters could rank three or four candidates in order of preference (rather than sticking to the party's order of listing), members of the Christian Democratic Party spent substantial resources building their personal support networks. In other words, Italy resembled Japan in the sense that the electoral rules gave individual candidates of the same party an incentive to compete against each other electorally (Katz 1980).

6 See also a May 1992 press release by a group of young LDP Dietmembers voluntarily disclosing their income and expenditures (Wakate giin no kai 1992). Their stated purpose was to spur electoral reform by horrifying the public with this glimpse of Japan's money politics. According to this report, the average annual expenditure of these primarily first- and second-term LDP members was over a million U.S. dollars (at 130 yen to the dollar) in 1991, not an election year. Japan's weak campaign finance disclosure laws made these partial revelations of LDP finances particularly valuable.

7 See, for example, Kawato (1992) and Soma (1986).

8 The argument is not that Japanese firms are relying increasingly on foreign imports and therefore want tariffs reduced. Japan's intraindustry trade is notoriously weak, more or less across the board in the manufacturing sector (Lincoln 1990). The point is rather that Japanese exporters, fearing foreign retaliation, urged the government at least to open domestic agriculture and retailing. Corporations also seemed to worry that high domestic agricultural prices contributed indirectly to higher labor costs (Honsho 1985).

9 See, for example, Arai (1988) and Kobayashi (1987). The variance in electoral

margins of LDP candidates increased as districts have urbanized, making LDP
incumbents less electorally secure. Electoral insecurity of LDP incumbents, in
turn, fuelled an increase in factionally backed independent candidates. Incumbents who were "running scared" became a natural constituency for electoral
reform (Cox and Rosenbluth 1995).

10 In addition to demanding public goods such as lower consumer prices, urban
voters also wanted a wide array of private goods such as better schools and
roads in *their* neighborhoods. But because urban voters are more fragmented
than rural voters, LDP representatives in urban districts had to pay a higher per ,
capita price for urban votes, largely in organization costs. In either case, due to
more consumer concerns or to the higher price of urban porkbarrel, the LDP
coalition became more costly to hold together.

11 For pressure on the LDP to hold the line on agricultural protection, see
"Yureru kome seisaku [Japan's Shifting Rice Policy]," *Nihon keizai shimbun*
(November 11, 1992): p. 5; "Kome mondai [The Rice Problem]," *Nihon keizai
shimbun* (Nov. 24, 1992): p. 1; "Kome kaiho 'joken toso' [Fighting Over Conditions on Agricultural Liberalization]," *Nihon keizai shimbun* (November 25,
1992, eve.): p. 1; "Kome kanzeika o kyohi [Refusing to Tariffize Rice]," *Nihon
keizai shimbun* (December 4, 1992): p. 2.

12 According to a 1985 LDP report, only 20.3 percent of farmers and 49.6 percent
of nonagricultural small business owners paid *any* taxes in 1983 (Maruyama
chosakai 1985).

13 A group of LDP backbenchers formed an antisales tax group within the LDP,
but they quickly disbanded upon threat of sanctions from the LDP leadership
(Ishikawa and Hirose 1989). Apparently the leadership decided the benefits of
the tax outweighed the political costs. See also *Nihon keizai shimbun* (April 24,
1991).

14 Businessmen decried Japan's multimember electoral rules almost daily in the
media. For a small sample of these denunciations, see "Shusho ni seiji kaikaku
ikensho [Making Recommendations on Political Reform to the Prime Minis-
ter]," and "Shikin atsume, atarashii hoho de [Raising Funds a New Way],"
Nihon keizai shimbun (eve. January 7, 1993: p. 3); "Seiji kaikaku danko o
[Pressing for Political Reform]," *Nihon keizai shimbun* (October 7, 1992): p. 5;
"Jiminto e no fuman funshutsu [Exploding with Disapproval at the LDP],"
Nihon keizai shimbun (October 9, 1992): p. 5

15 Se Takahashi (1991: 48–50). Returning to the Italian case noted in footnote 5,
the combination of proportional representation and preferential voting did not
force the DC to divide districts among candidates. As a result, factions could
and did compete on the basis of issues as well as on the basis of patronage and
pork. This probably somewhat lowered the price tag for DC election campaigns
and reduced the redistributive pressures on the government budget from within
the party. Nonetheless, the preferential voting scheme no doubt encouraged
some reliance on particularistic favors, and was therefore inconsistent with real
economic openness. European integration appears to have spurred the recent
move in Italy for electoral reform.

16 Most political science accounts emphasize how England's industrialization
shifted the preferences of economic and social groups (McKeown 1989: 379;
Rogowski 1989: 34–6); and Schonhardt-Bailey (1991: 52). Schonhardt-Bailey's
work, however, which stresses "the united force of concentrated and de-
concentrated interests" in achieving free trade policies, is intriguingly consistent with an argument about changes in England's electoral institutions. For

sources that consider the role of political institutions more explicitly, see Blake (1967), and especially Cox (1987, ch. 4).

17 Some scholars, most notably Chalmers Johnson (1986, 1995) dispute the notion that politicans have ever actually wrested power from bureaucrats.

18 For an application of principal-agent theory to American politics, see Keiwiet and McCubbins (1991). Ramseyer and Rosenbluth (1993) apply principal-agent analysis to Japanese politics under the LDP.

19 For bureaucrats' woeful confirmation of this point, see, for example, *Asahi shimbun* (July 5, 1994: p. 3).

CHAPTER 7

1 By one estimate, foreign firms provided 500–800 million rubles worth of goods and services to the Soviet economy in 1989, or well less than 0.1 percent of GNP (Kuzmin 1990: 52).

2 For the argument that "the aggregate benefits of liberalization will be greatest precisely in the most closed economies," see Frieden and Rogowski, this volume (p. 34).

3 For the current, post-Soviet period, such a rigorous test of political-economy theories may be possible. A particularly promising project of data gathering and analysis is being undertaken by Stephan De Spiegeleire and Klaus Segbers at the Stiftung Wissenschaft und Politik, Ebenhausen, Germany.

4 Even the collective farms (kolkhozy) – the main institutions which were not directly owned by the state – have since the 1950s come to resemble or be replaced by state farms (sovkhozy). Kolkhoz members received salaries and had no say over the disposition of the assets nominally owned by the collective.

5 See the discussion, for example, by the Soviet sociologist and economist Tatyana Zaslavskaya (1990: ch. 4).

6 Especially prescient on this point is the article by Lukc and Boggs (1982), written a decade before the demise of the Soviet Union.

7 For the distinction between hidden and repressed inflation, see Kornai (1992: 255–7).

8 Much of the following argument comes from Moody (1991: 21–5). I am grateful to Peter Lange for calling it to my attention.

9 Not all imported goods were subsidized in that fashion. Consumer goods, for example, were priced to reflect the world market values, as were some intermediate goods. See the discussion in Treml (1980).

10 In a well-documented account of a 1987 Politburo meeting, where the minister of finance presented a report on inflation, many of these internal sources are discussed, but the international economy is not mentioned at all (Cherniaev 1993: 145–6). Former Soviet Prime Minister Nikolai Ryzhkov, in his memoirs (Ryzhkov 1992: 229), does mention the effect of the dramatic fall in oil prices in 1986. He suggests that the energy export-dependent structure of Soviet foreign trade was one of the "mistakes" that contributed to the economic crisis, but not a major one (neglavnykh).

11 I owe this point and the subsequent discussion to Yasheng Huang.

12 A similar argument about the psychological effect of the failure of the Soviet economy to compete with the West is found in Halliday (1992).

13 Yanov constantly refers to his proposed economic reforms as "reconstruction," which might have been perestroika in the original Russian manuscript.

14 For a discussion of the high-level politics of the early reform years and the

constituencies of the various leaders, see Aslund (1989). For discussions of the economic and political views of the intelligentsia, see Flaherty (1991), Schwartz (1991), and Singer (1991).

15 As Luke and Boggs argued in an account consistent with Yanov's, the strategy of what they call "technocratic reform from above" was "most compatible with Soviet adaptation to the imperatives of technological innovation and the world market," although they anticipated, correctly, that "it would not solve the basic contradictions of imbalanced growth" (Luke and Boggs 1982: 123–4). Many of the Soviet memoirists employed a similar analysis.

16 See, for example, the rich accounts by Remnick (1994) and Smith (1990).

17 During the 1970s, the USSR continued to reap windfall profits from its sale of oil outside eastern Europe for world-market prices. Yet there were still opportunity costs entailed in not selling all of the oil at those prices.

18 Jack Snyder (1987/88) draws on Schumpeter for his analysis of the Gorbachev phenomenon.

19 This discussion draws on Burawoy and Krotov (1992); Crowley (1993); Friedgut and Siegelbaum (1990); Gustafson (1989); Hewett (1982); Mandel (1990, 1991); and Rutland (1990).

20 Who initially controls the shares would not be an issue if there were no restrictions on their resale. As of the first half of 1994, however, there were many such restrictions, including the fact that foreigners were not allowed to purchase shares in "the defense and mining sectors, in the fuel and energy complex, and in certain extractive industries," and that permission of the finance ministry was required for sales to foreigners even in less strategically important industries (Bush 1994). I thank Celeste Wallander for discussion of this point.

21 This is a central argument in Thelen and Steinmo (1992).

22 Consider a couple of mundane, but telling examples: In Russia today, it is difficult to purchase logs, even from privatized lumber companies, in any lengths except three or six meters, because those are the "government standards," inherited from Gosplan. Construction firms, even foreign ones, are expected to follow published government norms for how many people to hire to construct a building, based on the building's dimensions, even though that work force may be 4–5 times what would be adequate in the United States (National Public Radio 1994). For evidence of deep-seated beliefs that affect workers' economic behavior, see Evangelista (1996).

CHAPTER 8

1 In contradiction to Cumings (1979), Lardy (1992: 30–1) argues that the Chinese import substitution development strategy adopted during the 1950s when the Soviet Union was selling China industrial plants, did not undergo fundamental change after the break with the Soviet Union in 1960. Food imports surged after the disaster of the 1959 Great Leap Forward, but during the 1960s, China continued a program of complete plant imports largely from Japan.

2 With all trade corporations under the Ministry of Foreign Trade, if one corporation sustained a net loss, it was easy for the Ministry to reallocate financial profits from another money-making corporation (Lardy 1992: 6). The system of cross subsidies meant that China had a de facto multiple exchange rate system (Lardy 1992: 28).

3 Lardy (1992: 23) notes that the military received preferential treatment in all of its trade transactions.

4 In a 1984 article, I identified a communist coalition consisting of three groups,

heavy industry, inland provinces, and central agencies (Shirk 1984). I now believe that the military belongs in this coalition of groups favored and protected by communist policies.

5   CCP leaders anticipated little risk that government officials would act contrary to party preferences because the party had appointment power over government officials, exercised constant, tight "police patrol" oversight over the government through party committees and groups, and had ultimate veto power over government decisions. Moreover, having institutionally established who gets to sit around the table, the party expected few surprises from government decision making (Shirk 1993).

6   After 1964, domestic and international prices were completely separate in an "airlock" system in order to protect domestic industry, particularly machinery from foreign competition (Lardy 1992: 24).

7   The national security rationale for the drastic shift in foreign policy probably made it easier for CCP conservatives to swallow it than if it had been motivated by economics.

8   According to Mao's doctor (Li 1994: 514), in 1969 the leader described China as surrounded by enemies on all sides (USSR, India, Japan) and began to think about bolstering its security by reaching out to the U.S. "Beyond Japan is the United States," he said, "didn't our ancestors counsel negotiating with faraway countries while fighting with those that are near?"

9   Zheng Tuobing, "To Promote China's Foreign Trade Under the Reform and Open Policy," *To Build Socialism with Chinese Characteristics,* Zhongguo zhanwang chubanshe, 1985: 40–2, cited in Huan Guocang, 1987: 42.

10 Because ordinary citizens have no institutional voice in communist authoritarian regimes, citizen collective action through protest becomes all the more important. Therefore groups that find it easier to organize mass protests (e.g., urban workers) are more influential in authoritarian regimes than those who find it harder (e.g., peasants).

11 Scholars who study noncommunist third world countries often ascribe reform initiatives to "change teams" of technocrats (Waterbury 1993) or the "embedded autonomy" of technocratic government agencies (Evans 1992). Such phenomena are impossible to find in communist systems because even with reciprocal accountability, top-down political controls over bureaucratic careers are very strong, and communist oligarchs keep the bureaucracy compartmentalized to prevent coordinated action among the second tier. It is also worth noting that Chinese government bureaucracy in the late 1970s had a very small number of university educated technocrats because for decades Mao stressed political loyalty over expertise in bureaucratic promotion.

12 Although improved relations with the United States and Europe created conditions for financial and technical assistance from these countries, economic recession and protectionism limited markets for Chinese manufactured exports in those countries.

13 Although the formulation of specific foreign economic policies was a complex processing involving many CCP and government officials other than Deng Xiaoping, the open policy, more than any other feature of the reforms, was always personally associated with and attributed to Deng.

14 China's evolution from personalistic rule to institutionalized authority was retarded due in large part to Mao Zedong's attempts to sustain his revolutionary charisma and stem the trend of institutionalization (which is disparagingly called "revisionism") by launching mass campaigns.

15 See "New Industrial Policy Released," *China Daily,* June 17, 1994: 1.

16 For a good example, see David Zweig, "Internationalizing China's Country-side: The Political Economy of Exports from Rural Industry." *The China Quarterly,* 1991: 716–41.

17 The term "experiment" is a misnomer. Chinese reform experiments closely resembled the model farms, factories, and localities of the previous era that Mao Zedong used to propagandize and build bureaucratic support for his policy initiatives.

18 See Joseph Fewsmith, "Reform, Resistance, and the Politics of Succession," in Joseph (1994): 7–34.

19 It is important to note that most of the Chinese gains from opening have originated in trade of goods rather than capital. Despite high levels of foreign investment, China remains only very partially integrated with international capital markets. As Frieden and Rogowski point out, the benefits from the reform of commodity trade are far less than the potential benefits from capital trade. Therefore China has far to go to approach its own Pareto frontier. I am grateful to Tim Fitzpatrick for this observation.

20 For example, the SEZs pioneered the use of labor markets rather than administrative allocation of labor.

21 As Chen, Jefferson, and Singh (1992: 212–13) point out, Hong Kong, and now increasingly, Taiwan, have had a profound effect on P.R.C. economic development as trading partners, financiers, and intermediaries. As of 1988, exports to Hong Kong were 40.8 percent of China's total exports (three-fourths were reexported), and 30.8 percent of China's total imports came from Hong Kong (more than two-thirds of them were processed in China and reexported through Hong Kong). Of the $3.2 billion of direct foreign investment in China in 1993, two-thirds originated in Hong Kong and Macao; Guangdong province claims 43 percent of China's total foreign direct investment.

22 When I interviewed the then-mayor of Shanghai, Wang Daohan, in 1985, even before I asked the first question, he launched into a long tirade about the center's special treatment of Guangdong province and its SEZs.

23 In a 1992 speech Deng conceded his mistake: "In retrospect, one of my big errors was the exclusion of Shanghai when the four special economic zones were instituted. Otherwise, the Yangtze Delta, the entire Yangtze Valley and even the whole country would now have presented a different picture as far as reform and opening to the outside world is concerned." ("Importance of Development Stressed," Xinhua News Agency, November 5, 1993, in FBIS, *China,* November 5, 1993: 32.

24 As Cumings (1989: 218) points out, China's huge domestic market gives it an advantage over other newly industrialized countries with less purchasing power at home that run into trouble when protectionism cuts their access to the U.S. market.

25 In 1993 the State Council required that it must approve all local development zones. The uncontrolled spread of local development zones produced several negative economic consequences: localities competed in "policy auctions" to attract foreign investors by lowering taxes; development zone construction caused economic overheating and shortages of funds, energy, transport, and raw materials; and farmland was gobbled up (Shi Jian, 1992: 28–9; "State Council Issues Development Zones Circular," 1993: 43).

26 A massive wave of South Korean and Japanese foreign investment during 1992–3 was concentrated in Northeast China, particularly Shandong and Tianjin. The dynamic economic development stimulated in the Northeast region by this

investment has broadened support for the open policy beyond the Southeastern coastal areas.

27 In 1985 and 1986, the central government temporarily froze the foreign exchange in the hands of local officials by putting strict controls on its use. This move was a response to the Hainan auto import scandal in which officials on the island took advantage of their preferential access to foreign exchange to import automobiles for resale in Guangdong and other provinces, and to overall trade deficits.

28 By the mid-1980s, 42 percent of all foreign exchange was in the hands of the provinces and export producers, and only 58 percent was controlled by the central government. As a general rule, of the foreign exchange retained by locals, half went to the enterprise and half to the level of government that "owned" it (Lardy 1992: 56–7).

29 David Zweig (1994: 6) notes that central leaders were surprised by the responsiveness of rural township and village industries to international market demand. Central policies to expand foreign exchange retention and import approval rights of these rural nonstate firms in 1988 reflected not lobbying from below but a Beijing decision to promote exports and create jobs in rural areas.

30 Exports did not grow rapidly until the rate of exchange was improved and tax subsidies for exporters increased in the second half of the 1980s.

31 Competition among provinces and localities for foreign business, however, had a salutary affect on the economic decisions of local officials. In the early days of reform, local officials took advantage of their new economic authority to subsidize loss-making enterprises and build patronage machines; they paid little attention to raising efficiency or investing in needed infrastructure. But over time, competition for foreign investors led them to push firms to become more efficient so that they could concentrate funds on building the airports, telecommunications and roads that would create an attractive environment for foreign investors (Rawski 1992: 11–12).

CHAPTER 9

1 We define financial internationalization to include two broad policy areas: rules governing the capital account; and rules governing the international behavior of financial institutions. With respect to the first, the OECD Capital Movements Code directs attention to restrictions on: direct investment or disinvestment; buying and selling of securities; operations in real estate; credits directly linked to international trade in goods or services; cross-border financial credits and loans; the accounts of financial institutions; personal capital transfers; physical movement of capital assets; and disposal of funds owned by nonresidents (Organisation for Economic Cooperation and Development 1990: 11–12). The OECD does not specifically address the rules governing foreign entry in financial services except as one component of the broader regime governing foreign direct investment. As the IMF notes, however, "trade liberalizations in many service industries, in particular the financial industry, have necessitated accompanying liberalizations of capital account transactions" (International Monetary Fund 1992: 27).

There is a small but growing number of studies of the political economy of finance in developing countries, but few deal primarily with the issue of the internationalization of financial markets. Two exceptions are Maxfield 1990 and Winters 1996. See also Frieden 1991b; Haggard and Maxfield 1993; Woo 1991: 176–203.

2 The IMF collates all policy changes and categorizes them as either "liberalizing" or "tightening." Totaling these measures runs the risk of weighting the significant and the trivial equally; nonetheless, the results do provide an overall sense of the direction in which countries are moving. Data are from International Monetary Fund 1992.

3 For a similar argument with respect to German banks see Goodman and Pauly 1993.

4 Two contending economic models of balance of payments crises have dominated recent debates. Krugman (1979) emphasizes changes in the economic fundamentals while Obstfeld (1986) emphasizes the significance of speculative behavior.

5 The balance of payments crisis that triggered the 1971 reform occurred in 1965–6 and thus predates the data on capital account openness.

6 For overviews of the Indonesian economy during this period, see Booth and McCawley 1981; Palmer 1978; Robsion 1986; Winters 1996.

7 The following draws on Economist Intelligence Unit, *Quarterly Economic Report,* 1988, 2: 13; 1989, no. 1: 9; 1989, no. 2: 10; 1989, no. 3: 15; and 1989, no. 4: 10.

8 In December 1976, the Minister of Finance Jorge Cauas resigned, and Sergio de Castro replaced him. Pablo Baraona moved from the Central Bank to the Ministry of Economy, and Alvaro Bardon assumed the Central Bank presidency. De Castro, Baraona and Bardon had all done graduate work at the University of Chicago; the "Chicago Boys" now had full control of the key economic policy-making positions and the backing of Pinochet himself.

9 The one foreign bank branch active in Mexico at the time, Citibank, was allowed to keep its license.

10 For an overview of Korean financial policy, see Choi 1993; Cole and Park 1983; Woo 1991.

11 A review of the IMF's *Annual Report on Exchange Arrangements and Exchange Restrictions* during the 1960s provides a fascinating antidote to the idea that Korea liberalized during this period.

12 For an overview of the reforms, see Park 1995. On the politics of financial market reform in the 1980s, see Choi 1993 and Rhee 1992.

13 See, for example, the essays in Dornbusch and Park 1995.

CHAPTER 10

1 In a very interesting paper, Torben Iversen demonstrates that not all social democratic governments in Europe used Keynesian policies; for those that didn't, the constraints imposed by internationalization should be less. (See Iversen 1994.) Others who stress the choices open to governments rather than the constraints they face are Helleiner 1994 and Moses 1994.

References

Adzhubei, Aleksei. 1989. *Te desiat' let* Moscow: Sovetskaia Rossiia.

Akhromeev, S. F., and G. M. Kornienko. 1992. *Glazami marshala i diplomata.* Moscow: Mezhdunarodye otnosheniia.

Akhtar, M. A., and Ethan S. Harris. 1987. "Monetary Policy Influence on the Economy – An Empirical Analysis." *Federal Reserve Bank of New York Quarterly Review* (Winter): 19–34.

Akhtar, M. A., and Howard Howe. 1991. "The Political and Institutional Independence of U.S. Monetary Policy." Federal Reserve Bank of New York Research Paper no. 9110. New York: Federal Reserve Bank of New York.

Alesina, Alberto, Vittorio Grilli, and Gian Maria Milesi-Feretti. 1993. "The Political Economy of Capital Controls." Working Paper no. 4353. Cambridge: National Bureau of Economic Research.

1994. "The Political Economy of Capital Controls." In Leiderman and Razin, eds., *Capital Mobility: The Impact of Consumption, Investment and Growth.* Cambridge University Press.

Alesina, Alberto, and Nouriel Roubini. 1992. "Political Cycles in OECD Economies." *Review of Economic Studies* 59, 4: 663–8.

Alesina, Alberto, and Jeffrey Sachs. 1988. "Political Parties and the Business Cycle in the United States, 1948–1984." *Journal of Money, Credit, and Banking* 20, 1 (February): 63–82.

Alesina, Alberto, and Guido Tabellini. 1989. "External Debt, Capital Flight, and Political Risk." *Journal of Development Economics* 27: 199–221.

Alt, James E. 1985. "Political Parties, World Demand, and Unemployment: Domestic and International Sources of Economic Activity." *American Political Science Review* 79, 4 (December): 1016–40.

Alvarez, R. Michael, Geoffrey Garrett, and Peter Lange. 1991. "Government Partisanship, Labor Organization, and Macroeconomic Performance." *American Political Science Review* 85, 2 (June): 539–56.

Amann, R., and J.M. Cooper, eds. 1982. *Industrial Innovation in the Soviet Union.* New Haven: Yale University Press.

Amann, R., J. M. Cooper, and R. W. Davies, eds. 1977. *The Technological Level of Soviet Industry.* New Haven: Yale University Press.

Anderson, Gary, William Shughart II, and Robert Tollison. 1988. "A Public Choice Theory of the Great Contraction." *Public Choice* 59, 1 (October): 3–23.

Anderson, Stephen. 1987. "The Politics of the Welfare State in Japan." Ph.D. diss., Massachusetts Institute of Technology.

Andrews, David M. 1994. "Capital Mobility and State Autonomy: Toward a Structural Theory of International Monetary Relations." *International Studies Quarterly* 38, 2 (June): 193–218.

Arai, Kunio. 1988. *Senkyo, joho, yoron [Elections, Information, and Public Opinion]*. Tokyo: Nihon hoso kyokai.

Arato, Andrew. 1978. "Understanding Bureaucratic Centralism." *Telos* 35 (Spring): 73–87.

Arbatov, Georgii. 1991. *Zatianuvsheesia vyzdorovlenie (1953–1985 gg.): Svidetel'stvo sovremennika*. Moscow: Mezhdunarodnye otnosheniia.

Arellano, Pablo. 1983. "De la Liberalizacion a la Intervencion: El Mercado de Capitales en Chile, 1974–83." *Coleccion Estudios Cieplan* 11: 5–49.

Arndt, H. W., and Njoman Suwidjana. 1982. "The Jakarta Dollar Market." *Bulletin of Indonesian Economic Studies* 28: 35–65.

Aronson, Jonathan. 1977. *Money and Power: Banks and the World Monetary System*. Beverly Hills: Sage.

Arthur, W. Brian. 1994. *Increasing Returns and Path Dependence in the Economy*. Ann Arbor: University of Michigan Press.

Asahi shimbun. Various issues.

Aschauer, David Alan. 1990. *Public Investment and Private Sector Growth*. Washington, D.C.: Economic Policy Institute.

Aslund, Anders. 1989. *Gorbachev's Struggle for Economic Reform*. Ithaca, NY: Cornell University Press.

——— 1995. "Russia's Sleaze Sector." *New York Times,* July 11.

Auerbach, Robert. 1990. "A Budgetary Bias for United States Intervention in Foreign Exchange Markets." *Public Budgeting and Financial Management* 2, 3: 407–30.

Bahry, Donna. 1987. *Outside Moscow: Power, Politics, and Budgetary Policy in the Soviet Republics*. New York: Columbia University Press.

Balassa, Bela, and John Williamson. 1990. *Adjusting to Success: Balance of Payments Policy in the East Asian NICs*. Washington, D.C.: Institute for International Economics.

Baldwin, David. 1980. "Interdependence and Power: A Conceptual Analysis." *International Organization* 34, 4 (Autumn): 471–506.

Bank for International Settlements (BIS). 1993. *Sixty-Third Annual Report*. Basle, Switzerland: Bank for International Settlements.

Bank for International Settlements (BIS). 1995. *Annual Report*. Basle, Switzerland: Bank for International Settlements.

Barber, William J. 1985. *From New Era to New Deal*. Cambridge University Press.

Barro, Robert. 1973. "The Control of Politicians: An Economic Model." *Public Choice* 14, 1: 19–42.

——— 1989. "Government Spending in a Simple Model of Endogenous Growth." *Journal of Political Economy* 98: 103–25.

Bartolini, Leonardo, and G. Bondar. 1992. "An Analysis of the Process of Capital Account Liberalization in Italy." Working Paper 92/27. Washington: International Monetary Fund.

Bartolini, Leonardo, and Allan Drazen. 1994. "Capital Account Liberalization as a Signal." Mimeo. Washington: International Monetary Fund Research Department.

Batchelder, Ronald, and David Glasner. 1992. "Debt, Deflation, the Great Depression, and the Gold Standard," in John Rollins, ed., *Money and Banking: The American Experience*. Virginia: Durell Foundation.

Bates, Robert H. 1981. *Markets and States in Tropical Africa*. Berkeley and Los Angeles: University of California Press.

Bates, Robert H., and Paul Collier. 1991. "The Politics of Economic Reform in Zambia." Unpublished manuscript.

Bates, Robert, and Da-Hsiang Donald Lien. 1985. "A Note on Taxation, Development and Representative Government." *Politics and Society* 14, 1: 53–70.

Bawn, Kathleen. 1993. "The Logic of Institutional Preferences: German Electoral Law as a Social Choice Outcome." *American Journal of Political Science* 37, 4 (November): 965–89.

Bayoumi, Tamin. 1990. "Savings–Investment Correlations." *IMF Staff Papers* 37: 360–87.

Beck, Nathaniel. 1991. "The Fed and the Political Business Cycle." *Contemporary Policy Issues* 9 (April): 25–38.

Beck, Nathaniel and Jonathan Katz. 1995. "What to do (and what not to do) with Time-Series-Cross-Section Data in Comparative Politics." *American Political Science Review* 89, 3 (September): 634–47.

Becker, Gary S. 1983. "A Theory of Competition Among Pressure Groups for Political Influence." *Quarterly Journal of Economics* 98: 371–400.

Bhagwati, Jagdish. 1984. "Why Are Services Cheaper in Poor Countries?" *Economic Journal* 94 (June): 279–86.

Biddulph, Howard. 1983. "Local Interest Articulation at CPSU Congresses." *World Politics* 36, 1 (October): 28–52.

Birman, Igor. 1990. "The Budget Gap, Excess Money and Reform." *Communist Economies* 2, 1: 25–46.

Bisat, Amer, R. Barry Johnston, and V. Sundarajan. 1992. "Issues in Managing and Sequencing Financial Sector Reforms: Lessons from Experiences in Five Developing Countries." Working Paper 92/82. Washington: International Monetary Fund.

Blake, Robert. 1967. *Disraeli*. New York: St. Martin's Press.

Booth, Anne, and Peter McCawley, eds. 1981. *The Indonesian Economy During the Soeharto Era*. New York: Oxford University Press.

Bowman, John, and Richard Keehn. 1974. "Agricultural Terms of Trade in Four Midwestern States, 1870–1900." *Journal of Economic History* 34 (September): 592–609.

Branson, William, and James Love. 1988. "U.S. Manufacturing and the Real Exchange Rate." In Richard Marston, ed., *Misalignment of Exchange Rates: Effects on Trade and Industry*. Chicago: University of Chicago Press.

Broz, Lawrence. 1993. "Wresting the Sceptre from London: The International Political Economy of the Founding of the Federal Reserve." Ph.D. diss., University of California, Los Angeles.

Bryant, Ralph. 1980. *Money and Monetary Policy in Interdependent Nations*. Washington, D.C.: Brookings Institution.

1987. *International Financial Intermediation*. Washington, D.C.: Brookings Institution.

Bunce, Valerie. 1985. "The Empire Strikes Back: The Evolution of the Eastern Bloc from a Soviet Asset to a Soviet Liability." *International Organization* 39, 1 (Winter): 1–46.

Burawoy, Michael, and Pavel Krotov. 1992. "The Rise of Merchant Capital:

Monopoly, Barter, and Enterprise Politics in the Vorkuta Coal Industry." *Harriman Institute Forum* 6, 4 (December): 1–15.

Burlatskii, Fedor. 1991. *Khrushchev and the First Russian Spring.* New York: Scribner's.

Bush, Keith. 1993. "Gas Industry to be Privatized." Radio Free Europe/Radio Liberty *Daily Report* 66 (April 6) (electronic version).

——— 1994. "Privatization and Foreign Investment." Radio Free Europe/Radio Liberty *Daily Report* 38 (February 24) (electronic version).

Bykov, Aleksandr. 1988. "Ne neft'iu edinoi." *Literaturnaia gazeta* (February): 14.

Cain, Bruce, John Ferejohn, and Morris Fiorina. 1987. *The Personal Vote: Constituency Service and Electoral Independence.* Cambridge, Mass.: Harvard University Press.

Calder, Kent. 1988. *Crisis and Compensation: Public Policy and Political Stability in Japan, 1949–1986.* Princeton: Princeton University Press.

Calleo, David P. 1982. *The Imperious Economy.* Cambridge, Mass.: Harvard University Press.

Calmfors, Lars, and John Driffill. 1988. "Bargaining Structure, Corporatism and Macroeconomic Performance." *Economic Policy* 3 (October): 13–61.

Cameron, David M. 1978. "The Expansion of the Public Economy: A Comparative Analysis." *American Political Science Review* 72, 4 (December): 1243–61.

Campbell, John Creighton. 1991. *Why Policies Change: The Japanese Government and the Elderly.* Princeton: Princeton University Press.

Cardoso, Fernando Henrique, and Enzo Faletto. 1979 *Dependency and Development in Latin America,* trans. by Marjory Mattingly Urquidi. Berkeley and Los Angeles: University of California Press.

Casella, Alessandra. 1992. "Arbitration in International Trade." Working Paper 1.6, Series on Political Economy of European Integration, Center for German and European Studies, University of California.

Castles, Francis, and Peter Mair. 1984. "Left-Right Political Scales: Some Expert Judgments." *European Journal of Political Research* 12: 73–88.

Ceglowski, J., and S. Hilton. 1987. "Interest Rate and Exchange Rate Effects in Selected Manufacturing Industries." In Federal Reserve Bank of New York. *Research Papers on International Integration of Financial Markets and U.S. Monetary Policy.* New York: Federal Reserve Bank of New York: 403–500.

Centeno, Miguel Angel, and Sylvia Maxfield. 1990. "The Marriage of Finance and Order: Changes in the Mexican Political Elite." *Journal of Latin American Studies* 24: 57–86.

Central Intelligence Agency (U.S.). 1986. "Economic and Energy Indicators." Report no. DI EEI 86-002, January 17.

——— 1988a. "International Energy Statistical Review." Washington, D.C.

——— 1988b. "Revisiting Soviet Economic Performance Under Glasnost: Implications for CIA Estimates." Report no. SOV 88-10068, September.

Central Intelligence Agency and Defense Intelligence Agency (U.S.). 1991. "Beyond Perestroyka: The Soviet Economy in Crisis." Paper prepared for presentation to the Technology and National Security Subcommittee of the Joint Economic Committee, U.S. Congress, May 14.

Checkel, Jeff. 1993. "Ideologies on the Loose: (Re-) Defining Russia's National Interests in the Post-Soviet Era." Paper presented at the SSRC-sponsored conference "Bringing Russia Back In: IR Theory, Comparative Politics and the Study of the Former USSR." University of Pittsburgh, February.

Chen, Kang, Gary H. Jefferson, and Inderjit Singh. 1992. "Lessons from China's Economic Reform." *Journal of Comparative Economics* 16: 201–25.

Cherniaev, A. S. 1993. *Shest' let s Gorbachevym: podnevnikovym zapisiam.* Moscow: Progress.

China: Foreign Trade Reform. 1994. Washington D.C.: The World Bank.

Choi, Byung-sun. 1993. "Financial Policy and Big Business in Korea: The Perils of Financial Regulation." In Stephan Haggard, Chung Lee, and Sylvia Maxfield, eds., *The Politics of Finance in Developing Countries.* Ithaca: Cornell University Press.

Cohen, Stephen D., and Ronald I. Meltzer. 1982. *United States International Economic Policy in Action.* New York: Praeger.

Cole, David, and Yung-chul Park. 1983. *Financial Development in Korea, 1945–1978.* Cambridge, Mass.: Harvard University Press.

Cole, David, and Betty Slade. 1994. "Political Economy of Indonesian Financial Reform." Unpublished manuscript. Cambridge, Mass.: Harvard Institute for International Development.

Cooper, Richard. 1968. *The Economics of Interdependence.* New York: McGraw-Hill for the Council on Foreign Relations.

1972. "Economic Interdependence and Foreign Policy in the Seventies." *World Politics* 24, 2 (January): 159–81.

1994. "Foreign Trade, Wages and Unemployment." Discussion Paper no. 1701. Harvard Institute of Economic Research, November.

Corbo, Vittorio. 1983. "Chile: Economic Policy and International Economic Relations since 1970." Documento de Trabajo no. 86. Santiago: Pontifica Universidad Católica de Chile, Instituto de Economía.

Corbo, Vittorio, and Jaime de Melo. 1985. "Liberalization with Stabilization in the Southern Cone of Latin America: Overview and Summary." *World Development* 13: 863–6.

Corbo, Vittorio, and Jaime de Melo. 1987. "Lessons from the Southern Cone Policy Reforms." *World Bank Research Observer* 2: 111–42.

Corden, W. M. 1986. *Inflation, Exchange Rates, and the World Economy.* 3rd ed. Chicago: University of Chicago Press.

Cox, Gary W. 1987. *The Efficient Secret: The Cabinet and the Development of Political Parties in Victorian England.* Cambridge University Press.

Cox, Gary W., Matthew McCubbins, and Terry Sullivan. 1984. "Policy Choice as an Electoral Investment." *Social Choice and Welfare* 1: 231–4.

Cox, Gary W., and Frances M. Rosenbluth. 1995. "Factional Cheating on the Party Endorsement: The Case of Japan's Liberal Democratic Party." *British Journal of Political Science.*

Crane, George T. 1990. *The Political Economy of China's Special Economic Zones.* Armonk: M. E. Sharpe.

Crawford, Arthur. 1940. *Monetary Management under the New Deal.* Washington, D.C.: American Council on Public Affairs.

Crowley, Stephen. 1993. "From Coal to Steel: The Formation of an Independent Workers' Movement in the Soviet Union, 1989–1991." Ph.D. diss., University of Michigan.

Cukierman, Alex. 1992. *Central Bank Strategy, Credibility and Independence.* Cambridge, Mass.: Massachusetts Institute of Technology Press.

Cumings, Bruce. 1979. "The Political Economy of Chinese Foreign Policy." *Modern China* 5 (October): 411–62.

1984. "The Origins and Development of the Northeast Asian Political Economy." *International Organization* 38 (Winter): 1–40.

1989. "The Political Economy of China's Turn Outward." In Samuel S. Kim, ed., *China and the World.* 2nd ed. Boulder: Westview Press.

Curtis, Gerald. 1988. *The Way of Japanese Politics*. New York: Columbia University Press.

Dahse, Fernando. 1979. *El Mapa de la Extrema Riqueza*. Santiago: Editorial Aconagua.

D'Arista, Jane. 1971. *Federal Reserve Structure and the Development of Monetary Policy: 1915–1935*. Staff Report of the Subcommittee on Domestic Finance, Committee on Banking and Currency, United States House of Representatives. Washington, D.C.: Government Printing Office.

Darst, Robert. 1994. "Transnational Bargains, Expert Intervention, and Ideological Conversion: The 'Westernization' of Economic and Environmental Policy in the Former Soviet Union." Ph.D. diss., University of California, Berkeley.

David, Paul. 1985. "Clio and the Economics of QWERTY." *American Economic Review* 75: 332–7.

Deardorff, Alan, and Robert Stern. 1987. "Current Issues in Trade Policy." In Robert Stern, ed., *U.S. Trade Policies in a Changing World Economy*. Cambridge, Mass.: Massachusetts Institute of Technology Press.

DeGaulle, Charles. 1971. *Memoirs of Hope: Renewal and Endeavor*. Transl. by Terence Kilmartin. New York: Simon and Schuster.

de Kock, Gabriel, and Thomas DeLeire. 1994. "The Role of the Exchange Rate in the Monetary Transmission Mechanism: A Time-Series Analysis." Federal Reserve Bank of New York Research Paper no. 9412. New York: Federal Reserve Bank of New York.

Destler, I. M., and C. Randall Henning. 1989. *Dollar Politics: Exchange Rate Policymaking in the United States*. Washington, D.C.: Institute for International Economics.

Destler, I. M., and Hisao Mitsuyu. 1982. "Locomotives on Different Tracks: Macroeconomic Diplomacy, 1977–1979." In I. M. Destler and Hideo Sato, eds., *Coping with U.S.-Japanese Economic Conflicts*. Lexington, Massachusetts: Lexington Books.

Destler, I. M., and John Odell. 1987. *Anti-Protection: Changing Forces in United States Trade Politics*. Washington: Institute for International Economics.

Deutsch, Karl, and Alexander Eckstein. 1961. "National Industrialization and the Declining Share of the International Economic Sector, 1890–1959." *World Politics* 13, 2 (January): 267–99.

de Vylder, Stefan. 1989. "Chile, 1973–1987: Los Vaivenes de un Modelo." In Roberto Garcia, ed., *Economía y Política Durante el Gobierno Militar en Chile, 1973–1987*. Mexico, D.F.: Fondo de Cultura Económica.

Diaz, Eduardo Turrent. 1982. *Historia del Banco de México, Vol. 1*. Mexico, D.F.: Banco de México.

Djilas, Milovan. 1957. *The New Class: An Analysis of the Communist System*. New York: Praeger.

Dornbush, Rudiger, and Jacob Frenkel. 1979. *International Economic Policy: Theory and Evidence*. Baltimore: John's Hopkins University Press.

Dornbush, Rudiger, and Yung-Chul Park, eds. 1995. *Financial Opening: Policy Lessons for Korea*. Seoul: Korea Institute of Finance and International Center for Economic Growth.

Dos Santos, Teotonio. "The Structure of Dependence." *American Economic Review* 60, 5 (September): 235–46.

Douglas, Hernan Cortes. 1985. "Stabilization Policies in Chile: Inflation, Unemployment, and Depression, 1975–1982." In Gary Walton, ed., *The National Economic Policies of Chile*. Greenwich: JAI Press.

Dowrick, Steve, and Duc-Tho Nguyen. 1989. "OECD Comparative Economic Growth 1950–85: Catch-Up and Convergence." *American Economic Review* 79: 1010–30.

Drazen, Allan, and Vittorio Grilli. 1993. "The Benefits of Crisis for Economic Reforms." *American Economic Review* 83, 3 (June): 598–607.

Eckes, Alfred Jr. 1975. *A Search for Solvency: Bretton Woods and the International Monetary System, 1941–1971.* Austin: University of Texas Press.

Economic Report of the President. 1993. Washington, D.C.: Government Printing Office.

Economic Report of the President. Various issues. Washington: Government Printing Office.

The Economist. 1993. "Intel: The Coming Clash of Logic." (July 3): 21–3.

The Economist. 1990. "Japan's $3 Billion Election." (February 3): 31–2.

Economist Survey. 1993. "The European Community: A Rude Awakening," July 3.

Edwards, Sebastian. 1984. "The Order of Liberalization of the External Sector." *Princeton Essays on International Finance* 156. Princeton: International Financial Section.

Edwards, Sebastian, and Alejandra Cox Edwards. 1987. *Monetarism and Liberalization: The Chilean Experiment.* Cambridge: Ballinger Publishing.

Edwards, Sebastian, and Sweder van Wijnbergen. 1986. "The Welfare Effects of Trade and Capital Market Liberalization." *International Economic Review* 27, 1 (February): 141–8.

Eichengreen, Barry. 1992. *Golden Fetters: The Gold Standard and the Great Depression.* New York: Oxford University Press.

———. 1993. "International Monetary Arrangements for the 21st Century." Paper prepared for the Brookings Institution project on "Integrating the World Economy" (September).

Eichengreen, Barry, and Peter Garber. 1991. "Before the Accord: U.S. Monetary-Financial Policy, 1945–51." In R. Glenn Hubbard, ed., *Financial Markets and Financial Crises.* Chicago: University of Chicago Press.

Eichengreen, Barry, Andrew Rose, and Charles Wyplosz. 1994. "Speculative Attacks on Pegged Exchange Rates." Unpublished manuscript. University of California, Berkeley.

Epstein, Gerald A., and Thomas Ferguson. 1984. "Monetary Policy, Loan Liquidation, and Industrial Conflict: The Federal Reserve and the Open Market Operations of 1932." *Journal of Economic History* 44, 4 (December): 957–83.

Epstein, Gerald A., and Juliet Schor. 1992. "Structural Determinants and Economic Effects of Capital Controls in OECD Countries." In Tariq Banuri and Juliet Schor, eds., *Financial Openness and National Autonomy.* New York: Oxford University Press.

Erlanger, Steven. 1995. "Russia's Premier: Too Popular for His Own Good?" *New York Times,* June 26.

Euh, Yoon-dae, and James C. Baker. 1990. *The Korean Banking System.* New York: Routledge.

Evangelista, Matthew. 1995. "The Paradox of State Strength: Domestic Structures, Transnational Relations, and Security Policy in the USSR and Russia." *International Organization* 49, 1 (Winter): 1–38.

Evangelista, Matthew. 1996. "From Each According to Its Abilities: Competing Theoretical Approaches to the Post-Soviet Energy Sector." In Celeste Wallander, ed., *The Sources of Russian Conduct After the Cold War.* Boulder, CO: Westview.

Evans, Peter. 1979. *Dependent Development: The Alliance of Multinational, State, and Local Capital in Brazil.* Princeton: Princeton University Press.

Evans, Peter, Dieter Reuschemeyer, and Theda Skocpol, eds. 1985. *Bringing the State Back In.* New York: Cambridge University Press.

Evans, Peter. 1992. In Haggard and Kaufmann, 1992: 139–81.

Fainsod, Merle. 1963. *How Russia is Ruled.* Rev. ed. Cambridge, Mass.: Harvard University Press.

Falin, Valentin. 1993. *Politische erinnerungen.* Munich: Droemer Knaur.

Federal Reserve System. Various issues. *Federal Reserve Bulletin.* Washington, D.C.: Federal Reserve System.

Federal Reserve Bank of St. Louis. 1986. *International Economic Conditions* (October).

Feinberg, Richard E., John Echeverri-Gent, Friedemann Müller, et al. 1990. *Economic Reform in Three Giants.* New Brunswick, NJ: Transaction Books.

Feldstein, M., and C. Horioka. 1980. "Domestic Saving and International Capital Flows." *The Economic Journal* 90 (June): 314–29.

Flaherty, Patrick. 1991. "Perestroika and the Neo-Liberal Project." In Ralph Miliband and Leo Panitch, eds., "Communist Regimes: The Aftermath." *Socialist Register 1991.* London: Merlin.

Flanagan, Robert, David Soskice, and Lloyd Ulman. 1983. *Unionism, Economic Stabilization and Incomes Policies.* Washington, D.C.: Brookings Institution.

Forsyth, P. J., and St. J. Nicholas. 1983. "The Decline of Spanish Industry and the Price Revolution: A Neoclassical Analysis." *Journal of European Economic History* 12: 601–10.

Foxley, Alejandro. 1983. *Latin American Experiments in Neo-conservative Economics.* Berkeley and Los Angeles: University of California Press.

Frankel, Jeffrey A. 1985. "Six Possible Meanings of 'Overvaluation': The 1981–1985 Dollar." *Princeton Essays in International Finance* 159. Princeton: International Finance Section.

——— 1991. "Quantifying International Capital Mobility in the 1980s." In B. Douglas Bernheim and John Shoven, eds., *National Saving and Economic Performance.* Chicago: University of Chicago Press.

——— 1994. "The Making of Exchange Rate Policy in the 1980s." In Martin Feldstein, ed., *American Economic Policy in the 1980s.* Chicago: University of Chicago Press.

Franzese, Robert. 1995. "Central Banks and the Wage Bargain." Manuscript. Harvard University.

Freidel, Frank. 1990. *Franklin D. Roosevelt: A Rendezvous with Destiny.* Boston: Little, Brown and Company.

French-Davis, Ricardo, and Jose Pablo Arellano. 1981. "Apertura Financiera Externa: La Experiencia Chilena en 1973–1980." *Estudios Cieplan* 50.

Frieden, Jeffry. 1991a. *Debt, Development and Democracy: Modern Political Economy and Latin America, 1965–1985.* Princeton: Princeton University Press.

——— 1991b. "Invested Interests: The Politics of National Economic Policies in a World of Global Finance." *International Organization* 45, 4 (Autumn): 425–51.

——— 1994a. "Making Commitments: France and Italy in the European Monetary System." In Barry Eichengreen and Jeffry Frieden, eds., *The Political Economy of European Monetary Unification.* Boulder: Westview Press.

——— 1994b. "Exchange Rate Politics: Contemporary Lessons from American History." *Review of International Political Economy* 1, 1 (Spring): 82–103.

Friedgut, Theodore, and Lewis Siegelbaum. 1990. "Perestroika from Below: The Soviet Miners' Strike and its Aftermath." *New Left Review* 181: 5–32.

Friedman, Milton, and Anna Schwartz. 1963. *A Monetary History of the United States, 1867–1960*. Princeton: Princeton University Press.

Funabashi, Yoichi. 1988. *Managing the Dollar: From the Plaza to the Louvre*. Washington, D.C.: Institute for International Economics.

Galbis, Vicente. 1986. "Financial Sector Liberalization under Oligopolistic Conditions and a Bank Holding Company Structure." *Savings and Development* 10: 117–41.

Garrett, Geoffrey. 1993. "The Politics of Structural Change: Swedish Social Democracy and Thatcherism in Comparative Perspective." *Comparative Political Studies* 25 (January): 521–47.

Garrett, Geoffrey, and Peter Lange. 1986. "Performance in a Hostile World: Economic Growth in Capitalist Democracies, 1974–1980." *World Politics* 38, 4 (July): 517–45.

1991. "Political Responses to Interdependence: What's 'Left' for the Left?" *International Organization* 45, 4 (Autumn): 539–64.

Garrett, Geoffrey, and Christopher Way. 1995. "The Sectoral Composition of Trade Unions, Corporatism and Economic Performance." In Barry Eichengreen, Jeffry Frieden, and Jürgen von Hagen, eds., *The Political Economy of European Integration*. New York: Springer–Verlag.

Gaytan, Ricardo Torres. 1980. *Un Siglo de Devaluaciones del Peso Mexicano*. Mexico, D.F.: Siglo XXI.

Gerschenkron, Alexander. 1943. *Bread and Democracy in Germany*. Berkeley and Los Angeles: University of California Press.

Giovannini, A., and M. de Melo. 1993. "Government Revenue from Financial Repression." *American Economic Review* 83: 953–63.

Goldberg, Linda. 1990. "Nominal Exchange Rate Patterns: Correlations with Entry, Exit, and Investment in U.S. Industry." NBER Working Paper no. 3249, National Bureau of Economic Research: Cambridge.

Golden, Miriam. 1993. "The Dynamics of Trade Unionism and National Economic Performance." *American Political Science Review* 87 (June): 439–54.

Golden, Miriam, and Michael Wallerstein. 1994. "Trade Union Organization and Industrial Relations in the Postwar Era in Sixteen Nations." Paper presented at the Annual Meeting of the American Political Science Association. New York, September 1–4.

Goldstein, Avery. 1991. *From Bandwagon to Balance-of-Power Politics: Structural Constraints and Politics in China, 1949–78*. Stanford: Stanford University Press.

Goldstein, Judith. 1989. "The Impact of Ideas on Trade Policy: The Origins of U.S. Agricultural and Manufacturing Policies." *International Organization* 43, 1 (Winter): 31–72.

1993. *Ideas, Interests and American Trade Policy*. Ithaca: Cornell University Press.

Golub, Stephen. 1986. "The Current-Account Balance and the Dollar: 1977–78 and 1983–84." *Princeton Studies in International Finance* 57. Princeton: International Finance Section.

Goodman, John B., and Louis W. Pauly. 1993. "The Obsolescence of Capital Controls? Economic Management in an Age of Global Markets." *World Politics* 46, 1 (October): 50–82.

Gorbachev, Mikhail. 1987. *Perestroika: New Thinking for Our Country and the World*. New York: Harper and Row.

Gourevitch, Peter A. 1977. "International Trade, Domestic Coalitions, and Liberty: Comparative Responses to the Crisis of 1873–1896." *Journal of Interdisciplinary History* 8: 281–313.

1978. "The Second Image Reversed: The International Sources of Domestic Politics." *International Organization* 32, 4 (Autumn): 881–912.

1979. "The Re-emergence of 'Peripheral Nationalisms': Some Comparative Speculations on the Spatial Distribution of Political Leadership and Economic Growth." *Comparative Studies in Society and History* 21: 303–22.

1986. *Politics in Hard Times: Comparative Responses to International Economic Crises.* Ithaca: Cornell University Press.

Gourevitch, Peter, Christopher Allen, Stephen Bornstein, Andrei Markovits, Andrew Martin, and George Ross. 1984. *Unions and Economic Crisis: Britain, West Germany and Sweden.* Boston: Allen and Unwin.

Gowa, Joanne. 1983. *Closing the Gold Window: Domestic Politics and the End of Bretton Woods.* Ithaca: Cornell University Press.

1994. *Allies, Adversaries, and International Trade.* Princeton: Princeton University Press.

Green, George. 1981. "The Ideological Origins of the Revolution in American Financial Policies." In Karl Brunner, ed., *The Great Depression Revisited.* Boston: Martinus Nijhoff.

Greene, Margaret. 1984. *U.S. Experience with Exchange Market Intervention: September 1977–December 1979.* Board of Governors of the Federal Reserve System Staff Studies, no. 128. Washington: Federal Reserve.

Gregory, Paul, and Robert Stuart. 1986. *Soviet Economic Structure and Performance.* 3rd ed. New York: Harper and Row.

Grenville, Stephen. 1981. "Monetary Policy and the Formal Financial Sector." In A. Booth and P. McCawley, eds., *The Indonesian Economy During the Soeharto Era.* New York: Oxford University Press.

Grier, Kevin. 1987. "Presidential Elections and Federal Reserve Policy: An Empirical Test." *Southern Economic Journal* 54, 2 (October): 475–86.

Griffith-Jones, Stephany. 1981. *The Role of Finance in the Transition to Socialism.* Totawa, NY: Allanheld, Osman.

Grilli, Vittorio, Donato Masciandaro, and Guido Tabellini. 1991. "Political and Monetary Institutions and Public Financial Policies in the Industrial Countries." *Economic Policy* 13 (October): 342–92.

Gudgin, Graham, and Peter Taylor. 1976. *Seats, Votes and the Spatial Organization of Elections.* London: Pion Press.

Gustafson, Thane. 1989. *Crisis Amid Plenty: The Politics of Soviet Energy Under Brezhnev and Gorbachev.* Princeton: Princeton University Press.

Haggard, Stephan. 1988. "The Institutional Foundations of Hegemony: Explaining the Reciprocal Trade Agreements Act of 1934." *International Organization* 42, 1 (Winter): 91–120.

1990. *Pathways from the Periphery: The Politics of Growth in the Newly Industrializing Countries.* Ithaca: Cornell University Press.

Haggard, Stephan, and Robert Kaufman. 1992. *The Politics of Economic Adjustment.* Princeton: Princeton University Press.

1995. *The Political Economy of Democratic Transitions.* Princeton: Princeton University Press.

Haggard, Stephan, and Sylvia Maxfield. 1993. "Political Explanations of Financial Policy in Developing Countries." In Stephan Haggard, Chung Lee, and Sylvia Maxfield, eds., *The Politics of Finance in Developing Countries.* Ithaca: Cornell University Press.

Haggard, Stephan, et al. 1994. *Macroeconomic Policy and Adjustment in Korea, 1970–1990.* Cambridge, Mass.: Harvard University Press.

Hall, Peter A. 1986. *Governing the Economy.* New York: Oxford University Press.
  ed. 1989. *The Political Power of Economic Ideas: Keynesianism Across Nations.* Princeton: Princeton University Press.
  1994. "Central Bank Independence and Coordinated Wage Bargaining." *German Politics and Society* 31, 1 (Spring): 1–23.
Halliday, Fred. 1992. "A Singular Collapse: The Soviet Union, Market Pressure and Inter-State Competition." *Contention* 1, 2 (Winter): 121–42.
Hanson, James A. 1992. *Opening the Capital Account: A Survey of Issues and Results.* Washington, D.C.: The World Bank.
Hastings, Laura. 1993. "Regulatory Revenge: the Politics of Free Market Financial Reforms in Chile." In Stephan Haggard, Chung Lee, and Sylvia Maxfield, eds., *The Politics of Finance in Developing Countries.* Ithaca: Cornell University Press.
Helleiner, Eric. 1994. *States and the Emergence of Global Finance.* Ithaca: Cornell University Press.
Hewett, Ed A. 1984. *Energy, Economics, and Foreign Policy in the Soviet Union.* Washington DC: Brookings Institution.
  1987. *Reforming the Soviet Economy: Equality versus Efficiency.* Washington, D.C.: Brookings Institution.
Hewett, Ed A., with Clifford G. Gaddy. 1992. *Open for Business: Russia's Return to the Global Economy.* Washington, D.C.: Brookings Institution.
Hibbs, Douglas. 1987. *The American Political Economy.* Cambridge, Mass.: Harvard University Press.
Hicks, John. 1931. *The Populist Revolt.* Minneapolis: University of Minnesota Press.
Hirschman, Albert O. 1970. *Exit, Voice, and Loyalty.* Cambridge, Mass.: Harvard University Press.
  1978. "Exit, Voice, and the State." *World Politics* 31, 1 (October): 90–107.
  [1945] 1980. *National Power and the Structure of Foreign Trade.* 2nd cd. Berkeley and Los Angeles: University of California Press.
  1985. "Reflections on the Latin American Experience." In Leon N. Lindberg and Charles S. Maier, eds. *The Politics of Inflation and Economic Stagnation.* Washington, D.C.: Brookings Institution.
Hobsbawm, Eric J. 1962. *The Age of Revolution, 1789–1848.* New York: New American Library.
  1979. *The Age of Capital, 1848–1875.* New York: New American Library.
Hoffmann, Erik P., and Robbin F. Laird. 1982. *The Politics of Economic Modernization in the Soviet Union.* Ithaca, NY: Cornell University Press.
Honsho, Jiro. 1985. *Keidanren.* Tokyo: Toyo keizai shimposha.
Hough, Jerry F. 1986. "Attack on Protectionism in the Soviet Union? A Comment." *International Organization* 40, 2 (Spring): 489–503.
  1988. *Opening Up the Soviet Economy.* Washington, D.C.: Brookings Institution.
Huan Guocang. 1987. "China's Open Door Policy: 1978–1984." Ph.D. diss., Princeton University.
Hufbauer, Gary Clyde, and Jeffrey J. Schott. 1993. *NAFTA: An Assessment.* Washington: Institute for International Economics.
Huntington, Samuel P. 1991. *The Third Wave: Democratization in the Late Twentieth Century.* Norman: University of Oklahoma Press.
Ichikawa, Taichi. 1990. *Seshu daigishi no kenkyu* [*Research on Second-Generation Diet Members*]. Tokyo: Nihon keizai shimbunsha.

Inoue, Kyo. 1993. "Aitsugu shinseiji shudan no kessei to sono haikei, jissu [The Backgrounds of the New Political Groupings]" *Zen'ei*. 2,629: 69–82.

International Monetary Fund, The World Bank, Organisation for Economic Co-operation and Development, European Bank for Reconstruction and Development. 1991. *A Study of the Soviet Economy.* 3 vols. Paris: IMF, World Bank, OECD, EBRD.

International Monetary Fund, 1992. *Issues and Developments in International Trade Policy.* Washington, D.C.: International Monetary Fund, August.

1992. *Developments in International Exchange and Payments Systems.* Washington, D.C.: International Monetary Fund.

Various issues. *International Financial Statistics.* Washington, D.C.: International Monetary Fund.

Various issues. *Annual Report on Exchange Arrangements and Exchange Restrictions.* Washington, D.C.: International Monetary Fund.

Iseri, Hirofumi. 1988. *Habatsu saihensei [The Reorganization of Factions]* (Tokyo: Chuko shinsho).

Ishikawa, Masumi, and Michisada Hirose. 1989. *Jiminto: choki shihai no kozo [The LDP: The Structure of Longterm Dominance].* Tokyo: Iwanami shoten.

Iversen, Torben. 1994. "Wage bargaining, Monetary Regimes and Economic Performance." Paper prepared for the Annual Meeting of the American Political Science Association, New York, September 1–4.

1995. "Power, Flexibility and the Breakdown of Centralized Wage Bargaining." *Comparative Political Studies.*

Jichi sho gyosei kyoku, ed. 1988. *Zenkoku shichoson yoran [National Survey of Cities, Towns and Villages].* Tokyo: Daiichi hoki shuppan.

Johnson, Chalmers. 1986. "Tanaka Kakuei, Structural Corruption, and the Advent of Machine Politics in Japan." *Journal of Japanese Studies* 12: 1–28.

1995. *Japan, Who Governs? The Rise of the Developmental State.* New York: Norton.

Joseph, William, ed. 1994. *China Briefings.* Boulder: Westview.

Journal of Monetary Economics. 1978. Special issue on "Congressional Supervision of Monetary Policy."

Katz, Richard. 1980. *A Theory of Parties and Electoral Systems.* Baltimore: The Johns Hopkins University Press.

Katzenstein, Peter J., ed. 1978. *Between Power and Plenty: Foreign Economic Policies of Advanced Industrial Countries.* Madison: University of Wisconsin Press.

1984. *Corporatism and Change: Austria, Switzerland, and the Politics of Industry.* Ithaca: Cornell University Press.

1985. *Small States in World Markets: Industrial Policy in Europe.* Ithaca: Cornell University Press.

Kawato, Sadafumi. 1992. *Nihon no seito seiji, 1890–1937 [Japan's Party Politics, 1890–1937].* Tokyo: Tokyo daigaku shuppankai.

Keesing's Contemporary Archives.

Keohane, Robert O. 1984. *After Hegemony.* Princeton: Princeton University Press.

Keohane, Robert O., and Joseph Nye, Jr. 1972. *Transnational Relations and World Politics.* Cambridge, Mass.: Harvard University Press.

1977. *Power and Interdependence: World Politics in Transition.* Boston: Little, Brown.

1987. "Power and Interdependence Revisited." *International Organization* 41, 4 (Autumn): 725–53.

Kettl, Donald F. 1986. *Leadership at the Fed.* New Haven: Yale University Press.

Kiewiet, Rod, and Matthew McCubbins. 1991. *The Logic of Delegation* Chicago: University of Chicago Press.

Kindleberger, Charles P. 1951. "Group Behavior and International Trade." *Journal of Political Economy* 59: 30–46.

——— ed. 1970. *The International Corporation.* Cambridge, Mass.: Harvard University Press.

Kiselev, Stepan. 1995. "Chernomyrdin Gains the Upper Hand." *Moscow News,* 24–5 (June 30–July 6).

Kitschelt, Herbert. 1994. *The Transformation of European Social Democracy.* Cambridge University Press.

Kobayashi, Yoshiaki. 1987. *Keiryo seijigaku [Quantitative Political Science].* Tokyo: Seibundo, Showa 60.

Kornai, János. 1992. *The Socialist System: The Political Economy of Communism.* Princeton: Princeton University Press.

Kramer, Gerald. 1971. "Short-Term Fluctuations in U.S. Voting Behavior, 1896–1964." *American Political Science Review* 65 (March): 131–43.

Krasner, Stephen D., ed. 1983. *International Regimes.* Ithaca: Cornell University Press.

Krauss, Ellis, and Michio Muramatsu. 1987. "The Conservative Policy Line and the Development of Patterned Pluralism." In Kozo Yamamura and Yasuki Yasuba, eds., *The Political Economy of Japan: Vol. 1, The Domestic Transformation.* Stanford: Stanford University Press.

Krauss, Ellis, and Bradford Simcock. 1980. "Citizens' Movements: The Growth and Impact of Environmental Protest in Japan." In Kurt Steiner, Ellis Krauss, and Scott Flanagan, eds., *Political Opposition and Local Politics in Japan.* Princeton: Princeton University Press.

Kravis, Irving B., and Robert E. Lipsey. 1983. "Toward an Explanation of National Price Levels." *Princeton Studies in International Finance,* no. 52. Princeton: International Finance Section.

Krehbiel, Keith. 1991. *Information and Legislative Organization.* Ann Arbor: University of Michigan Press.

Krueger, Anne O. 1992. *Economic Policy Reform in Developing Countries.* Oxford: Blackwell.

Krugman, Paul R. 1979. "A Model of Balance of Payments Crises." *Journal of Money, Credit and Banking* 11: 311–25.

——— 1991. *Geography and Trade.* Cambridge, Mass.: Massachusetts Institute of Technology Press.

——— 1993a. "Toward a Counter-Revolution in Development Theory." *Proceedings of the World Bank Annual Conference on Development Economics 1992.* New York: The World Bank (International Bank for Reconstruction and Development).

——— 1993b. "What Do We Need to Know About the International Monetary System?" *Princeton Essays in International Finance,* no. 190. Princeton: International Finance Section.

——— 1994a. "Competitiveness: A Dangerous Obsession." *Foreign Affairs* 73 (March/April): 28–44.

——— 1994b. "The Myth of Asia's Miracle." *Foreign Affairs* 73 (November/December): 62–78.

Krugman, Paul R., and Maurice Obstfeld. 1988. *International Economics: Theory and Policy.* Glenview, Il: Scott, Foresman and Co.

1991. *International Economics: Theory and Policy.* 2nd ed. New York: Harper Collins.

Kurzer, Paulette. 1991. "Unemployment in Open Economies: The Impact of Trade, Finance and European Integration." *Comparative Political Studies* 24 (April): 3–30.

1993. *Business and Banking: Political Change and Economic Integration in Western Europe.* Ithaca: Cornell University Press.

Kuzmin, Dmitri. 1990. "Joint Ventures: The Upward Trend." *Vestnik* 1, 1 (March): 51–4.

Laba, Raul, and Felipe Larrain. 1993. "Can Liberalization of Capital Outflows Increase Net Capital Inflows?" Mimeo. Santiago: Pontifica Universidad Catolica de Chile, Economics Department.

Lake, David A. 1988. *Power, Protection, and Free Trade.* Ithaca: Cornell University Press.

Lambi, Nikolai. 1963. *Free Trade and Protection in Germany, 1868–1879.* Beiheft 44, *Vierteljahrschrift für Sozial- und Wirtschaftsgeschichte.* Wiesbaden: Franz Steiner.

Lange, Peter, George Ross, and Maurizio Vanicelli. 1982. *Unions, Change and Crisis: French and Italian Union Strategy and the Political Economy, 1945–1980.* New York: Allen and Unwin.

Lardy, Nicholas R. 1992. *Foreign Trade and Economic Reform in China, 1978–1990.* Cambridge University Press.

1994. *China in the World Economy.* Washington, D.C.: Institute for International Economics (April).

Lee, Dwight R., and Richard B. McKenzie. 1989. "The International Political Economy of Declining Tax Rates." *National Tax Journal* 42: 79–83.

Leiderman, Leonardo, and Assaf Razin, eds. 1994. *Capital Mobility: The Impact of Consumption, Investment and Growth.* Cambridge University Press.

Li Zhisui. 1994. *The Private Life of Chairman Mao.* New York: Random House.

Ligachev, Yegor. 1993. *Inside Gorbachev's Kremlin.* New York: Pantheon.

Lincoln, Edward. 1990. *Japan's Unequal Trade.* Washington, D.C.: The Brookings Institution.

Lindblom, Charles E. 1977. *Politics and Markets: The World's Political-Economic Systems.* New York: Basic Books.

Lipset, Seymour Martin, and Stein Rokkan, eds. 1967. *Party Systems and Voter Alignments.* New York: Free Press.

Lipton, Michael. 1976. *Why Poor People Stay Poor: Urban Bias in World Development.* Cambridge, Mass.: Harvard University Press.

Little, I. M. D., Richard Cooper, W. Max Cordon, and Sarath Rajapatuana. 1993. *Boom, Crisis and Adjustment.* New York: Oxford University Press.

Lohmann, Susanne. 1995. "Federalism and Central Bank Autonomy." Manuscript. University of California, Los Angeles.

Lohmann, Susanne, and Sharyn O'Halloran. 1994. "Divided Government and U.S. Trade Policy: Theory and Evidence." *International Organization* 48, 4 (Autumn): 595–632.

Londregan, John, and Keith Poole. 1990. "Poverty, the Coup Trap and the Seizure of Executive Power." *World Politics* 42 (January): 151–83.

Lowi, Theodore. 1979. *The End of Liberalism: The Second Republic of the United States.* 2nd ed. New York and London: W. W. Norton and Co.

Lucas, Robert E. Jr. 1988. "On the Mechanics of Economic Development." *Journal of Monetary Economics* 22, 1 (July): 3–42.

Luke, Timothy W., and Carl Boggs. 1982. "Soviet Subimperialism and the Crisis of Bureaucratic Centralism." *Studies in Comparative Communism* 15, 1 and 2 (Spring/Summer): 95–124.

Mabuchi, Katsu. 1989. "Okurasho shuzeikyoku no kikan tetsugaku [The Organizational Ideology of the Ministry of Finance Tax Bureau]." *Lebaiasan* 4: 41–58.

MacIntyre, Andrew. 1993. "The Politics of Finance in Indonesia." In Stephan Haggard, Chung Lee, and Sylvia Maxfield, eds., *The Politics of Finance in Developing Countries.* Ithaca: Cornell University Press.

Mackie, Thomas, and Richard Rose. 1991. *The International Almanac of Electoral History.* 3rd ed. New York: Free Press.

Maddison, Angus. 1991. *Dynamic Forces in Capitalist* Development. Oxford: Oxford University Press.

Magee, Stephen. 1980. "Three Simple Tests of the Stolper–Samuelson Theorem." In: Oppenheimer, ed., 1980.

Mahler, Walter. 1988. "The Allocation of the Windfall from Internationalization of the Korea Capital Market." Working paper no. 8813. Korea Development Institute.

Mandel, David. 1990. "The Rebirth of the Soviet Labor Movement: The Coalminers' Strike of July 1989." *Politics and Society* 18, 3: 381 404.

   1991. "The Struggle for Power in the Soviet Economy." In Ralph Miliband and Leo Panitch, eds., "Communist Regimes: The Aftermath." Socialist Register 1991. London: Merlin.

Mandel, William. 1989–91. "Soviet Miners Speak." *The Station Relay* 5. 1–5.

Mansfield, Edward D., and Marc Busch. 1995. "The Political Economy of Non-Tariff Barriers: A Cross-National Analysis." *International Organization* 49, 4 (Autumn): 723–49.

Mansfield, Edward D., and Jack Snyder. 1995. "Democratization and the Danger of War." *International Security* 20, 1 (Summer): 5–38.

Marrese, Michael, and Jan Vanous. 1983. *Soviet Subsidization of Trade with Eastern Europe: A Soviet Perspective.* Berkeley: Institute of International Studies, University of California.

Martinez, Fransisco Borja. 1991. *El Nuevo Sistema Financiero Mexicano.* Mexico, D.F.: Fondo de Cultural Economica.

Martinez, Guillermo Ortiz. 1980. *La Dolarizacion en Mexico: Causas y Consecuencias.* Serie de Documentos no. 40. Mexico: Banco de Mexico,

Maruyama chosakai, ed. 1985. *Zeisei kaikaku ni mukete [Towards Tax Reform].* LDP document.

Marx, Karl, and Friedrich Engels. [1848] 1959. "Manifesto of the Communist Party." In Lewis Feuer, ed., *Marx and Engels: Basic Writings on Politics and Philosophy.* New York: Doubleday Anchor.

Mathieson, Donald, and Liliana Rojas-Suarez. 1993. "Liberalization of the Capital Account: Experiences and Issues." Occasional Paper no. 103. Washington D.C.: International Monetary Fund.

Maxfield, Sylvia. 1990. *Governing Capital.* Ithaca: Cornell University Press.

   1992. "Business Interests and U.S. International Monetary Policy." Paper presented at meetings of the American Political Science Assn.

   1993. "The Politics of Mexican Financial Policy." In Stephan Haggard, Chung Lee, and Sylvia Maxfield, eds., *The Politics of Finance in Developing Countries.* Ithaca: Cornell University Press.

1995a. "The Politics of Central Banking in Developing Countries." Unpublished manuscript. New Haven: Yale University Department of Political Science.

1995b. "Mexican Financial Liberalization." In Kent Calder, et al., *Letting Capital Loose*. Ithaca: Cornell University Press.

Mayhew, David R. 1974. *Congress: The Electoral Connection*. New Haven and London: Yale University Press.

McCubbins, Mathew, Roger Noll, and Barry Weingast. 1987. "Administrative Procedures as an Instrument of Political Control." *Journal of Law, Economics, and Organization* 3: 243–77.

McCubbins, Mathew, Roger Noll, and Barry Weingast. 1989. "Structure and Process, Politics and Policy: Administrative Arrangements and the Political Control of Agencies." *Virginia Law Review* 75, 2 (March): 431–82.

McCubbins, Mathew D., and Frances M. Rosenbluth. 1995. "Electoral Strategy and the Organization of Policy Making in Japan." In Peter Cowhey and Mathew McCubbins, eds., *Policy Making in Japan and the U.S.* Cambridge University Press.

McGuire, Robert. 1981. "Economic Causes of Late-Nineteenth Century Agrarian Unrest." *Journal of Economic History* 41, 4 (December): 835–52.

McKean, Margaret. 1981. *Environmental Protest and Citizen Politics in Japan*. Berkeley and Los Angeles: University of California Press.

McKendrick, David. 1989. "Acquiring Technological Capabilities: Aircraft and Commercial Banking in Indonesia." Ph.D. diss., University of California, Berkeley, School of Business Administration.

McKeown, Timothy J. 1989. "The Politics of Corn Law Repeal and Theories of Commercial Policy." *British Journal of Political Science* 19, 3: 353–80.

1991. "A Liberal Trade Order: the Long-Run Pattern of Imports to the Advanced Capitalist States." *International Studies Quarterly* 35, 2 (June): 151–72.

McKinnon, Ronald I. 1988. "Monetary and Exchange Rate Policies for International Financial Stability." *Journal of Economic Perspectives* 2: 83–103.

1991. *The Order of Economic Liberalization: Financial Control in the Transition to a Market Economy*. Baltimore: Johns Hopkins University Press.

Medvedev, Roy. 1974. *On Socialist Democracy*. New York: Norton.

Mikhailov, V. M. 1993. *Ia – "Iastreb."* Moscow: Kron-Press.

Milgrom, Paul, Douglass North, and Barry R. Weingast. 1990. "The Role of Institutions in the Revival of Trade: The Medieval Law Merchant, Private Judges, and the Champagne Fairs." *Economics and Politics* 1 (March): 1–23.

Millar, James R. 1985. "The Little Deal: Brezhnev's Contribution to Acquisitive Socialism." *Slavic Review* 44, 4 (Winter): 694–706.

Milner, Helen V. 1988. *Resisting Protectionism: Global Industries and the Politics of International Trade*. Princeton: Princeton University Press.

Ministry of Home Affairs. Various years. *Chiho jichi nenkan [Local Government Annual]*. Tokyo: Jichi kenshu kyokai.

Moe, Terry M. 1990. "The Politics of Structural Choice: Toward a Theory of Public Bureaucracy." In Oliver Williamson, ed., *Organization Theory: From Chester Barnard to the Present and Beyond*. New York: Oxford University Press.

Moody, Stephen S. 1991. "Fallen Star." *The New Republic* (September): 21–5.

Morgan Guaranty Trust Company. Various issues. *World Financial Markets*. New York: Morgan Guaranty Trust Company.

Morvant, Penny. 1995. "Gaidar on Domestic Politics." *OMRI Daily Digest*, 33, Part I, February 15 (electronic version).

Moses, Jonathon. 1994. "Abdication from National Policy Autonomy." *Politics and Society*, 22 (June): 125–48.

Mundell, Robert A. 1957. "International Trade and Factor Mobility." *American Economic Review* 47: 321–35.

1962. "The Appropriate Use of Monetary and Fiscal Policy Under Fixed Exchange Rates." *IMF Staff Papers* 9 (March): 70–7.

1963. "Capital Mobility and Stabilization Policy Under Fixed and Flexible Exchange Rates." *Canadian Journal of Economics and Political Science* 29, 4 (November): 475–85.

Murphy, Kevin M., Andrei Shleifer, and Robert Vishny. 1989. "Industrialization and the Big Push." *Journal of Political Economy* 97, 5 (October): 1003–26.

Mursaliyev, Azer. 1995. "Chernomyrdin Rising to the Top." *Moscow News,* 20–1 (June 2–8): 10.

Mussa, Michael. 1979. "Macroeconomic Interdependence and the Exchange Rate Regime." In Dornbush and Frenkel 1979: 160–204.

National Public Radio (U.S.). 1994. "Report from Moscow," September 30.

Naughton, Barry. 1993. "Deng Xiaoping: The Economist." *China Quarterly* 135 (September): 491–514.

1995. *Growing Out of the Plan: Chinese Economic Reform, 1978–1993.* Cambridge University Press.

Neal, Larry. 1985. "Integration of International Capital Markets: Quantitative Evidence from the Eighteenth to Twentieth Centuries." *Journal of Economic History* 45, 2 (June): 219–26.

Nelson, Joan ed., 1990. *Economic Crisis and Policy Change: The Politics of Adjustment in the Third World.* Princeton: Princeton University Press.

Noren, James, and Laurie Kurtzweg. 1993. "The Soviet Economy Unravels: 1985–1991." In Joint Economic Committee, U.S. Congress, *The Former Soviet Union in Transition, Vol. 1.* Washington, D.C.: Government Printing Office.

North, Douglass C. 1981. *Structure and Change in Economic History.* New York and London: W. W. Norton and Co.

1990. *Institutions, Institutional Change and Economic Performance.* Cambridge University Press.

North, Douglass, and Barry Weingast. 1989. "The Evolution of Institutions Governing Public Choice in 17th Century England." *Journal of Economic History* 49: 803–32.

Notermans, Ton. 1993. "The Abdication of National Policy Autonomy." *Politics and Society* 21 (June): 133–67.

Obstfeld, Maurice. 1986. "Rational and Self-fulfilling Balance of Payments Crises." *American Economic Review* 76: 72–81.

Odell, John. 1982. *U.S. International Monetary Policy: Markets, Power, and Ideas as Sources of Change.* Princeton: Princeton University Press.

O'Donnell, Guillermo. 1974. *Bureaucratic Authoritarianism.* Berkeley and Los Angeles: University of California Press.

Ofer, Gur. 1988. *Soviet Economic Growth: 1928–1985.* Santa Monica, CA: Rand.

Officer, Lawrence. 1986. "The Efficiency of the Dollar–Sterling Gold Standard, 1890–1908." *Journal of Political Economy* 94, 3: 1038–73.

Olson, Mancur. 1982. *The Rise and Decline of Nations: Economic Growth, Stagflation, and Social Rigidities.* New Haven: Yale University Press.

Oppenheimer, Peter, ed. 1980. *Issues in International Economics.* London: Oriel.

Organization for Economic Cooperation and Development (OECD). 1988. *The Newly Industrializing Countries: Challenge and Opportunity for the OECD Countries.* Paris: Organization for Economic Cooperation and Development.

1990. *Liberalization of Capital Movements and Financial Services.* Paris: Organization for Economic Cooperation and Development.

1991. *The Soviet Agro-Food System and Agricultural Trade: Prospects for Reform.* Paris: Organization for Economic Cooperation and Development.

1991. *Historical Statistics 1960–1989.* OECD Economic Outlook. Paris: Organization for Economic Cooperation and Development.

Organization for Economic Cooperation and Development (OECD). 1992. *OECD Economic Outlook* 52. Paris: Organization for Economic Cooperation and Development, December.

Organization for Economic Cooperation and Development (OECD) and International Energy Agency (IEA). 1992. "Russian Energy Prices and Taxes." Report no. IEA/NMC(92)6, June 11. Paris: Organization for Economic Cooperation and Development and IEA.

Ozawa, Ichiro. 1993. *Nihon Kaizo Keikaku* (Blueprint for a New Japan). Tokyo: Kodansha.

Palmer, Ingrid. 1978. *The Indonesian Economy Since 1965*. London: Frank Cass and Company.

Parrish, Scott. 1995. "EBRD President Cautious About Russian Economy." OMRI Daily Digest, 129, Part I, July 5 (electronic version).

Parrott, Bruce. 1983. *Politics and Technology in the Soviet Union*. Cambridge: MIT Press.

1985. "Soviet Foreign Policy, Internal Politics, and Trade with the West." In Bruce Parrott, ed., *Trade, Technology, and Soviet–American Relations*. Bloomington: Indiana University Press.

Pauley, Louis W. 1988. *Opening Financial Markets: Banking Politics on the Pacific Rim*. Ithaca: Cornell University Press.

Pearson, Margaret M. 1991. *Joint Ventures in the People's Republic of China: The Control of Foreign Direct Investment Under Socialism*. Princeton: Princeton University Press.

Pejovich, Steve. 1990. "A Property Rights Analysis of Perestroika." *Communist Economies* 2, 2: 157–76.

Pempel, T. J. 1987. "The Tar Baby Target: 'Reform' of the Japanese Bureaucracy." In Robert Ward and Yoshikazu Sakamoto, eds., *Democratizing Japan: The Allied Occupation*. Honolulu: University of Hawaii Press.

Perez-Campanero, J., and A. M. Leone. 1992. "Liberalization and Financial Crisis in Uruguay, 1974–87." In V. Sundaragjan and T. Balin, eds., *Banking Crisis: Cases and Issues*. Washington, D.C.: International Monetary Fund.

Perkins, Dwight H. 1968. "The International Impact on Chinese Central Planning." In Alan A. Brown and Egon Neuberger, eds., *International Trade and Central Planning*. Berkeley and Los Angeles: University of California Press: 177–98.

Peterson, Peter. 1973. "Understanding United States' Attitudes on Trade." *Euromoney* (November).

Piven, Frances Fox, ed. 1991. *Labor Parties in Postindustrial Societies*. New York: Oxford University Press.

Porter, Michael P. 1990. *The Competitive Advantage of Nations*. New York: Free Press.

Putnam, Robert, and Nicholas Bayne. 1984. *Hanging Together: The Seven-Power Summits*. Cambridge, Mass.: Harvard University Press.

Quijano, Jose Manuel. 1985. "Finanzas Latinoamericanas y Banca Extranjera." In Jose Manuel Quijano, Hilda Sanchez, and Fernando Antia, eds., *Finanzas, Desarollo Economica y Penetracion Extranjera*. Puebla: Universidad Autonoma de Puebla.

Rae, Douglas. 1967. *The Political Consequences of Electoral Laws*. New Haven: Yale University Press.

Ramos, Joseph. 1986. *Neoconservative Economics in the Southern Cone of Latin America*. Baltimore: Johns Hopkins University Press.

Ramseyer, J. Mark, and Frances M. Rosenbluth. 1993. *Japan's Political Marketplace*. Cambridge, Mass.: Harvard University Press.

1995. *The Politics of Oligarchy: Institutional Choice in Imperial Japan.* Cambridge University Press.

Rawski, Thomas G. 1992. "Progress Without Privatization: The Reform of China's State Industries." Working Paper no. 281. University of Pittsburgh, Department of Economics, July.

Razin, Assaf, and Andrew Rose. 1994. "Business Cycle Volatility and Openness." In Leiderman and Razin, eds., *Capital Mobility: The Impact of Consumption, Investment and Growth.* Cambridge University Press.

Reinhart, Carmen M., and R. Todd Smith. 1995. "Capital Controls: Concepts and Experiences." Mimeo. Washington, D.C.: International Monetary Fund.

Remnick, David. 1994. *Lenin's Tomb: The Last Days of the Soviet Empire.* New York: Vintage Books.

Rhee, Jong Chan. 1992. "The Limits of Financial Liberalization under an Authoritarian Regime: The Political Process in South Korea." Paper prepared for American Political Science Association Meeting, Chicago, September 3–6.

Rigby, T. H. 1964. "Crypto-Politics." *Survey* 50, (January): 183–94.

Riker, William H. 1980. "Implications from the Disequilibrium of Majority Rule for the Study of Institutions." *American Political Science Review* 74: 432–46.

Robison, Richard. 1986. *Indonesia: The Rise of Capital.* Sydney: Allen and Unwin.

Rodrik, Dani. 1989. "Promises, Promises: Credible Policy Reform via Signaling." *Economic Journal* 99: 756–72.

Roeder, Philip G. 1993. *Red Sunset: The Failure of Soviet Politics.* Princeton: Princeton University Press.

Rogowski, Ronald. 1987. "Trade and the Variety of Democratic Institutions." *International Organization* 41, 2 (Spring): 203–23.

1989. *Commerce and Coalitions: How Trade Affects Domestic Political Alignments.* Princeton: Princeton University Press.

Romer, Paul M. 1986. "Increasing Returns and Long-Run Growth." *Journal of Political Economy* 94: 1002–37.

1990. "Endogenous Technological Change." *Journal of Political Economy* 98: 79–102.

Rosecrance, Richard, and Arthur Stein. 1975. "Interdependence: Myth or Reality?" *World Politics* 27, 1 (October): 1–27.

Rosefielde, Steven. 1980. "Was the Soviet Union Affected by the International Economic Disturbances of the 1970s? An Exploratory Essay on the Macrostability of the Soviet Economic System." In Egon Neuberger and Laura D'Andrea Tyson, eds., *The Impact of International Economic Disturbances on the Soviet Union and Eastern Europe: Transmission and Response.* New York: Pergamon.

Rosenberg, Hans. 1943. "Political and Social Consequences of the Great Depression in Europe, 1873–1896." *Economic History Review* 13: 58–73.

1967. *Grosse Depression und Bismarckzeit: Wirtschaftsablauf, Gesellschaft und Politik in Mitteleuropa.* Berlin: Walter de Gruyter.

Rosenbluth, Frances McCall. 1989. *Financial Politics in Contemporary Japan.* Ithaca: Cornell University Press.

1993. "Japan's Response to the Strong Yen: Party Leadership and the Market for Favors." In Gerald Curtis, ed., *Japan's Foreign Policy: Coping with Change.* New York: Sharpe.

Rostow, Walt Whitman. 1978. *The World Economy: History and Prospect.* Austin and London: University of Texas Press.

Roubini, Nouriel, and Xavier Sala-i-Martin. 1992. "Financial Repression and Economic Growth." *Journal of Development Economics* 39, 1 (July): 5–30.

Ruggie, John Gerard. 1982. "International Regimes, Transactions and Change." *International Organization* 36: 379–415.

Rutland, Peter. 1990. "Labor Unrest Movements in 1989 and 1990." *Soviet Economy* 6, 4, reprinted in Ed A. Hewett and Victor H. Winston, eds., 1991. *Milestones in Glasnost and Perestroyka: Politics and People.* Washington, D.C.: Brookings Institution.

Ryzhkov, Nikolai. 1992. *Perestroika: Istoriia predatel'stv.* Moscow: Novosti.

Samuelson, Paul. 1948. "International Trade and the Equalization of Factor Prices." *Economic Journal* 58: 163–84.

Samuelson, Robert J., ed. 1990. *The Economist Book of Vital World Statistics.* New York: Times Books.

Scharpf, Fritz. 1991. *Crisis and Choice in European Social Democracy.* Ithaca: Cornell University Press.

Schonhardt-Bailey, Cheryl. 1991a. "Lessons in Lobbying for Free Trade in 19th-Century Britain: To Concentrate or Not." *American Political Science Review* 85, 1: 37–58.

　　1991b. "Specific Factors, Capital Markets, Portfolio Diversification, and Free Trade: Domestic Determinants of the Repeal of the Corn Laws." *World Politics* 43: 545–69.

Schumpeter, Joseph A. [1942]1950. *Capitalism, Socialism and Democracy.* 3rd. ed. New York: Harper's.

Schwartz, Justin. 1991. "A Future for Socialism in the USSR?" In Ralph Miliband and Leo Panitch, eds., "Communist Regimes: The Aftermath." *Socialist Register 1991.* London: Merlin.

Shepsle, Kenneth A. 1986. "Institutional Equilibrium and Equilibrium Institutions." In Herbert F. Weisberg, ed., *Political Science: The Science of Politics.* New York: Agathon Press.

Shevardnadze, Eduard. 1991. *Moi vybor: v zashchitu demokratii i svobody.* Moscow: Novosti.

Shi Jian. 1992. "Policy Auctions in Development Zones Viewed," *Zhongguo tongxun she* (Hong Kong), November 4, *Foreign Broadcast Information Service: China Report,* November 25, 1992, 28–29.

Shindo, Muneyuki. 1986. *Gyosei kaikaku to gendai seiji [Administrative Reform and Contemporary Politics].* Tokyo: Iwanami shoten.

Shirk, Susan L. 1984. "The Domestic Political Dimensions of China's Foreign Economic Relations." In Samuel S. Kim, ed., *China and the World: Chinese Foreign Policy in the Post-Mao Era.* Boulder: Westview Press.

　　1990. "China: The Bargaining Game." In Hadi Soesastro and Mari Pangestu, eds., *Technological Challenge in the Asia-Pacific Economy.* Sydney: Allen and Unwin.

　　1993. *The Political Logic of Economic Reform in China.* Berkeley and Los Angeles: University of California Press.

Shmelev, Nikolai, and Vladimir Popov. 1989. *The Turning Point: Revitalizing the Soviet Economy.* New York: Doubleday.

Shonfield, Andrew. 1965. *Modern Capitalism.* New York: Oxford University Press.

Shugart, Matthew, and John M. Carey. 1992. *Presidents and Assemblies: Constitutional Design and Electoral Dynamics.* Cambridge University Press.

Silva, Eduardo. 1991. "Capitalist Coalitions and Economic Policymaking in Authoritarian Chile, 1973–1988." Ph.D. diss., Department of Political Science, University of California, San Diego.

　　1993. "Capitalist Coalitions, the State, and Neoliberal Economic Restructuring: Chile, 1973–88." *World Politics* 45: 501–25.

Singer, Daniel. 1991. "Privilegentsia, Property and Power." In Ralph Miliband and Leo Panitch, eds., "Communist Regimes: The Aftermath." *Socialist Register 1991*. London: Merlin.

Smith, Hedrick. 1990. *The New Russians.* New York: Random House.

Snyder, Jack. 1987/88. "The Gorbachev Revolution: A Waning of Soviet Expansionism?" *International Security* 12, 3 (Winter): 93–131.

Solomon, Robert. 1977. *The International Monetary System 1945–1976.* New York: Harper and Row.

Soma, Masao. 1986. *Nihon senkyo seidoshi [A History of the Japanese Electoral System].* Fukuoka: University of Kyushu Press.

Soskice, David. 1990. "Wage Determination: The Changing Role of Institutions in Advanced Industrialized Countries." *Oxford Review of Economic Policy* 6, 1: 36–61.

"State Council Issues Development Zones Circular." (1993). Xinhua, May 15, 1993, *Foreign Broadcast Information Service: China Report,* May 18, 1993: 43.

Steel, Ronald. 1980. *Walter Lippman and the American Century.* Boston: Little, Brown and Company.

Stolper, Wolfgang Friedrich, and Paul A. Samuelson. 1941. "Protection and Real Wages." *Review of Economic Studies* 9: 58–73.

Swenson, Peter. 1992. "Union Politics, the Welfare State, and Intra-Class Conflict in Germany and Sweden," in Miriam Golden and Jonas Pontusson, eds., *Bargaining for Change: Union Politics in North America and Europe.* Ithaca: Cornell University Press.

Sylla, Richard. 1988. "The Autonomy of Monetary Authorities: The Case of the U.S. Federal Reserve System." In Gianni Toniolo, ed., *Central Banks' Independence in Historical Perspective.* Berlin: Walter de Gruyter.

Takahashi, Yoshikatsu. 1991. *Seiji kaikaku [Political Reform].* Tokyo: Ashi shobo.

Tello, Carlos. 1984. *La Nacionalizacion de la Banca.* Mexico, D.F.: Siglo XXI.

Temin, Peter, and Barrie Wigmore. 1990. "The End of One Big Deflation." *Explorations in Economic History* 27: 483–502.

Thelen, Kathleen. 1993. "West European Labor in Transition." *World Politics* 46, 1 (October): 23–49.

Thelen, Kathleen, and Sven Steinmo. 1992. "Historical Institutionalism in Comparative Politics." In Sven Steinmo, Kathleen Thelen, and Frank Longstreth, eds., *Structuring Politics: Historical Institutionalism in Comparative Analysis.* Cambridge University Press.

Todd, Walker. 1992. "Disorderly Markets: The Law, History, and Economics of the Exchange Stabilization Fund and U.S. Foreign Exchange Market Intervention." *Research in Financial Services* 4: 111–179.

Traxler, Franz. 1994. "Collective Bargaining: Levels and Coverage." *OECD Employment Outlook.* July.

Treml, Vladimir G. 1980. "Foreign Trade and the Soviet Economy: Changing Parameters and Interrelations." In Egon Neuberger and Laura D'Andrea Tyson, eds., *The Impact of International Economic Disturbances on the Soviet Union and Eastern Europe: Transmission and Response.* New York: Pergamon.

Trotsky, Leon. 1937. *The Revolution Betrayed: What is the Soviet Union and Where is it Going?* New York: Doubleday, Doran, and Co.

Tsebelis, George. 1995. "Decision Making in Political Systems." *British Journal of Political Science* 25, 3 (July): 289–325.

Turner, Philip. 1991. *Capital Flows in the 1980s.* BIS Economic Papers, no. 30. Basle, Switzerland: Bank for International Settlements, April.

Tzeng Fuh-wen. 1991. "The Political Economy of China's Coastal Development Strategy, A Preliminary Analysis." *Asian Survey* 31, 3 (March): 270–84.

Unger, Irwin. 1964. *The Greenback Era: A Social and Political History of American Finance, 1865–1879.* Princeton: Princeton University Press.

United Nations. *World Investment Report 1991.* New York: United Nations.

United States Department of Treasury. Various issues. *Report to the Congress on International Economic and Exchange Rate Policy.*

Upham, Frank. 1993. "Privatizing Regulation: The Implementation of the Large Scale Retail Stores Law in Contemporary Japan." In Gary Allinson and Yasunori Sone, eds., *Political Dynamics in Contemporary Japan.* Ithaca: Cornell University Press.

Vergara, Pilar. 1986. "Changes in the Economic Function of the Chilean State Under the Military Regime." In J. Samuel Velenzuela and Arturo Valenzuela, eds., *Military Rule in Chile: Dictatorships and Oppositions.* Baltimore: Johns Hopkins University.

Vinals, Jose. n.d. "Spain's Capital Account Shock." CEPR Discussion Paper no. 477.

Visser, Jelle. 1991. "Trends in Trade Union Membership." *OECD Employment Outlook.* Paris: OECD.

Voslensky, Michael. 1984. *Nomenklatura: The Soviet Ruling Class, An Insider's Report.* New York: Doubleday.

Wade, Robert. 1990. *Governing the Market: Economic Theory and the Role of the Government in East Asian Industrialization.* Princeton: Princeton University Press.

Wakate giin no kai [Young Dietmembers' League]. 1992. Press release, May 29.

Wallerstein, Immanuel. 1974. *The Modern World-System: Capitalist Agriculture and the Origins of the European World-Economy in the Sixteenth Century.* New York: Academic Press.

Waltz, Kenneth. 1970. "The Myth of National Interdependence." In Charles Kindleberger, ed., 1970. *The International Corporation; a Symposium.* Cambridge, MA: Massachusetts Institute of Technology Press.

Warren, George, and Frank Pearson. 1935. *Gold and Prices.* New York: John Wiley and Sons.

Waterbury, John. 1993. *Exposed to Innumerable Delusions: Public Enterprise and State Power in Egypt, India, Mexico and Turkey.* Cambridge University Press.

Weaver, Kent R., and Bert A. Rockman, eds. 1993. *Do Institutions Matter? Government Capabilities in the United States and Abroad.* Washington, D.C.: Brookings Institution.

Weingast, Barry, and Mark Moran. 1983. "Bureaucratic Discretion or Congressional Control? Regulatory Policymaking by the Federal Trade Commission." *Journal of Political Economy* 91: 675–700.

Whitlock, Erik. 1993. "Oil Sector Slated for Competition?" Radio Free Europe/Radio Liberty, *Daily Report* 94, May 18 (electronic version).

Wigmore, Barrie. 1985. *The Crash and its Aftermath: a History of Securities Markets in the United States, 1929–1933.* Westport, CT: Greenwood Press.

Wigmore, Barrie. 1987. "Was the Bank Holiday of 1933 Caused by a Run on the Dollar?" *Journal of Economic History* 47, 3 (September): 739–55.

Williamson, John. 1992. "A Cost-Benefit Analysis of Capital Account Liberalization." In Bernhard Fischer and Helmut Reisen, eds., *Towards Capital Account Convertibility.* Development Centre Policy Brief no. 4. Paris: Organisation for Economic Cooperation and Development.

Williamson, Oliver. 1985. *The Economic Institutions of Capitalism: Firms, Markets, Relational Contracting*. New York: The Free Press and London: Collier Macmillan Publishers.

Winiecki, Jan. 1989. "Large Industrial Enterprises in Soviet-type Economies: The Ruling Stratum's Main Rent-seeking Area." *Communist Economies* 1, 4: 363–83.

Winters, Jeffrey A. 1992. "Banking Reform in Indonesia: External Linkages and Created Crises." Paper prepared for the Annual Meetings of the American Political Science Association, Chicago, September 3–6.

——— 1994. "Power and the Control of Capital." *World Politics* 46: 419–52.

——— 1996. *Power in Motion: Capital Mobility and the Indonesian State*. Ithaca: Cornell University Press.

Wisecarver, Daniel L. 1985. "Economic Regulation and Deregulation in Chile." In Gary Walton, ed., *The National Economic Policies of Chile*. Greenwich: JAI Press.

Woo, Jung-en. 1991. *Race to the Swift: State and Finance in Korean Industrialization*. New York: Columbia University Press.

Wood, Adrian. 1994. *North-South Trade, Employment, and Inequality: Changing Fortunes in a Skill-Driven World*. Oxford: The Clarendon Press.

Woolley, John T. 1984. *Monetary Politics: The Federal Reserve and the Politics of Monetary Policy*. Cambridge University Press.

——— 1995. "Nixon, Burns, 1972, and Independence in Practice." Paper presented to the University of California Conference on the Political Economy of Monetary Policy, University of California, Santa Cruz, June.

World Bank (International Bank for Reconstruction and Development). 1983. *World Tables*. 2 vols. Baltimore: Johns Hopkins University Press.

——— 1984. *Toward Sustainable Development in Sub-Saharan Africa: A Joint Program of Action*. Washington, D.C.: The World Bank.

——— 1992. *World Development Report 1992: Development and the Environment*. New York: Oxford University Press.

Yang, Dali L. 1991. "China Adjusts to the World Economy: The Political Economy of China's Coastal Development Strategy." *Pacific Affairs* 64, 1 (Spring): 42–64.

Yanov, Alexander. 1977. "Détente after Brezhnev: The Domestic Roots of Soviet Foreign Policy." Policy Papers in International Affairs no. 2, Institute of International Studies, University of California, Berkeley.

Zaslavskaya, Tatyana. 1990. *The Second Socialist Revolution: An Alternative Soviet Strategy*. Bloomington: Indiana University Press.

Zevin, Robert. 1992. "Are World Financial Markets More Open? If So, Why and With What Effects?" In Tariq Banuri and Juliet B. Schor, eds., *Financial Openness and National Autonomy: Opportunities and Constraints*. Oxford: Clarendon Press.

Zysman, John. 1983. *Governments, Markets and Growth*. Ithaca: Cornell University Press.

Index

Ad Hoc Administrative Reform Promotion
    Council, Japan, 143
administrative decentralization, in Chinese
    economic reform, 196–9
aggregate national welfare, 31–6, 44
agriculture, 52, 53, 126, 128, 141–4, 146
Alesina, Alberto, 9
Allende, Salvador, 224, 226, 235
American Federation of Labor–Congress of
    Industrial Organizations (AFL–CIO),
    122
Andrews, David, 257
appreciation, 127–31, 134, 135
Argentina, 209, 214
Aslund, Anders, 184
Aukrust model, 60
Australia
    balance of political power in, 85, 104–7
    labor unions in, 86–7, 104–7
    ratio of merchandise exports to, 12, 13
    trade and capital mobility in, 82–4, 98–
        102
Austria
    balance of political power in, 85, 104–7
    financial linkages, 9
    labor unions in, 53, 57, 60, 86–7, 104–7
    ratio of merchandise exports to, 12, 13
    trade and capital mobility in, 82–4, 98–
        102
automobile industry, 38, 126, 128

balance of payments crises, 211, 214–17,
    220, 222, 223, 225, 227, 228, 230, 231,
    234–6, 235, 246–8, 254
Banking Acts of 1933 and 1935, 120
Bank of America, 221
Bank of Tokyo, 221
banks, 54, 67–70
    in Chile, 224–7

in Indonesia, 221–3
in Japan, 70, 147–8
in Mexico, 227–9
in South Korea, 230–2
Bates, Robert, 250
Becker, Gary S., 42–3
Belgium
    balance of political power in, 85, 104–7
    financial linkages, 9
    labor unions in, 57, 86–7, 104–7
    level of internationalization, 96, 97
    ratio of merchandise exports to, 12, 13
    trade and capital mobility in, 82–4, 100–2
Bentsen, Lloyd, 129
bicameralism, 66, 70
Bipartisan Appeal (1983), 130
black market, 30, 169
Blumenthal, Michael, 125
Brazil, 11
Bretton Woods system, 24, 124, 129, 133,
    135, 168
Brezhnev, Leonid, 169, 245
Bryan, William Jennings, 118
budget deficits, 80, 81, 88–91, 93–5, 102,
    130, 169, 170, 178, 248
Bukharin, Nikolai, 165
bureaucratic autonomy, 66–8
Burns, Arthur, 125
business cycle, 93
Business Roundtable, 128

cabinet governments, balance of power in, 85
Calmfors, Lars, 52
Cameron, David, 8
Canada
    balance of political power in, 85, 104–7
    labor unions in, 57, 86–7, 104–7
    ratio of merchandise exports to, 12, 13
    trade and capital mobility in, 82–4, 100–2

Cantons, 70
capital controls, 26
capital market liberalization, 19, 20, 212–20
  in Chile, 224–7
  in Indonesia, 220–4
  in Mexico, 227–30
  in South Korea, 230–4
capital mobility, 15–19, 23, 80–4, 108, 250, 257
  influence on economic policy, 88–100, 101, 103
capital taxation, 80, 81, 88, 90, 91, 93–5, 97, 103
Cardenas, Lazaro, 227
Carter, Jimmy, 125, 126
Castro, Sergio de, 226
Caterpillar Tractors, 128, 129
central planning system, 162, 165, 167, 176, 178
chaebol, 232, 233
Chase Manhattan Bank, 221
checks and balances, 54
Chernomyrdin, Viktor S., 183–4
"Chicago boys," 225
Chile, 209, 216–20, 224–7, 235, 248, 251, 252, 255
China, *see* People's Republic of China
Chun Doo Hwan, 231
closed-economy monetary policy, 109–14, 116, 121, 124, 133
coal industry, in Soviet Union, 163, 179–83
Cold War, 192
collective bargaining, 57
Commerce and Coalitions (Rogowski), 8, 48
communism, Chinese versus Soviet version of, 195–6
comparative advantage, 37, 57, 89, 100, 206
compensation hypotheses, 90–2, 95
Congressional Subcommittee on International Exchange and Payments, 123
Congress of the United States, 66, 113, 116–21, 123–6, 128–31, 133, 135
Conservative Party, Great Britain, 73
convergence, process of, 19–20, 81
Cooper, Richard, 247
coups d'état, 63
Credit Lyonnaise, 223
cross-border capital flows, 81, 82, 88, 101, 103
Cuba, 14
Cultural Revolution, 192, 196
currency values, 111, 112

Danforth, John, 129
Debt, Development and Democracy (Frieden), 48
deficit spending, 56
deindustrialization, 41

democracy
  policy change and, 61–2
  preference aggregation in, 63–6
democratic centralism, 162, 167, 178
Deng Xiaoping, 186, 187, 193–7, 199, 201–3, 206, 245
Denmark
  balance of political power in, 85, 104–7
  labor unions in, 59, 86–7, 104–7
  ratio of merchandise exports to, 12, 13
  trade and capital mobility in, 82–4, 100–2
depreciation, 111, 112, 116–18, 125–6, 130, 134, 135
deregulation, 12, 147
devaluation, 119, 120, 123–4, 133
developing countries, financial international-ization in, 209–39, 245, 251–2, 255
  Chile, 216–20, 224–7
  economic interdependence, 211, 212–14
  Indonesia, 216–24
  Mexico, 216–20, 227–30
  South Korea, 216–20, 230–4
distribution sector, Japan, 144–7
Djilas, Milovan, 164, 181
Driffill, John, 52
"Dutch disease," 41, 46, 244
dynamic costs of closure, 33

Echeverria Alvarez, Luis, 235
economic pluralism, 49, 54–6, 61–6, 69, 70, 74
economic shocks, 16, 18
economies of scale, 26, 30, 39–41, 57, 100
efficiency hypotheses, 90–2, 95
Emergency Committee for American Trade (ECAT), 122
endogenous growth theory, 89, 90
endogenous institutional change, 69–74
Engels, Friedrich, 258
European Economic Community, 24
European Monetary System, 246
European Union, 101, 257
Evangelista, Matthew, 6, 23, 159–85, 245, 248, 249, 251, 252
exchange rates, 8, 16–18, 24, 58, 68, 88, 108, 246
  fixed, 17, 24, 88, 111, 135
  floating, 17, 18, 135
  monetary policy and, 109–12, 121, 124, 128–36
  in Soviet Union, 166
exogenous easing of international exchange, 25–37, 40–7, 162, 169, 173
expansionary monetary policy, 56

federalism, 64, 65, 70
Federal Reserve Act, 1977 amendment to, 124

Federal Reserve Board, 113, 119, 120,
  124–7, 133, 135
financieras, 224, 225
Finland
  balance of political power in, 85, 104–7
  capital controls in, 101
  labor unions in, 86–7, 104–7
  level of internationalization, 96, 97
  ratio of merchandise exports to, 12, 13
  single-transferable-vote system in, 139
  trade and capital mobility in, 82–4, 100–2
First National City Bank, 221
Fiscal Investment and Loan Program, Japan, 145
fiscal policy, 17–18, 30, 88
fixed exchange rates, 17, 24, 88, 111, 135
floating exchange rates, 17, 18, 135
footwear industry, 122
Foreign Capital Control Act of 1991, 233
foreign direct investment (FDI), 13–14, 16, 118
Foreign Trade and Investment Act (Burke–Hartke bill), 124
formal political institutions, 50, 60–9
France, 246
  balance of political power in, 85, 104–7
  labor unions in, 57, 86–7, 104–7
  ratio of merchandise exports to, 12, 13
  trade and capital mobility in, 82–4, 98–102
Frieden, Jeffrey A., 3–6, 8, 15, 16, 18, 25–47, 48, 50, 52, 55, 74, 75, 108–36, 155, 160–3, 169, 171, 173, 175–7, 179, 181–3, 190, 199, 206, 211, 212, 234, 244, 247, 253
full employment, 17

Gaidar, Yegor, 184
Garrett, Geoffrey, 5–6, 18–21, 27, 28, 42, 47, 48–75, 79–107, 136, 162, 177, 185, 189, 234, 246–8, 251, 253–5
GDP (gross domestic product), ratio of merchandise exports to, 11–13
General Agreement on Tariffs and Trade (GATT), 23, 24, 197, 213
Gephardt, Richard, 129
Germany
  balance of political power in, 85, 104–7
  central bank in, 54, 67, 70
  labor unions in, 53, 57, 60, 70, 86–7, 104–7
  ratio of merchandise exports to, 12, 13
  trade and capital mobility in, 82–4, 98–102
  trade with U.S., 122, 125
  veto players in, 66
Gerschenkron, Alexander, 8
Glasnost, 174

Glass, Carter, 119
GNP (gross national product)
  import volumes as percentage of, 10
  openness of U.S. economy (1869–1992), 114, 115
  of Soviet Union, 159, 160
Gold Reserve Act of 1934, 120
gold standard, 10, 14, 116–20, 123, 124, 133, 134, 136, 168
Goldstein, Avery, 192
goods flows, 15–16
Gorbachev, Mikhail, 160–2, 169, 171–4, 185, 245
Gosplan, 176
Gourevitch, Peter, 8
Government spending, 80, 81, 88, 90, 91, 93–5, 97
gradualism, in Chinese economic reform, 196, 197, 199
Grant, Ulysses, 117
Great Britain, 246
  balance of political power in, 85, 104–7
  central bank in, 67
  labor unions in, 59, 73, 86–7, 104–7
  plurality voting in, 63
  ratio of merchandise exports to, 12, 13
  under Thatcher, 73
  trade and capital mobility in, 82–4, 100–2
  veto player in, 66
Great Depression, 119–20, 166, 178
Great Leap Forward, 196
Greenback populism, 116–17
Group of Five, 130

Haggard, Stephan, 6, 19, 30, 155, 209–39, 245, 246, 248, 250–2, 254, 255
Hata, Tsutomu, 151
Heckscher–Olin trade model, 8, 37, 38, 40, 46, 212
Hewett, Ed, 166
Hiraiwa, Gaishi, 148
Hirschman, Albert, 7, 250
historical institutionalism, 49
Hong Kong, 11, 194, 200, 201
Hosokawa, Morihiro, 151
Hough, Jerry, 165
Hua Guofeng, 193–4, 201

IG Metall, 57
import substitution policies, 188, 190, 251
Indonesia, 216–24, 235, 248, 252, 255
inflation, 58, 67, 68, 93, 127, 130, 135, 248
  in Soviet Union, 168, 170, 171, 178
infrastructure category of costs, 26
institutions, 27, 28, 42–4, 48–75 (*see also* People's Republic of China, Japan, Soviet Union)

institutions (*cont.*)
  effects on character of, 7–9
  endogenous change, 69–74
  formal political, 50, 60–9
  hypothetical two sector economy and, 54–6
  internationalization and political change and, 50–4
  organization of socioeconomic interests, 56–60
interdependence, 7, 211, 212–14
interest groups, 109, 111, 121, 128, 130, 135, 189, 214
Interest Rate Control Act of 1947, Japan, 147
interest rates, 8, 10, 14, 20, 32–3, 58, 68, 80, 81, 88–91, 93–5, 97, 103, 110
international cartels, 30
international division of labor, 84
International Monetary Fund (IMF), 24, 82, 96, 101, 129, 211, 217, 221, 229, 255, 256
International Trade Commission, 129
international trade flows, 8, 10–11
Ireland, 139
Italy, 246
  balance of political power in, 85, 104–7
  labor unions in, 57, 59, 86–7, 104–7
  political system in, 54
  ratio of merchandise exports to, 12, 13
  trade and capital mobility in, 82–4, 100–2

Jakarta Stock Exchange (JSE), 222, 223
Japan, 23, 137–56, 191, 194, 213, 244–5, 250, 253, 254, 256
  agriculture in, 53, 141–4, 146
  balance of political power in, 85, 104–7
  banks in, 70, 147–8
  demographic change in, 142
  distribution sector in, 144–7
  electoral districts in, 143, 148
  electoral rules in, 138, 140–1, 143, 148–56
  examples of policy changes in, 142–8
  labor unions in, 70, 86–7, 104–7
  pro-producer economic policies, 141–2, 149
  protectionism in, 137, 138, 141, 142, 144, 145, 152, 156
  ratio of merchandise exports to, 12, 13
  steel industry in, 30
  trade and capital mobility in, 82–4, 100–2
  trade with U.S., 122, 125

Katzenstein, Peter, 8, 9, 253
Keidanren, 143, 148
Keohane, Robert O., 3–24, 25, 138, 156, 160, 243–58
Keynesian welfare state, 55–9, 61, 62, 65, 68–70, 79–81

Kim Jae Ik, 231
Korea, *see* South Korea
Kurzer, Paulette, 9

labor unions, 9, 52–3, 57–60, 69–70, 73, 86–7, 104–7, 109
  density and composition of, 86
  internal structure of, 87
Labour Party, Great Britain, 73
Lange, Peter, 5–6, 20, 21, 27, 28, 42, 47, 48–75, 136, 162, 177, 185, 189, 234, 251, 253
Large Scale Store Law, Japan, 145
Larosiere, Jacques de, 184
left-labor governments, 9, 17–18, 20, 78, 80, 81, 83–6, 90–103, 246–8
Lenin, V. I., 164, 165
Liberal Democratic Party (LDP), Japan, 137–56, 245, 253, 254
Lien, Da-Hsiang Donald, 250
Lindblom, Charles E., 19
Li Peng, 203
Lipset, Seymour Martin, 21, 252
Lopez Portillo, 235

MacArthur, Douglas, 140
Madrid, Miguel de la, 229
Magee, Steven, 38
Malaysia, 191
managed depreciations, 88
manufacturing jobs, decline in, 84
Mao Zedong, 187, 188, 190, 192, 195–6
market integration, 87, 109
Marx, Karl, 258
Maxfield, Sylvia, 6, 19, 30, 155, 209–39, 245, 246, 248, 250–2, 254, 255
McKinley, William, 118
Mexico, 11, 16, 209, 214, 216–20, 227–30, 235, 247, 248, 251, 252, 255, 257
military spending, 127
Miller, G. William, 125, 126
Mills Bill, 124
Milner, Helen V., 3–24, 25, 48, 138, 156, 160, 243–58
Ministry of International Trade and Industry (MITI), Japan, 141
Miyazawa, Kiichi, 150–1
monetary policy, 17–18, 30, 67–8
  in closed and open economies, 109–14, 116, 121–31, 133
  politics of in U.S., 108–9, 113–36
Morgan, Lee, 128
Mundell–Fleming theorem, 17

National Association of Manufacturers, 128
Neoclassical theory, 89, 90, 94, 102, 175
Neoliberal economic policies, 20

Netherlands
  balance of political power in, 85, 104–7
  financial linkages, 9
  labor unions in, 86–7, 104–7
  natural gas discoveries in, 41
  ratio of merchandise exports to, 12, 13
  trade and capital mobility in, 82–4, 100–2
new growth theory, 80, 89, 91, 94, 103
new institutionalism, 49
New Japan Party, 151
Newly Industrializing Countries (NICs), 11,
  73, 82, 191, 194, 215
New Zealand
  central bank in, 67
  labor unions in, 59
  plurality voting in, 63
Nixon, Richard, 123, 124
nomenklatura, 164–5, 167, 181
nominal price level, 110, 112
nontradables sector, 55–61, 64, 65, 68–71
  monetary policy and, 111, 112, 116, 117,
  119, 122–4, 126–8, 132, 134
North American Free Trade Agreement
  (NAFTA), 213, 229
North Korea, 14
Norway
  balance of political power in, 85, 104–7
  labor unions in, 53, 60, 86–7, 104–7
  ratio of merchandise exports to, 12, 13
  trade and capital mobility in, 82–4, 100–2
Nye, Joseph, Jr., 7

oil prices, 30, 41, 42, 168–70, 173–5, 177,
  183
oil shocks, 82, 86, 216, 231
oil transport, 30
open-economy monetary policy, 110–15,
  121–31
Organization for Economic Cooperation
  and Development (OECD), 10, 82, 97
Organization of Petroleum Exporting Countries (OPEC), 30, 86
Ozawa, Ichiro, 151, 156

Palmer, Ingrid, 220–1
Paris Club debt rescheduling, 222, 223
Park Chung Hee, 231
particularistic contracting, in Chinese economic reform, 196, 198–9
Partisanship of governments, 9, 10
part-time work, 84
People's Liberation Army, China, 189
People's Republic of China, 186–206, 245,
  247, 249, 251, 252, 255, 256
  autarky and communist party-state in,
  187–90

domestic political institutions and reform
  strategies, 195–9
foreign-trade monopoly in, 187–90, 188,
  198, 203–5
internationalization and reform bandwagon, 199–205
internationalization without policy change
  in 1970s, 190–3
leadership competition and policy innovation in, 193–5
relations with Soviet Union, 192
special economic zones (SEZs) in, 201–4
Tiananmen demonstrations, 203
Percy, Charles, 129
perestroika, 161, 170, 171, 173, 245, 249
personal-vote strategy, 139–41, 148
Pertamina, 222, 223
Peterson, Peter, 123, 130
Pinochet, Augusto, 217, 224–6, 235
Plurality voting, 63
Poland, 173, 174
Policy change
  democracy and, 61–2
  institutions and (*see* institutions)
  totalitarian systems and, 62–3
  veto players and, 66
Policy preferences and coalitions, 25–47,
  244–6, 253
Power and Interdependence (Keohane and
  Nye), 7
presidential election
  of 1896, 118
  of 1960, 123
presidentialism, 66
price changes, 16, 29–31
price convergence, 29, 32, 35, 38
price equalization system, 162, 166, 167, 177
price levels, 110, 112
price shocks, 29, 31, 35, 36, 41, 46, 162
price stability (1920–35), 116, 119
proportional representation, 63–5, 70
Proporz norm, 70
protectionism, 89, 122–4, 129, 130
  in Japan, 137, 138, 141, 142, 144, 145,
  152, 156
public sector employment, growth in, 84

quotas, 26, 29

railroad industry, 117
Reagan, Ronald, 127
reciprocal accountability, 189
Reciprocal Trade Adjustment Act of 1934, 43
referendums, 70
Resisting Protectionism (Milner), 8, 48
Resumption Act of 1875, 117
Reuss, Henry, 123–5

Ricardo–Viner approach, 38, 40, 46
Rigby, T. H., 194
right-wing governments, 9, 17–18
ripple effect, 41
Rogowski, Ronald, 3–5, 8, 15, 16, 18, 25–
    47, 48, 50, 52, 55, 74, 75, 138, 155, 160–
    3, 171, 173, 175–7, 179, 181–3, 190,
    199, 206, 211, 234, 244, 247, 253, 269
Rokkan, Stein, 21, 253
Rosenbluth, Frances McCall, 6, 137–56,
    213, 244, 253
Rostenkowski, Dan, 129
Roubini, Nouriel, 9
Rutland, Peter, 159, 180

Schumpeter, Joseph, 178, 258
"second image reversed" tradition, 7, 184
separation of powers, 54
service sector, expansion of, 84
shadow prices, 30
shipping, 30
Shirk, Susan L., 6, 23, 186–206, 245, 249,
    252
Silva, Eduardo, 225
Silver populism, 116–18
Singapore, 11, 191, 200
single member districts, 63–5, 149, 150
social democratic governments, *see* left-
    labor governments
Social Democratic Party, Great Britain, 73
Socialist Party, Japan, 140, 148, 149, 151,
    156
social welfare costs, 32
socioeconomic institutions, 50, 52, 53, 56–60
Solidarity, 174
Southern Cone experiments, 209
South Korea, 11, 23, 191, 201, 213, 216–20,
    230–4, 236, 248, 251, 254–6
Soviet Union, 36, 39, 159–85, 189, 245, 248,
    249, 251, 252, 256, 258
    budget deficit in, 170, 171, 178
    central planning system in, 162, 165, 167,
        176, 178
    democratic centralism in, 162, 167, 178
    energy sector in, 163, 173, 176–7, 179–84
    foreign-trade monopoly in, 162, 165–7,
        178
    GNP of, 159, 160
    Gorbachev's reforms in, 160–2, 169, 171–
        4, 185
    inflation in, 168, 170, 171, 178
    perestroika, 161, 170, 171, 173, 245, 249
    regional politics in, 175–8
    relations with China, 192
    Stalinist system in, 163–5, 178, 180
Spain, 246
special economic zones (SEZs), China, 201–4

specific factors approach, 38, 40, 46, 212
Stalinist system, 163–5, 178, 180
standard open economy macroeconomic
    model, 17
static efficiency costs of closure, 33
steel industry, 30, 116, 122, 126
Stolper–Samuelson theorem, 8, 37, 38
Suharto, 221, 222
Sukarno, 220, 235
supply-side policies, 60
Sweden, 23, 246, 254
    balance of political power in, 85, 104–7
    financial linkages, 9
    labor unions in, 59, 60, 86–7, 104–7
    ratio of merchandise exports to, 12, 13
    trade and capital mobility in, 82–4, 100–2
Switzerland, 12, 13, 70

Taiwan, 11, 191, 200, 201, 213
tariffs, 23–4, 26, 29, 111, 118, 119
tax reductions, 127
technological innovation, 12, 29, 30, 33
Textile industry, 122
Tiananmen demonstrations, 203
total factor productivity (TFP), 26, 33–4,
    38–9
tradables sector, 55–61, 63–5, 68–71
    monetary policy and, 111, 112, 116, 117,
        119, 122–32, 134
Trade Act, Section 301 of, 24
Trade Bill of 1988, 232
transport costs, 26, 30, 31
Treasury Accord of 1951, 120
Treml, Vladimir, 168
Trotsky, Leon, 164, 252

unemployment, 59, 67, 73, 89, 90
United Kingdom, *see* Great Britain
Uruguay, 209

Venezuela, 214
veto players, 66, 70
veto points, 54
Volcker, Paul, 125–7, 129
voluntary export restraints, 26
Voslensky, Michael, 164, 181

wage and price controls, 124
Westminster systems, 54
wheat prices, 29
World Bank, 24, 25, 255

Yanov, Alexander, 171–3
Yeltsin, Boris, 162, 184
Yoshida, Shigeru, 140

Zhao Ziyang, 203